Cold Peace

COLD PEACE

Stalin and the Soviet Ruling Circle, 1945–1953

Yoram Gorlizki and Oleg Khlevniuk

OXFORD

UNIVERSITY PRESS

2004

OXFORD
UNIVERSITY PRESS

Oxford   New York
Auckland   Bangkok   Buenos Aires   Cape Town   Chennai
Dar es Salaam   Delhi   Hong Kong   Istanbul   Karachi   Kolkata
Kuala Lumpur   Madrid   Melbourne   Mexico City   Mumbai   Nairobi
São Paulo   Shanghai   Taipei   Tokyo   Toronto

Published by Oxford University Press, Inc.
198 Madison Avenue, New York, New York 10016

www.oup.com

Oxford is a registered trademark of Oxford University Press

Parts of chapter 2 were published originally as "Ordinary Stalinism: The Council of
Ministers and the Soviet Neo-patrimonial State, 1945–1953," *Journal of Modern History*
74, 4 (2002): 699–736, © by The University of Chicago. All rights reserved.

Parts of chapter 2 were published originally as "Stalin's Cabinet: The Politburo and
Decision Making in the Post-war Years," *Europe-Asia Studies* 53, 2 (2001): 291–312, and
are reprinted with the permission of Taylor and Francis. http://www.tandf.co.uk

Library of Congress Cataloging-in-Publication Data
Gorlizki, Yoram.
Cold peace: Stalin and the Soviet ruling circle, 1945–1953 / Yoram Gorlizki and Oleg
Khlevniuk.
   p. cm.
Includes bibliographical references and index
ISBN 0-19-516581-0
1. Soviet Union—Politics and government—1936–1953. 2. Stalin, Joseph, 1879–1953.
3. Stalin, Joseph, 1879–1953—Friends and associates I. Khlevniuk, O. V. (Oleg
Vital'evich) II. Title.
DK268.4.G67 2003
947.084'2'092—dc21   2003048081

9 8 7 6 5 4 3

Printed in the United States of America
on acid-free paper

To two members of the staraia gvardiia,

Bob Davies and Misha Lewin

ACKNOWLEDGMENTS

Work on this project was made possible by a research grant from the UK Economic and Social Research Council (award number R000222676). We are very grateful to the ESRC, and in particular to the Politics, Economics and Geography Research Unit, for their support of our work. Thanks are also due to the Department of Government at the University of Manchester and to the Deutsche Forschungsgemeinschaft for sabbaticals and a research stipend that enabled us to complete the manuscript. The bulk of the research for the book was carried out in Russian archives. Much of this work was conducted in collaboration with the series "Documents in Soviet History," which continues to flourish under the energetic leadership of Andrea Graziosi. For their guidance through holdings and for ferreting documents we are, as ever, extremely grateful to Galina Gorskaia, Galina Iudinkova, Liudmilla Kosheleva, Larisa Rogovaia, Sofia Somonova, Andrei Miniuk, and Mikhail Prozumenshchikov. Our project has also benefited enormously from the warm support and encouragement of our parents and of numerous friends and colleagues: John Barber, Dietrich Beyrau, Martin Burch, Miriam and Boaz Evron, Don Filtzer, Klaus Gestwa, Alexander Gorlizki, Mark Harrison, Julie Hessler, Eugene Huskey, Melanie Ilic, Evan Mawdsley, Mick Moran, Aleksandr and Dima Myslivchenko, Arfon Rees, Yaacov Ro'i, Ron Suny, Jeremy Smith, Peter Solomon, Robert Tucker, Ursula Vogel, Derek Watson, Stephen White, and Elena Zubkova. Peter Solomon made excellent comments on an early draft of chapter 2. We also owe an immense debt to Sheila Fitzpatrick for her generous support of our work at various stages and for helping us through the delicate but necessary process of engaging a publisher. At Oxford University Press it has been a pleasure to work with Susan Ferber, whose efficiency and enthusiasm, as well as her excellent editorial eye, have all helped in the final phases of preparing the book. Also at OUP, Rebecca Johns-Danes has proved a most professional production editor and Petra Dreiser a meticulous copyeditor. The index was compiled by Peter Turnbull. All the photographs in the volume are reproduced courtesy of the Russian Archive of Social and Political History (RGASPI) in Moscow. Portions of chapter 2 have previously been published as "Ordinary Stalinism: The Council of Ministers and the Soviet Neo-Patrimonial State, 1945–1953," *Journal of Modern History* 74, 4 (2002): 699–736, © by the University of Chicago; and as "Stalin's Cabinet: The Politburo and Decision Making in the Post-War Years," *Europe-Asia Studies* 53, 2 (2001): 291–312, reprinted with the permission of Taylor and Francis, http://www.tandf.co.uk. With the usual exceptions for well-known names such as Beria and Vyshinsky, as well as for some less well-known ones such as Lozovsky and Nikolaevsky, which have now assumed standard forms in English, we have opted for the Library of Congress transliteration system. Lastly, two groups of people deserve special mention. Our wives and daughters, Vera and Hannah, and Katia and Dasha, have given their wholehearted support and created loving homes for us to work in. Bob Davies and Misha Lewin have set the highest standards of professional commitment and scholarship, and have taught us the important art of staying optimistic.

Y.G. and O.Kh.
Manchester and Moscow
July 2003

CONTENTS

Introduction   3

Part I: Reconstruction

1 A Return to Order   17

2 State Building Stalin-Style   45

Part II: Stalin's Shift

3 The Politburo's Last Purge   69

4 Peaceful Coexistence: Collective Leadership and Stalinist Control   97

Part III: Stalin's Legacy

5 Awakening to Crisis   123

6 Stalin's Last Struggle   143

Conclusion   165

Notes   173

Glossary   225

Bibliography   227

Index   239

Photo galleries appear after pages 44, 98, 142

Cold Peace

INTRODUCTION

This is a book about Stalin's relationship with his entourage in the years after World War II. It tells the story of an aging and distrustful despot who habitually picked on and humiliated his companions. Sparing no one, Stalin aimed to infect the ruling circle with the suspicions and insecurities that characterized his own mental world. Such actions seem to confirm a widespread perception of Stalin in these years as a vain, capricious, and highly unstable individual, who was bent on petty revenge and short-term personal domination. Against such a view, this book argues that Stalin's behavior after the war followed a clear political logic. This was, in part, the logic of a dictator seeking to preserve his power in conditions of old age and chronic ill health. It was also, however, the logic of a leader determined to consolidate his position as head of a separate, respected, and powerful socialist system. In order to press home his country's claims as a global power and to put it on a level economic and military footing with the West, Stalin vested authority in committees, elevated younger specialists, and initiated key institutional innovations. No matter how perverse they may have appeared, Stalin's actions did not contradict his wider political objectives. For all their high drama, Stalin's relations with his companions followed a political and administrative logic. The purpose of this book is to unravel that logic.

Stalin's relations with his companions and the evolution of high-level decision making in the postwar period must be set against the backdrop of wider domestic and international events. The devastation of World War II necessitated a massive recovery program involving the rebuilding of plant and housing stock and the demobilization and migration of millions of soldiers and civilians. It was in this context that over the winter of 1946–1947 the Soviet Union experienced the worst natural famine in over

3

fifty years.[1] The stresses of the famine filtered through to the very highest leadership circles and led to blistering attacks by Stalin on some of his colleagues, most notably on Anastas Mikoian. The years 1946 and 1947 also saw the sharpening of international tensions and the onset of the Cold War. Frosty relations with the West were punctuated by a succession of diplomatic standoffs and international crises. These, too, were keenly reflected in the leadership dynamics of the period, providing the pretext for coruscating offensives against Stalin's deputy, Viacheslav Molotov. The timing of international tensions also corresponded closely with a series of campaigns against the domestic intelligentsia, which were inspired almost in their entirety by Stalin. Following various flashpoints, most notably the confrontation over Berlin, the Soviet Union finally plunged into a "hot" war, albeit by proxy, when it supplied advisers, equipment, and air crews to the northern communist side in the Korean conflict. The Korean War also left its mark on Soviet governmental structures, with the reorganization of the Council of Ministers and the grafting onto it of an influential military-industrial bureau. The postwar period was a time of domestic and international pressures, some of which were translated into conflicts and reorganizations at the upper reaches of the political system.

Despite this, most of the period spanning the end of the war and Stalin's death was one of relative geopolitical and psychological security for the Soviet leadership. Having successfully rebuffed the Nazis and proved itself in the ultimate test of war, the Soviet Union emerged in 1945 as a robust and respected international power. "The war," Stalin told a Central Committee plenum on 19 March 1946, "has shown that our social system is now secure."[2] This sense of security was augmented in 1948 when the country received additional protection from Western advances with the formation of a buffer zone, consisting of eight satellite states, in Eastern Europe. The country's sense of its own might was bolstered even further in August 1949, when the Soviet Union carried out its first successful nuclear test. In addition, the regime's political reach grew in the one area where it had traditionally been weakest, namely, the countryside.[3]

Psychologically, the country never descended to the panic which—in the face of inevitable war—it had experienced in the late 1930s. While Stalin took advantage of tensions with the West to discipline colleagues and the intelligentsia through domestic campaigns, the imperative of purging large segments of society, of wiping out "fifth columns," which had been so much in evidence in the late 1930s, had diminished and was now largely restricted to the newly acquired western borders of the country.[4] Also indicative of the greater restraint shown by the leadership was the steep fall in the number of people convicted for counterrevolutionary offenses.[5] More secure and self-confident in its position than at any time under Stalin, and arguably even since the October Revolution, the leadership had less reason to resort to extraordinary measures to shore up their authority.

Rooted in a new-found self-confidence and sense of security, a postwar equilibrium was established within the Soviet leadership. This equilibrium found expression in Stalin's relations with his Politburo companions and in the shape and character of decision-making structures. While historians have noted the relative stability and security of tenure within Stalin's Politburo in the postwar years,[6] we are now in a better position to flesh out these relationships. To be sure, in order to keep them on their toes, Stalin administered reproofs and leveled far-fetched allegations against his colleagues. In attacks of this kind (twelve are described in some detail in this book) Stalin vilified, shunned, and humbled his victims, even to the point of compelling them to betray their own spouses. In all cases but one, however, he stopped short of irrevocable steps. With the exception of Nikolai Voznesenskii, a victim of the Gosplan Affair of 1949, all Politburo members retained, or eventually returned to, their original posts.

In many respects, Stalin's treatment of his Politburo colleagues was in keeping with a pattern of leadership he had staked out in the 1930s.[7] Even at the height of the terror, Stalin had never touched the "backbone" of the Politburo, those venerated members of the leadership who had long been associated with him and whose public denigration might have tainted his own image.[8] Such figures continued to be well represented in the postwar Politburo.[9] Further, to the extent that some members of the Politburo in the 1930s were punished, they tended to be "expendable," unproductive leaders, who were unable to cope with their work obligations.[10] By contrast, Stalin had always shown a reluctance to remove top leaders in their prime. It may have been for these reasons that the younger members of the Politburo—dependable workaholics such as Georgii Malenkov, Lavrentii Beria, and Nikita Khrushchev, whom Stalin had recruited on the eve of the war—were also left untouched.

After the war Stalin appears to have moved even beyond the rationales, such as they were, of the 1930s. Although we have no incontrovertible evidence (and none is ever likely to surface), Stalin's actions in the postwar period suggest that he had been unnerved by the Great Purges and was extremely wary of embarking on a new round of bloodletting on such a scale. Thus, even the mass arrests that came in the wake of the postwar Leningrad and Mingrelian Affairs were clearly targeted and did not cross well-defined limits. For their part, even aging, chronically ill, and redundant Politburo members, such as Kliment Voroshilov and Andrei Andreev, whose use to the leader was extremely questionable, were spared. As for established Politburo members, there was all the more reason why Stalin should have followed a policy of caution after the war. These were all leaders on whom, over a period of many years, Stalin had expended con-

siderable energies, pressing and molding them to suit his own requirements. Each was a known quantity to the leader, and all the easier to
control and to manipulate for that. Replacing them with relative unknowns
at this stage would have introduced needless uncertainty to Stalin's system
of rule.

Notwithstanding Stalin's formidable powers, the postwar equilibrium
within the ruling circle was not just one of the leader's making. Although
Stalin encouraged rivalries among his companions, members of the Polit-
buro were reluctant to become embroiled in mutually destabilizing conspiracies. For most of the period of reconstruction, which lasted until 1948,
Stalin's deputies participated in healthy competition to win the leader's ear.
There is no evidence, however, that they sought each other's destruction.
After the Leningrad and Gosplan Affairs of 1949, which ended in the ju-
dicial murder of the Politburo member Voznesenskii and of the Central
Committee Secretary Aleksei Kuznetsov, members of the ruling group
sensed that any doubts instilled in Stalin over one or another of their
companions could easily spill over into a new wave of violence.[11] They
recognized that the best way to protect their own individual interests was
by preserving the balance of power within the group. The postwar equilibrium within the ruling circle was hence the product of a wary dictator,
who sought continuity of leadership, and of a ruling group, who understood that the existing balance of power was fragile and, under the wrong
circumstances, easily broken, with potentially devastating consequences for
themselves.

Complementing the equilibrium in leadership relations was an institutionalization of political and administrative structures at the highest levels
of the system. One reason for this was a realization on Stalin's part that
he could not manage such a vast social system as the Soviet Union on his
own, especially since his own physical powers were on the wane. Some
form of delegation was clearly indispensable. As Molotov recalled: "For
[Stalin] to have read all these papers would, of course, have been senseless.
He would simply have become a bureaucrat. He was in no condition to
read it all. . . . So Stalin would ask: 'Is it important?'——I would reply that
it was. He would then examine it in minute detail. And then, of course, a
resolution would have been adopted on whom to assign one question to,
whom the second, and whom the third—for him to have processed it all
himself would have simply been impossible."[12]

As important as the imperative for delegation was a recognition of the
need for an effective and flexible system of administration. The main chal-
lenge now, as Stalin made clear in his speech on 9 February 1946, was to
create conditions for long-term economic growth, so that the Soviet system
could compete with the West.[13] The need to attain the targets laid out in

that speech became all the more pressing the following year as the Soviet Union was drawn into an increasingly hostile relationship with the Western bloc. Central to raising the long-term productive capacity of the economy was a rationalization of economic decision making. To this end, Stalin initiated a series of far-reaching reorganizations at the highest levels of the political and economic system in February 1947. The most important of these reforms was the reorganization of the Council of Ministers, where decision making was vested in a hierarchy of specialized committees.[14] These reforms, which were designed to make the system of decision making more precise and effective, were complemented by a range of other changes to everyday bureaucratic practices. Whereas in the 1920s and early 1930s notes between leading officials may have been scrawled on scraps of paper, messages, memoranda, and letters at the highest levels were now typed on velvety thick, embossed sheets, invariably bearing issue numbers and graded in accordance with the rank and office of the sender.

To attach too much importance to the rationalization of government would be an error, however. The trend toward administrative efficiency could at any time be disturbed by Stalin's coercive approach to rule and by his moody and capricious personality. It was these qualities that would lend Stalin's truce with his entourage such a brittle, cold, and unpredictable quality.

As in the 1930s, Stalin preserved special lines of communication with the secret police. He appointed a succession of relatively disposable figures with no power base of their own, such as Viktor Abakumov and Semën Ignat'ev, as heads of the security service. Records of interrogations reached Stalin through special channels that bypassed other leaders. When any member of the ruling circle, in particular Beria, appeared to come too close to the security police, Stalin took decisive measures, for example by removing Beria's dependent, Vsevolod Merkulov, as head of the Ministry of State Security in 1946. Such unhindered access to the security agencies was pivotal to Stalin's control of the ruling group. Members of the ruling circle were never in doubt that the authority to punish or expel any of them rested with Stalin alone. It was Stalin who pulled the key levers in the Leningrad and Gosplan Affairs, with calamitous consequences for two members of the leadership. At the same time, the very fact that Politburo members were guarded around the clock by specially assigned security officials and that all their ciphered correspondence was decoded by employees of the secret police, afforded Stalin an excellent means of keeping track of colleagues. From 1950 on, he reportedly even had bugging devices planted in the apartments of his most senior deputies, Molotov and Mikoian.[15] Stalin's relationship with the documents flowing in on a daily basis from the secret police was intimate and quite obsessive. Sitting, secluded, for hours, poring over the transcripts of interrogations with "wreckers" and "doctor-murderers" would prove, in his final months, to be one of Stalin's favorite pastimes.

Although after the war Stalin had clearly aged and was inclined to spend longer periods in the south, this did not mean that the leader had mellowed or that his maniacal need to control his deputies had subsided. Although from 1945 to 1951 Stalin spent an average of nearly three months a year at his various southern dachas,[16] these were not merely phases of idle rest or contemplation. While there, Stalin frequently received visitors on business matters and kept track of literary trends in the thick journals. Through ciphered telegrams he received a steady stream of draft legislation for approval and maintained lively correspondence with members of the ruling circle. As well as for editing and amending legislation, Stalin used these telegrams as a means of confronting, humiliating, and controlling his colleagues. Over his last years, some of Stalin's most stunning rebukes were issued in this way. Rather than loosening the reins over his Politburo deputies, Stalin gained a reputation for being particularly moody and severe when away from the capital;[17] members of the ruling group learned, in turn, to be even more deferential and circumspect when the boss was out of town.

Recognition of the need to modernize the economy and to rationalize the system of administration sat quite uneasily alongside some of Stalin's personality traits. Most of these traits had, indeed, been apparent since the 1930s. When members of the ruling circle had, in his eyes, erred, Stalin insisted on debasing, confessional apologies, usually in written form, so that he could circulate them for other members of the Politburo to absorb. Over the postwar period, virtually no member of Stalin's circle was spared this humiliation. As in the 1930s, Stalin remained uncompromising in his demand for absolute personal loyalty and insisted that this supersede any ties members of the Politburo had to friends, siblings, or spouses. In a series of test cases, most notably in Molotov's vote against his own wife, Polina Zhemchuzhina, Stalin forced his companions to pledge their primary allegiance to him. More important still was the demand that personal devotion to Stalin should come before any loyalty members of the ruling circle had to an "office." In a show of strength, Stalin could create or destroy institutional positions and all the personal incentives and authority that came with them. His ability to redraw duties and jurisdictions underscored Stalin's supremacy over everyday bureaucratic categories.

One of the best examples of Stalin's capacity to fashion preexisting institutions to suit his own ends was his treatment of the Politburo. Stalin determined the general jurisdiction of the Politburo and set its agendas. By not inviting official members who were out of favor, Stalin in effect selected a ruling group that convened and exercised power in the Politburo's name. The Politburo also met at times and places of Stalin's choosing, which usually meant convening very late at night at his country house. Stalin did not, however, jettison the formal aspects of the Politburo's functions. Thus, he ensured, even when this had to be achieved by the time-consuming procedure of "correspondence votes," that all members of the Politburo attached their signatures to the most important decisions. Although all knew that the ultimate decision was Stalin's, they resigned themselves, often reluctantly, to act as his accomplices. Through this blend of formal structure and overriding ad hominem loyalty, Stalin turned the Politburo into an instrument of personal rule.

Uniting his control of ideology and coercion, Stalin set in motion periodic domestic campaigns. Although their purpose was normally to reimpose "discipline" or "vigilance" and, in times of particular tension, to identify "enemies," the particular targets of such campaigns were usually quite arbitrary. Launched to a great fanfare, the prosecution of most such campaigns tended to be uneven, haphazard, and highly disruptive to the normal operations of most bureaucracies.[18] Stalinist campaigns were thus the very antithesis of the model of routine, effective, committee-based administration.

The late Stalinist system of leadership and administration therefore consisted of two opposing elements. One, aimed primarily at maximizing the long-term productive potential of the Soviet economic system, was based on a regular, specialized committee-based system of decision making. The other, based primarily on personal loyalty to the leader, was repressive, informal, and fundamentally disruptive to any notion of a continuous routine bureaucracy. Stalin's efforts to combine these two elements are characterized in this book as "neo-patrimonial."[19] The traditional concept of the patrimonial state rested on the notion that patriarchal authority—that of the master over his household—might be adapted to the needs of administering a large political community.[20] Such systems were marked by forms of bureaucratic administration that differed in key respects from "rational-legal" bureaucracies. In place of well-defined spheres of competence, patrimonial administrations were characterized by shifting tasks and powers granted on an ad hoc basis by the ruler. In the absence of clear-cut spheres of competence, there was no bureaucratic separation between the private and official spheres; the exercise of political power was thus discretionary and treated as the "private" affair of the ruler.[21] As we shall see, Stalin's capacity to transact official business in the form of personal encounters and to redeploy the offices of his subordinates fits the concept well.[22] Rather than being continuous and regulated, Stalin's control of decision making was entirely a matter for his own discretion. In many respects, Stalin's patrimonial authority was also specifically modern. His own patrimonial authority was compatible with quite rational and predictable forms of decision making lower down the hierarchy; although he himself remained free of regulations that might constrain his authority, his form of rule did accommodate rational-legal forms of administration at other levels. However, the patrimonial and modern aspects of this system were perpetually in tension.

If one fault line that runs through this book is the tension between the modern and the personalized in high-level leadership and administration, a second axis is the distinction between Stalin up to 1949, the year of his seventieth birthday, and the period that followed. The Leningrad Affair, which erupted that year, was a somber reminder to Stalin's companions of how easily intrigues could swerve out of control. After this event in particular, Politburo members exhibited special care not to antagonize the leader and, in an attempt to maintain the status quo within the ruling circle, refrained from initiatives that might be construed as attacks on their colleagues. After 1949 Stalin also became somewhat more lethargic and less assiduous in controlling his subordinates. From 1950 on, the "septet"—a subgroup of leading Politburo members who met without Stalin— began to convene and to make decisions on a regular basis, both while Stalin was in the south and, more significantly, as the Bureau of the Presidium of the Council of Ministers while Stalin was in Moscow. The septet appears to have engaged in active debate and resorted to consultative devices—for example, the setting up of commissions—reminiscent of the practices of "collective leadership" of the 1920s. These meetings, especially those at the Bureau of the Council of Ministers, anticipate the collective decision-making dynamics of the early post-Stalin leadership.

The despot's immense power, advancing age, and infirm health were a potentially lethal mix. A string of capricious actions toward the end of his life have invited conjectures that the leader may have become deranged. It appeared out of keeping with earlier behavior, for example, for Stalin to attack his oldest comrades, Molotov and Mikoian, in public, as he did in October 1952. From Stalin's point of view, however, both actions had a certain logic. As he neared the end of his days, Stalin viewed his oldest comrades—especially Molotov—as his natural successors. Some action had to be taken to prevent political momentum building up behind any potential heirs. Tarnishing their image before party elders inflicted great harm on their succession credentials. But neither Politburo member lost office under Stalin nor, despite later claims, were they in fear for their lives. Arresting Politburo members who had been with Stalin since the 1920s and who were themselves the centers of formidable political networks, would have been hugely destabilizing. In fact, not only were neither arrested but Stalin's attacks on them were confined to upper party circles and never reached, even in a most oblique form, the wider Soviet public.

Having thrown off the deep-seated insecurities of earlier periods, the Soviet Union of the early 1950s had attained superpower status. The peace the country and its leadership had toiled so hard to achieve during World War II was nonetheless a cold and unwelcoming one. It was a peace in which the leader attacked his deputies and jolted bureaucracies and public alike with periodic campaigns; it was a peace that always appeared to teeter on the edge of violence. Intended to secure discipline, vigilance, and loyalty, the shocks to the system administered by the despot never transgressed two principal parameters—one was pursuit of the country's superpower ambitions; the other was the dictator's unshakeable will to secure his own power in conditions of advanced age and ill health. From the point of view of a tired and aging leader reaching the end of his days, an unwavering adherence to these two principles constituted the logic of his system.

This is by no means the first work on Stalin's relations with his entourage in the postwar period. A number of valuable studies, based largely on information gleaned from the Soviet press, have been published on this theme.[23] This book does, however, part company from even the most thoroughly researched of earlier volumes on this period in two key respects. First, earlier works, especially those in English, relied heavily on newspaper articles and on a small number of leaked reports and memoirs, especially those associated with the victor of the post-Stalin succession struggle, Nikita Khrushchev.[24] This book supplements these accounts by turning to a rich vein of archival, memoir, and published materials that were unavailable to earlier authors. For example, our book refers to original Central Committee resolutions, the contents of many of which have never been published, to unearth new reorganizations and personnel changes, as well as to identify more precisely initiatives of which we previously had only the faintest knowledge.[25] Moreover, scrutiny of personal correspondence between Stalin and members of the leadership, as well as among members of the Politburo themselves, allows us, often on the basis of the tone of the letters, to reconstruct more fully the nature of these relationships, as well as to reveal previously unknown clashes. In addition, a clutch of memoirs published over the last decade has enabled us to explore the psychological dimension of leadership under Stalin and to compensate for Khrushchev's often partial and one-sided accounts.[26]

Second, this book also differs from earlier Western, as well as more recent Russian, scholarship in terms of the arguments it advances. It dispels any notion that there were rivals to Stalin's leadership, that his companions either usurped his powers or conspired to kill him, or that major policy initiatives, for example in Eastern Europe, were initiated independently of the leader.[27] Neither was the research able to detect any consistent "factions" associated with moderate or liberal policy programs, or indeed any other coherent political philosophies, within Stalin's entourage.[28] Where they were not shaped by current departmental responsibilities, the "positions," such as they were, of members of the leadership on key political issues were invariably formed in response to cues from the leader.[29] This is not to say that the evolution of policy and decision-making structures in the late Stalin period was random or arbitrary, nor that Stalin decided everything. On the contrary, a strong technocratic tendency, rooted in the desire to enhance the security and status of the country, found expression in a major rationalization and, to an extent, a delegation of powers at the Council of Ministers. It was in this context that the practices of collective leadership, only fully realized after Stalin's death, were gradually restored.

There are other ways in which the arguments advanced in this book are at odds with prevailing scholarly interpretations of the period under scrutiny. While some observers, such as T. H. Rigby, have suggested that after the war "all institutions had gradually dissolved in the acid of despotism" and that "only the most minimal of gestures were made to reverse the atrophy of formal organs of authority, in both party and state," this was in fact far from being the case.[30] Routine and formal committee meetings were very much a feature of this period, even at the very highest reaches of the political system. In contrast to recent accounts, which discern a general radicalization of policies and perceptions in the postwar period, our book suggests that in terms of governmental practices and procedures, as well as of some substantive policy discussions, the postwar period was one of relative equilibrium and institutional consolidation.[31]

Much of the research in this book is based on an examination of documents in Russian archives. At the Russian State Archive of Social and Political History (RGASPI), our work focused on Politburo materials. These fall into two groups. The first are the original records (*podlinnye protokoly*) of the Politburo meetings. These contain draft resolutions, often written by hand, as well as notes on voting, amendments, and various other marginalia from Stalin, his aide Aleksandr Poskrebyshev, or other members of the Politburo, most often Malenkov. The second type of Politburo materials were the official records (*podpis'nye protokoly*), sometimes referred to as the signed records, which were typed up and carried the signature of Stalin or, in his absence, of a senior Central Committee Secretary, and which provide the resolutions, including the dates on which they were issued, in their final form. By contrast with other recent works, we have relied predominantly on the former, the draft records, which has allowed us to better reconstruct the dynamics of decision making and the roles played by key actors.[32] At RGASPI we also examined official correspondence in the personal archives of leading Politburo members, such as Molotov, Andrei

Zhdanov, Malenkov, Lazar Kaganovich, and Stalin himself.[33] At the State Archive of the Russian Federation (GARF), we made ample use of the Council of Ministers depository to obtain copies of Sovmin resolutions, as well as to follow organizational matters within the government's branch bureaus. At the Russian State Archive of the Economy (RGAE), we obtained background information on broader economic developments. To fill some important gaps, for example on the period after the XIX Congress and on the functioning of the Council of Ministers Bureau, we gained restricted access to three archives whose materials remain mostly classified: the Presidential Archive (APRF), the Russian State Archive of Contemporary History (RGANI), and the rarely used current archive of the Russian government (Arkhiv pravitel'stva Rossiiskoi Federatsii). Finally, to add a personal perspective on what were, for the most part, highly moving and dramatic stories, we commissioned interviews with former functionaries who occupied senior positions in the late Stalin period, as well as with relatives of Politburo members from that era.[34]

The book is divided into three parts, each consisting of two chapters and corresponding roughly with the periods 1945–1948, 1949–1951, and 1952–1953. Chapter 1 describes Stalin's relationships with members of the ruling group during the period of reconstruction, attempting to flesh out the human and psychological dimensions of these relationships. What emerges is a picture of Stalin's relentless severity applied in equal measure to all members of the group, be they old Bolsheviks such as Molotov, second-generation functionaries such as Malenkov, or new recruits such as the younger Zhdanov. Despite the sharpness of some of these attacks, this period is characterized by an equilibrium within the leadership. Chapter 2 looks at the political structures and decision-making procedures under which the postwar leadership operated. Through an examination of the Politburo and the Council of Ministers, the chapter describes the peculiar blend of personal rule and modern, regular, committee-based government that Stalin achieved in this period.

The third chapter begins with a discussion of the Leningrad and Gosplan Affairs of 1949. Although in many respects an aberration in the postwar period—this was the only occasion on which a Politburo member was expelled and senior politicians executed—the chapter argues that Stalin's charges, though contrived, did rest on a rational basis. In addition to demonstrating that it was Stalin who orchestrated these affairs, the chapter describes how the leader took action to fill the vacancies created by these scandals and thus to reestablish a balance within the leadership. The fourth chapter describes how, in the wake of the Leningrad Affair, Stalin kept up the pressures on individual members of the group with periodic attacks. This chapter also describes the further rationalization of the Council of Ministers, with the establishment of a new military-industrial bureau there, and the emergence of the rough outlines of "collective leadership" within the council's Presidium Bureau.

The final part of the book begins with a chapter on the wider costs to society and the economy of the late Stalinist system of rule. Concentrating on agriculture and the Gulag system, it shows how, by the early 1950s, high-grade information on how unproductive and dysfunctional these sectors were had begun to filter into the leadership around Stalin. Although any attempts at restructuring were blocked by the leader, an agenda for reform began to take shape in the last two years of Stalin's rule. The last chapter then shows how, despite his frailties, Stalin used the XIX Party Congress as a means of exercising his dominance over the party by, among other things, restructuring "offices" and reassigning his colleagues' duties. It argues that Stalin's final offensive against Molotov and Mikoian from October 1952 was part of a quite rational bid on his part to stave off any thoughts of a succession. The attack on his Politburo colleagues was accompanied by a final lunge at a group of Jewish "doctor-murderers." In order to prosecute and broaden this campaign, Stalin readied the security police and the party's ideological apparatus with a series of carefully planned cadre changes. As he reached the end of his life, the dictator fell back on the essence of his system of rule, a crude toxic mixture of ideology and repression.

PART I

Reconstruction

1

A RETURN TO ORDER

The everyday pressures on Joseph Stalin during the Second World War surpassed even the most grueling experiences of the 1930s. Serving in no fewer than five leadership roles, Stalin had no choice but to delegate full responsibility over certain spheres of government and the economy to his colleagues.[1] These leaders, and especially those who doubled up as members of the supreme civilian authority, the State Defense Committee (GKO), were given plenipotentiary powers to cut through red tape and to achieve military-economic targets on their own steam.[2] By the war's end Stalin's deputies had come to enjoy a measure of freedom in their respective fields and to resemble more the semiautonomous leaders of the early 1930s than the cowed and submissive Politburo minions of the first post-purge years. To add to the greater independence of the ruling circle, the accumulated pressures of war had taken their toll on Stalin's health and stamina. Shortly after the war, in October 1945, Stalin went on a long sojourn to the south, his first in almost ten years. According to some reports, the ruler had retired from the capital in order to convalesce from a heart attack that had struck over the summer; Western newspapers even ran a story that, after almost twenty years at the helm, Stalin had voluntarily opted to step down from the rigors of leading what had become one of the most powerful states in the world.[3]

That the latter reports proved to be completely groundless did not mean that Stalin could afford to ignore the major changes, both within the ruling circle and in his own appetite for work, resulting from the war. Stalin's response to this state of affairs would prove to be typically robust. First, within the space of little more than a year, he carried out a series of savage personal attacks on each member of his inner circle. Designed to resurrect the severe, patriarchal relationships of the late 1930s, these attacks underscored the loyalty of each member of the ruling group to Stalin above all else. Second, in order to conserve his own energies, Stalin forged a new division of labor in which purely economic or technical matters devolved to committees in which he had no role. This allowed Stalin to focus on a smaller set of policy issues—among them state security, ideology, and foreign affairs—which were to become his primary concerns after the war.

Stalin's efforts to reorient the ruling circle took place against a fast-changing international setting. The procedural and narrow country-based disputes that had dominated the Potsdam Conference and the subsequent foreign ministers meeting in London in September 1945 had, by the spring of 1947, escalated into a full-blown ideological conflict between two opposing camps. The eruption of the Cold War had a dramatic effect on the nature of high-level decision making, spawning an obsession with secrecy and antiforeigner hysteria in culture and the sciences. These deepening tensions did not, however, lead to a new wave of dismissals, let alone to a purge of the ruling group. On the contrary, once the emergency pressures of the Second World War had subsided, Stalin pushed for a return to the leadership equilibrium that had prevailed on the eve of war. Rather than causing instability, crises—both at home and abroad—served as excellent pretexts for reestablishing discipline and order within the leadership. This, indeed, would emerge as one of the main themes of leadership politics in the first phase of postwar reconstruction, which lasted until the middle of 1948.

As had been the case in the late 1930s, Stalin favored informal means of decision making over formal ones. The most important instance of this was Stalin's desire to operate through a narrow "ruling group," as opposed to the formal Politburo elected at the XVIII Congress in 1939. By the end of the war Stalin had selected a quintet of leaders, who occupied positions in both the Politburo and the GKO.[4] Apart from Stalin himself, the quintet consisted of two younger figures, Georgii Malenkov and Lavrentii Beria, whom Stalin had promoted to the Politburo just prior to the war, and two older comrades, Viacheslav Molotov and Anastas Mikoian, who had been part of the loyal, hardworking Stalinist core of the Politburo throughout the 1930s.[5] In the year following the war Stalin set about putting each member of the quintet in his place. Naturally enough, Stalin's first target was the First Deputy Chair of the Council of People's Commissars, Viacheslav Molotov. An associate of Lenin's, and the oldest and most loyal of Stalin's colleagues, Molotov was in the unenviable position of being widely touted as Stalin's natural successor.

Old Comrades First

After a short summer recess, on 4 September 1945, the Soviet leadership reverted to prewar structures by dissolving the GKO and officially transferring all its affairs to the Council of People's Commissars (SNK). In fact, supreme power at this point lay with an informal quintet, constituted by Stalin, which was already making the most important national decisions, including the very decision to dissolve the GKO itself.[6]

On the face of it there were no obvious reasons why Stalin should have distrusted the other members of the ruling group. For his part, Stalin had emerged from the war as the undisputed leader of a triumphant nation. On armistice day, *Pravda* had hailed the "great Stalinist victory" to which Stalin had led his people. After Roosevelt's death and Churchill's election defeat, Stalin had become the most senior and best-known Great Power leader in the world. For the first time since coming to power, Stalin found his regime without any clear-cut foes, either at home or abroad. Furthermore, Stalin himself had picked the members of his quintet. Judging from their past behavior, the loyalty of each was beyond question. Throughout the 1930s and during the war, every member of the ruling group had repeatedly demonstrated his unswerving devotion to the leader and to his policies, and it was for this very reason that they had risen to the apex of the political system and been allowed to stay there.

Nonetheless, Stalin's suspicions, especially toward Molotov, were stoked by an unfortunate conjunction of rumors surrounding his own state of health and some genuine concerns that his deputy had gained too much independence. On 3 October 1945, the Politburo officially awarded Stalin the first extended period of leave in nine years, which he chose to spend near the Black Sea. While there, the leader regularly received translations of articles from the foreign press, including pieces that attributed Stalin's departure from Moscow to his ailing health.[7] Although unfounded,[8] these claims fueled intense Western speculation as to who might succeed Stalin. The most likely candidate appeared to be his first deputy at Sovnarkom, Molotov, whom Stalin had unofficially left in charge during his absence.[9] It was Molotov who was chosen to deliver the keynote anniversary speech to mark the October Revolution and it was he, too, who had most dealings with foreign correspondents. On 19 October, in a major article in the Norwegian paper *Arbeiderbladet*, the head of the Norwegian health department, Karl Evang, spoke of the tremendous authority wielded by Molotov and of him being, after Stalin, "the second citizen of the Soviet Union."[10] On 24 October, the British newspaper *The Daily Express* ran a sensational story that Stalin was planning to step down in favor of Molotov and assume an "elder statesman" role.[11]

As a seasoned politician Stalin could have chosen to ignore these stories. Yet what he would not tolerate was Molotov's perceived "independent" political line. This was an issue that gradually built up over the course of autumn of 1945. It had begun even before the leader had set off for Sochi, in September, when Molotov, as Commissar for Foreign Affairs, had been dispatched to the first meeting of the Council of Foreign Ministers in London. Although mandated to represent the Soviet side, Molotov's every move was monitored by Stalin in Moscow, and the two were in daily correspondence. It was not long before the leader found serious fault with his deputy's conduct. The matter in question, raised on the first day of the conference, was the seemingly trivial procedural issue of whether the French and the Chinese, albeit without voting rights, should be admitted to the negotiations. Molotov's consent to this was immediately pounced on by Stalin as a serious error of principle. At Potsdam, Stalin wrote, "no one had presented the question of a majority versus a minority. Now, in violation of the decisions of the [Potsdam] conference, thanks to your connivance, the Anglo-Saxons have succeeded in drawing in the Chinese and the French, and Byrnes has found a chance to raise the question of the majority versus a minority." "I accept," Molotov responded, "that I have made a great slip . . . and shall insist that henceforth the general sessions of the five ministers will cease." This was to prove more difficult than Molotov expected, and wrangling over procedural matters and some substantive foreign policy issues brought the London conference to a dead end.[12]

On his departure for Sochi in October, Stalin formally left affairs of state in the hand of a "quartet"—that is, the quintet minus Stalin—unofficially led by Molotov. Nevertheless, the leader closely followed events, receiving between twenty and thirty documents a day, including draft Politburo resolutions for approval and reports from security sources. What Stalin read served to fuel his disenchantment with Molotov still further. Stalin was first incensed by the transcript of a discussion between Molotov and Harriman in early November, in which Molotov agreed with U.S. suggestions that the Americans should enjoy a right of veto on a proposed Far Eastern Control Commission for Japan. Stalin, who regarded the American proposal as "underhand" and aimed at isolating the Soviet Union, immediately charged Molotov with lapsing into the ways of the London session. "Molotov's behavior in detaching himself from the government," Stalin wrote to the quartet, "and in presenting himself as more liberal and more compliant than the government, will get us nowhere."[13] Stalin was further angered by Molotov's decision to allow excerpts from a recent speech by Churchill, flattering both to the Russian contribution to the war effort and to Stalin personally, to be published in *Pravda*. "I regard the publication of Churchill's eulogy of Russia and of Stalin to be a mistake," Stalin wrote to the quartet on 10 November. "All this is necessary to Churchill so that he may still his unclear conscience and mask his hostile intentions toward the USSR. . . . We have among us a number of leading workers who are sent into foolish raptures by praise from the Churchills, the Trumans, and the Byrneses and, conversely, sink into depression after unfavorable commentaries by these gentlemen. I regard such opinions as dangerous, since they foster among us servility toward foreign figures." Anticipating the signature slogan of the anti-Western campaign of 1947, Stalin went on: "If in future we publish such speeches, we shall be planting the seeds of servility and groveling."[14]

Stalin's reaction was all the more unexpected since the publication of such speeches had been a regular occurrence during the war. In a response, sent on 11 November, Molotov intimated that he understood the chief reason behind Stalin's rebuke: "Publication of a shortened version of Churchill's speech was authorized by me. I acknowledge this was a mistake, since even in the printed version Churchill's praise of Russia and Stalin has served to mask his hostile intentions toward the Soviet Union. In any case, it should not have been published *without your consent*."[15] Having known Stalin for over twenty years, Molotov understood that whatever secondary goals he may have had, the primary purpose of the leader's interventions were to find fault in his deputy and thereby bring him into line.

It was at the beginning of December 1945, however, that Stalin's patience with Molotov finally snapped. On 1 December, Stalin's daughter, Svetlana, wrote to her father: "I am very, very pleased that you are healthy and are having a good rest. I say this since Muscovites, unaccustomed to your absence, have begun to spread rumors that you have fallen seriously ill and that such-and-such doctors have been dispatched to attend to you."[16] On the same day, an article appeared in the *Daily Herald*, claiming that "today political power in the Soviet Union lies in the hands of Molotov" and that Molotov would soon be reinstated as head of government (the post he had yielded to Stalin in 1941). Stalin's understandable unease at hearing these reports was only made worse by a separate chain of events that commenced the following day in a telephone conversation with Molotov. As Commissar for Foreign Affairs, Molotov bore responsibility for screening press coverage by Moscow-based journalists. Following concerted lobbying from journalists and overseas embassies, Molotov tried to plead with Stalin to relax the censorship on foreign correspondents. Sensing Stalin's indignation, Molotov quickly backtracked and proceeded to assure the leader that censorship would not be eased but, rather, tightened.[17]

Nevertheless, on 3 December, the Soviet news agency TASS circulated an article from the *New York Times*, which claimed that the Politburo had sent Stalin on vacation five days after Molotov's return from London.[18]

Stalin became all the more dismayed when, also on 3 December, Reuters announced that a relaxation of press censorship had taken place in the Soviet Union. Reuters attributed the new shift in policy to Molotov, referring to a declaration by Molotov to this effect at a reception for the foreign press corps on 7 November.[19] Very early on the morning of 5 December, Stalin wrote to the quartet, complaining of the cock-and-bull stories and slanders that had appeared over the previous days and ordered that further "lampoons against the Soviet government" be stopped. In addition, Stalin asked that the relevant culprit be identified: "If Molotov forgot to give out the instructions, then the press department is innocent and we shall need to draw Molotov to account."[20]

The next day the quartet conceded that Molotov had authorized a slight easing of press restrictions in November but denied the statement attributed to him in the Reuters report. Rallying to Molotov's defense, the quartet tried to place the blame for the offending pieces on the press department at the Commissariat of Foreign Affairs whose deputy chief, Gorokhov, it informed Stalin, had duly been sacked.[21] These measures were not, however, the ones Stalin had in mind. In a very sharp ciphered message that afternoon, addressed to Malenkov, Beria, and Mikoian, Stalin made it plain that he regarded the quartet's response as "entirely unsatisfactory" and that he considered it an attempt to "brush the affair aside." "None of us has the right to change the course of our policies unilaterally," Stalin argued. "But Molotov has accorded himself this right. Why, and on what grounds? . . . Until your message I thought that we could confine ourselves to a reprimand of Molotov. But that is no longer enough. I am convinced that Molotov does not much value the interests of our state and the prestige of our government, so long as he gains popularity among certain foreign circles. I can no longer regard this comrade as my first deputy." In order to make the assault on Molotov all the more humiliating, Stalin rounded off his message with the words, "I send this only to the three of you. I have not sent it to Molotov, as I do not trust the conscientiousness of some of those around him. I ask you to summon Molotov and to read him this telegram in full, but not to present him with a copy of it."[22]

On 7 December, the triumvirate reported that they had performed Stalin's instructions. "We summoned Molotov and read out your telegram in full. After some hesitation Molotov admitted that he had committed very many mistakes, but he regarded the lack of trust in him as unjust, and shed some tears." The triumvirate proceeded to serve on Molotov a list of his errors, beginning with his mistakes at the London conference, before moving on to his advocacy of a "personal, compliant, and unfavorable position" on the Far Eastern Commission and to his loosening of controls over the Moscow-based Western press. "All these mistakes," the triumvirate wrote to Stalin, "including those on censorship, are part of a general policy of concessions to the Anglo-Americans, so that foreigners will take the view that Molotov has his own policy which is different from the policy of the government and of Stalin, and [so that the Anglo-Americans will think] that with him, with Molotov, it will be quite possible to work something out."[23] On the same day Molotov sent his own reply to Stalin. Conceding that he had erred on the side of "false liberalism" and that he had committed a "gross, opportunistic mistake which has brought harm to our state," he went on: "Your ciphered message is filled with deep distrust toward me, both as a Bolshevik and as a person, which I take as a most serious party warning for all my further work. I shall try through deeds to regain your trust, in which every honest Bolshevik sees not only personal trust, but also the trust of the party, which is dearer to me than my own life."[24]

On the following day Stalin wrote to the triumvirate that he disagreed with their "interpretation of the essence of the matter" and that he would take up the issue when he returned to Moscow.[25] By the next morning, however, Stalin adopted a more conciliatory tone. Writing this time to the full quartet, he admonished them for having "succumbed to pressure and intimidation from the United States and for having wavered and adopted a liberal course." He went on: "Chance came to your rescue and in time you returned to the policy of firmness."[26] Although Stalin did not refrain from giving his deputy advice and administering occasional reproofs on other matters over the following year, he decided to let this matter lie.[27]

The attack on Molotov at the end of 1945 was by no means the first time that Stalin had lashed out at his deputy. After the Great Terror, Stalin had, on several occasions, taken measures against Molotov.[28] Yet in its tone and in the manner in which it was delivered, this attack was sterner and more humiliating than anything that had come before. One reason for this may have been that Stalin sought to compensate for the fact that, for the first time in nearly a decade, he was not in Moscow. For this reason, Stalin would establish for himself a reputation of being even tougher, even more severe, when he was out of town.[29] Of equal importance, however, was the fact that Molotov had gained a measure of autonomy during the war. The succession of errors after September 1945 gave Stalin the impression that his deputy was not taking his views, and in particular the idea that the Soviet Union needed to pursue a "firm" line, sufficiently seriously. Worse still, Molotov had, on a number of issues, given every sign of pursuing his "personal" position in foreign affairs. This was something that Stalin would not stand for. When the quartet hesitated on Stalin's signal, and seemed reluctant to follow the rules of group condemnation that had become customary in the late 1930s, Stalin decided to act, and he did so with unprecedented ferocity.

Notwithstanding their severity, these attacks had no bearing on Molotov's official standing within the government, nor do they appear to have put Molotov in any personal danger. Stalin was especially keen to keep knowledge of the affair restricted to a very small subgroup, so that even most members of the Politburo were not told of it at the time. While Stalin certainly wanted to dent Molotov's authority within the ruling circle, and to have Molotov reassume the subjugated persona of the late 1930s, he appears to have had no intention of taking the matter further. What Stalin appeared to want was the reestablishment of some sort of leadership balance, modeled on the relationships he had forged with his companions on the eve of the war.

Anastas Mikoian was not as senior or as well-known a politician as Molotov, nor was he ever seriously viewed as a potential successor to Stalin. Nevertheless, a candidate member of the Politburo since 1926, Mikoian was of the same political generation as Molotov. As a devout Stalinist and member of the ruling group since the late 1920s, Mikoian came to be seen, like Molotov, as a coarchitect of the Stalinist system that had been formed in the early 1930s. It was a measure of Mikoian's seniority in the pecking order that, like Molotov and Kliment Voroshilov, he was the only member of the postwar Politburo to address Stalin in familiar terms.[30] As did Molotov—but unlike Voroshilov—Mikoian emerged from the war and from the dissolution of the GKO as a firmly entrenched member of Stalin's quintet.

The first postwar incident with Mikoian to provoke Stalin's wrath occurred in the spring of 1946, when the Soviet Union entered into negotiations with the Americans over financial credits the Soviets were hoping to receive from the United States. Although the Americans attached conditions that were unacceptable to the Soviet side, Mikoian, in consultation with the Deputy Minister of Foreign Affairs, Solomon Lozovsky, and with the support of Molotov in Paris, sent a broadly favorable response to the Americans at the end of April. Although Mikoian requested that Lozovsky clear the matter with the Central Committee ("that is with the Politburo, i.e., Stalin," he would later recall), the matter never reached the leader. Stalin was predictably indignant. "Since when," he asked a vexed Mikoian a month later, "have you been taking decisions in the name of the Politburo on questions of foreign policy?" Stalin then quietly dropped the matter but, as with Molotov, he would return to it in later years and charge Mikoian with being "in league" with Lozovsky.[31]

A more pressing concern in the summer and autumn of 1946 was the increasingly desperate food situation for which Mikoian, as deputy chair of the Council of Ministers in charge of food supplies, was held responsible. For some months Mikoian had rejected appeals from the Minister for Procurements, B. A. Dvinskii, to regulate the demand for bread by decreasing ration supplies and placing caps on the monthly distribution of grain. In view of Mikoian's resistance, Dvinskii, who had earlier served as Stalin's personal aide, decided to bypass his immediate superior and appeal directly to the leader. "We are quickly using up our grain reserves," he reported in a letter of 23 September 1946. "Please," he went on, "consider my report, for without you no one will settle [this] painful issue."[32] Stalin quickly sided with his former aide. On 3 October, in a telegram to all the members of the Politburo, Stalin wrote: "It appears that comrade Mikoian, in supervising the ministries responsible for [food supplies], has turned out to be entirely unprepared, not only for the resolution of these questions but even for understanding them and placing them for discussion."[33] Twelve days later, Stalin wrote to top party and state leaders in even more scathing terms: "Do not show any faith in this matter in comrade Mikoian, who, thanks to his poor management, has been breeding thieves around our supplies."[34] Emphasizing his displeasure with Mikoian, Stalin also ordered that control of the Ministry of Trade be shifted from the Council of Ministers, where it had been part of Mikoian's brief, to the Central Committee Secretariat.[35]

Stalin's attack on Mikoian enabled the leader to shift some of the blame for the grain shortages onto one of his deputies. It serves as a good example of how the leader could turn the tensions of postwar reconstruction—which in this case had reached near-crisis proportions—into a convenient pretext for bringing a member of his ruling circle into line. Shortly afterward, however, Stalin dropped his assault on Mikoian. Like the attack on Molotov, the primary purpose of the rebuke was to discipline a close colleague, not to signal his elimination. As with Molotov, this was a preventative and prophylactic measure designed to restore the prewar equilibrium.

For his part, Mikoian quickly caved in to the mounting pressure from Stalin: "Of course, neither I nor others," a contrite Mikoian conceded to the leader, "can frame questions quite like you. I shall devote all my energy so that I may learn from you how to work correctly. I shall do all I can to draw the lessons from your stern criticism, so that it is turned to good use in my further work under your fatherly guidance."[36] Like Molotov, Mikoian was a seasoned member of the inner circle, who could easily slip back into the norms of Politburo deference which had been drummed into him over the 1930s. Although the other two members of the quartet—Malenkov and Beria—had been handpicked by Stalin and owed their rise entirely to him, they were relative newcomers to the ruling group and may not have assimilated prewar leadership norms as deeply as their more senior companions. Certainly, in his treatment of these two younger colleagues, Stalin would employ rather different tactics.

The Upstarts

Although only five years younger than Mikoian and ten years younger than Molotov, Malenkov and Beria hailed from a very different political generation. Malenkov first took up a major post in 1934, when he became head of the department of leading party agencies at the Central Committee. Five years later, in 1939, he became party Secretary, head of the cadres administration, and a member of the Central Committee. Beria had become First Secretary of the Transcaucasian regional party committee in 1932 and a member of the Central Committee in 1934. He moved to Moscow in 1938, first becoming deputy Commissar of Internal Affairs in August and then commissar in November. Whereas Molotov had joined the Politburo (as a candidate member) in 1921, and Mikoian in 1926, it was well over a decade later, on the very eve of the war, in March 1939 and February 1941, that Beria and Malenkov entered the Politburo as candidates.

Stalin's attack on Malenkov and Beria was all the stranger for coming hot on the heels of his decision to have them elected, in March 1946, as full members of the Politburo. After picking them as members of his ruling group and having them formally ratified as full members of the Politburo, Stalin immediately set about concocting "affairs" against them. The first to suffer was Malenkov. The origins of Stalin's charge against him lay in a claim by Stalin's air force pilot son, Vasilii, that the fighter planes he had flown during the war had been of poor quality.[37] As deputy premier responsible, since 1942, for aircraft production, such an accusation had inescapable consequences for Malenkov. Stalin ordered an inquiry and, at the Politburo meeting of 29 December 1945, engineered the dismissal of A. I. Shakhurin, the Minister for Aviation Industry, who had been named by Vasilii.[38] A criminal investigation followed, for which Marshal S. A. Khudiakov, commander of the Twelfth Air Division, served as a key witness, testifying against a large number of generals and leading officials from the aviation industry, among them Shakhurin. "Our investigation of the work of the Air Force and complaints from front-line pilots over the low quality of our planes," Stalin wrote on 11 April 1946, "have brought us to the conclusion that the former Commissar for Aviation Industry Shakhurin, who delivered planes for the front, and the former chief engineer of the Air Force, Repin, and his subordinate, Seleznev, who accepted these planes, had struck a deal the aim of which . . . was to fool the government and to receive awards for 'fulfilling' and 'overfulfilling' the plan. This criminal activity continued for around two years and led to the death of our pilots. . . . [Accordingly,] those immediately responsible for these crimes have been arrested."[39] As the investigations progressed, their remit was broadened to examine what role, if any, Malenkov had played in the affair.[40]

It was against the background of these ongoing investigations that Malenkov's simultaneous promotion and disgrace took place. On 18 March, at a meeting of the Central Committee, Malenkov was elected a full member of the Politburo and reelected as Central Committee Secretary. The following day, however, Malenkov was removed as deputy chair of the Council of Ministers.[41] Toward the end of March, the four party Secretaries, led by Malenkov, sent Stalin a draft resolution on the organization of the Central Committee apparatus which envisaged Malenkov as chair of the two leading party committees, the Secretariat and the Orgburo. Stalin rejected the draft. In response to his instructions, the four returned with a new draft, approved by the Politburo on 13 April, which ruled that Malenkov would no longer preside over the Secretariat or lead the mighty cadres administration.[42]

In the 1930s, one of Stalin's favored ploys for undermining colleagues had been to have their aides and deputies arrested. It was thus a dark omen for Malenkov when the head of the aviation industry sector at the Central Committee apparatus, Grigorian, who had been Malenkov's "right-hand man" in supervising the aviation industry during the war, was detained.[43] On 25 April, a rattled Malenkov delivered a fiery speech to party members at the aviation ministry. In what could have been construed as an oblique reference to his own situation, he declared: "Many here have taken fright and are thinking to themselves: they have already imprisoned the leadership; we have produced low-quality goods, so what will they now do to us?"[44]

Malenkov did not have to wait long to find out. At the next meeting of the Politburo, on 4 May, Stalin dictated a resolution dismissing Malenkov as Central Committee Secretary. So as to publicize Malenkov's downfall, the resolution was voted on "by correspondence" by all members of the Central Committee over the following two days. "As the person in charge of the aviation industry and of . . . the air force more generally," the resolution stated, "comrade Malenkov bears moral responsibility for the shocking things which have been exposed in these agencies (the production and acceptance of substandard planes), and for the fact that he, knowing of these outrages, did not inform the Central Committee."[45] Sacked as party Secretary, Malenkov was also stripped of his chairmanship of the Orgburo. Although he remained a member of the Politburo, and he continued to attend leadership functions, he slipped to last place in protocol rankings in the press.[46] Malenkov, it seemed, had been cast into political limbo.[47]

It was common for Stalin to sit on personal cases for long stretches before coming to a decision.[48] It was almost three months, on 2 August, before Malenkov's fortunes were partially restored with his reappointment as deputy chair of the Council of Ministers. A week later, on 8 August, Malenkov again began attending meetings of the main Sovmin Bureau (which he had missed since March) and, on the following day, he played a central role at a key meeting of the Orgburo on the Leningrad journals. At the beginning of the following month, on 2 and 6 September, Malenkov also attended both meetings of the full Politburo. Despite a two-month posting to Siberia from October to December, in autumn 1946 Malenkov's fortunes began to pick up.[49] Even as his career began to revive, however, Malenkov would not lose sight of the fact that for several months he had come very close to the wire. Intimate colleagues and right-hand men from the war years had been arrested. His own name had come up in the course of the investigations, and the question of whether to press charges against Malenkov himself must surely have been raised. More so than had been the case with either Molotov or Mikoian, Malenkov's fate had hung in the balance.

Stalin's offensive against the last member of the quartet, Beria, was not as sharp as his attack on Malenkov, and the contrast between promotion and humiliation was not as striking. On 18 March 1946, Beria was elected a full member of the Politburo, and two days later he was made chair of the powerful new unified Bureau of the Council of Ministers.[50] In the distribution of responsibilities that followed, Beria was given oversight of the Ministry of Internal Affairs, the Ministry of State Security, and the Ministry of State Control.[51] Having been released as Commissar of Internal Affairs in December 1945, Beria, in accordance with his new Politburo status, assumed an "overlord" role over the Ministry of Internal Affairs (MVD) and the other two ministries.[52] In order to weaken Beria's hold over his traditional fiefdom, the MVD, Stalin chose as Beria's successor Sergei Kruglov, an official not in any respect beholden to Beria. Further, only one of the seven deputy ministers of internal affairs appointed in April, Mamulov, was directly connected to Beria.[53] While Beria retained overall responsibility for the ministry, it was no longer so clearly a tool of his political ambitions.

Although the Ministry of Internal Affairs had assumed major economic responsibilities since the 1930s, it was not as politically sensitive as was the Ministry of State Security, from which it had been divided in April 1943. Since the division, Beria had retained his own line of access to the security service through the minister, Vsevolod Merkulov, one of his oldest and most intimate associates from Georgia. Toward the end of 1945, while he was away in the south, Stalin began to formulate misgivings about Merkulov's leadership of the commissariat.[54] These came to a head at the same session of the Politburo, on 4 May 1946, at which Malenkov was sacked as Central Committee Secretary. The Politburo dismissed Merkulov as Minister of State Security and replaced him with Viktor Abakumov, who had taken over as deputy minister in March.[55] The removal of Merkulov was a blow to Beria, not least because his relations with the new minister, Abakumov, were at best neutral. Worse still for Beria was that Stalin ordered a commission be set up to explore mistakes committed under Merkulov's leadership.[56] As with Malenkov, Stalin chose to attack Beria obliquely, by launching an offensive against one of his closest associates. Any findings against Merkulov could easily have rubbed off, by association, on Beria, who was Merkulov's patron and protector. Beria was thus forced to sweat it out as the commission, whose deliberations lasted for nearly four months, slowly wound its way to a conclusion. On 20 August, Stalin dictated a Politburo resolution "On comrade Merkulov" which, in the event, concluded with a relatively mild indictment of Merkulov.[57] The resolution, and a proposal that Merkulov be demoted from full to candidate member of the Central Committee, were then brought to a correspondence vote of the Central Committee from 21 to 23 August.[58] The fallout of the Merkulov affair for Beria was later made apparent by Merkulov. "The history of my departure from the Ministry of State Security," he recounted, "produced a number of uncomfortable moments for Beria. Beria himself told me that on my account he became the target of much unpleasantness from Stalin."[59]

The attacks on Malenkov and Beria were part of a broader action by Stalin to destroy the system of leadership that had emerged in wartime. Stalin sought to nip in the bud any signs of autonomy within the ruling group and to restore the Politburo to the norms of the immediate post-purge period of the late 1930s. While Stalin took energetic measures to chasten the more recent Politburo recruits, even here he stopped short of decisive or irreversible steps. It had been for good reasons that Stalin had picked this quartet in the first place; they possessed the requisite combination of loyalty, personal authority, and capacity for hard work which Stalin cherished. Having gone to the trouble of forging a set of working relationships within the ruling group, he could gain little from breaking the equilibrium and searching for replacements.

Members of the quartet were not the only leadership figures to suffer from Stalin's attentions after the war. Other Politburo members were also subjected to dressing-downs and reprisals.[60] Outside the Politburo itself Stalin was particularly mindful of the need to attend to the army. During the war, especially at the early stages, some generals had of necessity taken the lead from Stalin.[61] By the end of the war, the status of the army and of its high command within Soviet society had grown enormously. For Stalin, who coveted his reputation as war leader arguably above all else, the latter development was regrettable.[62] Returning the ruling group to prewar norms meant not only curtailing the autonomy of his deputies but also reinforcing the cult of the leader.

As a means of reasserting his military credentials, Stalin had himself crowned as head of the newly integrated Commissariat of Armed Forces on 25 February 1946.[63] It was also at around this time that Stalin moved against the foremost military hero of the war, Marshal Georgii Zhukov. One line of attack, vigorously pursued by the then head of counterintelligence in Germany, Abakumov, was an allegation that Zhukov had purloined state property while stationed in East Germany after the war.[64] The charge that was to prove particularly damaging to Zhukov, however, was of an altogether different nature. Two days after Stalin's Kremlin reception to mark the Soviet victory, Zhukov invited a group of generals to his dacha outside Moscow for a celebration of their own. The following day, tapes of the group hailing Zhukov as "victor over Germany" reached Stalin's desk. Concerns over Zhukov's "arrogance" were confirmed by the concurrent investigations into the Aviators' Affair. Testimony by the former head of the air force, A. A. Novikov, proved to be particularly harmful: "In a very cunning and guarded form," Novikov claimed, Zhukov "tries to belittle the leading role in the war of the supreme commander in chief [Stalin], while he is not embarrassed to overemphasize his own role as army leader in the war, and he even declares that all the main plans for military operations were worked out by him."[65]

On 1 June 1946, four weeks after the demotion of Malenkov and the sacking of Merkulov, an infuriated Stalin presented Novikov's testimony to a stunned meeting of the Soviet military council.[66] Two days later, the Council of Ministers ratified a proposal from the military council that Zhukov be released both as commander in chief of ground forces and head of the Soviet military administration in Germany. On 9 June, the Ministry of Armed Forces issued an extraordinary attack on Zhukov: "Having lost all sense of humility and carried away by personal ambition, Marshal Zhukov, believing that his achievements had been undervalued, ascribed to himself in conversations with subordinates the preparation and conduct of all the major operations of the Great Patriotic War, including those operations in which he was not at all involved."[67] Nonetheless, as with Malenkov and Merkulov, Stalin stopped short of drastic measures. While Zhukov was demoted to the lesser post of head of the Odessa military district and, in February 1947, was dropped from the Central Committee, in later years Stalin would arrange his return to the committee and to a key role in the military.[68]

Stalin's postwar attacks on the quartet and, to a lesser extent, on Marshal Zhukov, were designed to restore the system of leadership norms that had prevailed on the eve of the war. One aspect of Stalin's postwar strategy involved taking on all those who came close to rivaling his authority in head-on confrontations. Stalin also, however, sought to lessen his reliance on particular individuals by swelling the ranks of his ruling group. On coming back to Moscow in December 1945, Stalin added a new member, Andrei Zhdanov, so that the quintet became a sextet.[69] Shortly after, in the spring of 1946, Zhdanov replaced Malenkov as head of the party apparatus. By August of that year Zhdanov had become, along with Stalin, one of only two signatories of joint party-state resolutions, with Stalin representing the government and Zhdanov the Central Committee. With all decisions of the Central Committee's two executive arms, the Orgburo and Secretariat, requiring his consent, Zhdanov became the only member of the sextet, apart from Stalin, to devote himself to general rather than to sectoral issues. In the coming year Zhdanov, and the party apparatus that he headed, would become the main conduit for implementing Stalin's domestic policies. Rather than initiating these campaigns, as some earlier scholars have surmised, the archives show that Zhdanov was Stalin's compliant, hard-pressed, and ultimately rather bewildered agent.

Andrei Zhdanov and
Stalin's Cold War

Early depictions of Zhdanov in the postwar period emphasized his role as a hard-line radical and scourge of the Soviet intelligentsia, whose personal crackdown on culture in the summer of 1946 would later become synonymous—as the so-called Zhdanovshchina—with a regime of unthinking dogmatism and philistine intolerance in the arts.[70] Later portrayals sought, by contrast, to present him as an advocate of moderation and as a patron of liberals in the sciences and humanities.[71] In fact, in matters relating to culture and the arts, Zhdanov appears to have had very few ideas of his own. Virtually his every move in these areas was orchestrated by Stalin, so much so that Zhdanov was coaxed into actions that ran against his own interests. For his part, Stalin was guided by what he perceived as the evolving logic of the Cold War, one which would pit the Soviet intelligentsia against all things Western.

The fact that he was little more than Stalin's factotum did not mean that Zhdanov lacked an institutional identity. Following the illness and death of Aleksei Shcherbakov in May 1945, Zhdanov returned to Moscow in November 1945 in order to oversee the agitation and propaganda department, then headed by his protégé, Georgii Aleksandrov, and to take overall charge of ideological matters in the party. One of the main challenges confronting Zhdanov was the need to return the party to the path of ideological orthodoxy. Without observing normal procedures for screening and training new members, millions of new recruits had been admitted to the party during the war; many soldiers had also encountered relatively unregimented and prosperous societies while in action.[72] The demobilization of young soldier-members after the war and their integration into party cells at their workplaces threatened to dilute the ideological purity of civilian party organizations. It was in this context that Zhdanov was entrusted with increasing ideological vigilance. His duties in the ideological sphere were properly formalized in a Politburo resolution of 13 April 1946.[73] Within four months Zhdanov had set up a new propaganda weekly, *Kul'tura i zhizn'*, authored two key Central Committee resolutions on improving the ideological and practical training of new members and leading officials, and established the new Higher Party School at the Central Committee.[74]

In the spring of 1946 some of Zhdanov's associates also prospered. In March, Aleksei Kuznetsov, who had served for many years under Zhdanov in Leningrad, was made Secretary of the Central Committee.[75] On 13 April, Kuznetsov took over responsibility for supervising the mighty cadres administration and for chairing sessions of the Central Committee Secretariat from Malenkov.[76] Other figures close to Zhdanov also received high-ranking promotions in this period. Thus, for example, Nikolai Patolichev, who had known Zhdanov since the 1920s, was invited, at a meeting with Stalin, Zhdanov, and Kuznetsov on 4 May, to take over as Central Committee Secretary and to head the new powerful administration for checking party organs.[77] Zhdanov's ascendancy in the party was then secured at a Politburo meeting later that day, when his main rival, Malenkov, was dismissed as Central Committee Secretary and was succeeded by Zhdanov as chair of a new, more powerful Orgburo.[78]

Notwithstanding the sudden rise of Zhdanov over the spring and summer of 1946, the main episodes that year for which he would become famous were ones in which it was Stalin, not Zhdanov, who took the lead. While Stalin was keen to present these initiatives as Zhdanov's own, it was Stalin who pushed and cajoled Zhdanov into adopting positions he most certainly would not otherwise have taken. An underlying theme of these attacks, which would only become fully apparent in the summer of 1947, was the need to discipline the Soviet intelligentsia, and as international tensions deepened, to drive it into an ideological war with the West.

On 14 August 1946, the Central Committee published a resolution "On the Journals *Zvezda* and *Leningrad*," which condemned the named Leningrad-based publications for serious ideological irregularities.[79] Two days later, Zhdanov delivered a fiery speech to the Leningrad branch of the Writers' Union, castigating two writers, the humorist Mikhail Zoshchenko and the poet Anna Akhmatova, in the most vitriolic of terms. Zhdanov's speech, an amended version of which was later published in the national press, vilified Zoshchenko as a "vulgar and trivial petty bourgeois," who "oozed anti-Soviet poison" and indulged in "vile obscenities" and "political hooliganism"; Akhmatova, in Zhdanov's infamous formulation, was a "mixture of nun and harlot, . . . a crazy gentlewoman dashing backwards and forwards between her boudoir and her chapel."[80] For this tirade and the campaign of artistic repression that followed, Zhdanov's name would become a "byword of intolerance, cultural persecution and dictatorial stupidity," and the phase of ideological regimentation over which he presided would become known as the Zhdanovshchina, literally, "the time of Zhdanov."[81]

In fact, however, the campaign against the intelligentsia was closely choreographed by Stalin. It began at the Politburo meeting of 13 April 1946, when, according to Zhdanov, "Comrade Stalin issued a very sharp criticism of our thick journals, and raised the question of whether the thick journals should be reduced in number." Stalin had argued that, since the thick—that is, the densely filled literary journals—could evidently not be relied on to deliver genuine "internal criticism," that task should now fall on the propaganda administration of the Central Committee.[82] The eventual choice of journals to be attacked, and in particular the fact that they were to be Leningrad-based, was also almost certainly Stalin's.[83] Zhdanov had been First Secretary in Leningrad for over a decade and, together with his colleague Kuznetsov, continued to have responsibility for overseeing its affairs. Attacking Leningrad-based institutions, and especially the Leningrad party, which was inevitably implicated in the running of the journals, could only sully his own reputation as a political overlord. In fact, on 26 June, the bureau of the Leningrad city committee approved the inclusion of Zoshchenko on the editorial board of *Zvezda*, and on 6 July the organ of the city committee printed an article praising the writer. Such was their involvement in monitoring and sanctioning the journal that in the fallout from the August decree, officials from the Leningrad city committee were reprimanded. Attacking his old bailiwick was an embarrassment for Zhdanov and ran against his personal interests.[84]

In fact, Zhdanov himself was very subdued at the key meeting of the Orgburo on 9 August devoted to denouncing the journals, while his rival, Malenkov, played the more pronounced role. "In Leningrad," Malenkov declared, "they have given refuge to those who have been beaten." "Zoshchenko was criticized," he told the editor of *Zvezda*, Prokof'ev, "but you offered him shelter." When Stalin asked whether the Leningrad committee had been told of the inclusion of Zoshchenko on the new board of *Zvezda*, Malenkov sniped: "Yes, that was decided on by the Leningrad committee."[85]

It was Stalin himself, however, who played the key role at the Orgburo meeting of 9 August. The significance Stalin attached to this meeting was underlined by the fact that he attended it at all; this was, in fact, the only occasion after the war for which Stalin was present at a session of the Orgburo. Stalin dominated the session not only with his presence but with a short oration on the offending journals, which would set the tone for

Zhdanov's speech: "Why do I not like people such as Zoshchenko?" he asked rhetorically. "It is because they write these hollow, trivial things, not even stories or essays, but things which make you want to vomit. Can we tolerate such people in literature? No, we can't. Can we allow such people to educate our youth? No, we cannot." Of Akhmatova, he went on: "Why the hell should we adapt our journal to the tastes of an old poetess, on what basis?"[86] In his speeches in Leningrad, Zhdanov himself would make plain Stalin's central role in the attacks:

> This question has been raised at the Central Committee on the initiative of comrade Stalin. He is personally informed of the work of the journals *Zvezda* and *Leningrad*, has always followed closely the state of these journals, and reads the literary works they publish. [It is comrade Stalin who] proposed that the Central Committee discuss shortcomings in the leadership of these journals, and, moreover, he himself participated at the session of the Central Committee [at which they were discussed] and issued the directives which lie at the heart of the decision of the Central Committee which it is now my duty to elucidate to you.[87]

It was therefore with good reason that a leading member of Agitprop at the time, A. M. Egolin, would later recount: "Stalin inspired these decisions . . . it was he who drew our attention to Zoshchenko."[88] "Of course," Khrushchev would observe, "Zhdanov performed his assigned role, but he was all the same implementing the direct instructions of Stalin."[89] Even after Zhdanov delivered his speech he sought instructions from Stalin. On 14 September, he sent an amended draft of the Leningrad speech to Stalin: "I beg of you, if it is at all possible, to have a look at this and to see whether it is suitable for publication and to decide what needs to be corrected." "I think," replied Stalin on 19 September, "that the paper has come out superbly. We need to get it out in the press quickly, and then to bring it out as a brochure."[90]

Zhdanov's Leningrad speech would become notorious for the way in which two gifted writers were humiliated. Of equally long-term significance, however, was the fact that the resolution of 14 August poured scorn on works that "cultivate the spirit, alien to the Soviet people, of servility before the modern bourgeois culture of the West."[91] In the amended version of his speeches, which Zhdanov prepared for Stalin's perusal, this theme was explored at greater length:

> Some of our literary people have come to see themselves not as teachers, but as pupils [and] . . . have slipped into a tone of servility and cringing before philistine foreign literature. Is such servility becoming of us Soviet patriots, who are building the Soviet system, which is a hundred times higher and better than any bourgeois system? Is it becoming of our

vanguard Soviet literature, which is the most revolutionary literature in the world, to cringe before the narrow-minded and philistine bourgeois literature of the West?[92]

Stalin had played a major part in writing the Central Committee resolution, and the reference to "servility before the West" most probably originated with him. Certainly, the phrase was one that Stalin had used the previous autumn.[93]

The second stage in the unfolding campaign to rein in the intelligentsia would build on the theme of a rift with the West, which Stalin had adumbrated in August. Here, too, Stalin was the main instigator and Zhdanov his tool. In 1946, the head of Agitprop, Aleksandrov, an old associate of Zhdanov's, published a volume titled *The History of Western European Philosophy*. Although the book was initially well received—it was awarded a Stalin prize—Stalin subsequently turned against it, for belittling Russian philosophy, after he had received a denunciation from the Moscow University philosopher Zinovii Beletskii.[94] In light of Stalin's criticism, the Secretariat organized a conference on the book at the Institute of Philosophy in January 1947. Launching an attack on Aleksandrov could not have been easy for Zhdanov, since the former had headed Agitprop under Zhdanov's supervision since 1940 and was very much regarded as Zhdanov's dependent.

Stalin's central charge against Aleksandrov was that his book had underestimated the influence of Russian philosophy on the West. The attack on the book was merely a vehicle for a broader point Stalin wanted to make: that Russians needed greater confidence in their own achievements. In the event, the January discussants tried to gloss over any serious criticism of Aleksandrov, presumably in the hope that the whole matter might blow over. The urgency of Stalin's rationale, however, became all the more apparent in the months after January, as relations with the West plunged to a new low. On 12 March, President Truman set out his "doctrine" to Congress and called for aid for Greece and Turkey to counteract the "totalitarian" threat of communism. The following month, the breakdown of the Council of Foreign Ministers conference in Moscow signaled that relations between the superpowers had reached an impasse. In light of heightened international tensions, Stalin decided to return to the Aleksandrov volume and to depict the author himself as a high-profile illustration of the dangers of undue deference to the West.

On 22 April, once the failure of the meeting of the Council of Foreign Ministers had become clear, the Secretariat ordered a second, more searching discussion of Aleksandrov's book. Unlike the January session, this conference, which lasted from 16–25 June, was a widely publicized event. Over fifty speakers presented their critical comments on the book, and the proceedings were published verbatim in 501 pages of a new journal, *Voprosy filosofii*.[95] Unhappy at Zhdanov's aloofness from the January debate, which had been organized by Aleksandrov's own deputies at Agitprop, P. N. Fedoseev, V. S. Kruzhkov, and G. S. Vasetskii, Stalin insisted that this time Zhdanov preside over the proceedings. Toward the end of the discussion, on 24 June, Zhdanov gave the most authoritative outline of the charge against Aleksandrov: by not including Russian philosophy in his discussion of European philosophy, Aleksandrov had belittled the influence of Russian thinkers on the development of world thought.[96] A reluctant Zhdanov was thus compelled by Stalin to berate his own dependent. By the end of the summer Aleksandrov and another Zhdanov associate, Aleksandrov's deputy, Fedoseev, were removed from their powerful positions at Agitprop and replaced by a new team headed by the recently appointed Central Committee Secretary, M. A. Suslov.[97]

By early summer 1947, the ideological campaign was also operating on a third front. This time the targets were two scientists, Nina Kliueva and her husband Grigorii Roskin, who had been working in Moscow on a so-called miracle cure for cancer. The main instrument of the new offensive was the "honor court," an updated Soviet version of a czarist institution that had been used to shame and in some cases to force the resignation of officials, especially from the army, who had violated accepted occupational norms.[98] Zhdanov was the chief behind-the-scenes manager of the first and most famous of these trials, against Kliueva and Roskin, held in Moscow on 5–7 June before an audience of over 800 spectators. Some scholars have viewed this as an extension by Zhdanov of the earlier campaigns of 1946 to reestablish the authority of the party apparatus over the cultural and artistic spheres. Having reasserted party control over writers and philosophers, it has been argued, Zhdanov now sought to do the same to science and, by doing so, to enhance the power of the ideological apparatus led by him, within the party bureaucracy.[99]

Although most of the groundwork for the Kliueva and Roskin trial was prepared by Zhdanov, it was Stalin who determined its content and general direction. The case had its origins in a concern that key secrets relating to the cancer cure had been divulged to representatives of the Western scientific community over the summer and autumn of 1946.[100] The matter appears first to have been discussed seriously at a meeting of the ruling group on 24 January 1947, the day of Zhdanov's return from vacation.[101] From its very beginning, Stalin seems to have taken a keen interest in the case. Thus, on 1 February, Zhdanov forwarded him the record of conversations he had had the previous week with Kliueva and the Minister of Public Health, Georgii Miterev, and two days later Stalin received a transcript of Kliueva and Roskin's meeting with the American ambassador, Walter Bedell Smith, which had taken place the previous summer.[102] On 6 February, Stalin acquired a transcript of the interrogations of the head of the cancer administration at the Ministry of Health, B. V. Milonov, who had been arrested on Stalin's orders a week earlier.[103] On 17 February, Stalin convened a session of the Politburo to discuss the affair. In addition to sacking Miterev, Stalin had Vasilii Parin, the official who had handed Kliueva and Roskin's manuscript to the Americans, arrested.[104]

It is likely that the decision to organize an honor court around the case was Stalin's.[105] Once the trial started, Stalin closely monitored its progress. Certainly, it is unlikely that without his keen interest the whole Politburo would have followed the proceedings of the honor court, receiving stenographic reports of its sessions daily.[106] Arguably of greater significance, however, was the choice of target for the court. Originally, the Politburo's energies had been directed at the Minister of Public Health, Miterev. Sometime after the Politburo meeting of 17 February, probably in April, Stalin appears to have decided that Kliueva and Roskin, rather than Miterev, should be the main defendants at the trial.[107] Zhdanov's notebook, where he dutifully took down Stalin's utterances on these and other matters, accordingly reads: "The commissar [Miterev] did not lead them, but it was they, together with Parin, who led him."[108]

Having Kliueva and Roskin as the chief defendants would prove extremely embarrassing for Zhdanov. It had been following a recommendation from an old associate of his, V. N. Viktorov, on 15 March 1946, that the case for improving their work conditions had first been brought to the Secretariat by Zhdanov himself on 4 April 1946.[109] Moreover, it was to Zhdanov that Kliueva and Roskin had turned later in the year for help to further improve their working conditions. "It was thanks to your help that in May and June measures were taken to enable us to work normally," they wrote to him on 15 November.[110] These were facts that Kliueva and Roskin gladly brought up at the "rehearsals" for the trial on 15, 20, and 27 May. Zhdanov's discomfort on these occasions was manifest. "Kliueva and Roskin distort the facts relating to their appeals to the Central Committee and, in particular, to me," he declared. Then, in a written statement to the court on 30 May, he sought to distance himself from the two as far as he could: "I first laid eyes on Kliueva and Roskin not in March or June 1946, as they claim, but on 21 November 1946. At no stage did Kliueva or Roskin ever complain to me either orally, or in writing, that we 'plan to sell them out to the Americans.' "[111] In light of the potential damage to Zhdanov's own standing from a trial against Kliueva and Roskin, the decision to bring proceedings against the two scientists was unlikely to have been at Zhdanov's behest. Decisions of this kind were ordinarily the prerogative of the leader.

In the event, the trial and, especially, the closed letter of the Central Committee "On the case of Professors Kliueva and Roskin," which was sent out on 16 July, were vehicles for a broader campaign engineered by Stalin to "eliminate servility before the West."[112] Employing the phrase "slavishness and servility before things foreign" as its main slogan (the word *nizkopoklonstvo* [slavishness] was used seven times), the letter picked up on earlier motifs: "Already last year, in the well-known resolutions on the journals *Zvezda* and *Leningrad* and on the theater repertoire, the Central Committee paid special attention to the harm done by slavishness before the modern bourgeois culture of the West on the part of certain of our writers and artists." "The ruling classes of Czarist Russia," the letter went on, "instilled in the minds of the Russian intelligentsia a sense of the unworthiness of our people and a conviction that Russians should always play the role of 'pupils' to Western European 'teachers.' "[113] The closed letter thus sought to engage the scientific and cultural intelligentsia in a struggle with Western values, to liberate them from "kowtowing and servility before the bourgeois culture of the West." That this theme should receive such emphasis in mid-July 1947 was most probably a result of the worsening international situation and, in particular, the declaration of the Marshall Plan the previous month.[114]

Despite Zhdanov's infamy by association with the anti-intelligentsia campaigns of 1946–1947, the three campaigns with which he was most intimately involved—against the Leningrad writers, against Aleksandrov, and against Kliueva and Roskin—were all orchestrated by Stalin.[115] In all three cases, Stalin demonstrated his control of his deputy by drawing Zhdanov into attacks that damaged Zhdanov's own interests. By autumn 1947 it had become clear that Zhdanov, who was by now evidently exhausted and whose health had become a major concern, could no longer usefully serve as Stalin's lapdog.[116] As the international crisis deepened, new approaches were required to instill vigilance and to tether a scientific intelligentsia that, despite the Kliueva-Roskin Affair, still enjoyed a certain degree of intellectual freedom.[117] Stalin's next move saw the final humiliation of Zhdanov, who was forced to turn against his own son.

Zhdanov Jr.: The Making of a Stalinist

On the last day of the historic VASKhNIL (Lenin All-Union Academy of Agricultural Sciences) conference of early August 1948, Trofim Lysenko announced to an audience of 700 carefully selected delegates that "the Central Committee of the party [has] examined [my] report and approved it." This infamous declaration and the proceedings of the meeting, which were published verbatim in nine successive issues of *Pravda*, had major repercussions for Soviet biology and for other branches of the natural and social sciences. With one stroke, following years of conflict, Lysenko's "materialist," "progressive," and "patriotic" agrobiology had finally triumphed over its "reactionary," "scholastic," "foreign," and "unpatriotic" scientific adversaries.[118] Lysenko's statement brought to an end the autonomy of the scientific community and, in effect, asserted the right of the party apparatus to dictate the content of science itself. In juxtaposing "Soviet" and "Western" scientific camps, Lysenko also extended the categories of Cold War politics to the organization of science.[119] We now know that Lysenko's statement had been authorized and, in effect, dictated by Stalin. Stalin's decision to turn a local institutional conflict into a broad propaganda campaign, which would envelop the whole scientific community, had its origins in the deepening international crisis. The early summer of 1948 had witnessed the climax of a Cold War confrontation that brought the United States and the USSR to the very edge of military conflict.[120] The division of the scientific community into two fiercely opposing groups and the subordination of scientific debates to party control were Stalin's knee-jerk responses to the crisis.

Whatever the reasons behind Stalin's intervention, the new policy required leading agents to implement it. Clearly, the main channel of the new policy was Lysenko himself. On New Year's Eve in 1946, Stalin had summoned Lysenko to the Kremlin to talk about his work on branching wheat. During 1947–1948, Lysenko remained in regular, direct correspondence with Stalin, enabling the scientist to circumvent the vast agricultural bureaucracy and to invoke the authority of the leader when he wanted key decisions, especially on resources, to go his way. Lysenko had met with Stalin on the eve of his address, on 6 August 1948. According to later reports, Stalin himself dictated the speech's opening paragraph and allowed Lysenko to draw on the authority of the Central Committee in support of his position.[121] Along with Lysenko, Stalin enlisted the support of an army of "Lysenkoists," which consisted primarily of poorly educated scientists, agricultural bureaucrats, and professional marxists. Given the stiff resistance faced by the Lysenkoists, Stalin also had to sway established scientists and their allies in the party apparatus. In what ensued, Stalin created active devotees and dependable functionaries out of people who had previously shown a mild skepticism and independence of spirit. A good example of this was the conversion of Andrei Zhdanov's son, Iurii.

Born in 1919, Iurii Zhdanov had graduated from Moscow University on the eve of the war in 1941 and had joined the party in 1944. As the son of the party's chief ideologist, Iurii in his father's library had access to a catholic selection of works not only in the natural sciences but also in political theory and philosophy and, by his account, made use of this resource in developing his own ideas on the nature of scientific progress.[122] Although he had studied chemistry at university, Iurii leaned toward the biological side of the discipline and published two articles on the relationship between biology and human evolution in the journal *Oktiabr'* in 1945 and 1947. On 18 October 1947, Iurii was summoned to Stalin's dacha at *Kholodnaia rechka* near the Black Sea. Stalin, who regularly followed the "thick journals," told Iurii that he had read and been impressed by his article "On the Influence of Humanity on Nature" in the July issue of *Oktiabr'* and that, notwithstanding Iurii's tender age, he would like him to join the Central Committee apparatus and to head the science department there. Although Iurii's father was opposed, Stalin insisted, and Iurii duly moved to his new post on 1 December 1947.[123]

At the time Iurii joined the Central Committee apparatus, two academic debates involving the Lysenkoists drew his attention. The first revolved around an attack by the Lysenkoists on the field of genetics. The offensive, which had begun in September 1947, culminated in the hearing of an honor court against the leading Soviet geneticist, Anton Zhebrak. Having accused Zhebrak of "unpatriotic acts" and of a "slavish servility to bourgeois science," his Lysenkoist detractors sought to publicize the findings of the court, to dissolve the genetics department at the Timizarev Academy, and to stage a second trial, against Nikolai Dubinin, the head of the genetics department at the Institute of Experimental Biology. Partly on Iurii Zhdanov's advice, the idea of a second trial was dropped and the antigenetics campaign was halted.[124] In the second debate, Lysenko attacked the "Malthusian error" committed by certain Soviet biologists who argued that "intra-species competition occurs in nature." Labeling this a "bourgeois remnant," Lysenko presented it as a distortion of Darwinism. There ensued a lively debate in academic circles, including a high-level meeting of the bureau of the biological division of the Academy of Sciences. In this conflict, Iurii Zhdanov again appeared to side with the biologists against Lysenko. Iurii's views were articulated in a long lecture called "Controversies of Modern Darwinism" on 10 April 1948. He argued that the academic debate was not between Soviet and bourgeois "camps," as Lysenko claimed, but simply between various schools of Soviet biology. He also upbraided Lysenko for claiming that he alone was the follower of the great Russian selectionist, Ivan Michurin. At the same time, Iurii made it clear that his speech only represented his own personal view.[125]

Although Lysenko did not attend Iurii Zhdanov's lecture, he overheard its contents. A week after the lecture, on 17 April, Lysenko wrote to Stalin and to Andrei Zhdanov with his objections to the younger Zhdanov's accusations. He also copied the letter to Andrei Zhdanov's rival Malenkov, and added some incriminating materials on Iurii. Over the next six weeks,

Lysenko, together with Malenkov, sought to focus Stalin's attention on Iurii Zhdanov's lecture. At the beginning of May, Malenkov's staff ordered Iurii Zhdanov to send Malenkov's department the text of the lecture, a copy of which was then passed on to Lysenko. On 11 May, Lysenko threatened, in a letter to the Minister of Agriculture, Ivan Benediktov, to step down as president of VASKhNIL, thereby bringing the matter to the Politburo, which was responsible for the post. On 31 May, Lysenko sent Malenkov fifty pages of excerpts from Iurii Zhdanov's lecture, together with his own comments.[126]

On the evening of 31 May, at an expanded meeting of the Politburo ostensibly dedicated to the awarding of Stalin prizes for science and inventions, Stalin prefaced the formal agenda with some remarks on Lysenko and on Iurii Zhdanov's lecture. On the former, Stalin equivocated, conceding that Lysenko had faults as a scientist and as a person, but that any attempt to destroy him was impermissible. "One should not forget," Stalin told the Politburo, "that Lysenko is today's Michurin."[127] Even more seriously, Stalin reproached Iurii for expressing his "personal" views. In his own copy of the younger Zhdanov's lecture, Stalin heavily underlined the phrase "I express here *not the official, but only my own personal* point of view" and added in the margin "Aha!"[128] This was the main point of Stalin's excursus at the meeting. "Comrade Stalin," one participant later recalled, "told us that in the party we do not have such things as personal opinions or personal points of view; there are only the opinions of the party."[129]

To convert Zhdanov into a true Stalinist functionary, Stalin had to obliterate any trace of Zhdanov's "own" position on key matters. But Stalin did not stop there. On 10 June, at a Politburo meeting devoted to the issue, Stalin asked Andrei Zhdanov to prepare a resolution of the Central Committee, entitled "On the Michurinist Trend in Soviet Biology," criticizing the younger Zhdanov's behavior. In line with his many efforts in the 1930s to turn family members against each other, Stalin forced the older Zhdanov to draft a piece condemning his own son. Andrei Zhdanov's notes of the meeting reflected his predicament succinctly: "Zhdanov is mistaken," he wrote, underlining the words. In late June Andrei Zhdanov asked Dmitrii Shepilov and Mark Mitin to draft a resolution, which he received on 7 July. An edited version was then forwarded to Stalin and the other members of the Politburo on 10 July. The idea of issuing a resolution was subsequently dropped in favor of convening a meeting at VASKhNIL, which was to be addressed by Lysenko. In all probability, the idea of holding a meeting rather than issuing a resolution was motivated by the desire to dramatize the debate as a conflict between a native "socialist" science and a foreign "capitalist" one.[130]

Publication of a Central Committee resolution on biology was to have been accompanied by a letter of "repentance" from Iurii Zhdanov. Withdrawal of the resolution did not mean, however, that Iurii's letter had been forgotten. "You need to put down in writing your position on what happened at the Politburo," he was told by his boss, Shepilov.[131] On 15 July the younger Zhdanov wrote his letter and submitted it to Stalin: "I had not thought that my lecture would be considered the Central Committee's official point of view" he admitted.[132] At Stalin's meeting with Lysenko on 6 August, Stalin decided to go ahead with publishing the letter in the following day's edition of *Pravda*. Iurii Zhdanov's promise to "work hard to correct previous mistakes" was, together with Lysenko's declaration on 7 August, taken as a clear-cut sign by Lysenko's opponents that they should recant, which, in a series of public confessions, they duly did. The meeting then ended with a "letter to comrade Stalin," concluding with a paean of praise to the "Great Stalin, Leader of the People, Luminary of Advanced Science."[133]

The Lysenko episode broke Iurii Zhdanov as a "free thinker" on scientific matters and turned him into an ordinary instrument of Stalin's apparatus. When, for example, the younger Zhdanov organized a conference on physiology two years later, designed to unseat the powerful Leon Orbeli, the director of the Institute of Physiology, he followed the August model faithfully. Carefully arranging the order of reports and editing their contents, he submitted the most significant for Stalin's approval and ensured their publication in *Pravda*. In a piece published several weeks later as "Certain Results of the Meeting on Physiology," intended to draw out the lessons of the conference, Iurii Zhdanov visited the same criticisms on Orbeli that had earlier been laid against him.[134]

The cumulative strain of the war and of Stalin's incessant hectoring was to prove more devastating for Iurii's father. On 6 July 1948, Stalin received a request from the medical center at the Kremlin to grant Andrei Zhdanov two months leave. Stalin's initial response was dismissive. "Where to, what treatment?" he scrawled in blue crayon over the form. The doctors' report had concluded that Zhdanov's health had seriously deteriorated and that as a result of an intensive spasm in his brain, Zhdanov had experienced a loss of feeling in his right hand and on the right side of his face. In coded terms the doctors were conveying to Stalin that Zhdanov was suffering from prestroke symptoms. On returning to the document, Stalin crossed out his earlier note and wrote in its stead, this time in red, "OK. J. Stalin." In fact, Zhdanov continued to attend meetings of the ruling circle for another week, before leaving for the south on 13 July.[135] Despite claims that Zhdanov was the victim of a plot, either by Stalin or by his adversaries in the Politburo, there is little evidence to support this view. Instead, after years of being run into the ground by his boss, Zhdanov suffered two heart attacks and died, of natural causes, on 31 August.[136]

Conclusion

Stalin's immediate goal after the war was to restore the leadership system that he had created in the wake of the Great Terror. By the end of 1946, he had launched a series of attacks designed to strip his colleagues of any independence they had acquired during the war. These attacks were savage and systematic: no member of the ruling group was left unscathed. Stalin deployed a variety of methods—including head-on confrontations, demotions, assaults on aides and allies, and the threat of physical repression—to bring his colleagues into line. To a degree, the form these attacks took depended on the political status of the victims. While the public assault on the younger Zhdanov reached a very wide audience, knowledge of Malenkov's demotion was restricted, and the humiliation of Molotov was made known only to a small subset of the Politburo. In his attacks Stalin appeared to thrive on the atmosphere of crisis that had enveloped the country, and he actively made use of particular crisis points—such as the famine and intractable international disagreements—as pretexts to embarrass and discipline his companions.

Stalin's relationship with Andrei Zhdanov demonstrates perhaps better than any other how fine-tuned his control of his deputies could be. Far from being a relatively independent and purposeful figure with ideas and potential claims of his own to the top post, Zhdanov comes across as a confused, bewildered, and largely unwitting agent, perpetually searching for cues from the leader. His control over Zhdanov was such that on several occasions Stalin was able to cajole Zhdanov into fronting attacks that harmed Zhdanov's own allies, his son, and, often, his own interests. Rather than merely being a means to extend the influence of the Central Committee (and, by implication, Zhdanov himself) over the cultural and scientific intelligentsia, the attacks on Zoshchenko and Akhmatova, on Aleksandrov, and on Kliueva and Roskin were part of a broader policy initiated by Stalin to drive the intelligentsia into an ideological war with the West. By contrast, Stalin's relationship with the younger Zhdanov showed how he was able to strip a relatively freethinking young man of any "personal views" and to convert him into a model Stalinist functionary, who could be relied on to perform Stalin's deeds with the minimum of direction from above.

While always keeping his deputies on edge, during the years of reconstruction from 1945 to 1948 Stalin stepped back from the brink of radical or irrevocable acts against members of his ruling circle. No member of the

Politburo was expelled, let alone arrested or executed. Rather than behaving in an anarchic or uncontrolled way, Stalin was, in the ways that mattered most, quite careful and restrained in his behavior toward his colleagues. The leader appeared to value order and continuity within his entourage. This approach would correspond to his attitude toward the country's ruling structures where, as long as he himself was not constrained, Stalin appeared to recognize the advantages of a smooth and effective system of administration.

Stalin's speech to voters, 9 February 1946, in which he set out ambitious growth targets for the coming fifteen years and signaled a hardening of Soviet policy toward the West.

Molotov at the Luxembourg Palace, Paris peace conference, 31 July 1946.

Funeral of Mikhail Kalinin, 5 July 1946. From left to right: Lavrentii Beria,
Nikolai Shvernik, Georgii Malenkov, Nikolai Voznesenskii, Aleksei Kuznetsov,
Joseph Stalin, Lazar Kaganovich, Viacheslav Molotov, and Andrei Zhdanov.
With the exception of Mikoian, who could not make it to the funeral, the ruling
quintet that had emerged during the war—Stalin, Molotov, Beria, and
Malenkov—are in the foreground.

Kalinin's lying in state. On the right are Stalin and the head of the organizing
committee for the funeral, Aleksei Kosygin, looking on as relatives pay their last
respects. Among the relatives is Kalinin's wife, E. V. Kalinina, who had been
arrested in 1938 and sentenced to fifteen years in a labor camp. It was only in
June 1945, a year before Kalinin's death, that Stalin finally gave in to pleas from
the terminally ill Kalinin to have her released.

Gala evening at the Bolshoi Theater, Moscow, 21 January 1947, to mark the twenty-third anniversary of Lenin's death. From left to right: Beria, Kaganovich, Malenkov, Molotov, Kuznetsov, Stalin, Kosygin, Voznesenenskii, Voroshilov, and Matvei Shkiriatov, the deputy chair of the Party Control Commission.

Zhdanov on holiday in Sochi, January 1947. On 5 January, Zhdanov wrote to
Stalin: "Dear Comrade Stalin! My visit to Sochi is doing wonders for my health.
I have been keeping to a strict regime. The conditions here are excellent and,
despite the fact that the weather has not held over the last week, and winter
is now with us, it has been a good time for convalescing. As things are going
so well I would rather not hurry my course of treatment and I ask of you,
comrade Stalin, that you extend my stay, which is due to end on 15 January,
by ten days, so that I may return to Moscow on the 25th, for which I would be
extremely grateful. Regards! Your Andrei Zhdanov." Although Stalin granted
Zhdanov's request, the recovery would prove to be short-lived, for Zhdanov
died the following year, on 31 August 1948.

At Stalin's country house in Sochi, 1947. Sitting, from left to right: Kaganovich, Malenkov, Stalin, and Zhdanov. Standing, from right to left: Stalin's aide Aleksandr Poskrebyshev, Stalin's daughter Svetlana, Stalin's son Vasilii, and an unknown military commander. In 1947, Stalin had left Moscow for Sochi on 16 August and returned to the capital on 21 November. In subsequent years, Stalin's visits to the south would be extended, lasting for four and a half months in 1950 and 1951.

At his office in the Kremlin Stalin would also receive foreign dignitaries such as, on 10 January 1947, the British Field Marshal Sir Bernard Montgomery.

Air show to mark national air force day, Tushinskii Aerodrome, Moscow, 25 July 1948. From the bottom of the picture upward are: Mikhail Suslov, the Moscow city chief Georgii Popov, Shvernik, Malenkov, unknown figure, Beria, Kaganovich, Voznesenskii, head of the air force K. A. Vershinin, Nikolai Bulganin, Stalin, the chief of staff A. M. Vasilevskii, and Kliment Voroshilov.

2

STATE BUILDING STALIN-STYLE

The subjugation of Stalin's Politburo companions after the war went hand in hand with his refashioning of high-level political structures. With the dissolution of the State Defense Committee in September 1945, Stalin's ruling group quickly reverted to prewar conventions designed to make life as comfortable as possible for the leader. Yet highly informal arrangements of this kind were by no means universal across the higher reaches of the political system after the war. In fact, formal and routine committees were very much a feature of high-level decision making in the late Stalin era. Nowhere was this more apparent than in the activities of the government. Under arrangements formalized in February 1947, the Council of Ministers (Sovmin) was given almost exclusive control of the economy, while "political" decisions were made the preserve of the Politburo. This delegation of authority to Sovmin committees was part of a general attempt to regularize decision making over a large range of economic and administrative issues. For the duration of Stalin's life, the inner councils of the government, the Sovmin bureaus, functioned as a routine committee system, meeting on a near weekly basis, handling a substantial workload, and enjoying a clear and continuous internal division of labor.

The other side of this arrangement was a Politburo entirely obedient to Stalin's whims. In addition to manipulating his companions through harassment and intimidation, Stalin conditioned the institutional environment in which they operated. The dictator personally selected the Politburo's membership, set its agendas, fashioned its procedures, and organized the locations and timing of its meetings to suit his own urges. In these respects the Politburo under Stalin was turned into an instrument of personal rule. Moreover, whenever Stalin felt that the government had gained too much in the way of autonomy he intervened, unilaterally redrawing the boundary dividing "political" issues, which were the prerogative of a Politburo ruled by him, from those "nonpolitical" issues that were the concern of the government. The enormous discretion Stalin enjoyed in redrawing these boundaries and, more generally, in determining his own involvement in the party-state will be referred to here as "patrimonial." The picture that emerges is not the traditional one of autocratic rule resting on institutional confusion and disarray, but of patrimonial authority coexisting alongside quite modern and routine forms of high-level decision making.

Stalin's Informal Norms: The Politburo as an Instrument of Personal Rule

The first formal meeting of the Politburo after the war, attended by seventeen people, took place on the evening of 29 December 1945.[1] At that session the Politburo resolved to meet once every other Tuesday for a short time, from 8:00–9:00 P.M. Although it failed to keep to this schedule, the full Politburo did convene with some regularity over the coming months, with sessions on 19 January, 4 March, 13 April, and 4 May 1946.[2] The holding of such frequent meetings was a departure from the prewar pattern, when the formal Politburo had convened only rarely. One reason for the early revival of the full Politburo after the war may have been Stalin's wish to present an image of Leninist normality after the turbulence of the preceding years. Carving out a clear institutional niche for the Politburo could help counter the institutional confusion of the war years, when the Politburo had in effect merged with other decision-making bodies, such as the State Defense Committee and the Council of People's Commissars. The degree of overlap then had been such that some leaders, such as Marshal Zhukov, had complained that they were never quite sure which leadership body they were attending.[3] The resuscitation of the formal mechanisms of the Politburo also served to accentuate the contrast between it and the relatively formless procedures of the now disbanded GKO. In the words of the former Deputy Commissar of Defense, A. V. Khrulev: "Military leaders, people's commissars, and other responsible individuals would turn up incessantly [to meetings of the GKO], not only if they were summoned, but even on their own initiative. There were no meetings of the GKO in the ordinary sense, that is, with a definite agenda, secretaries, and minutes. Procedures for agreeing issues with [other institutions] were simplified to the utmost."[4] Emphasizing the procedural aspects of the Politburo allowed Stalin to restrict access to leadership meetings and control their content more easily.

In the immediate aftermath of the war, a revival of the formal Politburo could be presented as a return to Leninist norms. Soon, however, Stalin reverted to his prewar "commission" modes of decision making, by which Politburo affairs were managed by a small, informal subgroup.[5] Indeed, even as Stalin sought to formalize the activities of the full Politburo in the months after the war, he persisted with regular meetings of his inner circle. At the Politburo meeting of 29 December 1945, where Stalin called for regularizing sessions of the full Politburo, he simultaneously took steps to consolidate his inner circle and to formalize its activities by endowing it with a title, the Commission for Foreign Affairs at the Politburo.[6] In spite of the brief flowering of full Politburo sessions in the early months of 1946, the balance between the formal Politburo and the commission tilted decisively toward the latter. Following the summer recess of 1946, there were two quick sessions of the full Politburo, on 2 and 6 September; thereafter, for the rest of Stalin's life, there were to be only two more full recorded sessions, on 13 December 1947 and 17 June 1949.[7] By contrast, meetings of the Politburo subgroup became a routine feature of leadership politics. Whereas "neither the Central Committee, nor the Politburo . . . worked regularly," Khrushchev recounted later, "Stalin's regular sessions with his inner circle went along like clockwork."[8]

Although this inner circle possessed an official title, the narrowly constituted sessions in Stalin's office came to be better known as meetings of the "select group" (uzkii sostav), the "close circle" (blizhnii krug) or, most commonly, of the "ruling group" (rukovodiashchaia grupa).[9] In a practice later made famous by Khrushchev in the secret speech, Stalin liked to refer to the group by its numerical epithet, the "quintet" or, as it became in December 1945, the "sextet." The composition and activities of the ruling group differed in key respects from that of the formal Politburo. Membership of the official Politburo was roughly twice that of the ruling group. Excluded from Stalin's inner circle were those Politburo members who had either fallen foul of Stalin or who were cut off for reasons of location or ill health.[10] Whereas a wide array of secondary officials, such as members of the Central Committee or specialist staff, had traditionally been invited to formal enlarged sessions of the Politburo, access to meetings of the ruling group was more tightly restricted. Moreover, while agendas and supporting documents for items on formal de jure meetings were circulated in advance, and their decisions listed in consecutive protocols, sessions of the ruling group were completely informal in character, without any minutes, agendas, secretaries, or a sequenced record of actions taken.[11] By contrast with full de jure Politburo meetings, which were relatively constrained by rules and procedures, meetings of the ruling group were usually ad hoc, unminuted, and completely informal in character.

There was also a difference in function between the ruling group and the formal Politburo. Where meetings of the de jure Politburo handled more prosaic matters of an economic or party nature, the ruling group tended to confine itself to the most sensitive matters of state.[12] As we have seen, in Stalin's first attempt to formalize the ruling group's activities, he labeled it, in the Politburo resolution of 29 December 1945, the Commission for Foreign Affairs.[13] One reason for this was that in the immediate aftermath of the war, foreign affairs occupied a particularly important place on Stalin's own agenda. In addition, foreign affairs had traditionally been among the most sensitive areas within the Politburo's domain. Nevertheless, most likely Stalin never intended the ruling group to limit itself solely to matters of foreign policy. Indeed, over the course of 1946, a number of urgent domestic issues began to impinge on its agenda. The most pressing of these was the growing crisis plaguing the food distribution network following the harvest failure that summer. Early in October, while in the south, Stalin wrote to his Politburo colleagues: "Our experience has shown that the sextet created by the Politburo for resolving foreign policy problems cannot limit itself to questions of foreign affairs but has been forced by circumstance to engage also in questions of domestic policy. This has been particularly vindicated in recent months, when the sextet has had to deal with issues relating to prices, grain resources, food supplies, and rations." Accordingly, on 3 October, a Politburo resolution, dictated by Stalin, ruled that "together with foreign affairs, the sextet be assigned issues of domestic construction and domestic policy."[14] The remit of the ruling group was thereby widened to include all matters of national importance which Stalin deemed worthy of his and, therefore, its attention.

An informally constituted ruling group offered Stalin numerous advantages over meetings of the official de jure Politburo, which had been elected after the XVIII Party Congress. Stalin could call meetings of the group as and when he wished, without the need to draw up an agenda or to distribute supporting materials ahead of time. Such flexibility was particularly useful to the leader as he gravitated toward a nighttime regime and began to call meetings of the ruling group after hours. At the meetings themselves, Stalin was freed from having to observe Politburo formalities on minuting discussions or tabulating decisions. The existence of a personally selected ruling group also allowed Stalin to circumvent time-consuming rules on admission to the cabinet. Membership of the full Politburo was not a prerequisite for entry into the group. Stalin unilaterally elevated colleagues without having to go through the tedious formality of having them "elected" as full members of the Politburo by the Central Committee.

Thus, for example, Malenkov and Beria were inducted into the quintet well before their election as full members of the Politburo on 18 March 1946. Similarly, on 3 October, nearly five months before Voznesenskii's election as a full member of the Politburo, Stalin dictated a Politburo resolution that the "sextet add to its roster the Chair of Gosplan [the State Planning Commission], comrade Voznesenskii, so that it now be known as the septet."[15] Rules on admission to the ruling group were sufficiently loose that its growth was not accompanied by any formal "decisions" as such. Without any official decision to go by, it is only indirectly—through their attendance at sessions of the ruling group—that we may infer that Kaganovich was admitted to it, approximately a year after Voznesenskii, on his return to Moscow from Kiev in December 1947, so that the septet had now become an octet, and that Nikolai Bulganin joined in February 1948, swelling the group into a novenary. In subsequent years, especially in the wake of the Leningrad Affair, the lack of clear-cut rules on the composition of the ruling group was exploited by Stalin to add and expel members with unseemly ease.

The ruling group also served a social function for Stalin. In spring 1944, Stalin's daughter Svetlana married her first husband, Grigorii Morozov, of whom Stalin strongly disapproved. As a result, Svetlana moved out of the Kremlin. From around this time on, Stalin ceased to dine with his daughter in the evenings, as he had done in the past, and chose instead to go to his dacha in Kuntsevo, to which he invited his ruling circle.[16] Even more so than in the 1930s, Stalin had become a lonely man who craved company. Much of his time with members of the ruling group was spent sitting through Westerns or through endless dinners marked by a conspicuous lack of policy-oriented discussion. In its increasingly informal settings and styles of operation, the ruling group, the country's informal cabinet, doubled as Stalin's social circle.[17]

The ruling group operated as an essentially informal collective thoroughly attuned to Stalin's needs. Although the composition and style of operations of the ruling group deviated, sometimes markedly, from those of the de jure Politburo, the bulk of decisions reached by the ruling group were issued as Politburo resolutions. By the same token, virtually all resolutions issued in the name of the Politburo in the late Stalin years were either decided on at meetings of the ruling group or were voted on by its members.[18] For their part, members of the ruling group, as well as officials invited on a one-off basis, tended to refer to sessions of the ruling group as meetings of the "Politburo."[19] For these reasons, one may think of the ruling group as a de facto Politburo in this period.

Although Stalin pushed the Politburo in the direction of greater flexibility, he stopped short of dispensing with it altogether. In fact, Stalin insisted on keeping up certain "institutional" aspects of the Politburo's activities. Not only did he have the ruling group's decisions drawn up as "Politburo" resolutions, he also insisted that these be signed by all members of the ruling group and sometimes even by members of the formal Politburo, even when, as was often the case, most of the latter group played no part whatsoever in discussing or approving the original decision. Sticking with a practice introduced in the 1930s, Stalin often sought the votes of absent members "by correspondence," whereby a draft decision was circulated by courier to all members of the group for their "vote" and signature.

The frequency of correspondence votes indeed begs the question of why Stalin should have incurred the inconvenience and delay of such a procedure when everyone knew that it was Stalin's opinion that ultimately mattered.[20] One reason for this insistence was Stalin's need to bind his coleaders in a system of collective responsibility. Stalin used correspondence votes and meetings of the ruling group to test the loyalty of his inner circle. The formal device for achieving this goal was to force cabinet colleagues to sign Politburo resolutions, even after the event, thus making them jointly accountable for state policy. Less formally, Stalin would use Politburo meetings as occasions to spring awkward questions on unsuspecting colleagues and to then check their reactions.[21] Politburo meetings thus evolved into an amalgam of formal devices (the demand for cosignatures and correspondence votes) and personalized modes of control (throwing surprise questions and soliciting early opinions on controversial matters) through which Stalin could manipulate his colleagues. The Politburo thus became indispensable as a tool for controlling the leadership.

There were other reasons why the outward form of Politburo decision making was maintained. While internal relations within the Politburo were fluid and fast changing, outside the ruling circle the Politburo had to project an image of stability and order. Here, in striking contrast to its internal reality, the Politburo was a symbol of steadfast authority. To those outside the upper circles of the regime, the Politburo remained the most authoritative of institutions. In view of the long intervals separating party congresses and Central Committee plenums after the war, the party leadership functions of the Politburo became all the more important. Further, although Stalin's authority was virtually unchallenged throughout the postwar period, he could mobilize the support of the Politburo to buttress potentially unpopular moves. When, for example, at the meeting of the main military council on 1 June 1946, most generals refused to give credence to testimony against Zhukov from arrested officers, Stalin successfully enlisted the help of members of the ruling group, who trooped into the room with denunciations of the marshal, and thereby successfully swung the balance of opinion against Zhukov.[22] At a meeting of the full Council of Ministers seven months later, on 31 December 1946, Stalin also invoked the authority of the Politburo: "The ruling circle—the Politburo," he told the ministers, "has discussed the draft plans for 1947 and believes that the plans projected by the ministries are unacceptable."[23]

The Politburo—now refashioned as the ruling group—was finely tuned to fit in with Stalin's work rhythms and to lend added institutional weight to his own policy preferences. While coaxing a small group of individuals did draw on Stalin's energies, it was by no means an insurmountable task. After all, these were men whom Stalin had known for many years and over whom he had established complete mastery. Manipulating a far larger body, such as the Central Committee, which had almost 150 members after the war, was an altogether different proposition.[24] The marginalization of the Central Committee had, under Stalin, been a long-term process begun in the 1920s. Now, however, Stalin went a step further by completely emasculating the Central Committee. The final phase of this process, which turned the Central Committee into a purely passive rubber stamp for Politburo decisions, took place in the early months of 1947, a time when a number of key reorganizations occurred.

The first postwar session of the Central Committee took place as a set of staggered meetings on 11, 14, and 18 March 1946. The main purpose of the plenum was to push through personnel changes on party committees and to approve a number of procedural issues that were to come up at the forthcoming meeting of the Supreme Soviet.[25] The primary aim of the second meeting, which took place on 21, 22, 24, and 26 February 1947, was, similarly, to rubber stamp personnel changes and to address the worsening agricultural situation.[26] Following the latter meeting, the Central Committee did not convene again for over five years, until the eve of the XIX Party Congress in August 1952. In the meantime, the body was reduced to voting by correspondence on largely procedural matters that had, in any case, been predetermined by the Politburo. Such "votes," which involved the laborious procedure of sending telegrams to and receiving replies from Central Committee members dotted all over the country, ordinarily lasted for two to three days and allowed for no deliberation or input—other than a vote in favor—from the electorate. The decline of the Central Committee was such that even these votes became a rarity, with only two held in 1946, two in 1947, and four in 1948.[27]

On the last day of the 1947 plenum, Zhdanov announced that "at the end of 1947 or, at any rate, in 1948, the forthcoming XIX Congress of our party will certainly have to be convened." It was in connection with the fact that "the deadline for convening the XIX Congress is approaching" that Zhdanov sought to replenish the commission on the party program and to select a commission on revising the existing party statutes, which, in his view, were now outdated.[28] According to the party rules, the congress, "the supreme organ" of the party, was to take place at least once every three years so that, even excluding the war, it had been over four years since the last congress, which had been held in March 1939.[29] If Stalin had, by this time, no truck for Central Committee plenums, he certainly would have seen little point in expending unnecessary energy on a full-blown party congress. Having allowed Zhdanov to raise the prospect, he subsequently blocked it, referring, in one version, to the fact that "he was not ready to make the Central Committee report [to the congress] and that in view of his age it would be difficult and he needed more time to prepare."[30] Although in mid-July 1947 the Politburo voted to set up a commission, headed by Zhdanov, to draft a new party program, nothing came of it.[31] It would be over four years before the wheels were properly set in motion for a congress and over five years before the congress itself convened. If Stalin's preferred state of affairs involved converting the Politburo into an informal ruling group and reducing the Central Committee to a passive college for registering correspondence votes, his wish for the party congress was that it should not meet at all.

To complement his strategies of interpersonal control, Stalin refashioned cherished party bodies so that the institutional constraints on him could be reduced to a minimum. Although he desired a measure of institutional fluidity at the highest level, he did not lose sight of the need for effective administration. Thus, the relatively ruleless activity of a Politburo dominated by him went hand in hand with greater institutionalization elsewhere. Perhaps Stalin's most ambitious piece of institutional engineering was the separation he effected between his own, procedurally labile Politburo and the governmental machinery at the Council of Ministers, which was founded on sound and systematic principles of administration.

The Council of Ministers and Economic Decision Making

On 19 March 1946, the Council of Ministers succeeded the Council of People's Commissars (Sovnarkom) as the official government of the USSR. The new title confirmed that, having passed the supreme test of war, the Soviet system could now be regarded as fully consolidated.[32] "The [term] commissar," Stalin declared at the Central Committee meeting that approved the change on 14 March, "reflected a time in which our system was unsettled, a period of civil war, revolutionary rupture, and so forth. But that time has now passed. The war has shown that our social order is now secure. Now that [our system] has come into being and is made flesh and blood, there is no point in sticking with a term that alludes to a social order which was unsettled and had yet to take root. The time has now come for us to move on from the term people's commissar to the term minister."[33]

The immediate remit and goals of the new Council of Ministers were not easy to discern, however. One reason was that the division of labor between it and the leading executive committee of the party, the Politburo, had become blurred. Following the integration of Sovnarkom into party structures in the 1930s, the Politburo and the government had become interlocking directorates of a unified party-state with Stalin, who became chair of Sovnarkom on 4 May 1941, at its pinnacle.[34] Relations between the two bodies were considerably complicated by the reorganizations of the war and its immediate aftermath. While the Politburo in effect ceased to function as a formal institution and convened, instead, as a ruling group with membership, agendas, and working rhythms determined entirely by the leader, Sovnarkom emerged from the war with two parallel operational bureaus, one led by Molotov and the other by Beria.[35]

A first stab at reorganizing the government coincided with the renaming of Sovnarkom in March 1946.[36] This was then overshadowed by a resolution of 8 February 1947, entitled "On the Organization of the Council of Ministers," which sought to formalize a new relationship between the Politburo and Sovmin. While the new legislation of February 1947 built on certain existing foundations, by continuing to vest rights in the leading committee of Sovmin, the Sovmin Bureau, it went beyond earlier practices in three important respects.[37] First, the resolution expressed in written form a clear-cut division of labor between the Politburo and Sovmin, in which the Politburo was accorded the right to consider all matters of a "political" nature, such as governmental appointments, issues relating to defense, foreign policy, and internal security, while Sovmin was expected to deal with straightforward economic issues. Certain functions, such as oversight of the Ministry of State Security, which, as late as March 1946, had been formally assigned to Sovmin, were now returned to the Politburo.[38] In addition, the question of whether to send miscellaneous issues to Sovmin or the Politburo, which had previously been decided on an ad hoc basis, was now given greater procedural clarity.[39] The competence of Sovmin to handle its own economic affairs would now become so well established that the earlier practice, common in the 1930s, of having government decisions referred to the Politburo for confirmation virtually ceased.

Second, the February resolution formalized the estrangement of Stalin from the government. In contrast to the situation immediately prior to the war, when Stalin had chaired meetings of the main executive committee of the government, the Sovnarkom Bureau, from the time the Bureau was reestablished in 1942 until his death, Stalin never again attended, let alone chaired, any of its meetings. Prior to the February resolution, Stalin had, on one occasion, fulfilled his formal obligations in the government. Less than six weeks earlier, on 31 December 1946, Stalin had, for the first time in five years, chaired a session of the full Council of Ministers. In a twenty-five-minute speech, he upbraided Gosplan for submitting "unacceptable" plans that failed to push "backward" enterprises to the level of the most "advanced" ones.[40] Stalin ordered that a new draft be presented to him. "I have looked at the draft plan," he wrote to the main Sovmin Bureau on 27 January 1947. "I consider it correct and write in favor of its approval. I ask you," he went on, "to consider the draft at the Bureau of Sovmin and to approve it."[41] Following the reorganization of February 1947, Stalin ceased to have any role either on the key economic committee at Sovmin, the main Bureau, or on the largely formalistic full Council.[42]

Formally speaking, the February resolution made no mention at all of any specific responsibilities for Stalin at Sovmin. In this it contrasted with the previous resolution, "On the Assignment of Duties at the Council of Ministers," passed a year earlier, which had explicitly assigned Stalin the duty, as part of his responsibilities at Sovmin, of overseeing the work of the Ministry of Armaments.[43] In fact, three weeks after the February resolution, Stalin also relinquished his cherished position as Minister of Armed Forces, which he had clung to since the beginning of the war. His reasoning was made clear on 26 February, when he told the plenum of the Central Committee: "I have a small statement to make regarding my own situation. I am very overworked, especially as, since the end of the war, I have had to immerse myself in civilian affairs. I ask that the plenum not object if I were freed from my duties as Minister of Armed Forces. I could be successfully replaced by my first deputy, Bulganin. Comrades, I am very overworked and ask that you do not oppose this. My age, too, has taken its toll."[44]

Stalin's formal withdrawal from Sovmin and his abdication as minister reflected a broader change in Stalin's own interests and concerns, as the leader increasingly focused his energies on diplomacy and foreign affairs at the expense of domestic and, especially, economic matters. The February resolution preceded the announcement of the Truman Doctrine by less than a month and came in the midst of detailed preparations for the foreign ministers meeting in March, in which Stalin himself was heavily engaged. Over the twenty months that had elapsed since May 1945, the exertions of war had finally caught up with Stalin. One diplomat, who had not seen him since the conclusion of hostilities, commented in April 1947 that Stalin had become "an old, very tired old man."[45] Under such circumstances, Stalin was forced to cut down on his commitments and to focus on those tasks and duties he regarded as truly essential.

Third, the February resolution marked the consolidation of a new supraministerial order at Sovmin. A year earlier, in March 1946, composition of the Sovmin Bureau had been restricted to deputy chairs, each of whom had been assigned a clear set of responsibilities;[46] since then, meetings of the Bureau had been held at near weekly intervals and routinely commanded a high turnout.[47] The February resolution went a step further, however, with the creation of a new supraministerial institution within Sovmin, the sectoral bureau.[48] The sectoral bureau was intended to facilitate the "coordination" of congruent branches of the economy and to expedite decision making.[49] Whereas earlier assignments of authority had been made to powerful commissars or vice-chairs of Sovnarkom, the February resolution now formalized the delegation of authority within Sovmin by setting up eight sectoral bureaus.[50] Although each bureau was headed by a deputy premier, decision-making authority was now vested in committees. Each consisted of several ministers and senior administrators and was supported by "a secretariat and a necessary apparatus" as well as by state counselors.[51] The organization of the sectoral bureaus was clearly laid out, with every bureau given jurisdiction over a broad and distinctive area of the economy. The collective remit of the bureaus was also very extensive, covering virtually all sectors of the economy and, indeed, almost all areas within the jurisdiction of Sovmin.[52] Each of the new sectoral bureaus, with the exception of machine building and trade and light industry, was headed by a Politburo member.[53]

The period following the February resolution saw the consolidation of the inner cabinet of Sovmin, the Sovmin Bureau, and of the newly created sectoral bureaus. The main Sovmin Bureau continued to meet on a continuous, near weekly basis,[54] while the legislative activity of Sovmin,

Table 2.1 Sectoral Bureaus of the Council of Ministers, February 1947

Bureau	Head	Number of Subordinate Ministries and Departments
Agricultural Bureau	G. M. Malenkov	6
Bureau for Metallurgy and Chemicals	N. A. Voznesenskii	7
Bureau for Machine Construction	M. Z. Saburov	11
Bureau for Fuel and Electric Power Stations	L. P. Beria	7
Bureau for Food Industry	A. I. Mikoian	5
Bureau for Transport and Communications	L. M. Kaganovich	8
Bureau for Trade and Light Industry	A. N. Kosygin	5
Bureau for Culture and Health	K. E. Voroshilov	19

Source: "Ob organizatsii raboty Soveta Ministrov SSSR," joint resolution of the Council of Ministers and the Central Committee of 8 February 1947, RGASPI f.17 op.163 d.1495 ll.120–124.

Table 2.2 Membership and Meetings of the Main
Sovmin Bureau, 1946–1949

	Number of Members[1]	Number of Meetings
1946[2]	6–9	55
1947	9–12	47
1948	12–13	53
1949[3]	13–15	53

Source: Politbiuro TsK VKP(b) i Sovet Ministrov SSSR 1945–1953
(Moscow: Rosspen, 2002), 455–537.

[1]That is, minima and maxima for any given year.
[2]The figures for 1946 include meetings of the first Sovnarkom
operational bureau, headed by Molotov, prior to its replacement by
the joint Sovmin Bureau, headed by Beria, on 27 March 1946.
[3]The figures for 1949 include the immediate successor to the
Sovmin Bureau, the Presidium, which began operating on 10 August
1949. Unlike the Bureau of the Presidium, which was founded the
following April, the Presidium was identical to the Sovmin Bureau
which it replaced, except that it included the Minister of Finances
and the Minister of State Control.

spurred on by the Bureau, almost doubled.[55] The membership of the main
Bureau, made up of deputy premiers, also began to expand. First to join,
on the day of the February resolution itself, was Maksim Saburov, who
attended his inaugural session on 22 February. Saburov was followed in
quick succession by a number of other young rising stars, most of them
specialists, including Nikolai Bulganin on 5 March 1947, Viacheslav Malyshev on 19 December, Aleksei Krutikov on 13 July 1948, Aleksandr Efremov on 8 March 1949, Ivan Tevosian on 13 June 1949, and Mikhail
Pervukhin on 17 January 1950.[56] By the beginning of 1950, the number
of deputy premiers, all of whom regularly attended the main Sovmin Bureau, had climbed to fourteen from eight in March 1946.[57]

Most of the new recruits have been characterized as young "technocrats" or "managers," whom Stalin had catapulted to positions of emi-
nence in order to integrate their technical expertise into the policy-making
process.[58] Although all were young, this was by no means their first taste
of high-level decision making. Indeed, a good portion of the new deputy
premiers, including Saburov, Bulganin, Malyshev, and Pervukhin, not to
mention the younger incumbents Aleksei Kosygin and Nikolai Voznesenskii, had already served as deputy chairs of Sovnarkom for most of the
war.[59] Thus the main Sovmin Bureau consisted of a combination of senior
Politburo members, most of whom had sat on the State Defense Committee,
and young technocrats, who had served through the war as deputy premiers. Whereas the presence of Politburo members undoubtedly lent the

Bureau authority, the inclusion of young technocrats provided it with technical expertise.[60] The reform of 1947 revived and consolidated a pattern of institutional development that had first emerged just prior to the war. Increasingly absorbed in military, diplomatic, and foreign affairs, Stalin had, over the course of the war, delegated responsibility for management of the economy to GKO and Sovnarkom committees. With the dissolution of the GKO, this authority was transferred entirely to a Council of Ministers in which Stalin now played a minimal role.

Sessions of the Sovmin Bureau were well attended. Apart from Molotov, who was frequently off on foreign affairs business, and Andrei Andreev, who suffered from chronic illnesses, the deputy premiers routinely attended the weekly meetings. The Bureau was, at the same time, an exclusive committee. Save for the occasional expert summoned to give advice on specialist matters, outsiders were rarely invited.[61] The Bureau became a tight decision-making unit bound by a common experience of regular and exclusive meetings. Within the organization, each deputy received individual assignments, normally relating to the sectoral bureau under their command, or to commissions they headed.[62] Assignments were usually accompanied by deadlines, and the Bureau's secretariat saw to it that members received reminders if a deadline had been breached. None of the deputy premiers was exempt from these schedules, and even the most senior figures, such as Beria and Voznesenskii, were held to them.[63] Far from being an inchoate and loosely organized body, as the Politburo had become at this time, the main Sovmin Bureau gave every sign of being a tight and disciplined ship.

Following the reorganization of February 1947, no one person or faction controlled the activities of the main Sovmin Bureau. Initially, the chairmanship went to Molotov, who was, in any case, away for much of the time.[64] On 29 March 1948, Bureau chairmanship passed to a trio of Beria, Voznesenskii, and Malenkov, in whose hands the leadership was rotated.[65] With no clear head to turn to, emerging conflicts among Bureau members were addressed simply to "the Bureau" for consideration.[66] Rather than one individual coming to dominate the body, the power to set the agenda and to determine decisions was spread equally among Bureau members, thus elevating the significance of meetings of the committee itself.

Following their formation in February 1947, the sectoral bureaus also attained institutional coherence. Although responsibility for filling the bureaus was left in the hands of bureau chairs,[67] all the bureaus consisted of specialists, mainly ministers and deputy ministers, with memberships ranging from eight to ten.[68] In order to ensure that the bureaus properly monitored the implementation of Sovmin decisions, several of their members were completely released from other duties and asked to focus their energies entirely on bureau matters.[69] As with the main Bureau, the sectoral bureaus met regularly, convening on average once every seven to ten days.[70] The formation of the sectoral bureaus marked a second round in the transfer of economic authority from an overburdened leadership around Stalin. This time, however, the delegation of authority occurred *within* Sovmin, from the main executive committee, the Sovmin Bureau, to subordinate specialist committees.[71] Numerous important but technical matters were now settled within the bureaus by teams of specialists, rather than troubling the more generalist leadership within the main Sovmin Bureau.[72] At the same time, all heads of sectoral bureaus were deputy chairs of Sovmin, who sat ex officio on the main Bureau.[73] Thus, the sectoral bureaus fitted in to a wider system of supraministerial decision making that, at its highest levels, was controlled by two tiers of committees. Boundaries between the committees were clearly marked, with the lower sectoral committees acquiring powers related to their own, specialized jurisdictions.

The new model of administrative organization was not confined to the Council of Ministers. On 1 July 1948, Malenkov was appointed Central Committee Secretary, after which he began to chair sessions of the Secretariat and of the Orgburo.[74] One of Malenkov's first acts at the Central Committee was to table a proposal for a reorganization of the Central Committee apparatus.[75] The production-branch structure advocated by Malenkov was designed to ensure better control of the economy by replicating specialized administrative divisions, already found in industry and the governmental apparatus, within the Central Committee apparatus.[76] Malenkov in fact created a structure in the Central Committee apparatus which closely paralleled the sectoral bureau structure at the Council of Ministers.[77] By the middle of 1948, it appeared that the leadership had become sufficiently persuaded of the merits of a sectoral system—consisting of specialized, regularly convened committees—that it agreed to have its principles universalized across the party-state bureaucracy.

Stalin as a Neo-patrimonial Leader

By stark contrast with the machinelike regularity of the Council of Ministers, meetings between Stalin and his Politburo colleagues did not take place on a continuous basis. Stalin's engagement in administration was a matter of discretion, with official business often assuming the form of "personal" encounters. Stalin often called Politburo meetings late at night, in the dining room at his dacha. "Unofficially and in actual fact," wrote the Yugoslav envoy, Milovan Djilas, who visited Stalin twice in this period, "a significant part of Soviet policy was shaped at these dinners." "It all resembled," he went on, "a patriarchal family with a crotchety head who made his kinsfolk apprehensive."[78]

Although Stalin had turned the Politburo into a highly personalized instrument of rule, this did not mean that the Council of Ministers would take the same form. There was, of course, a great degree of personnel overlap between the Politburo and the Sovmin Bureau, with seven of the nine initial members of the latter also being members of the former. But the Council of Ministers dealt with decisions from which Stalin had practically abdicated responsibility. The distance Stalin kept from Sovmin allowed it to function as an effective system of economic administration that operated according to predominantly technocratic criteria.

Stalin's fusion of traditional, personalized forms of decision making with modern, technocratic committees was a particular feature of the upper reaches of the party-state in the early postwar period. An important aspect of this system was the fact that jurisdictional boundaries were always at the leader's discretion. At any time, "official" committee business could assume the form of "personal" encounters with the leader. Where he wished, Stalin could also place institutional alignments and responsibilities on a more stable basis. It was thus Stalin himself, who drafted the key resolution of 8 February 1947, "On the Council of Ministers," which delegated economic decision making to a routine, largely technocratic hierarchy of committees which could make decisions without reference to the leader.[79]

Although economic decision making was, in the post–February 1947 dispensation, devolved to the Council of Ministers, Stalin maintained the right to launch initiatives of his own in the economic sphere. According to the February resolution, matters relating to the "circulation of money and hard currency questions" remained the preserve of the Politburo.[80] Thus, it was Stalin who, with the aid of the Minister of Finance, A. G. Zverev, pushed through the money reforms, which the leader had first conceived in the middle of the war, in December 1947.[81] Two months later, on 16 February 1948, the right to supervise the Ministry of Finances, which in the February resolution had been granted to Voznesenskii, was returned to Stalin.[82] Similarly, Stalin continued to be actively involved in reforms to the system of economic decision making. He, for example, proposed the division of Gosplan, also in December 1947. In addition to a new, slimmed-down planning commission, Stalin introduced two further agencies, a supply committee (Gossnab) and a committee for the introduction of new technologies (Gostekhnika). "Our Gosplan is overloaded," Stalin is reported to have told the chair of the new technology committee. "Our ministries poorly engage with new technology. . . . We must create a new state center for the introduction and guidance of new technologies."[83]

The February 1947 resolution on the Council of Ministers could not, of course, anticipate all eventualities; ambiguities crept in over certain economic issues. The February resolution stipulated that the Sovmin Bureau should handle plans for the "distribution of funded goods and also certain issues of economic construction."[84] Subsequently, however, the Politburo insisted that this did not include the right to allocate some "funded" materials. Thus, a Politburo resolution of 25 May 1948 ruled that any decision to release critical raw materials from state reserves could only be taken by the Politburo.[85] Similarly, the February resolution indicated that proposals on wages should be made by the commission on salaries and prices, attached to the Sovmin Bureau.[86] This decision was also soon amended. Thus, a sequence of Politburo resolutions at the end of 1947 and in 1948 made it plain that decisions on salaries and awards at the upper end of the scale, as well as perks and bonuses for shock workers in strategic industries, remained the prerogative of the Politburo.[87]

Stalin was particularly protective of his right to manage repressive and quasi-judicial jurisdictions. Of particular interest was the Ministry of State Security, where Stalin took great care to ensure that both the minister and those in charge of the administration for investigating especially important cases were directly beholden to him. Although a Sovmin resolution of 28 March 1946 had assigned Beria the duty of overseeing the ministry, Stalin made certain that all fundamental issues relating to the security police were referred to him. Stalin also went to great trouble to make sure that relatively independent figures with few ties to other Politburo members were appointed to the most sensitive posts in the security police. Indeed, the same month that Beria was given responsibility for overseeing the secret police, March 1946, Abakumov, who would become Minister of State Security in May, was made deputy minister. Abakumov's relations with Beria and with the other Politburo member most intimately involved with the repressive and intelligence apparatus, Malenkov, were positively frosty, not least because Stalin had entrusted Abakumov with leading the investigation into the Aviators' Affair, which was targeted against Malenkov, and with running an inquiry into mistakes committed at the MGB under Merkulov, who had been a close associate of Beria's. As Merkulov would later testify, Beria made special efforts not to cross Abakumov and "began to avoid [him] like the plague."[88]

In order to remove any ambiguities that may have arisen as a result of the March 1946 resolution, Stalin had all responsibility for MGB matters returned to the Politburo in February 1947.[89] Nonetheless, the March 1946 resolution had reflected the fact that, as was true of other areas, Stalin could not control the MGB alone. This question resurfaced later in 1947 when, on 17 September, the Central Committee Secretary Aleksei Kuznetsov was given responsibility, this time at the Central Committee apparatus, for overseeing the affairs of the secret police. It is likely that in the following months, Abakumov, as Minister of State Security, agreed all questions of principle directly with Stalin, while Kuznetsov was expected to oversee routine issues. Even so, it was most probably not easy to establish a clear division of labor between Stalin and Kuznetsov, and this appears to have been a matter which troubled the leader. As evidence, we can turn to a scandal that erupted at the beginning of 1948. In order to demonstrate his vigilance, Abakumov had decided to stage an honor court against two MGB officials at the end of 1947. For his part, Stalin chose to see in this a sign that Abakumov, who had not cleared the matter first with him, had achieved unwarranted autonomy within the MGB. When Stalin demanded an explanation from Abakumov, the latter replied that he had obtained permission from Kuznetsov. Judging from the available documents, it seems that Stalin was infuriated by this. Since the powers available to the honor court were relatively trivial, he refrained from taking drastic measures. He did, however, use the case to underline his own authority over the MGB and Abakumov, and to send a clear signal to Kuznetsov not to exceed his powers again. Accordingly, on 15 March 1948, the Politburo adopted a special resolution that reprimanded Abakumov for having organized an honor court "without the knowledge or consent of the Politburo," and rebuked Kuznetsov for having granted "unilateral" consent for staging the court.[90]

Stalin's sensitivity on such matters extended to other quasi-judicial institutions. In addition to censuring Abakumov and Kuznetsov, the Politburo resolution of 15 March also "henceforth forbade ministries to organize [other] honor courts without authorization from the Politburo." Equally, although another quasi-judicial institution, the Ministry of State Control was, under the provisions of the February 1947 resolution, "directly managed by the Sovmin Bureau," and the minister, Lev Mekhlis, the former editor of *Pravda*, was an old crony of Stalin's, Stalin was quick to stamp on any perceived abuses of the ministry's authority. Thus, when the ministry apparently overstepped its powers in a high-level review of the financial activities of the Azerbaijani Council of Ministers, Stalin and the Politburo intervened with a resolution of 26 August 1948, which curbed the rights of the ministry and severely censured Mekhlis.[91]

While on individual issues Stalin could seek to redraw the border separating the Politburo from Sovmin, the general principle of the February resolution was to reestablish Sovmin on bureaucratic principles that would best facilitate the growth and efficiency of the Soviet economy. Even where Stalin did not deliberately interfere in the work of Sovmin, however, his influence would often skew and distort the work of the government in indirect ways. Deputy premiers were prone to stifle what could be construed as "liberal" reforms, rather than to arouse Stalin's fury by venturing proposals that might run against his wishes.[92] They learned to adjust their behavior to Stalin's temperament by repressing pieces of legislation, however sound, or items of information, however urgent, which might disturb him. These efforts to internalize Stalin's psychology meant that a host of solid, well thought-out reforms which percolated up to the Sovmin Bureau were subsequently stalled.

As well as repressing liberal reforms, Stalin forced a number of perverse and dysfunctional campaigns on the Council of Ministers. The postwar laws on secrecy provide a good example. At the beginning of 1947, as the Cold War moved into full swing, both sides to the conflict tightened up security and access to information. On the Soviet side, Stalin pressed the campaign beyond any rational limits, so that it assumed a completely inconsistent and illogical form.[93] In June 1947, Stalin introduced a law on state secrets. In addition, he authorized a new list of types of information that should be regarded as "secret," the precise details of which were to be left in the hands of the Council of Ministers. Drawing up a list proved to be no easy matter. In view of the strength of Stalin's feelings, Sovmin felt compelled, in its resolution of 1 March 1948, to adopt a blanket ban on virtually all information that touched on state interests. Organizing the secrecy campaign became, inevitably, an administrative nightmare. Sovmin laid on a series of tightly guarded talks, "On Responsibility for Divulging State Secrets or for the Loss of Documents Containing State Secrets,"[94] and increased staff at its own in-house "secret department" to 350.[95] Orchestrating the distribution and dissemination of the resolution was the first major headache, since its contents were themselves a secret.[96] As soon became apparent from the tide of vexed and frustrated letters to the government, the Sovmin decree was awash with paradoxes and inconsistencies.[97] Sovmin was also flooded with technical inquiries, some quite farcical, about the types of information that should be designated "secret." Ministers had to obtain special permission for each table or appendix they published, no matter how innocent the information seemed, and to fight hard to "declassify" figures already in the public domain.[98] Thus, the campaign had the effect of converting relatively simple administrative tasks into lengthy and exhausting operations. Although Stalin had formally delegated authority to the Council of Ministers, he dragged Sovmin into a perverse set of administrative practices which confused ministers, frustrated officials, and created further layers of unnecessary bureaucracy.

As well as determining the content of Sovmin policies, Stalin also influenced the supraministerial system in indirect ways. Indeed, his own domestic habits had a significant impact on working conditions across the Council of Ministers. It is well known that Stalin kept to a nocturnal schedule. When not dining with the leader, Politburo members were phoned by Stalin's secretary, Aleksandr Poskrebyshev, as late as four or five in the morning to be told that Stalin had gone to bed and that they, too, could go home.[99] The effects of Stalin's nighttime regime were not confined to Politburo members. Given the precedent set by the leader, Politburo members, most notably Kaganovich and Beria but also others, regarded it as their prerogative to phone ministers and deputies into the early hours.[100] Ministers would, in turn, hold late-night conferences with their deputies and have their briefcase with them at all times, lest they be summoned at short notice by Stalin or their Politburo overlord.[101] Ministers also required aides, secretaries, and other support staff to be available to prepare emergency documents should the need arise. Although ministers might return home to their large apartments on nearby Gorkii Street for lunch and an afternoon nap, such a luxury was not open to their subordinates.[102] Around-the-clock pressure on clerical workers was such that whole battalions of secretaries and other support staff were expected to work the night shifts.[103]

On Stalin could depend not only the daily rhythms of work but also extensions to deadlines and even holidays.[104] The cumulative effect of such a punishing work schedule on Sovmin leaders and their subordinates was severe. In an entry to her diary of 25 April 1947, Voroshilov's wife recorded that her husband, then the head of the newly established culture bureau, suffered from headaches, insomnia, and dizziness, as a result of which he had been ordered by his doctors to take two months leave in Sochi.[105] Similarly, an exasperated Andreev, who sat on the main Sovmin Bureau, complained, in a letter of January 1949, of continuing dizzy spells and of not being able to stand up unaided, following which he was granted leave of six months in the south.[106] The strains of overwork were felt throughout Sovmin. A document of April 1947 commented that "among a number of [leading cadres], even of a comparatively tender age, there are serious ailments of the heart, blood vessels, and nervous system which result in a major decline in their capacity for work." The document went on to attribute these ailments to the grinding schedules of senior ministerial officials.[107] Another document a year later showed that the arduous timetable had taken a heavy toll on the health of ministers. The March 1948 memorandum, from the medical administration of the Kremlin, revealed that twenty-two ministers were suffering from severe fatigue, three from ulcers, and one from nervous exhaustion.[108]

Kremlin leaders were not entirely unresponsive to these predicaments. A draft resolution, put together by Zhdanov in April 1947, sought to ease the pressure on leading officials by stipulating that the workday begin at 1:00 P.M. and end no later than midnight, as well as by allowing officials at least one month's vacation a year.[109] Another draft, this time put together by Malenkov, Beria, and Mikoian in December 1948, condemned the fact that ministerial functionaries worked predominantly in the second half of the day and at night and obliged them instead to begin their work at 10:30 A.M. and to end it at 7:30 P.M..[110] Neither piece of legislation, however, went beyond the draft stage and both, crucially, ran counter to the example set by the despot. Indeed, so long as Stalin lived, those leaders who sought to escape their punishing schedules had to obtain permission directly from him.[111] Stalin's ability to resist the delimitation of his authority by rules thus had a bearing not only on his own conduct but also on all those around him.[112]

The relationship between Stalin and the supraministerial system was neo-patrimonial in two respects. First, the leader was not bound by a set of rules or expectations that ordained his involvement in governmental affairs on a continuous basis, nor was his participation confined to a particular class of decisions automatically reserved for the leader. Stalin's interventions were a matter for his own discretion; he got involved in the affairs of government on a random basis, as and when he pleased. Often, as with the laws on secrecy, his participation, which reflected his personal predilections, could throw the organization of government into turmoil. Second, Stalin's relations with deputy premiers was patrimonial in the sense that his dependents intuitively adjusted to and, eventually, internalized his likes and dislikes, taking precautionary measures to avert his displeasure. Stalin set an example for his immediate entourage, so that they fired and hired in accordance with his wishes and ate and drank, rose and retired to bed in line with his daily rhythms. The behavior of the leader had ripple effects right across the upper tiers of governmental administration.

In comparative terms, the degree of centralization of power under Stalin was extraordinarily high. No leader, however, can rule alone. In the postwar period, Stalin operated through two committees: the Politburo, over which he almost always presided, and the main Bureau of the Council of Ministers, which nearly always convened without him. Whereas the period prior to the war had witnessed a merger of these bodies, after the war they separated.[113] The combination of Stalin's highly personalized leadership, as represented by the Politburo, and the technocratic features of Sovmin was neo-patrimonial, allowing Stalin to marry personal-autocratic features of rule with modern committee-based decision making.

This neo-patrimonial order was, however, inherently unstable. At any point, Stalin could intervene to redraw jurisdictional boundaries. Decision-making powers were only delegated to the Council of Ministers on license. Where strategic economic decisions were judged to have "political" con-

tent—especially where deception, fraud, or subterfuge were suspected—
they were referred to the Politburo. Despite the leadership equilibrium that
had persisted throughout the phase of reconstruction from 1945 to 1948,
there was one such instance at the beginning of 1949 which would upset
the apple cart and unleash a violent new purge.

PART II

Stalin's Shift

3

THE POLITBURO'S LAST PURGE

Economic indicators for 1948 provided firm evidence that the immediate destruction of the war had been overcome and that the main targets of postwar reconstruction had been achieved. Of particular significance was the fact that the regime had survived the famine of 1946–1947. By 1948, the grain harvest had almost reached prewar levels, while the production of potatoes, a major staple, was higher than in any of the immediate prewar years. Industrial production plans for 1948 were also considerably exceeded, with overall growth, according to official statistics, of 27 percent, as opposed to the 19 percent that had been forecast.[1] Although these figures masked the usual bottlenecks and imbalances that marked periods of rapid growth, they nonetheless had a clear influence on the calculations of the leadership. In contrast to the relative caution of the 1948 plan, the 1949 plan was highly ambitious.[2] It was the resultant pressures on the economic agencies which would trigger the Gosplan and Voznesenskii Affairs.

As always, the international situation left a clear mark on the policies of Stalin's regime. In some respects, the position of the USSR was strengthened over the course of 1949. On 24 August, the country carried out its first successful test of the atom bomb, an event that must have heightened the leadership's sense of invulnerability. The Soviet Union's prestige was further bolstered by the decisive victory of the Chinese communists, which culminated in the declaration of the People's Republic of China on 1 October 1949. However, the year 1949 also saw two decisive setbacks. First, there were a series of diplomatic defeats in relations with the West. In April 1949, the founding treaty on NATO was signed, thus establishing a Western military bloc against the Soviet Union. The following month, in May 1949, having run into stiff opposition from Western states that had organized an effective air bridge to feed the blockaded city of Berlin, Stalin was forced to lift the siege. Finally, in autumn of that year, the division of Germany was sealed with the creation of the German Federal and Democratic Republics. One consequence of these diplomatic defeats was a new round of recriminations against Molotov who, as Minister of Foreign Affairs, was held partly responsible. The confrontation with the West also increased spy-mania in the Soviet Union and led to the punishment of those sections of the population (above all, the intelligentsia and "cosmopolitan" groups) suspected of pro-Western sympathies. Following the liquidation of the Soviet Jewish Anti-Fascist Committee (EAK) in November 1948, the early months of 1949 witnessed an intensive anti-Semitic campaign, presented as a struggle against so-called cosmopolitanism and Zionism.[3]

The second blow to the authority of the Soviet leadership was the growing differences with Yugoslavia, which in effect boiled down to a personal row between Stalin and Tito. Having begun in the spring of 1948, this conflict had acquired a particular intensity by 1949. One consequence was the inauguration of a far harsher attitude toward the Soviet Union's East European satellites.[4] Integral to the new approach was a series of celebrated cases, all closely orchestrated by Stalin, against "enemies" within the leadership of the socialist states. With the help of advisers from Moscow, a case was fabricated against the former Hungarian Minister of Internal Affairs, Laszlo Rajk, charging that he had headed a spy organization. Two months after Rajk's execution, Traicho Kostov, the former Secretary of the Bulgarian Communist Party, was also tried and executed.[5] These trials were matched by analogous arrests in Poland, Romania, Czechoslovakia, and Albania. One link in this international chain was the so-called Leningrad Affair in the USSR, which led to the arrest of a group of high-ranking Soviet leaders.

A principal cause of these purges was Stalin's determination to prevent disobedience and to harden official discipline. Following purges in practically all the European satellite states, new, more compliant leaders were installed. Similarly, following the arrest of the "Leningraders," Stalin established a new balance of forces within the Soviet leadership. As in Eastern Europe, these leaders retained their positions until Stalin's death: the Leningrad Affair would indeed constitute the last purge of Stalin's circle.

After Zhdanov

Although Zhdanov's relationship with Stalin had deteriorated toward the end of his life, Stalin did not show any outward signs of displeasure toward his deceased comrade-in-arms. As befitted a Soviet leader, Zhdanov was buried with full honors. On 20 September 1948, a Council of Ministers resolution provided for the erection of a tombstone at Zhdanov's grave by the Kremlin wall "in accordance with established tombstones to outstanding figures of the party and of the Soviet state." Preparation of the gravestone was assigned to the court sculptor S. D. Merkurov, who had created a number of representations of Stalin himself.[6] A month later, on 22 October, a Council of Ministers resolution was adopted "on the immortalization of the memory of Andrei Aleksandrovich Zhdanov," which provided for the construction of monuments to Zhdanov in Moscow and Leningrad and the renaming of his own hometown of Mariupol', as well as of a whole host of streets, districts, enterprises, and even a university after the deceased leader.[7] In the immediate aftermath of Zhdanov's death, even his former rivals demonstrated a certain caution over his legacy. On 28 September 1948, Malenkov sent Stalin, who was on vacation at that time, a telegram proposing that two of Zhdanov's aides be reappointed and moved to the relatively senior positions of deputy head of Central Committee departments. "They are qualified workers and should cope with managerial positions in the Central Committee apparatus," Malenkov added. By consenting to have the matter settled at the Secretariat, which Malenkov chaired, Stalin in effect gave this proposal his blessing.[8] As Zhdanov's successor and Stalin's deputy in the party, Malenkov did not, at least openly, take any steps that might have been construed as critical of his predecessor.

At the same time, Malenkov devoted himself to establishing order at the Central Committee. Under his chairmanship, sessions of the Secretariat and of the Orgburo were conducted in precise accordance with established rules. In his capacity as chair, Malenkov ensured that the records were personally signed by him.[9] Further, agendas for forthcoming meetings of the Orgburo were confirmed ahead of time at the Secretariat. It was thus on Malenkov's prompting that on 26 July, the Orgburo established that materials for discussion be submitted at least three days in advance. Responsibility for strict adherence to this rule was placed on department heads at the Central Committee.[10] As demonstrated by other, similar measures, Malenkov served as an effective administrator.

For a while it appeared as though Zhdanov's allies would not be made to suffer for their patron's death. If anything, the opposite was true. On 3 September 1948, Aleksei Kosygin was promoted to full member of the Politburo and admitted to the ruling group—the novenary.[11] Kosygin, who had been born in Leningrad, and who had made a career under Zhdanov, can be regarded as one of Zhdanov's clients. In putting his name forward, Stalin clearly sought to fill a major gap that had arisen within the Politburo as a result of Zhdanov's death. Another step in the construction of a new balance of power was Stalin's attempt to broaden the group of leaders at the "second level," who might form a counterweight to the "old guard." Characteristic in this regard was the political career of A. D. Krutikov.

In terms of his age, Krutikov, who was born in 1902, was a contemporary of Malenkov's. His career, however, had progressed less dramatically. Having entered the party in 1927, Krutikov had held a succession of minor posts in the provinces and, from 1936 to 1938, was sent to study at the Economics Department of the Leningrad Institute of Red Professors. Krutikov had turned up in Leningrad at an opportune moment. The mass arrests of 1937–1938 opened up vacancies for leading positions. Those cadres who survived the purges were assured of near automatic progress up the official hierarchy. In January 1938, Krutikov was appointed head of the Kuibyshev district department of propaganda in Leningrad; before the year was out, he had been elevated to the powerful position of deputy commissar at the USSR Commissariat of Foreign Trade, an institution whose leading staff had been depleted as a result of the repressions.[12] The promotion of Krutikov was very likely assisted by his association with Zhdanov, who by this stage had gained considerable clout in Moscow.

At a certain point, Krutikov, who for ten years had served as Deputy Commissar of Foreign Trade (eight as first deputy), appears to have gained favor with Stalin. On 9 July 1948, three days after reading about the serious deterioration of Zhdanov's health, Stalin confirmed Krutikov's appointment as deputy chair of the USSR Council of Ministers and chair of its bureau for trade and light industry.[13] The circumstances of Krutikov's promotion were later described by Mikoian, who was Minister of Foreign Trade and Krutikov's superior at the time.

> Stalin unexpectedly nominated Krutikov as deputy chair of the USSR Council of Ministers, with special responsibility for internal trade. I strongly objected, and tried to make Stalin see that Krutikov was not yet ripe for such a senior post, that he would need to gain experience as a minister first, and that he was not even quite ready for that yet. . . . With his characteristic obstinacy, and despite my opposition, in July 1948 Stalin went ahead with the appointment of Krutikov, without even having talked the matter over with Krutikov himself.[14]

Mikoian attributed this decision to Stalin's obstinacy. This is, in all probability, too simplistic an account of Stalin's motives. A year later, Mikoian was himself replaced as Minister of Foreign Trade by another one of his deputies, M. A. Men'shikov. The promotion of Krutikov and, then, of Men'shikov, appear to have been part of a general strategy by the leader to prepare younger replacements for, or, at the very least, counterweights to, the aging members of the Politburo.

In the wake of Zhdanov's death, Stalin continued to apply the same relentless pressures on his companions as he had in earlier years. Notwithstanding—and, in some respects, because of—his promotion as Stalin's right-hand man in the party, Malenkov would bear the brunt of Stalin's reproaches. A characteristic episode took place two months after Malenkov's return as Central Committee Secretary. In September 1948, a fire broke out on board the ship *Pobeda*, which had returned from the United States with Armenian repatriates. According to a report from the Ministry of State Security, which Malenkov presented to Stalin, who was at the time on leave in the south, the Americans had poured combustible materials into the vessel while it was docked in New York. In a return telegram Stalin admonished Malenkov and demanded that a search be made for American "spies" among those on board the ship, whose main aim, according to Stalin, was "to set [our] oil fields on fire."[15] Malenkov complied with predictable efficiency. On 13 September 1948, he sent Stalin the following report: "You are undoubtedly right that among the Armenian immigrants there are American intelligence officers, who carried out this act of sabotage before the ship departed from Batumi for Odessa, either after or during the disembarkation of the Armenians. Together with our friends [the security services] we shall today take the necessary measures to resolve this matter in full accordance with your proposals. You shall be informed of these measures forthwith."[16] The next day, Malenkov reported that a group of eight security service officials, headed by the Deputy Minister of State Security N. N. Selivanovskii, had been dispatched to Baku and that an analogous group had been sent to Erevan. With a Council of Ministers resolution adopted that day, the repatriation of overseas Armenians was stopped and the admission of Armenian immigrants banned.[17]

As ever, it was Stalin who came up with the harshest, most spectacular reading of an event. Outstripping even the Ministry of State Security for morbid suspiciousness, Stalin declared an everyday accident an act of sabotage and accused those on board of instigating it; this, in turn, became a pretext for triggering a wave of arrests. As he and other members of the Politburo had done on many occasions, Malenkov accepted this latest unexpected reprimand without demur on the understanding that his leader was completely unconstrained by ordinary rules of behavior.

Stalin's deputies were particularly alert to such reprimands in the wake of large-scale reorganizations and high-level reshuffles. The underlying instability occasioned by Zhdanov's death forced rivals in the Politburo to move into action. One consequence was a struggle that began to brew between two "middle-generation" groups within Stalin's circle. The moving spirit behind the first of these was the Politburo member Voznesenskii, toward whom two other key figures, Aleksei Kuznetsov and Aleksei Kosygin, began to gravitate. To some degree, these three men would all suffer as a result of the so-called Leningrad Affair. All three were of common political descent, having made their early careers in 1930s Leningrad under the patronage of Andrei Zhdanov. There were, in addition, other bonds tying these figures. Kuznetsov and Kosygin, for instance, had family links through their wives.[18] The "Leningrad leaders" also had good relations with certain elder members of the Politburo. Voznesenskii, for example, was close to Molotov, while Kuznetsov's daughter and Mikoian's son were engaged to be married, and the two spent much of their time together at the homes of their respective parents.[19]

The opposing group consisted, in the main, of Malenkov and Beria. The two were linked through many years of collaborative work at the end of the 1930s and during the war, when both sat on the GKO. Following Stalin's death, their close working relationship would be commented on by a host of Politburo members, including Khrushchev, Mikoian, and Bulganin. Moreover, the two had a fraught relationship with Voznesenskii, dating back to the prewar period when Stalin promoted Voznesenskii, to Beria's unconcealed disgust, to the post of First Deputy Chair of the Council of People's Commissars.[20]

The documents after Zhdanov's death do not bear out the existence of "programmatic" differences, based on conflicting principles, among Stalin's companions. Members of these warring groups fought to raise themselves above the other group in Stalin's esteem, more than to defend a particular decision or initiative for its own sake. In the ensuing struggle there were few rules, other than those set by the leader. While rivals had the right to present Stalin with compromising materials, any decision as to how these materials would be used, on whether pardons would be granted or punishments imposed, let alone what measures of punishment would be applied, would rest with Stalin. While the types of incriminating materials could vary, any political evaluations, especially on the political charges of wrecking, espionage, and so forth, could come only from Stalin. All these laws of Stalin's cadre politics would be fully corroborated later in 1949, in the course of the so-called Leningrad Affair. Yet chronologically, the first action that indicated Stalin's resolve to force through a major reorganization was a new round of personal attacks on Molotov, and the subsequent sacking of both Molotov and Mikoian from their ministerial positions.

Molotov and Mikoian

Frequent attacks on his companions were a customary technique by which Stalin achieved control over Politburo members. Molotov had nonetheless become a particularly frequent target of Stalin's invectives in the postwar period. The main pretext for the latest in this line of attacks was Molotov's corrections to the draft German Constitution. Having received Molotov's amendments while on holiday, Stalin replied with a ciphered telegram on 21 October 1948 to Malenkov. Molotov's changes, observed Stalin, were "politically incorrect and make the constitution worse. We must tell the Germans that the amendments do not reflect the position of the Central Committee and that the Central Committee has no intention of making any changes to the constitution, for it considers the draft to be fine as it stands."[21] Stalin indicated that the telegram be shown "to our friends," and it was accordingly circulated to Molotov, Voznesenskii, Kaganovich, and Kosygin (Beria and Mikoian, it seems, were away at the time). Despite its limited readership, it was clear from the wording of the telegram that Stalin was keen to embarrass Molotov, at the very least with the German leadership. To some extent, this can be attributed to Stalin's unhappiness about what was happening in Germany, for which he blamed Molotov as Minister of Foreign Affairs. The driving force behind these attacks, however, was the tension building up between the two over the case being mounted against Molotov's wife, Polina Zhemchuzhina.

Over the 1920s and early 1930s, Zhemchuzhina, like Molotov himself, had been close to Stalin's family and, in particular, she had been a good friend to Stalin's wife, Nadezhda Allilueva. Allilueva's suicide at the end of 1932 embittered Stalin and engendered in him a hostility toward Zhemchuzhina. Despite the fact that over the 1930s Zhemchuzhina had built a successful career, culminating in her appointment as People's Commissar for the Fish Industry, in 1939 she was charged with political naïveté and with unwittingly pandering to "wreckers" and "spies" in her social circle. That case, however, did not lead to her arrest, only her demotion.[22] Over the course of 1948 and early 1949, Zhemchuzhina, who was Jewish, was targeted as part of an increasingly vociferous anti-Semitic campaign. The case against her was fabricated in close association with the case of the Jewish Anti-Fascist Committee. During investigations for the latter, the security service beat out testimonies against Zhemchuzhina, which were hastily passed on to Stalin. Having decided that Zhemchuzhina should be arrested, Stalin demanded that Molotov divorce her. "Stalin came to me at the Central Committee," Molotov later recalled. " 'You need to divorce your wife!' Afterwards [Polina Semënovna] said to me: 'If that is what the party demands, then that is what we shall do.' So at the end of 1948 we got divorced."[23]

Even the separation of Molotov and Zhemchuzhina does not appear to have satisfied Stalin. On 29 December 1948, the Politburo considered a report presented jointly by the Deputy Chair of the Committee of Party Control, Matvei Shkiriatov, and the Minister of State Security, Abakumov. Zhemchuzhina was accused of links with "Jewish nationalists"; of attending the funeral of one of their "leaders," Solomon Mikhoels; of "disseminating provocative rumors on Mikhoels's death"; and of attending a religious service at the Choral Synagogue in Moscow on 14 March 1945.[24] As Molotov later recounted, "When at the Politburo session [Stalin] read out the materials on Polina Semënovna, which the Chekists had supplied, my knees began to tremble. But the case had been made against her. You just could not fault them. The Chekists had done their best."[25] The Politburo adopted a resolution on Zhemchuzhina's expulsion from the party. Molotov somehow found in himself the willpower to abstain from the vote.[26] It was a measure of the conflict which followed that, three weeks later, on 19 January 1949, Stalin ordered that copies of the original correspondence of November and December 1945 on Molotov's mistakes be circulated to those members of the ruling group, who had not been privy to the original exchange—Bulganin, Kosygin, and Voznesenskii, as well as Molotov himself.[27] Given the current circumstances, these materials presented Molotov's actions not as a chance mistake, but as part of a deliberate and consistent "position."

Unable to withstand this latest blow, Molotov addressed the following statement to Stalin on 20 January:

> In the vote at the Central Committee on the proposal to expel P. S. Zhemchuzhina from the party I abstained, which is an act that I now see to have been politically mistaken. I declare that, having thought the matter over, I am voting in favor of the decision of the Central Committee, which both meets the interests of the party and of the state and conveys a correct understanding of communist party-mindedness. In addition, I acknowledge my heavy sense of remorse for not having prevented Zhemchuzhina, a person very dear to me, from making her mistakes and from forming ties with anti-Soviet Jewish nationalists, such as Mikhoels.[28]

On Stalin's instructions, Molotov's statement was distributed to all candidates and members of the Politburo and, on the following day, Zhemchuzhina was arrested.[29]

On 4 March 1949, Molotov was dismissed as Minister of Foreign Affairs. His position was taken over by Andrei Vyshinsky, while at the same time Mikoian was replaced as Minister of Foreign Trade by Men'shikov. The original Politburo records reflect that these resolutions were taken at a meeting of Stalin, Malenkov, Beria, and Bulganin, and the blank in Stalin's Kremlin visitors' book on 3 and 4 March 1949 indicates it took place at Stalin's country house. Stalin conveyed the decision to Poskrebyshev, who, by phone, canvassed the positions of Mikoian, Molotov, Voznesenskii, Kosygin, Shvernik, and Voroshilov. All voted in favor of the resolutions, although Voroshilov expressed his position in a somewhat guarded form: "If everyone is in favor, then so am I."[30] The fact that the resolutions were approved by correspondence, and that the original decisions were taken without the participation of either Molotov or Mikoian, is a measure of a certain caution on Stalin's part. It may well have been that he was nervous about uncomfortable explanations at a meeting of the full Politburo.

In the following weeks, the dismissal of Molotov and Mikoian as ministers was backed up by a series of decisions that created a new system for confirming foreign policy decisions. On 12 March 1949, the Politburo created a foreign policy commission of the Central Committee (VPK) to deal with foreign policy and with links to foreign communist parties. The functions of the VPK, which were confirmed by a special resolution of the Politburo on 18 April 1949, duplicated, to some degree, the functions of the former department of external relations at the Central Committee. The new commission's tasks included the establishment of ties with foreign communist parties, the arrangement of links with the Cominform, and managing the international activities of Soviet public organizations such as the trade unions, the Society for Cultural Relations with Foreign Countries, and the Union of Writers.[31] Charging Molotov with supervision of the new commission meant that he was, in effect, tied down dealing with propaganda aspects of foreign policy, a matter of secondary importance.

At the same time, Molotov was formally prevented from overseeing more substantive decisions that passed through the Ministry of Foreign Affairs. To this end, on 9 April 1949, the Politburo confirmed a special resolution on procedures for considering foreign policy questions, by which matters of foreign affairs and foreign trade were now to be presented directly to the Politburo by the new ministers, Vyshinsky and Men'shikov.[32] At the last moment, Stalin crossed out the following item from the draft resolution: "Questions received by the Council of Ministers that have a bearing on foreign relations will be presented directly to the Politburo by comrade Molotov, while questions relating to foreign economic relations will be presented by comrade Mikoian."[33] The distancing of Molotov from foreign policy matters also appears to have been behind Molotov's appointment on 6 April 1949 as chair of the newly created sectoral bureau for metallurgy and geology at Sovmin.[34] His first weeks at his new post were marred by another minor humiliation. The original draft resolution on the formation of the bureau stipulated that Molotov's deputy would be N. M. Siluianov, the deputy chair of Gosplan, but Molotov's nomination was rejected.[35] Amending the draft, Molotov replaced Siluianov with the Deputy Minister of Metallurgical Industry, A. N. Kuz'min. On 6 April, the Politburo confirmed this proposal,[36] but on 11 April, the Minister of Metallurgical Industry Ivan Tevosian appealed directly to Stalin, requesting that Kuz'min's transfer be rescinded.[37] Perhaps in other circumstances Molotov's word would have carried more weight. However, the same day that Tevosian's letter was received, a Politburo resolution repealed the decision on Kuz'min.[38] For the third time in two weeks, Molotov was forced to find a new deputy; only on 18 April did the Politburo make a final decision.[39]

The removal of Mikoian as Minister of Foreign Trade proceeded without scandals or complications. As Mikoian himself recalled, the matter arose as if by chance during a meeting with Stalin following Mikoian's return from talks in China with Mao Tse-tung: "After the conversation Stalin, somewhat unexpectedly, without any reference to the theme of the conversation, says: 'Don't you think the time has come for you to be released as Minister of Foreign Trade?' When I agreed, he said: 'Who would you propose as a replacement?' I named Men'shikov."[40]

If Mikoian's story is true (and there is no reason to doubt it), then the removal of the two senior Politburo leaders may be viewed very simply as an example of the traditional Stalinist tactic of creating vacancies to make way for younger cadres, an ordinary "changing of the guard." As usual, there probably lay a far more complex mix of pragmatic as well as darker motives behind Stalin's decision. His dismissal was in part the price Molotov paid for the failure of Soviet policy in Germany, which had seen the Soviet Union coming off as loser in the Berlin crisis. Stalin sought a way out and dispatched signals to his Western counterparts—of which Molotov's sacking was one—of his readiness for negotiations. Certainly, Western leaders saw the removal of Molotov in this way.[41] Yet underlying the firing of both Molotov and Mikoian there also seems to have been an element of personal distrust on Stalin's part, a feeling that may well have hardened as a result of Molotov's *fronde* on the Zhemchuzhina affair and the marriage at this time of Mikoian's son to the daughter of the disgraced party leader Aleksei Kuznetsov.[42] In this light, the dismissals are best seen as one link in a chain of attacks on Molotov and Mikoian, which had recommenced with renewed vigor after the war and which would continue until Stalin's death.

However, notwithstanding their formal exclusion from certain decision-making structures and the petty degradations to which they were subjected, the demotion of Molotov and Mikoian was more declaratory than substantive in nature. The impulsive nature of the move is reflected in the fact that many of their responsibilities were swiftly restored. On 12 June 1949, the Politburo freed Molotov from his position as chair of the bureau for metallurgy and geology, obliging him "to concentrate on leadership of the Ministry of Foreign Affairs and the foreign policy commission of the Politburo."[43] Although on 13 February 1950 Molotov once again received an "economic load"—the position of chair of the Sovmin bureau for transport and communications—his main field would remain, as before, foreign policy.[44]

Whatever Molotov's precise role in the mechanics of decision making, it is clear that even after March 1949, he remained a central figure in the elaboration of important foreign policy decisions.[45] Judging by available Politburo records, at least until autumn 1952 all questions relating to the foreign policy commission passed through Molotov. Even when questions raised by the Ministry of Foreign Affairs were reported directly to Stalin by Vyshinsky, one gets the impression that, on the whole, Vyshinsky tried to cooperate with Molotov rather than avoid him. In addition, some foreign policy issues were assigned directly to Molotov by Stalin and were agreed bilaterally at meetings between the two.[46]

Following his displacement as Minister of Foreign Trade, Mikoian also retained some of his most important functions. On 19 January 1950, he was appointed chair of the newly created standing commission of the Politburo on questions of foreign trade, which was charged with "considering claims from foreign states on matters relating to external trade, as well as Soviet claims on foreign states."[47] Reflecting his senior status, Mikoian chaired the new commission, while his replacement as Minister of Foreign Trade, Men'shikov, served on it with the rights and status of an ordinary member. Although, owing to their secrecy, the records of this commission have not been released, it is clear that, in practice, Mikoian's appointment to such a senior post underlined his position as the main steward of foreign trade issues.[48] In confirmation of this, on 26 January 1950, Mikoian was also appointed head of the Sovmin bureau for trade and food industries.[49]

Stalin's approach to Mikoian and Molotov in 1949 was, in many ways, a continuation of the strategy he had adopted since the end of 1945. In light of recent events, most notably Stalin's humiliation of Molotov over his wife, these dismissals may well have appeared as rather ominous. But as keen as Stalin was to stamp his authority over his comrades-in-arms,[50] he was loath to take matters too far with such senior figures as Molotov and Mikoian. Hence, details of the attacks were confined to a very select group, and, notwithstanding their dismissal as ministers, the two remained highly influential members of the Politburo. By contrast, what would carry far greater significance for the balance of power within the leadership, was an innocuous-looking regional scandal that would soon blow up into the Leningrad Affair.

The Leningrad and Gosplan Affairs

Despite the callousness with which Stalin continued to treat subordinates, the Leningrad Affair stands out as the only occasion in the postwar period and, indeed, at any time after the Great Purges, when Stalin chose to have two colleagues of such high political standing—a Politburo member and a Secretary of the Central Committee—killed. No matter how intense his confrontations with his colleagues, before these incidents Stalin had always stopped short of such drastic measures. What were the circumstances and the rationale which on this occasion led to Stalin's patience finally snapping? One factor that clearly played a part was the fact that the hierarchy of decision making, which Stalin had gone to such pains to create, was broken. He took any violation of decision-making structures, even for a relatively trivial matter, very seriously. What appears to have truly enraged the leader, however, was a somewhat different matter. Despite having surrendered a large number of economic decisions to Sovmin, Stalin viewed the flow of high-quality strategic economic information to him as sacrosanct. Any attempt to deceive him by massaging or misrepresenting this information was seized on by the leader with utter ruthlessness.

The immediate trigger for both the Leningrad and the Gosplan Affairs was a scandal surrounding an all-Russian wholesale fair held in Leningrad from 10–20 January 1949. What at first glance appears to have been a completely innocuous event, was carried out in breach of a principal postulate of the Stalinist system—the strict hierarchy of decision making. Although the general issue of holding interregional wholesale fairs had been raised at a meeting of the all-union government, the Leningrad fair was the result of a "separate" initiative put together by the Leningrad leadership, the government of the Russian Federation (at the apex of which stood a native of Leningrad, M. I. Rodionov), and the Central Committee Secretary Kuznetsov, who was also from Leningrad.[51] There is no evidence to suggest that any of these leaders considered their actions to be anything but lawful and economically straightforward. Their behavior would, indeed, have been interpreted this way had the matter not fallen into the orbit of big-league Moscow politics. On 13 January 1949, the Chair of the RSFSR Council of Ministers, Rodionov, sent the Central Committee Secretary Malenkov a routine memorandum on the progress of the Leningrad fair. Malenkov then forwarded the brief report, with the following note: "To L. P. Beria, N. A. Voznesenskii, A. I. Mikoian, and A. D. Krutikov. Please look at the memorandum from comrade Rodionov. In my view such an enterprise needs the permission of the Council of Ministers."[52] It is still not clear how, from whom, and with what commentaries news of the Leningrad fair was passed on to Stalin. Whatever the source, the fact that the fair had taken place at all without the requisite clearance from above was a cause of great displeasure to Stalin. To make matters worse, the fair could easily have been construed as the result of a deal among a number of leaders with close regional ties.[53]

On 28 January 1949, somewhat out of the blue, the Politburo set up a Far Eastern Buro of the Central Committee, appointing Aleksei Kuznetsov as Secretary.[54] The new buro never met and Kuznetsov never assumed his new role. This obscure appointment was, instead, a typically esoteric signal from Stalin that he was planning some kind of radical action against Kuznetsov. Likely in connection with the Leningrad fair, Krutikov, the deputy chair of the Council of Ministers for trade questions, was also demoted. Together with the USSR Minister of Trade, V. G. Zhavoronkov, Krutikov was summoned to Stalin's office for five minutes on 4 February 1949. Three days later, the two were again called to Stalin's office for a longer meeting. That day Krutikov was dismissed, to be appointed two weeks later, on 22 February, to the lower position of deputy chair of the trade bureau.[55]

Despite taking these early actions, for two weeks Stalin appears to have vacillated over what to do with the organizers of the Leningrad fair. A turning point was apparently reached late on the evening of 12 February, at a meeting of the Politburo's ruling group. To this meeting, Stalin summoned the key officials responsible for setting up the Leningrad fair: the First Secretary of the Leningrad regional and city party committees, P. S. Popkov, the chair of the Leningrad city executive committee, P. G. Lazutin, the Chair of the Council of Ministers of the Russian Federation, Rodionov, and either his deputy, V. I. Makarov, or the Minister of Trade of the Russian Federation, M. Makarov.[56] It appears that the organizers of the fair were roundly condemned at the meeting. In order to stave off criticism of his own "factional" links with the Leningraders, Voznesenskii declared that in 1948, Popkov had, as Leningrad party secretary, approached him with a request that he act as a "patron" to Leningrad. Stalin was incensed. The idea that any leader other than Stalin could exercise patronage over a fiefdom and that this scheme should have been proposed behind his own back was entirely anathema to the dictator. In the subsequent Politburo resolution, passed on 15 February, a number of disparate charges that had previously taken shape in Stalin's mind were now fused. The independent organization of the fair now became tied to attempts by Leningrad leaders to carry out "underhand schemes" "by means of self-styled 'patrons' such as comrades Kuznetsov, Rodionov, and others," and this, in turn, was linked, quite disastrously for Voznesenskii, with Popkov's proposal that Voznesenskii serve as one of the city's advocates.

The Politburo resolution of 15 February contained serious allegations against the Leningrad leaders and their supposed "patrons":

The Politburo believes that . . . comrades Kuznetsov A. A., Rodionov, and Popkov are guilty of a perverted, unbolshevik deviation, which finds expression in their demagogic overtures to the Leningrad organization, in their underhand criticism of the Central Committee, which supposedly does not help Leningrad, as well as in their attempts to present themselves as special defenders of Leningrad and in their efforts to erect a barrier between the Central Committee and the Leningrad organization, thereby distancing one from the other.

The actions of the group were ominously compared to those of Grigorii Zinoviev, who had headed the Leningrad party organization in the 1920s and had turned that body into a center of opposition to Stalin. The Politburo resolution of 15 February peremptorily dismissed all three—Rodionov, Popkov, and Kuznetsov—from their leading party and state roles and issued the following reprimand against Voznesenskii: "Despite the fact that he declined the approach from comrade Popkov to act as a 'patron' to Leningrad, and that he pointed out the errors of this proposal, he was all the same in the wrong not to let the Central Committee know immediately of the anti-party proposal 'to act as a patron' to Leningrad which had been made to him by comrade Popkov."[57] On 22 February, Malenkov convened a joint plenum of the Leningrad regional and city party committees, at which Kuznetsov, Rodionov, Popkov, and the second secretary of the Leningrad regional committee, F. Ia. Kapustin, were charged with belonging to an anti-party group.[58]

As a pragmatic leader, Stalin accepted his companions only so long as he saw some value in their actions or in their symbolic existence. The middle generation of Politburo members, who had not seen revolutionary service and whose symbolic worth was limited, had been promoted and retained by Stalin solely on the basis of their organizational or administrative talents. As a typical member of this middle generation, Voznesenskii's value to Stalin rested entirely on his ability to fulfill assigned responsibilities. Although Stalin himself had softened the wording of the reprimand against Voznesenskii, Stalin's companions were now fully aware that Voznesenskii's position had been shaken.[59] Voznesenskii's rivals now sought to sow doubts in Stalin's mind about Voznesenskii's reliability as head of the state planning agency, Gosplan.

In the Soviet economic system, Gosplan was charged with coordinating the different sectors of the economy and defending general state interests against "ministerial egoism." In what was often a fraught relationship with the ministries, Gosplan was supposed to ratchet up ministerial plans and to ensure that new targets were met. Voznesenskii's political power rested on Stalin's confidence that he could fulfill these duties better than anyone else. As Stalin once confided to the Minister of Transport, Ivan Kovalev:

Take Voznesenskii, in what way is he different from the other managers?
. . . Where there are differences, the other managers will iron them out

and bring the matter to my attention only once they reach a consensus. Even when differences remain they will come to some agreement on paper and present the issue to me in that form. But not Voznesenskii; if he doesn't agree, he will stand his ground and simply refuse to have the matter agreed for form's sake. He will come to me with his objections, with his differences of opinion. The managers understand that I cannot know everything; all they want from me is a stamp with my signature. Yes, I cannot know everything, that is why I pay particular attention to disagreements, objections, I look into why they start, to find out what is going on. The managers do their best to conceal these from me; they go along with the votes but they conceal the differences, all so that they can obtain a stamp with my signature. What they want out of me is my stamp. That is why I prefer the objections of a Voznesenskii to their consensus.[60]

Some have attributed Voznesenskii's downfall to the fact that he was a progressive economist who opposed conservatives in the administration. However, Voznesenskii's removal had virtually nothing to do with "pro-grammatic" differences.[61] Voznesenskii was a typical Stalinist administrator who differed little from other Gosplan chairmen. Both in terms of his personality and of his administrative function in the system—as the head of Gosplan, the agency charged with providing "honest" third-party information—Voznesenskii served as one of Stalin's chief truth tellers.[62] Voznesenskii would fall for violating his cardinal truth-telling function.

Very shortly after the incidents with the Leningraders, Voznesenskii ran into new difficulties, this time relating directly to his own duties at Gosplan. According to Mikoian, some time toward the end of 1948 (although Mikoian does not give a date, the meeting is most likely to have taken place in November), the annual plan for 1949 had been discussed at the Politburo. Following the relatively healthy economic performance of 1948, Stalin wanted to step up the rate of industrial growth. Accordingly, he impressed on Voznesenskii the need to avoid in 1949 the downturn in production that was a cyclical feature of the first quarter of each calendar year.[63] Voznesenskii knew that sustaining and even increasing production over the first quarter at the same level as the previous quarter was an unrealistic task but, in view of Stalin's insistence, he complied.[64] The Politburo accordingly laid down a target of 5 percent growth in the first quarter of 1949.

On 15 December 1948, three senior officials at Gosplan sent Voznesenskii a memorandum in which they reported that, given the overfulfillment of the plan for the fourth quarter of 1948, such a 5 percent goal could be achieved so long as the quotas for gross industrial output for the first quarter of 1949 be increased by 1.7 billion rubles. Following this advice, Voznesenskii authorized the necessary changes in the plan. However, even though the annual plan for 1949 was correspondingly amended (the initial indicators were increased and the targets for 1949 accordingly lowered from 19 percent to 17 percent), for a variety of reasons the plan for the first quarter remained unchanged.[65] Most likely, no one would have paid any attention to the mismatch had the deputy chair of the state supply agency, M. T. Pomaznev, not intervened. It appears that some time in February 1949 Pomaznev sent Stalin a note to the effect that government directives on 5 percent growth in industrial production over the first quarter were not, in fact, being fulfilled.[66] Stalin immediately instructed the main Bureau of the Council of Ministers to look into the Pomaznev note. Although Voznesenskii put up a stand, the bureau placed its weight behind Pomaznev, and on 1 March 1949 presented Stalin with a paper criticizing Gosplan.[67] The paper referred only to "certain mistakes" and spoke relatively mildly of the need to correct the plans for the first and second quarters of 1949, without drawing any wider or harsher conclusions.[68] Regardless, the very fact that Voznesenskii's work was being scrutinized with Stalin's approval was a clear signal that it was now open season on Voznesenskii.

This was an invitation that Beria, a longtime adversary of Voznesenskii's, took up with relish. Via an agent in Gosplan, Beria obtained a note from one of Voznesenskii's deputies, which plainly conceded that the real plan for the first quarter was at odds with the 5 percent target. Although Voznesenskii had reportedly instructed that this paper be removed from circulation and filed, the document made its way to Beria who, in turn, personally handed it to Stalin. It is likely that Mikoian, on whose account this reconstruction of events is based, had in mind the note of the three senior Gosplan officials of 15 December.[69] The note would indeed figure as one of the chief proofs of Vonznesenskii's guilt in the Council of Ministers resolution "On Gosplan," which was confirmed by the Politburo on 5 March.

The resolution of 5 March stated in an official and unequivocal form the charges that had now settled in Stalin's mind against Voznesenskii and Gosplan.[70] "The government of the USSR," the resolution declared,

> has repeatedly pointed out that the most important task of Gosplan must be to secure, through state plans, the growth and development of the economy, to uncover available reserves of productive capacity, and to struggle with any kind of departmental tendencies toward lowering production targets. As the state agency responsible for planning the economy of the whole USSR and for controlling the implementation of state targets, Gosplan must be utterly objective and 100 percent an honest agency; any fudging of figures is completely unacceptable. . . . The report carried out by the Bureau of the Council of Ministers . . . has established

that Gosplan has followed a biased and dishonest approach to planning and to evaluating the fulfillment of plans. This has found expression above all in the fiddling of figures so as to mask the real state of affairs.[71]

The resolution made it plain that Stalin's central charge against Voznesenskii was that he had violated his chief duty as the purveyor of honest and uncontaminated economic information to the leadership.

The resolution also provided for the replacement of Voznesenskii as chair of Gosplan and instructed Gosplan to strengthen control over the ministries, to improve the system of planning, and to "increase the production plan of industrial output for March and for the second quarter of 1949." A purge of Gosplan was also proposed, to which end a special Central Committee plenipotentiary for cadres was appointed.[72] The wording of the resolution suggested that the new campaign was not simply a standard political vendetta but that its aim was to pressure Gosplan into squeezing out higher rates of economic growth. It was at this point that the Gosplan Affair and the Voznesenskii case, which would, by contrast, involve a struggle for influence at the very highest levels, began to move in separate directions.

On the day after the Politburo resolution on Gosplan, the Politburo dismissed Kuznetsov and Rodionov as members of the Orgburo.[73] On 7 March, Voznesenskii was removed as deputy chair of the Council of Ministers and forced out of the Politburo.[74] According to Khrushchev, Stalin toyed with the idea of appointing Voznesenskii as the head of Gosbank.[75] Whether or not Stalin was genuinely of two minds over Voznesenskii's fate, events that summer would bring any such vacillation to an end. On 21 July 1949, the Minister of State Security Abakumov sent Stalin a report claiming that the former secretary of the Leningrad regional and city party committees, Kapustin, had been an English agent (Kapustin had, at one stage, been on a posting to England). Stalin authorized Kapustin's arrest. While being tortured, Kapustin confirmed that Kuznetsov, Popkov, and others had been engaged in enemy activities while in Leningrad. On 13 August, Kuznetsov, Popkov, and Rodionov, as well as the chair of the Leningrad executive committee, Lazutin, and his predecessor, N. V. Solov'ev, then serving as First Secretary of the Crimean regional party committee, were all arrested in Malenkov's office in Moscow.[76]

Formally speaking, Voznesenskii was not implicated in any of these conspiracies. His name had come up, however, albeit indirectly, in the original Politburo resolution on Kuznetsov and the others of 15 February. With the exposure of his alleged deceit at Gosplan and his removal from the Politburo in early March, his position had become extremely vulnerable. In the course of a review of the journal *Bol'shevik*, which was carried out over the summer, the editorial board was accused, among other things, of having eulogized Voznesenskii's book on the war economy.[77] Although seemingly directed at others, even this oblique attack further damaged Voznesenskii's credentials. Worn out by waiting, on 17 August 1949 a desperate Voznesenskii wrote to Stalin:

> Comrade Stalin! I am turning to you with an exceptional request— please give me work, whatever you find possible, so that I can do my share for party and country. It has been very hard on me to be sidelined from the ongoing work of my party and comrades.
>
> I can of course see from the reports of the Central Statistical Administration in the press that the colossal successes of our party have been yet further augmented by the amendments to earlier plans and by the unearthing of new reserves. I can assure you that I have absolutely learned the lesson on party-mindedness from my case, and I beg of you that you give me the chance to participate in the general life and work of the party.
>
> I beg of you to extend your trust to me; to vindicate it, I shall ensure that any work that you assign me will receive all the effort and energy which I have at my disposal.
>
> Your devoted N. Voznesenskii[78]

It is hard to say with any certainty what Stalin's plans for Voznesenskii were at this stage. The fact that he was not included in the group arrested on Kapustin's testimony suggests that Stalin continued to hesitate or that he was biding his time. Very shortly, a case on the loss of secret documents at Gosplan would bring an end to Stalin's wavering. The precise circumstances surrounding the fabrication of this case remain unknown, and there is no evidence that either Malenkov or Beria were directly involved. Whatever the origins of the case, it is clear that its initiator, the Central Committee plenipotentiary for cadres at Gosplan, E. E. Andreev, carried out his duties at Gosplan with particular zeal. On 22 August 1949, Andreev sent the Central Committee Secretaries Panteleimon Ponomarenko and Malenkov a letter informing them that from 1944 to 1948, 236 secret documents had gone astray at Gosplan. Andreev supplied numerous examples of breaches in procedures for the safeguarding of state secrets by the Gosplan leadership. Andreev also reported that "at present procedures for handling secret documents at Gosplan are being checked by the Ministry of State Security."[79]

On Malenkov's instigation, the Andreev report was passed on to Stalin.[80] On 25 August, the USSR Council of Ministers set up an investigation into the matter. At this point, the case was also taken up by the Commission of Party Control at the Central Committee and, in particular, by its deputy chair, Matvei Shkiriatov, one of Stalin's most zealous sidekicks. On 1 September, Shkiriatov summoned Voznesenskii and charged him with loss of the documents. In a last-ditch attempt to earn the leader's forgiveness, Voznesenskii immediately sent Stalin a defense of his own position, explaining that control over secret documents was not his responsibility.

> I am appealing to the Central Committee and to you, comrade Stalin, and am begging you to pardon me . . . the punishment which I have already served and the fact that I have been out of work for so long has so shocked and so changed me, that I may now be so bold as to beseech you to look into this, and to believe that you are dealing with a man who has learned his lesson and who understands how one must observe Soviet and party laws.[81]

Despite Voznesenskii's letter, the Politburo passed a resolution, "On the Numerous Losses of Secret Documents at Gosplan" on 11 September 1949, which in effect sealed Voznesenskii's fate by confirming the recommendation of the Commission of Party Control to have him expelled from the Central Committee and to hand him over for trial.[82] On 27 October 1949, Voznesenskii was arrested. Following a year of confinement and interrogations, Voznesenskii, Kuznetsov, Popkov, Kapustin, Rodionov, and Lazutin were convicted at a secret trial in Leningrad in September 1950 and executed on 1 October. In addition, from 1949 to 1951, a further 214 people (69 main defendants and 145 relatives) were sentenced to death or to various custodial terms or periods of exile; two more defendants died in prison awaiting trial.[83] Arrests and trials connected with the Leningrad Affair continued until 1952.[84]

Whereas the Leningrad Affair, to which the Voznesenskii case was eventually annexed, was deeply politicized in nature, the Gosplan Affair assumed the form of a standard administrative investigation and was directed chiefly at strengthening Gosplan's control functions. By the measures of the Stalin period, Voznesenskii's colleagues at Gosplan came out of the affair lightly. In his report of 25 April 1950 Andreev noted that two categories of functionaries had been dismissed: "Those who are insufficiently qualified, and in certain cases dishonorable employees, who were unable to carry through the directives of the party and of the government in the sphere of economic planning," and a second group comprised of those "who correspond with close relatives abroad (mainly in the United States), those who have been expelled from the party for anti-party views, and those who maintain ties with close relatives convicted of counterrevolutionary crimes."[85] It was a measure of the nonpolitical nature of the purge that neither Stalin nor the MGB chose to make anything of the latter group and that the purge was confined, in the main, to dismissals. While lenient, the purge was, however, wide-ranging. By April 1950, the whole workforce of line officials and support staff at Gosplan—around 1,400 people—had been checked. In total, 130 employees were removed from their posts, over 40 of whom were transferred to work in other organizations. Over the same year, 255 new employees were taken on at Gosplan. Of Voznesenskii's twelve deputies, seven were sacked, four were reassigned to other leading posts, and one arrested. Lower down the hierarchy, one-third of heads of administrations and of departments and their deputies were replaced, as were 35 of the 133 sector heads.[86]

The Gosplan purge was accompanied by a string of decisions about raising economic targets for 1949. On 24 March, the government ratcheted up production indicators for industrial output for the first quarter. Two weeks later, on 6 April, a resolution of the Council of Ministers criticized as excessively modest the plan for the second quarter.[87] Then, on 13 September, the Council of Ministers also acknowledged as too limited the plans for the third and fourth quarters. On 4 October, a resolution was passed on increasing the gross production plan for 1949—on the basis of the unchanged 1926–1927 price index—by 1,215.3 million rubles (which included a growth of 460 million for the third and 448 million for the fourth quarter). These decisions were accompanied by demands that the whole system of planning and accounting be improved and, in particular, that any planning techniques possibly used to disguise the true state of affairs in industry be eliminated.[88] On the whole, the results of the government's pressure on Gosplan and on the ministries were relatively modest. The original plan for 1949, which forecast growth of 17 percent, was raised to 18.5 percent and exceeded by 0.5 percent, bringing growth over the year to 19 percent. More notable was the rate of growth of capital investments. The volume of centrally funded capital projects for 1949 was 22 percent higher than it had been in 1948, and even these ambitious plans were in the event overfulfilled by 12 percent.

The reasons why Stalin chose to undertake the high-level purges of 1949 are complex. Yet the documents leave no doubt that it was Stalin who initiated and coordinated these campaigns. At every stage, the principal decisions, especially over the fates of high-level leaders, rested with Stalin. The roles played by Beria and Malenkov in the Leningrad and Gosplan Affairs were decidedly secondary. Although Beria may have had a vendetta against Voznesenskii, he and Malenkov always acted on cues from the leader.[89] Under the operating rules of high-level Stalinist bureaucracy, Malenkov had no choice but to forward incriminating materials against Voznesenskii to Stalin—to have acted otherwise would have opened him up to the very serious charge of repressing vital information. While Malenkov may have benefited from the demotion of Voznesenskii and Kuznetsov, there is no evidence that he sought the incarceration or execution of either. If anything, the outcome of the Leningrad Affair may well have shocked Stalin's companions, Malenkov and Beria included. In light of such high-level executions, they now took extra precautions not to sow doubts in their leader's mind over the political honesty of their fellows or to otherwise antagonize Stalin needlessly, for fear that this would start off another political roller coaster to which they themselves might fall victim.

The substance of Stalin's charge that the Leningraders had formed a regional conspiracy was clearly baseless and derived in some measure from the leader's own fears and morbid suspicions. Although murderous and brutal, there was, however, a certain logic to Stalin's actions against Voznesenskii, Kuznetsov, and the others. Should any of them have doubted it, this action drove home the fact that Stalin still possessed the power and the will, over a decade after the Great Terror, to have high-level political leaders killed off. The harsh reprisals against the Leningraders also had a foreign policy aspect, for they served as a lesson to leaders of the Eastern European states that had recently come under Soviet tutelage. Furthermore, Stalin was only too aware of the need in his system to maintain absolute control of the security service. Any alliance on this axis had to be broken. This may have lain behind Stalin's action against Kuznetsov. As the blunt Politburo resolution of 15 March 1948 had made clear, Stalin was unhappy about the way in which Kuznetsov was discharging his duties as Central Committee Secretary with special responsibilities for the security services. It also suggested that Stalin was increasingly perturbed by the growing bond between Kuznetsov and the Minister of State Security, Abakumov. By removing Kuznetsov Stalin dissolved this secret police-based alliance. Finally, the rationale behind Stalin's actions against Voznesenskii was relatively clear. Stalin was in many respects right not to trust his colleagues, especially in matters relating to economic performance, since the pressures on them were such that they had strong incentives to distort the upward flow of economic information. When Stalin discovered that his honest "third-party" agent had in fact lied to him, Voznesenskii's raison d'être as a dependable middle-generation Politburo functionary came under question. When, as in this case, economic decisions were found to have "political" content, Stalin moved in, temporarily suspending the division of labor he introduced in 1947, and ordered radical, sweeping changes.

Filling the Gaps

The elimination of the Leningraders significantly changed the balance of power in Stalin's circle. In characteristic fashion, Stalin soon set about preparing counterweights to Beria and Malenkov, who had by now gained a clearly dominant position among the middle generation of Politburo members. At the end of October 1949, Stalin, while in the south, received a letter from three engineers at one of the Moscow factories. In an unusually sharp tone, the letter advanced a series of serious allegations against the then Secretary of the Moscow party organization and Secretary of the Central Committee, Georgii Popov. The engineers claimed that under Popov, the Moscow party organization had repressed "self-criticism," that party officials had committed systematic abuses, and that Moscow party leaders had fostered an "epidemic of dacha construction" and had themselves fallen into a life of "ethical decay and dissoluteness." Drawing overt parallels with the Leningrad Affair, the engineers accused Popov of "having succumbed to the thought that in future he might lead our party and people." As proof, they cited the following incident: "At a banquet to mark the 800th anniversary of Moscow, when one of the sycophants proposed a toast 'to the future leader of our party, Georgii Mikhailovich,' Popov did nothing to call the toady to order." Popov, the engineers alleged, had surrounded himself with a bunch of yes-men in Moscow. "Popov places his people wherever he can, so that at an opportune moment he might seize the steering wheel and lead the country."[90]

The circumstances under which this letter surfaced and its real authorship remain a mystery.[91] Whatever its real provenance, the key question of how such a "signal" would be acted on—and there was always a steady flow of such signals to Stalin—depended entirely on the inclinations of the leader. On this occasion, Stalin decided to exploit the allegations fully. On 29 October 1949, he declared, in a letter to Malenkov, that the denunciation of the engineers, when taken together with other facts that had come to his attention, clearly pointed to "anti-party and anti-state elements" in Popov's conduct. Stalin proposed establishing a Politburo commission to examine Popov's actions and, so as to prevent a pattern of local patronage from taking root, he insisted that appointments to prominent positions with the Moscow and Leningrad district committees be subject to Central Committee controls. Stalin ordered that his own letter, together with that of the three engineers, be circulated to Politburo members and to Central Committee Secretaries for information.

Despite having himself set up the Politburo commission on Popov, Stalin in effect preempted its general findings and conclusions by wording his own letter to Malenkov in a very firm and deliberate way. "I consider it my duty," he wrote,

> to point out what appear to be two utterly self-evident and, for me, grave features of the Moscow party organization, which highlight a deep flaw in comrade Popov's work. It is quite plain, first, that self-criticism has not only been suppressed but that it has been victimized by the Moscow party leadership. . . . Second, it is clear that the Moscow party leadership has taken to usurping the role of the ministries, the government, and the Central Committee and to issuing direct instructions to enterprises

and ministries, and that when ministers choose to stand up to these practices, they are mocked and humiliated in public by comrade Popov. . . . This state of affairs will lead only to the ruin of party and state discipline.[92]

Stalin's order was swiftly implemented. On 1 November, a meeting of the Politburo's inner circle, without Stalin—consisting of Malenkov, Molotov, Beria, Kaganovich, and Bulganin—decided "to assign a commission comprising comrades Malenkov, Beria, Kaganovich, and Suslov to examine, on the basis of comrade Stalin's directives as set out in his letter of 29 October, the activities of comrade G. M. Popov."[93] In fact, the commission soon reached the conclusion that the letter of the "three engineers" was little more than a standard anonymous denunciation (the names given on the letter were all invented) and that the specific accusations cited in the letter had no basis in fact. Having received clear-cut instructions from Stalin, however, the commission had no choice but to confirm the general points that Stalin had set out in his letter to Malenkov. On 4 December, the ruling group (now including Mikoian, who had returned from China, but still without Stalin) confirmed the "conclusions and proposals" of the Politburo commission which, in effect, were merely a restatement of the two central charges that Stalin had laid out in his letter: namely that Popov had stifled criticism and self-criticism within the Moscow party organization and that he had adopted an "incorrect position with regard to all-union ministries and ministers" by trying to order them about and to "substitute [their] work." Those charges in the original letter of the engineers which had not been mentioned by Stalin, such as that Popov was "politically questionable" and that he had installed his own clients to leading positions, were deemed "uncorroborated and fictitious." The commission proposed that while he should retain the symbolic position of head of the Moscow city council, Popov be released from his duties as Secretary of the Moscow party organization and as Secretary of the Central Committee.[94]

The text of this resolution was sent to Stalin. It appears that Stalin then suggested postponing a final decision on the matter until his return to Moscow several days later. Indeed, Stalin's very first meeting back at his Kremlin office, on 10 December, was devoted to the Popov case. At 9:30 P.M., Beria, Kaganovich, Malenkov, and Suslov, as well as Popov himself, gathered in Stalin's office. The discussion lasted for almost two hours, at which point Suslov and Popov left the room. Over the next quarter of an hour, Stalin conferred with Beria, Kaganovich, and Malenkov, after which Khrushchev was invited to the office for ten minutes.[95] The progress of this meeting can be broadly reconstructed on the basis of amendments made during it to a Politburo resolution on Popov, a first draft of which had been prepared in advance. Popov, it seems, acknowledged his guilt and repented, as a result of which the text of the initial draft of the resolution against him was considerably softened. In particular, Malenkov removed all inflammatory references, which earlier had peppered the text, to Popov's "unbolshevik methods of leadership," to his "unbolshevik practices," and to his "unbolshevik attitudes."[96] The revised version of the resolution also contained a new clause to the effect that "comrade Popov has acknowledged his shortcomings." Popov's fate was also certainly discussed at the meeting. The initial proposal of the Politburo commission to have Popov retain his post as chair of the Moscow city executive committee was crossed out and replaced by a rather vague statement about Popov being "appointed to a new position."[97] Popov became Minister of Urban Construction and, thereafter, Minister of Agricultural Machine-Building. Although he suffered another demotion in 1951 (this time being transferred to the relatively lowly position of factory director in the town of Kuibyshev), Popov was never arrested or persecuted.[98]

Typically, Stalin seems to have resolved the question of Popov's successor in his own mind well before the meeting of 10 December. As Khrushchev recalled, Stalin phoned him in Ukraine before returning from the south and ordered him to come to Moscow immediately. On his arrival, most likely during his ten-minute meeting with Stalin on 10 December, Khrushchev learned that he had been appointed Secretary of the Central Committee and head of the Moscow party organization.[99] In fact, the whole course of the so-called Moscow Affair suggests that the case was contrived from the very beginning with this end in mind. There is no evidence that Stalin harbored any particular hostility toward Popov; otherwise Popov would most certainly have met with an altogether more sorry fate. Instead, Stalin's true goal was Khrushchev's transfer to Moscow and appointment to a pivotal position in Stalin's entourage.

As a counterweight to a revitalized Malenkov and Beria, Khrushchev was an ideal choice. Since his temporary demotion in 1947, Khrushchev had spent a lengthy period in semidisgrace and was ready to serve his leader with redoubled energy and enthusiasm. More significantly, in terms of his official status (having been a full Politburo member since 1939), Khrushchev could compete comfortably with Malenkov and Beria who, although they belonged to the same political generation as Khrushchev, had in fact entered the Politburo after him.

In the midst of the Leningrad Affair, Stalin also moved Bulganin to a far more prominent position within his entourage. Bulganin had already made steady progress up the higher reaches of the Stalinist hierarchy well before the Leningrad Affair. Almost two years earlier, on 26 February 1947, Bulganin had replaced Stalin as Minister of Armed Forces,[100] and a week later, on 5 March, he had been appointed deputy chair of the Council of

Ministers.[101] The appointment of Bulganin, a preeminently civilian official, as Minister of Armed Forces, may be attributed to Stalin's pronounced distrust of the military after the war. In order to raise Bulganin's authority with the generals, Stalin had also conferred on him the highest military honors. On 3 November 1947, he told the Politburo: "I propose to award comrade Bulganin the title of Marshal of the Soviet Union. In my view, the corresponding decree of the Presidium is justified on the grounds of Bulganin's outstanding service to the Soviet armed forces both during the Great Patriotic War and after it. . . . I believe that these reasons do not require special commentary—they are quite clear as they are."[102]

Bulganin's promotion and the bestowal on him of such an accolade were clear signs that Stalin was grooming him for higher things. This cultivation of Bulganin led, eventually, to his election, on 16 February 1948, as a full voting member of the Politburo. Formally speaking, Bulganin's promotion was justified on the technical grounds that "the Politburo finds it hard to fulfill its duties without the Minister of Armed Forces."[103] Although Stalin returned the post of Minister of War to the generals a year later, this by no means indicated that Bulganin had fallen out of favor. On 24 March 1949, in the midst of the Leningrad Affair, Bulganin, now relieved of his specific ministerial duties at the Ministry of Armed Forces, was charged with carrying out "general state duties" at the Bureau of the Council of Ministers. Bulganin was entrusted with overseeing the Ministries of Finances, Aviation Industry, and Arms Production, as well as the work of committees concerned with jet technologies and radar.[104] Stalin assumed a monitoring role over the Ministry of Armed Forces, but "in view of his work overload" he relinquished this duty a month later and had this, too, transferred to Bulganin.[105] With this step, Bulganin's position in the new order that was emerging in the wake of the Leningrad Affair appears to have been secured: in his capacity as deputy chair of the Council of Ministers, Bulganin had been put in charge of the strategically key military and military-industrial bloc of ministries.

In the year after Voznesenskii's dismissal, a "collective leadership" of Stalin's deputies began to take shape at the All-Union Council of Ministers. Following a resolution of 30 July 1949, the Bureau of the Council of Ministers was converted into the Presidium, which consisted of the Chair of the Council of Ministers, his deputies, and the Ministers of Finance and State Control.[106] A Politburo resolution of 1 September introduced a rotational system whereby the right to chair meetings of the new Presidium was conferred on Beria, Bulganin, Malenkov, Kaganovich, and Saburov.[107] Early the following year, these new arrangements were amended. Khrushchev's return to Moscow in December 1949 prompted Stalin to reconfigure his ruling group. On 7 April 1950, Stalin pushed the following proposals through the Politburo: Bulganin was to be made First Deputy Chair of the Council of Ministers; a Bureau of the new Presidium of the Council of Ministers was to be formed, to consist of a select group of senior Politburo members, which was to meet weekly; and in Stalin's absence, meetings of the new Bureau and of the full Presidium should be presided over by his new first deputy, Bulganin.[108] It seems likely that Stalin's judgment on his successors, which was subsequently related by Khrushchev, was made at around this time:

> I remember how, in our presence, Stalin reasoned: "Who will we appoint chairman of the Council of Ministers after me? Beria? No, he is not Russian, but Georgian. Khrushchev? No, he is a worker, we need someone who is more educated. Malenkov? No, he can only follow someone else's lead. Kaganovich? No, he won't do, for he is not Russian but a Jew. Molotov? No, he has already aged, he won't cope. Voroshilov? No, he is really not up to it. Saburov? Pervukhin? These people are only right for secondary roles. There is only one person left and that is Bulganin."[109]

Evidently, these considerations were not the only ones which led Stalin to promote Bulganin as his first deputy. It is likely that Stalin valued Bulganin as an experienced, obedient, and harmless administrator. On this count, Molotov later mused: "Bulganin does not really stand for anything— he is not in himself 'for' or 'against' anything; whichever way the wind blows, Bulganin will be sure to follow."[110] Over 1949 and 1950, Bulganin emerged as a second useful counterweight to Malenkov and Beria. The promotion of Bulganin was thus the last act in the formation of a new balance of forces among Stalin's companions following the elimination of the Leningraders.

Despite being on a very different scale, the repression of leading cadres in 1949 served a purpose similar to the "cadres revolution" of 1937–1938. Periodic shake-ups of the apparatus, the physical elimination of some officials, and the promotion of others in their place were typical features of Stalinist dictatorship. Such attacks naturally reinforced the sense of fear and subjugation among Stalin's subordinates. Through the Leningrad and Gosplan Affairs, Stalin succeeded in strengthening his hold over three key strata in his administration: those within his own entourage, heads of economic ministries, and regional leaders. These attacks also served as a model for analogous brutal purges in the Soviet satellite states.

The elimination of the Leningraders was accompanied by the emergence of a new balance of forces within the Politburo. As later events would show, those senior leaders admitted to Stalin's entourage at the end of 1949 and in 1950 would form the backbone of the "collective leadership" that took over after his death. The Leningrad Affair, however, did not simply change the personal configuration of Stalin's entourage; it also exercised a far deeper influence on Stalin's companions. Having confronted the first wave of repression within their own circle since the Great Terror, members of the Politburo learned a valuable political lesson. They were now firmly persuaded that even after the war, Stalin would not stop at lenient methods of punishment (official demotions and reprimands) against his colleagues, but would quite readily countenance their murder. No one, it appeared, was safe from this threat. Experienced as they were, Stalin's companions became aware that any new arrest spelled danger for themselves. They knew that any tactical advantage they might temporarily accrue as individuals from having a rival removed could never make up for the lethal climate of uncertainty and suspicion which inevitably followed once the delicate balance within the leadership had been broken. For these reasons, one may well doubt if either Malenkov or Beria—although both played an active role in the Leningrad Affair—actually sought the destruction of their political opponents. Certainly, after the Leningrad Affair, the natural instinct of political self-preservation, which was extremely well developed among all of Stalin's companions, compelled them to act with particular care and discretion so as not to cross the thin boundary between everyday rivalry and actions that might needlessly arouse Stalin's suspicions. Fear of Stalin's unpredictable behavior united members of the ruling group in an unspoken alliance which, in turn, would become an essential precondition for collective leadership.

4

PEACEFUL COEXISTENCE: COLLECTIVE LEADERSHIP AND STALINIST CONTROL

The war in Korea, which began on 25 June 1950 and ended several months after Stalin's death, exerted a major influence on the Stalinist system. Although the Soviet Union did not openly take part in the war, limiting itself instead to the clandestine transfer of military advisers, aircraft, and crew, as well as to bulk deliveries of military technology, this was, in effect, the first true military confrontation between a socialist bloc, consisting of the Soviet Union and its allies, and a Western bloc headed by the United States. Although military attention naturally focused on the Korean peninsula, the war deepened tensions between the two blocs in other parts of the world, most notably in Europe.

The passage of the Cold War into open conflict nudged both sides into a new spiral of the arms race. In the Soviet Union, the transfer of resources to military needs occurred at the expense of living standards and further depressed the agrarian sector and those branches of the economy devoted to consumer goods. From 1950 to 1952, taxes, especially on agriculture, were raised, leading to a drop in production on private plots and to a contraction in overall food supplies. In turn, the urban population became increasingly prone to food shortages and deficits of everyday consumer items. The grave international situation also gave rise to a series of actions against an alleged American-sponsored secret network operating on Soviet territory. Cases were fabricated against agents of the "U.S. secret service" who had ostensibly wormed their way into Soviet society. In Stalin's view, the most energetic tentacles of this network were the "agencies of Jewish bourgeois nationalism" and of "world Zionism" which had established roots in the country since the war. It was under slogans such as these that purges were carried out in state and economic bureaucracies. Meanwhile, those sectors of the intelligentsia suspected of "political decrepitude" and of harboring sympathies for Western values continued to be persecuted.[1] After an investigation that dragged on for over two years, a secret trial was finally held against members of the Jewish Anti-Fascist Committee in May and June 1952, leading to the execution of thirteen defendants. This celebrated case spawned seventy analogous trials across the country.[2]

The populations of the USSR's western border regions (the Baltic states, western Ukraine, Belorussia, and Bessarabia), which had been integrated into the Soviet Union on the eve of the war, became another target of large-scale repressions. The incomplete Sovietization of these countries and the presence, especially in western Ukraine, of an active partisan movement were viewed by the Stalinist leadership as a threat to Soviet security. To add to the continuing operations against "Kulaks," "bandits and their accomplices," and "Ounovtsy" (western Ukrainian separatists), which had begun shortly after the war, in 1951 the Ministry of State Security expelled thousands of Jehovah's Witnesses to Siberia.[3]

Against this backdrop of purges, privations, and military mobilization, Stalin's companions found themselves in a relatively stable position, certainly by comparison with the excitement of 1949. Notwithstanding his habitual tendency to cajole and intimidate, Stalin took an approach of relative moderation toward his colleagues in 1950 and 1951. On this basis, the higher leadership began to consolidate itself and to lay the foundations of collective leadership within the ruling circle. The rough outlines of collective rule established in this period would set the pattern for the leadership arrangements following Stalin's death.

Military Preparations

Although military-industrial investment had always been a priority for the Stalinist leadership, the military sector received an additional boost with the onset of the Korean War. A major turning point in policy appears to have taken place not long after the commencement of the war, at a conference of Soviet and East European leaders that took place in Moscow in January 1951. It is a measure of the secrecy surrounding the conference that no documents relating to it have surfaced in the archives. Indeed, the fact that it took place at all is only known from the memoirs of its participants. According to the head of the Hungarian Communist Party, Matias Rakosi, the conference was attended on the Soviet side by Stalin, several members of the Politburo, and a handful of military leaders (probably including Marshal A. M. Vasilevskii and certainly General S. M. Shtemenko), and on the East European side by the leaders of the national ruling parties (with the exception of the Polish leader Boleslaw Bierut) and their defense ministers. The Soviet chief of staff, General Shtemenko, delivered

Funeral of Andrei Zhdanov, 2 September 1948. Eyeing Stalin on the left in a light coat and hat is the Minister of State Security, Viktor Abakumov, followed from left to right by Kaganovich, Malenkov, Molotov, Stalin, Voroshilov, Beria, Kuznetsov, Voznesenskii, and Shvernik. Within six months, Voznesenskii and Kuznetsov had been fired and they would later be shot. The head of the security police, Abakumov, was himself arrested in July 1951, once the trial and execution of the Leningraders—one of his primary responsibilities—had been attended to.

Andrei Zhdanov on the right, with Aleksei Kuznetsov.

Zhdanov on the right, with Nikolai Voznesenskii.

Meeting with Mao Tse-tung in Moscow, 16 December 1949. From left to right:
the Chinese ambassador to Moscow Wan Tsziazan, the Soviet Minister of
Foreign Trade Mikhail Men'shikov, Mao, Molotov, Andrei Gromyko, Bulganin,
and the Moscow city commander K. R. Sinilov. Later that day Mao would meet
up with Stalin.

a paper which, according to Rakosi, focused on the growing threat from NATO and on the need to counterbalance this with corresponding military preparations from the socialist camp. The Soviet leadership instructed the East European satellite states to dramatically expand their armies and military capacity within the next three years. In his speech, Shtemenko named specific targets that each army should reach by the end of 1953.

According to Rakosi, Shtemenko's figures sparked dissent. The Polish Minister of Defense, K. K. Rokossovskii, claimed that the target Shtemenko had set for 1953 could not, under current projections, be achieved before 1956. Representatives from other states also doubted the feasibility of the plans and, in particular, of securing an appropriate military-industrial base within the deadline. The Soviets, however, stood their ground. In particular, Stalin responded that the timeline projected by the Poles—of achieving the targets by 1956—would remain unchanged only if Rokossovskii could give a cast-iron guarantee that there would be no war before that date. Since no such guarantee could be given, it was incumbent on the Poles and on all the other East European states to accept the Shtemenko plan.[4]

The Soviet leadership's tough stance was supported by supplementary information it received on the escalating military plans of the West and, especially, of the United States. Thus, in August 1951, the head of the Central Statistical Administration, V. Starovskii, sent various statistical tables to Poskrebyshev (in effect, to Stalin) which included an item under the heading "Military Expenditure of the USA in Millions of Dollars." The table showed that according to the provisional plans for 1951–1952, American military spending would come to over 64 billion dollars (almost twice the amount spent in 1949–50), a sum which would account for almost 90 percent of all central state expenditure. Moreover, referring to a secondary Cominform publication, the appendix to the table suggested that the Truman government planned to exceed even these figures by a hefty margin.[5] Without assessing the accuracy of this information, one may merely note that it was figures of this order which were circulated at the highest levels. To the country's leaders, these statistics underlined the sudden surge in military spending of the Soviet Union's archrival.

Although we do not know concretely what plans were drawn up for Soviet rearmament, or to what extent they were realized, statistics on the development of the Soviet economy as a whole show that in 1951–1952 there was indeed accelerated military growth. Capital investment in the war and naval ministries and in those ministries producing arms and military technology went up by 60 percent in 1951 and by 40 percent in 1952.[6] By comparison, capital spending outside the military and military-industrial sector accounted for only 6 percent of overall capital investments in 1951 and 7 percent in 1952.[7]

Within the military sphere, highest priority was attached to the atomic weapons project. In addition to carrying out atom bomb tests, significant resources were ploughed into rocket technologies, jet-propelled aviation, and a system of air defense around Moscow.[8] A large portion of state resources also went into the construction of new military bases in the eastern part of the Soviet Union within reach of the U.S. border.[9] In 1951, as part of a program to strengthen the Soviet navy, work started on a new shipyard in the Soviet Harbor (Gavan') district in the far east which, at full capacity, was to produce two battle cruisers and four submarines a year. The shipyard was constructed by Soviet prisoners.[10]

Despite such heavy military spending, and its influence on the socio-economic development of the country, there would be no letup in the tempo of the arms race until the very end of Stalin's life.[11] On 9 February 1953, a Council of Ministers resolution provided for the creation, by the end of 1955, of 106 bomber divisions, instead of the 32 currently in existence. In order to bring the new divisions up to strength, it was proposed that 10,300 planes be built and that the manpower of the air force and navy be increased by 290,000 troops. The cost of establishing the divisions and setting up the requisite infrastructure (aerodromes, housing, and barracks) was initially put at over 9.5 billion rubles. Equally ambitious was the program to build heavy and medium-sized battle cruisers, which proposed expending approximately 10 billion rubles on the scheme by 1959.[12] Immediately after Stalin's death, the leadership was forced to turn its back on these exorbitant projects.

In order to realize Stalin's ambitious military plans, it became apparent that the state apparatus responsible for arms production would have to be restructured. In the first postwar years, the activities of ministries and departments in the military-industrial sector were coordinated by a number of special committees at the Council of Ministers. These committees were, however, designed to deal with certain priority tasks—such as making atomic weapons and developing rocket and radar technologies—and did not address other, everyday problems that cropped up in the management of military industry. In May 1948, the deputy chair of the Council of Ministers, Maksim Saburov, and the Minister of Arms Production, Dmitrii Ustinov, submitted a paper to Stalin: "There is now a pressing need to create a new agency that would consider such questions as coordinating mobilization plans, assessing current issues in military industry, creating new weapon models, coordinating different branches of military industry, and so forth. We currently have an acute need for such an agency."[13] This appeal was ignored. However, three years later, in connection with the intensification of the arms race, the idea was eventually taken up. On 16 January 1951, the Politburo adopted a resolution on the formation of a bureau for military-industrial and military issues at the Council of Ministers under the leadership of Bulganin. The new bureau was charged with exerting leadership over the Ministries of Aviation Industry and Arms Production, and over the Ministries of War and of the Navy.[14] In order to coordinate the practical side of its work, a number of "groups" were established at the bureau: for arms production, aviation, the Ministry of War, the Ministry of the Navy, shipbuilding, radar, and jet technologies. With the sole exception of the atom bomb project, the bureau coordinated the activities of practically all the branches of military-industrial production. The scale of the bureau's operations is reflected in the fact that in March 1952 alone, its groups worked on 622 questions, in addition to which a number of separate issues were prepared directly for bureau members.

In terms of its significance, the new bureau for military-industrial and military questions quickly outstripped the other sectoral committees at the Council of Ministers. On 15 March 1951, half of the sectoral bureaus at Sovmin were dissolved.[15] Matters that had earlier been decided by these bureaus were now considered directly by the main Presidium of Sovmin and by its inner Bureau.[16] The new emphasis on military and military-mobilizational matters at Sovmin was also apparent in other decisions taken that day. On Stalin's prompting, it was resolved that Voroshilov, a Politburo member, who was also a deputy chair of Sovmin, should take charge of war preparations among the Soviet public, and that Beria, also a Politburo member and a deputy chair of Sovmin, should "devote half of his working time to committees Nos. 1, 2, and 3" (i.e., to the atom, rocket, and radar projects).[17] The latest in a long line of reorganizations at Sovmin was pursued with the specific aim of adjusting the governmental apparatus to the new military-mobilizational tasks that had been formulated at the beginning of 1951. The heightening of the arms race thus led to an increase in influence of those structures and leaders who were most closely identified with the military-industrial and military sectors. With the assignment of high-level figures such as Bulganin, Beria, and Voroshilov to military-related projects, the new emphasis on the military sector would also leave its mark on the distribution of forces within Stalin's immediate entourage.

The Septet and Collective Leadership

With the elimination of the Leningraders, Stalin's circle had begun to assume a new shape by the beginning of 1950. Although they remained members of the Politburo, two of Stalin's oldest companions, Andreev and Voroshilov, took virtually no part in its work. Andreev had, for a long time, suffered from various chronic illnesses. At the beginning of 1949, the Politburo granted him six months leave to recuperate, but the break seems to have had little long-term effect.[18] For much of the following year, 1950, Andreev was off on sick leaves of various durations. On those occasions when he was fit for work, Andreev headed only a secondary body, the Council for Kolkhoz Affairs. Although a full Politburo member, Andreev was, in not being a member of the "ruling group," cut off entirely from decision making on the most important issues.[19] Andreev's fortunes hit a low on 19 February 1950, when *Pravda* published an article "Against Distortions in the Organization of the Kolkhoz," in which he was criticized for advocating the use of small-scale work units (the so-called links) on collective farms. Although he immediately showed himself quite ready to recant in public, on 25 February the Politburo passed a resolution censuring Andreev for his "erroneous position."[20] A public apology from Andreev followed in *Pravda* three days later, on 28 February. Voroshilov's relationship to high-level decision making was only slightly less peripheral than Andreev's. Following his dismal showing during the war, Voroshilov had been cast to the outer ring of the system of supreme power. Charged, since 1947, with the second-order function of overseeing culture, Voroshilov was also often ill and on sick leave.[21] In not belonging to the ruling group, Voroshilov's rights as a Politburo member were severely restricted.

If Andreev and Voroshilov had become little more than symbols of revolutionary continuity, the other representatives of the "old guard"— Molotov, Mikoian, and Kaganovich—continued to function as active members of the Politburo. Although subjected to periodic attacks, Molotov and Mikoian continued to carry out important state functions and to be included on all the most important party and state agencies. Since the end of 1947, Kaganovich had also recovered the position within the ruling group that he had lost earlier in the decade. Although no formal decision was ever taken, we can surmise on the basis of attendance lists of top leadership meetings that he was reinstalled as a full member of the Politburo's ruling group following his return from Ukraine in December 1947. As a deputy to Stalin at the Council of Ministers, Kaganovich was also, like Molotov and Mikoian, a member of the top decision-making committees of the government.

Greater in number than the old guard was a second group of Politburo members, who were younger and had joined the country's ruling structures later. This group had its own outsiders. Prime among them was Aleksei Kosygin, who, despite being closely linked with the executed Leningraders, retained his formal position on the Politburo, but was stripped of his place in the ruling circle. Despite never being formally rescinded, the decision on bringing Kosygin into the ruling group, which had been taken in September 1948, was in effect nullified as the events in Leningrad unfolded. Kosygin was subsequently marginalized from Politburo proceedings and, after 1949, never set foot in Stalin's office again.

In functional terms, the second group was headed, as of the beginning of 1950, by Malenkov and Bulganin. With the exception of Stalin, Malenkov was the only Soviet ruler to combine leading positions in both party and state bureaucracies. He directed the Secretariat and the Orgburo of the Central Committee and was widely perceived as Stalin's second-in-command in the party. Incoming requests from ministers or regional party leaders to have matters considered or agreed by the Central Committee were routinely addressed to Malenkov, as well as to Stalin. As deputy chair of the Council of Ministers, Malenkov was also a member of all the ruling committees of the government, including the all-important Bureau of the Presidium of the Council of Ministers. As First Deputy Chair of the Council of Ministers, Bulganin also enjoyed the broadest of opportunities to keep in touch with the leader. While Stalin was in Moscow, it was probably Bulganin, as First Deputy, who briefed him on the work of the main Sovmin Bureau. Certainly, during Stalin's break from Moscow from August to November 1950, it was Bulganin who sent Stalin reports on key debates at the Sovmin Bureau and passed on copies of draft government resolutions for Stalin's perusal.[22]

Following his return to Moscow in December 1949, the role of another member of the second group, Nikita Khrushchev, also grew. Khrushchev's appointment to the Secretariat significantly changed the balance of forces on a body that Malenkov had earlier dominated. By contrast with other Secretaries (Suslov, Ponomarenko, and his predecessor, Popov), Khrushchev was a member of the Politburo. Although no formal decision on Khrushchev's inclusion in the Politburo's ruling group was ever taken, it appears, at least judging from the records of the Politburo, that he was brought onto it around July 1950.[23] Khrushchev regularly visited Stalin in his office. More revealing (and somewhat surprising to historians who thought that Khrushchev, in contrast to Malenkov, concentrated on work in the party apparatus) was Khrushchev's active participation in governmental structures. Although Khrushchev did not formally occupy any positions on the Council of Ministers, by 1950 he was regularly taking part in sessions of the Presidium of the Council of Ministers and, occasionally, attending sessions of the Bureau of the Presidium. By the following year, he had become a regular participant at meetings of both bodies.[24]

The position of the fourth active member of the "second group," Lavrentii Beria, was also strengthened in 1950. The ever-pragmatic Stalin attached great significance to the fact that the aims of the Soviet atomic project had been achieved under Beria's stewardship. According to the head of Stalin's guard, Nikolai Vlasik, Beria had visited the leader in the south in 1950 "with a report on the work of the first committee of the Council of Ministers, and showed Stalin a film of the atom bomb tests. This was a pivotal moment in Stalin's attitude toward Beria. Having shown Beria nothing but thinly disguised contempt for over two years, Stalin again became favorably disposed toward him. Stalin now emphasized that only Beria could have brought such brilliant results."[25] Vlasik's reminiscences about Beria's return to Stalin's good books appear to be corroborated by the next reorganization of governmental structures, which Stalin pushed through after his return from the south at the beginning of 1951. On 16 February 1951, on the same day as the creation of a bureau for military-industrial and military questions, the Politburo adopted the following resolution: "Chairmanship of meetings of the Presidium of the Council of Ministers and of the Bureau of the Presidium of the Council of Ministers is to be rotated in turn among the deputy chairs of the Council of Ministers, comrades Bulganin, Beria, and Malenkov, who will also take decisions on pressing issues. Resolutions and directives of the Council of Ministers are to be issued over the signature of the Chair of the Council of Ministers, comrade I. V. Stalin."[26] This decision marked a return to earlier procedures for collective chairmanship of government meetings and, in practice, meant the annulment of the recently created position of First Deputy Chair of Sovmin, to which Bulganin had been appointed.[27]

In once again dispersing operational leadership of the government and in assigning equal powers to a number of his companions, Stalin was applying his customary policy of promoting a balance of forces within the Politburo. Stalin's own state of mind at this particular time may have also played a role here. Having returned from one of his longest ever breaks from Moscow—four and a half months—Stalin may have been showing his companions (and perhaps himself) that he had no need for a first deputy. Certainly, Stalin never again raised the subject of a second-in-command. At the same time, the decision to include Stalin's signature even on such second-order documents as directives of the Council of Ministers was largely a gesture, especially since a stamp with Stalin's signature was normally used for this purpose. Depriving his deputies of the right to sign directives could hardly have been justified on efficiency grounds. For Stalin, this reserve power may have been largely symbolic, the defensive reaction of an aging dictator, who had been forced to withdraw from many affairs of state.

There were indeed several signs of such a withdrawal. From the Kremlin visitors' book, it has been calculated that from 1939 to 1940, Stalin received 2,000 visits a year, but that this number had fallen to 1,200 in 1947, 700 in 1950, and no more than 500 in 1951.[28] To some degree, this was connected with the greater length of Stalin's stays in the south. Since the war, Stalin's breaks had grown ever longer—lasting slightly over two months in 1945, over three months each year from 1946 to 1949, and over four months in 1950 and 1951.[29] Over one stretch, from 9 August 1951 to 12 February 1952, Stalin did not appear in his own Kremlin office for over half a year.[30] Stalin's diminishing energy levels and declining health meant that even when in town, he was forced to economize on his duties and to limit his commitments, especially at the Council of Ministers, to an absolute minimum.

Stalin's increasingly lengthy absences from Moscow meant that issues within the Politburo's brief were often discussed at meetings of a Stalin-less ruling group which, from 1950 until the spring of 1952, consisted of Molotov, Mikoian, Kaganovich, Malenkov, Beria, Bulganin, and Khrushchev.[31] Draft records of Politburo meetings allow us to make out certain differences in the septet's procedures from those followed in Stalin's presence. It is apparent that, while Stalin was away, the group operated as a genuinely collective agency: questions were properly debated and authentic fact-finding commissions were regularly set up for supplementary investigation of contentious issues. On 17 September 1951, for example, Beria, Bulganin, Kaganovich, and Molotov (other members of the leading group were, by all accounts, on holiday) adopted the following decision on the involvement of the USSR in an international trade conference: "On the basis of the *exchange of opinions here* comrades Vyshinsky and Men'shikov are instructed to rework proposals on this matter within the next two days and to submit them to comrade Molotov for his initial consideration before presenting them again to the Politburo."[32] On 15 November 1951, Beria, Kaganovich, Malenkov, Mikoian, and Khrushchev adopted the following Politburo decision on German nationals under special settlement regimes: "Comrades Ignat'ev, Gorshenin, Kruglov, and Safonov are instructed to look thoroughly at the above question within two days and to rework the draft resolution of the Ministry of State Security *in light of the exchange of opinions at sessions of the Politburo*."[33] There are many such examples in the archives; what bears emphasis is that when Stalin was in Moscow, such formulations are never encountered in the Politburo's records. Certainly, decisions taken by the septet were customarily sent to the south for Stalin's approval. Many of these have comments by Poskrebyshev indicating Stalin's response.[34] Despite this, the septet's work methods in Stalin's absence began to approximate the traditional patterns of behavior that characterized Politburo meetings prior to the mid-1930s, before Stalin had entrenched his position as a dictator. These methods of collective leadership would come into their own following Stalin's death.

Arguably of greater significance for the consolidation of a collective leadership were the regular meetings of the supreme governmental agencies in this period, the Presidium and the Bureau of the Presidium of the

Council of Ministers. Although the former continued to meet, it was the latter that assumed greater importance. In contrast to the Presidium that, with the addition of Pervukhin, Khrushchev, and the new Minister of State Control, Merkulov, attracted up to seventeen members to its meetings, the Bureau was a highly compact and select group. At the time of its foundation on 7 April 1950, the Bureau consisted of five members, Bulganin, Beria, Kaganovich, Mikoian, and Molotov, who were joined by a sixth member, Malenkov, in mid-April, and by a seventh, Khrushchev, on 2 September 1950.[35] While the Bureau consisted entirely of members of the Politburo's ruling group, it differed in that the Bureau *never* met with Stalin, not even when the leader was in Moscow. At the same time, the Bureau convened very regularly. From 4 April to the end of December 1950, it met thirty-nine times, thirty-eight times over the following year, and forty-three times in 1952.[36] Thus, the ruling group of the Politburo had regular opportunities to meet without Stalin and outside the very framework of the Politburo in order to discuss issues of national importance within a committee structure with a clear membership, well-defined procedures, and set agendas. Alongside those meetings of the Politburo which took place while Stalin was away, sessions of the Bureau of the Council of Ministers, with an identical membership, afforded an embryonic collective leadership the opportunity to meet regularly and to forge a set of mutual understandings that would put them in good stead once Stalin died.

A further stepping stone toward collective leadership was the fact that members of the septet, all of whom occupied key posts in the party-state apparatus, themselves managed important branches of the state administration and, inevitably, enjoyed a certain measure of independence in dealing with operational matters. In this capacity, members of the septet did, to varying degrees, come to recognize the inefficiency and anachronistic nature of the methods of rule which Stalin had instituted. Members of the ruling group also gained relatively accurate information on what was happening within their own domains. Together, they were able to assemble a composite picture of what was happening across the country. This could not but have fed into a common understanding of what needed to be done when Stalin died.[37]

While Stalin was in Moscow, meetings of the Politburo's ruling group were held either in his Kremlin office, or, more frequently, at his country house. Many of these meetings are hard to label—they can be viewed as meetings of the Politburo, of the ruling group of the Politburo or even, though they were never formally identified as such, as ad hoc meetings of the Bureau of the Presidium of Sovmin.[38] Decisions taken at these meetings could also be drawn up under various guises, either as decisions of the Politburo or as resolutions of the Council of Ministers. Certain observations on procedures for adopting Politburo decisions in 1952, prior to the XIX Party Congress, can be made on the basis of comparing Stalin's Kremlin visitors' book with the original records of Politburo meetings.

In accordance with the division of labor between party and state which had been forged after the war, the Politburo primarily addressed decisions on cadres, organizational matters, and international questions. Politburo decisions were approved in a variety of ways. This much is apparent from looking at how one group of issues, relating to international affairs, were drawn up as Politburo resolutions. A large share of them were discussed and adopted at meetings in Stalin's office in the Kremlin, where they were normally tabled by the Minister of Foreign Affairs, Andrei Vyshinsky.[39] On other days, Politburo decisions on international affairs appear to have been taken at Stalin's dacha. Hence one note from Vyshinsky reads as follows: "Comrade A. N. Poskrebyshev. Please have this typed up. The draft resolution has been put together in accordance with directives received on 13 August."[40] Given that there were no meetings in Stalin's office on that date, it is likely that Vyshinsky had attended a meeting at the dacha.[41] In other cases, Vyshinsky found out about decisions relating to the Ministry of Foreign Affairs from a member of the Politburo, most probably Molotov. For example, on 6 June 1952, Vyshinsky wrote on a draft resolution: "Comrade A. N. Poskrebyshev. Please have this drawn up. I understand from comrade V. M. Molotov that it has been confirmed by comrade Stalin."[42] It is most likely that Molotov either agreed these matters personally with Stalin, or that he was conveying the results of a meeting at Stalin's dacha which Vyshinsky himself had not attended. On those days when there were no meetings in Stalin's office, Vyshinsky also received communications directly from Stalin, by telephone or in the form of a written directive. So, on the draft of one of the Politburo resolutions, Vyshinsky, without referring to any communiqué from a third party, made the following note: "Comrade A. N. Poskrebyshev. Please have this drawn up. It has been confirmed by comrade I. V. Stalin. 19 June."[43]

The procedures for considering and confirming foreign policy questions appear to have been typical for other areas of policy, and they shed light on the Politburo's business methods in the penultimate phase of Stalin's life. By this stage, there were no regular formal sessions of the Politburo with minutes and preliminary agendas. The Politburo had become an amorphous body operating under a wide variety of guises. Politburo decisions could be taken in Stalin's office or at his dacha, in the company of the Foreign Minister or without him, by a small cabal or by Stalin alone. What lent coherence to Politburo decisions was the fact that all, at one stage or another, received Stalin's personal blessing. Stalin determined not only the content of Politburo decisions but the procedures by which these decisions were made and enacted. Stalin's approval was the glue that held the informal system of Politburo decision making together.

The pattern of decision making at the Council of Ministers was more formal and predictable. Most decisions were discussed and approved at regular meetings of the Bureau of the Presidium which, with the exception of Stalin, were attended by all members of the Politburo's ruling group. Although Stalin was supposed to sign resolutions of the Council of Ministers, this rule was largely declaratory in practice. The Bureau provided a forum at which members of the ruling group could meet and come to shared understandings on policy. These common perceptions would serve as a launching pad for the sharp changes in policy that would occur after Stalin's death.

On the Attack

The emergence of a new balance of forces within the Politburo did not bring to an end Stalin's periodic offensives against individual members of the leadership. The best known of these in 1951 were the assault on Khrushchev over an article of his on the collective farm, and the Mingrelian Affair, which was aimed at Beria.[44]

The scandal surrounding Khrushchev was sparked by his article "On Developing and Improving the Collective Farm," which appeared in *Pravda*, *Moskovskaia Pravda*, and *Sotsialisticheskoe zemledenie* on 4 March 1951. Khrushchev had advanced a scheme for the creation of "agrocities" and "collective farm settlements" to which peasants from small villages would be moved. The next day, *Pravda* printed a note explaining that the article had come out as a discussion piece, although this, owing to an oversight by the editors, had not been made clear. Behind this note lay the groundwork for an attack on Khrushchev by Stalin, who, it appears, was neither pleased with the initiative nor with the fact that Khrushchev's speech had been published without his permission. Very shortly after the offending article had appeared, Stalin reprimanded Khrushchev. On 6 March, Khrushchev composed a letter of repentance:

> Following your instructions, I have tried to dwell on the matter more deeply. Having thought it over, I now understand that my speech [on which the article was based] was, in its essence, flawed. In having this speech published, I have committed a profound mistake and brought great harm to the party. All this could have been avoided had I consulted the Central Committee. Although I had the chance to air my views at the Central Committee, I failed to take it up. That I also now consider to be a grave mistake. I am deeply upset by this blunder and am wondering how best to make amends. I have decided to ask you to allow me to correct this mistake myself. I am quite ready to appear in print again

and to criticize my own article. . . . I beseech you, comrade Stalin, to help me correct this terrible error and, thereby, as far as it is now possible, to limit the damage which I have inflicted on the party.[45]

At first, Stalin chose to ignore this humble appeal. According to Molotov, Stalin instructed that a document censuring Khrushchev be drawn up: "Stalin said: 'we need to have Molotov [on this commission], so that we can really let Khrushchev know what's what!' " Molotov suggested, however, that the primary responsibility for composing the draft document on Khrushchev lay with Malenkov.[46] That claim appears to be borne out in the reminiscences of another participant, Dmitrii Shepilov, who recalled that the attack was prepared at the agricultural department of the Central Committee, which was then headed by one of Malenkov's dependents, A. I. Kozlov. According to Shepilov, the tone of the original paper was cutting and politically charged, with Khrushchev's statements labeled as "ultra-left."[47]

Stalin was soon presented with a draft closed letter of the Central Committee, "On the Development of the Collective Farm in Connection with the Amalgamation of Small Collective Farms." The original record of the Politburo meeting at which this was discussed has been preserved, with a note by Poskrebyshev: "Not confirmed. Deemed unsatisfactory. March 1951."[48] The extensive amendments to the first draft by Stalin help to make sense of this rejection. Most significant was the fact that Stalin crossed out a whole paragraph of exacting criticism of the Khrushchev article, putting in its stead the relatively mild phrase: "One should note that analogous mistakes were also committed in the well-known article by comrade Khrushchev 'On Developing and Improving the Collective Farm,' and that Khrushchev now acknowledges in full the errors of his article." A certain lightening of Stalin's position is also confirmed in Molotov's account of the meeting: "When we brought him our draft, Stalin began to shake, to shake his head. . . . 'It needs to be softer. To be softened.' "[49] According to Shepilov, Kozlov, one of the main authors of the first draft, told him that "comrade Khrushchev has talked this over with comrade Stalin" and, for that reason, work on a highly critical document was stopped.[50] Although the original criticism was watered down, Khrushchev's reputation was tarnished nonetheless. On 18 April, the Politburo took a decision to have the revised version of the closed letter read out at gatherings of primary party organizations.[51] At the same time, Stalin ensured that Khrushchev retained his position and did not allow him to be fully discredited. Khrushchev had notched up a new "sin" and, in Stalin's books, would become all the more obedient and compliant for that.

The fallout for Beria of the so-called Mingrelian Affair would turn out to be quite similar. As Western scholars have argued, the Mingrelian Affair was orchestrated by Stalin,[52] and as was often the case with Stalin's intrigues, events unfolded in an enigmatic and roundabout way. On 26 September 1951, Stalin, who was at the time on vacation in Georgia, received the Georgian Minister of State Security, N. M. Rukhadze. Over dinner, as the arrested Rukhadze would later testify, Stalin, still in a very general way, touched on the subject that Georgia was dominated by members of a regional ethnic group, the Mingrelians, and indicated that this group enjoyed the patronage of none other than Beria.[53] Shortly afterward, the head of Stalin's guard, Vlasik, forwarded complaints to Stalin on corruption in the Georgian system of higher education.[54] This fairly mundane and unremarkable piece of information might easily have passed right by Stalin had he not already been contemplating a purge in Georgia. Stalin's ears pricked up, and the leader issued an instruction for Rukhadze to investigate the matter further.

On 26 October 1951, Rukhadze informed Stalin that the complaints on corruption were completely unfounded.[55] The actual facts of the matter had by this stage become irrelevant, however. Stalin had already decided on a new campaign, and finding a pretext for it was now just a matter of time. On 3 November, Stalin phoned Rukhadze and proposed that he prepare a report on the protection extended by the Second Secretary of the Georgian Communist Party, Baramiia, to the "bribe-taker" and former procurator of Sukhumi, Gvasalii. Rukhadze duly prepared a document showing that Baramiia had, indeed, covered up the crimes of various Mingrelian officials.[56] Matters were now quickly set in motion. On 9 November 1951, the Politburo adopted a resolution, "On Corruption in Georgia and on the Anti-party Group of Comrade Baramiia." The resolution spoke of groups of Mingrelian nationalists, led by Baramiia, which, operating within Georgia's governing structures, had extended protection to bribe-takers (the Gvasalii case was offered as an example) and placed their own people in leading positions across the republic.

> It is beyond doubt that if the anti-party principle of Mingrelian "patronage," as practiced by comrade Baramiia, does not receive a decisive rebuff, then new "patrons" from other provinces in Georgia will emerge ... who would also want to extend patronage over their "own" provinces and to cover up faulty elements there, so as to strengthen their own authority among the masses. If this were to happen, then the Georgian Communist Party will fragment into a number of provincial party principalities that will then possess all the "real" power, while the Georgian Central Committee and its leadership will become obsolete.

Baramiia, together with a number of other leading functionaries in the republic, were dismissed.[57] The style of this document, along with the fact that the original record of the Politburo meeting contains one copy of the draft resolution written by Poskrebyshev (in other words, dictated by Stalin) and another typed copy with amendments by Stalin, all lead to the conclusion that the resolution was prepared by Stalin.

In many respects, the Mingrelian Affair followed the same script as the Leningrad Affair. The case began with the standard charges of abuse of power and political protectionism. The next step, which was not long in coming, was the arrest of the fallen leaders and the fabrication of cases on their "anti-Soviet" and "spying" activities.[58] On 16 November 1951, a further Politburo resolution, "On the Expulsion of Enemy Elements from the Territory of the Georgian Soviet Socialist Republic," was passed on Stalin's instructions; on its basis, 11,200 people were deported to far-off regions in Kazakhstan. In addition, thirty-seven republican leaders were arrested.[59]

Having obtained the necessary materials, Stalin moved on to the next stage, which had, undoubtedly, been planned much earlier: the complete replacement of the Georgian leadership. As is apparent from documents in Stalin's personal archive, on 25 March 1952 from 6:00 to 10:25 P.M. and on 27 March from 10:00 P.M., there were meetings of the Politburo attended by members and candidate members of the Buro of the Georgian Central Committee, who had been summoned to Moscow. Also in attendance were the deputy chair of the Commission of Party Control, Shkiriatov, the Minister of State Security, Ignat'ev, and the head of the Central Committee department that supervised the activities of regional party organizations, Nikolai Pegov.[60] The result of these meetings was a new Politburo resolution of 27 March 1952 on the situation in Georgia. The resolution concluded that the "Baramiia group," "reckoning on the help of foreign imperialists, planned to seize power in the Georgian Communist Party." Responsibility for the fact that such an "anti-Soviet organization" had been allowed to operate over a number of years and had been exposed only following the intervention of Moscow, was placed on the leadership of the Georgian Communist Party. As a result, K. N. Charkviani was dismissed as First Secretary, and was replaced by A. I. Mgeladze, whom Stalin had long favored and supported in his rivalry with Charkviani. The documents show that this second resolution on Georgia, as had the first, had been prepared with Stalin's active involvement.[61]

With the resolution of 27 March, fabrication of the case against the "Mingrelian nationalist group" received a new impulse. To aid Rukhadze and the Georgian Ministry of State Security, a group of experienced investigators was dispatched from Moscow.[62] Relying on support from Stalin, Rukhadze launched purges across the republic, but soon ran into the new First Secretary, Mgeladze. Clearly overestimating his own powers (or, to be more specific, misinterpreting Stalin's intentions), Rukhadze began to assemble incriminating evidence—largely by way of torture—against Mgeladze. He then sent the fabricated records of his "investigations" to Stalin. Stalin's reaction was rather unexpected. He addressed his response not to Rukhadze, but to Mgeladze and to members of the Buro of the Georgian Central Committee.[63] Stalin wrote:

> The Central Committee of the All-Union Communist Party believes that comrade Rukhadze has, in enlisting prisoners as witnesses against Georgian party leaders, pursued a mistaken non-party path. . . . Apart from this, it should be understood that comrade Rukhadze does not have the right to circumvent either the Georgian Central Committee or the Georgian government. Without their knowledge, he has sent the All-Union Central Committee materials incriminating [both these institutions]. In so far as [Rukhadze's] Georgian Ministry of State Security is a union-republic ministry, it is subordinate not only to the center but also to the government and Central Committee of Georgia.[64]

Dutifully implementing Stalin's orders, the republican leadership in Tbilisi removed Rukhadze as Minister of State Security, a step then confirmed by the Politburo in Moscow.[65] For a while, Stalin suspended any further movement, refusing to sanction Rukhadze's arrest. On 25 June, Stalin wired the Georgian leaders, who were naturally impatient to make short work of their enemy: "We regard the arrest of Rukhadze to be premature. We advise you to complete the handover of documents [to the new minister], and then to send Rukhadze to Moscow, where his fate will be settled."[66] Shortly thereafter Rukhadze was indeed summoned to Moscow, where he was arrested. These arrangements were fully in line with the nomenklatura rules of the Stalin period: notwithstanding Stalin's formal pronouncement about the Georgian Ministry of State Security being a "union-republic ministry," the fate of an official of Rukhadze's rank and standing could only have been settled in Moscow.

The arrest of Rukhadze suggests that Stalin's goal in organizing the Mingrelian Affair was not so much to initiate a mass purge as to depose one specific group of Georgian officials, who were linked to Beria. As did other initiatives of this kind, the Mingrelian Affair also served another purpose. The resolution of 9 November, with its threatening reminder of the fixed and unalterable nature of central power, was sent out to all party-state leaders across the Soviet Union, including republican and regional first secretaries, and served as a clear signal that Moscow would not tolerate any form of local "patronage." Most contemporaries agreed, however, that the Mingrelian Affair was primarily directed at Beria.[67] The purge was aimed at Beria's networks in Georgia and sent a clear signal that Beria's own position was far from secure. Having made that point, Stalin typically insisted that Beria himself preside over the April 1952 plenum of the Georgian Communist Party, at which Beria's own clients were "unmasked."

Despite the dangers hanging over him, Beria came out of the Mingrelian Affair lightly. He had lost regional allies and had his image bruised, but the damage was not irrevocable. As he had Khrushchev, Stalin had merely reminded Beria of the essentially ephemeral nature of his own existence under the despot. Even in old age, Stalin was congenitally inclined to administer such "lessons" to his colleagues. Indeed, over the course of 1951 and 1952, lessons of this kind were by no means confined to Beria and Khrushchev. The Artillery Officers' Affair, which unfolded at the same time as the Mingrelian Affair, appears to have been initiated in part so as to scare a third Politburo member, Bulganin. On 31 December 1951, a resolution of the Council of Ministers, "On Shortcomings in the S-60 57 mm. Automatic Anti-aircraft Gun," was adopted, on the basis of which a number of high-ranking military officers and directors in the defense industry were sacked and prosecuted for "wrecking."[68] Bulganin, who supervised the defense industries, was, as Khrushchev later confirmed, in some danger, since he ultimately bore responsibility for accepting the faulty guns.[69] However, in contrast to Malenkov, who had earlier suffered in the similar Aviators' Affair, Bulganin retained his position. The Artillery Officers' Affair was part of a pattern of cases over 1951 and 1952, in which Stalin reminded his companions of their political mortality and their dependence on his favor, but where the leader stopped short of drastic action. As were the "Mingrelian nationalists," the arrested artillery officers and directors in the defense industry were released immediately after Stalin's death.

The course of these attacks on Politburo members in 1951 suggests that the balance of forces that had formed in his entourage suited Stalin rather well and that he was wary of upsetting it. Relatively content to keep things as they were, Stalin saw no need for demotions or sweeping reorganizations, let alone physical reprisals. At the same time, these campaigns, and especially the Mingrelian Affair, highlight Stalin's increasing reliance on the agencies of state security as a lever of rule. Always a central pillar of the dictatorship, Stalin's direct control of the secret police assumed particular importance in the leader's old age. Although quite willing to excuse himself from secondary commitments, Stalin would not let the direction of the security services out of his clutches for a moment.

The Abakumov Affair

Personal control over the security service had, since the late 1920s, been vested directly in Stalin and had been a major tool for securing his hold on the party-state apparatus, including its highest ranks. The very way in which the work, and even the holidays, of Soviet leaders were organized, meant that the secret police was entitled to follow their every move. Within the brief of the Ministry of State Security lay not only an around-the-clock guard of party-state functionaries but the transmission and decoding of correspondence (which, as a rule, was sent in ciphered form), the maintenance of a special telephone system (the so-called VCh), the running of country houses, the supply of special provisions, and so forth. To this, one may add the special forms of monitoring that Stalin might at any one time choose to bring in. So, for example, according to P. A. Sudoplatov, Stalin ordered that bugging devices be placed in the homes of two of his most senior deputies, Molotov and Mikoian, in 1950.[70]

Although he relied heavily on the agencies of state security, Stalin never became their hostage. The leader always treated the "Chekists" with great suspicion, and in many respects he was right to do so. Assigning them the most underhand and murky of cases, Stalin never harbored any illusions as to the honesty or moral fiber of his agents. One of the chief services rendered by the security services was the supply of incriminating information against Stalin's perceived adversaries. Together with the party, the security service played a major role in initiating and coordinating Stalinist purges. Yet in the conduct of such purges, the relationship between the party and the secret police was never a straightforward one. The arrest and prosecution of party officials was ordinarily left in the hands of the security police. At the same time, the security police could, at any given moment, be placed "under the control of the party" and themselves be subjected to a purge. Indeed, such a maneuver, whereby the security police was reinforced with cadres from the party apparatus, had long been a favored means of asserting Stalin's personal control over the security agencies.

Stalin pursued such a strategy in the lead-up to the arrest of Abakumov, the latest in a long line of hapless and expendable ministers of state security. Toward the end of 1950, Abakumov's fortunes began to take a sharp tumble. The turning point appears to have been the conclusion of the Leningrad Affair and the execution of the Leningraders on 1 October 1950. Stalin had been pleased with preparations for the trial, and there were those in the Abakumov circle who believed that, as a mark of gratitude, the minister might even be rewarded with a place on the Politburo.[71] Such expectations were soon dashed. Two months after the execution of the Leningraders, on 3 December 1950, the Politburo adopted a resolution with adverse effects on Abakumov. The main purpose of the resolution was to raise the number of deputy ministers of state security from four to seven. Promoted to the highly sensitive position of deputy minister for cadres was the head of the administrative agencies department at the Central Committee, V. E. Makarov, who replaced Abakumov's closest colleague, M. G.

Svinelupov. Also transferred to Moscow, as the new head of the chief administration of the MGB guard for rail and water transport, was Beria's associate, S. A. Goglidze, who had previously languished as head of the MGB in Khabarovsk.[72]

Notes on the original record of the Politburo meeting point to a number of important circumstances surrounding the adoption of this resolution. They indicate that the document had been prepared in August 1950; most likely Stalin decided to postpone any decision on this matter until the trial of the Leningraders had ended. The original record also carries an order from Poskrebyshev: "Type this up. Have one copy sent to comrade Malenkov, and then draw up [the document] in its final form once you get the go-ahead from him."[73] This suggests the direct involvement of Malenkov, and hence of the apparatus of the Central Committee, in laying the groundwork for a ministerial purge. As had been the case earlier under Stalin, the reorganization of the security service was carried out at the hands of the party bureaucracy.

At the Ministry of State Security, Abakumov was now surrounded by new people and deprived of familiar faces. Makarov, a party functionary, had probably been given charge of the cadres section at the ministry in order to prepare the way for a new party-led reorganization. Although moves to restructure the ministry had already been conceived during the summer of 1950, it is quite likely that, even in December, Stalin still had an open mind about the ultimate fate of Abakumov. Events may well have unfolded along the lines of 1946, when the deposed Merkulov, having been subjected to scathing criticism, was spared not only his life but even his position in the nomenklatura system. What would prove fateful in determining Abakumov's fortunes was a denunciation from one of his subordinates, Lieutenant-Colonel M. D. Riumin.

In the denunciation, which Riumin addressed to Stalin, Abakumov was accused of various offenses, the chief of which was hampering the investigation into the criminal activities of terrorist groups—consisting of doctors and a Jewish youth organization—that were planning to assassinate the country's leaders. The exact circumstances under which Riumin's statement surfaced at the highest levels are unknown.[74] Riumin may well have sent in the denunciation on his own, or on prompting from above. Nonetheless, the pressures that induced him to make his statement do tell us something about how Stalinist bureaucracies operated and, possibly, about how Stalin was able to manipulate such pressures in order to squeeze out suitable denunciations from below. In 1950, Riumin had misplaced a folder with important documents on a government bus, for which he received both party and ministerial reprimands. In May 1951, the cadres administration at the Ministry of State Security began to examine information relating to Riumin's nearest relatives, only to discover that Riumin had concealed a number of compromising facts about himself. Riumin filed a report on the matter, but even here he failed to mention that his father had been a cattle trader, that his brother and sister had had previous convictions, and that his father-in-law had served on the wrong side during the civil war.[75] For these reasons, Riumin's claim, during interrogation after Stalin's death, that his denunciation was filed under duress, does have a ring of truth to it. In December 1950, powerful outside figures such as the Central Committee official Makarov had been brought into leading positions at the Ministry of State Security in order to carry out a searching review of the ministry's operations and personnel. Riumin's allegations may well have been a knee-jerk response to the ensuing pressures building up around him. It is indeed quite likely that Stalin had reckoned on such responses when launching the purge. Certainly, this would help account for the fact that Riumin's report was brought so speedily to his attention.

How Riumin's accusations were followed up cannot be established from the documents. Even if the denunciation did not reach Stalin directly from Riumin, but via a Politburo member (most probably Malenkov), any subsequent moves could have been taken only on Stalin's say-so. It may very well have been that a preliminary denunciation from Riumin was, possibly with the help of Malenkov, reworked into a form that Stalin would find acceptable. Riumin's letter, as the Politburo resolution of 11 July subsequently established, was received by the Central Committee on 2 July, and two days later, the Politburo adopted the following resolution: "To charge a commission consisting of comrades Malenkov (chair), Beria, Shkiriatov, and Ignat'ev to check the facts set out in the statement of comrade Riumin and to convey their results to the Politburo. The commission should complete its work within 3–4 days."[76] The way in which this resolution was drawn up gives us grounds for certain suppositions.

First, the draft copy of the resolution was written in Malenkov's hand and was not accompanied by any mention of a vote. Such a procedure tended to be followed at meetings between Stalin and his closest companions. To the extent that on 4 July 1951 there were no meetings in Stalin's Kremlin office, we may assume that the matter was decided at Stalin's dacha. Second, in the handwritten version of the resolution, written up by Malenkov, there is no mention of the head of the department of party, trade union, and Komsomol agencies at the Central Committee, Ignat'ev. His name was inserted by a secretary in the typed version of the resolution with a note: "Amendment entered on the instruction of comrade Malenkov. 5 July." It is probable that the decision on Ignat'ev was taken on the night of 5 July at a meeting in Stalin's office, where Molotov, Bulganin, Beria, and Malenkov were present from 12:30 A.M. onward, then joined at 1:00 A.M. by Abakumov, and at 1:40 A.M. by Riumin.[77] The impromptu inclusion of Ignat'ev on the commission may be a sign that Stalin did not reach a decision on Abakumov's fate until the very last moment, or that he had delayed choosing his successor or, simply, that, as a mark of his natural caution, he did not want to let his intentions be known in advance.

In the short time allocated it, the Politburo commission cross-examined Abakumov, his deputies, and the heads of the MGB's subdivisions. It concluded that Riumin's allegations were, indeed, well founded. On 11 July 1951, the Politburo adopted a decision, "On the Unfavorable Situation at the USSR Ministry of State Security." Charges against Abakumov were advanced on a number of counts. First, he was accused of blocking the case against Ia. G. Etinger, a Jewish doctor who had been arrested in November 1950 and who had admitted, under torture, that he "harbored terroristic intentions" and that he had "deployed all available means to cut short the life" of A. S. Scherbakov, the Central Committee Secretary, who had died in 1945. Abakumov, so the resolution stated, "deemed Etinger's testimony to be far-fetched" and ordered that this line of investigation be terminated. In addition, the resolution stated that Abakumov had purposefully ordered the ailing Etinger to be placed in a cold and damp cell. Shortly afterward, Etinger had died, leaving the investigative trail cold. "Thus, having stopped the Etinger case," the resolution went on, "Abakumov prevented the Central Committee from revealing the undoubted existence of a conspiratorial group of doctors, who are carrying out the orders of foreign agents to perpetrate acts of terrorism against our state and party leaders." Abakumov was also accused of concealing important materials: evidence against a certain Salimanov, a former deputy general director of the joint-stock company VISMUT, who had fled to the Americans, but who had been arrested in August 1950 in Germany; and information on the case of the "Jewish anti-Soviet youth organization," members of which had been arrested in Moscow in January 1951 while allegedly preparing terrorist acts against Politburo leaders. In addition to these charges, Abakumov was accused of violations in carrying out investigations—of allowing protocols of interrogations to be falsified and of dragging out investigations beyond the time limits established by law.

The Politburo ruled that Abakumov be removed as Minister of State Security and that criminal proceedings against him be instituted, that several high-ranking MGB functionaries be ejected from their posts and expelled from the party, and that yet others receive reprimands.[78] The Politburo also ordered the MGB to restart the case on the terrorist activities of the doctors and of the Jewish anti-Soviet youth organization. Anticipating his appointment as the new Minister of State Security, Ignat'ev was appointed the Central Committee's representative at the MGB. On 13 July, the resolution was included in a closed letter of the Central Committee, which was intended for distribution to regional party organizations (from the republican to the provincial level) and to subdivisions of the MGB.[79] Apart from replicating in full the resolution of 11 July, the letter called on party leaders "to afford all help to the Ministry of State Security in its difficult and crucial work." To underline the need to establish "party control" over the security agencies, it was confirmed on 9 August 1951 that the party official Ignat'ev, would take over as the new Minister of State Security.[80]

The charges against Abakumov were clearly far-fetched. At any one time, the Ministry of State Security would have had numerous contrived cases against alleged "terrorists" and "wreckers," including those who were ostensibly planning to assassinate Soviet leaders. To have reported all such cases to the Central Committee (i.e., to Stalin) would have been unfeasible. Claims regarding violations of "socialist legality" in carrying out investigations were in general ludicrous, especially bearing in mind that it was Stalin himself who had given the order to apply torture. Apart from any logical motives for Abakumov's removal, periodic reshuffles were, for Stalin, a customary means of reinforcing control over the agencies of state security. Stalin's candidate for the vacated post of minister appeared to be entirely appropriate for such a goal. Prior to his promotion to the MGB, the forty-seven-year-old Ignat'ev had made a career out of party work. After a short stint at the Central Committee apparatus from October 1935 to October 1937, he had served as Secretary of two regional party committees from 1937 to 1946, and as Second Secretary of the Belorussian Communist Party from 1947 to 1949, before returning to lead the Central Committee's department of party, trade union, and Komsomol agencies in 1950. Stalin had chosen Ignat'ev as a reliable party functionary free of Chekist group interests. Soon, other party officials were appointed to leading posts in the MGB,[81] while, concurrently, a large group of Chekist cadres were arrested.

Apart from the new balance of forces between the Chekists proper and the new party appointees at the MGB, the recent reshuffles created a tangled system of competition and counterbalances among various groupings. On 26 August 1951, soon after Ignat'ev's appointment, a decision was made to have two First Deputy Ministers of State Security.[82] The reasoning behind this decision becomes clearer if we pay attention to who, specifically, took up these posts. Equivalent powers as Ignat'ev's deputies were assigned to two potential rivals—S. I. Ogol'tsov, who had worked earlier as Abakumov's deputy, and S. A. Goglidze, who was close to Beria. Both had periodically been moved from the center to the provinces and back again to Moscow.[83] In addition to this pair of direct competitors, Riumin was appointed deputy minister and head of the section for investigating especially important cases on Stalin's recommendation on 19 October 1951.[84] Immediately under Ignat'ev there was now an "eye of the Czar," who enjoyed special protection from, and had direct access to, Stalin. Ignat'ev was thus surrounded by deputies whom he would hardly have chosen of his own free will.

Stalin's guiding role in all these events is beyond doubt. Notwithstanding the active part that Malenkov played in preparing the purge of the MGB, it is clear that he was acting on Stalin's orders. Stalin personally directed the investigation against Abakumov and his collaborators, and routinely pored over and edited the formal charge sheets against them. Indeed, the last time Stalin received a report on the Abakumov case was on 20 February 1953, barely a matter of days before he was disabled by a stroke.[85]

Having got rid of Abakumov and appointed Ignat'ev, Stalin set off on his annual visit to the south, which on this occasion would last for over four months. Judging by the inventory of documents sent to Stalin in this period, he received regular and voluminous reports from Ignat'ev. From 11 August to 21 December 1951, in addition to numerous resolutions of the Politburo and of the Council of Ministers relating to the MGB, Stalin received over 160 documents directly from the MGB itself.[86] Control over the agencies of state security not only figured at the top of Stalin's list of priorities in a notional or abstract sense: it received concrete expression in the flows of paperwork being sent back and forth between Stalin's various dachas in the south and the MGB's headquarters, the Lubianka, in Moscow.

Stalin's lengthy absences from Moscow and the general decline of his energies in 1950 and 1951 coincided with a sharp deterioration in the international situation and an upturn in the arms race. None of these developments, however, significantly altered the system of supreme political power which had become entrenched in the preceding years. The methods for agreeing on and adopting decisions remained as they had been before. The partial reorganization of the governmental apparatus did not affect the functions or prerogatives of the Council of Ministers. Similarly, the reorganization of the party apparatus—the division of the Central Committee's department of propaganda and agitation into four departments in December 1950[87]—was routine and politically inconsequential. Unchanged, too, were the methods by which Stalin controlled and put down his colleagues. Moreover, the periodic attacks on Politburo members (against Khrushchev and Andreev on agrarian questions, the Mingrelian Affair, and the affair concerning the artillery officers) assumed a predominantly prophylactic character; none of these actions had the same tragic implications for Politburo members as had the Leningrad Affair. Instead, the chief punitive strike in this period was aimed at the agencies of state security.

The period from the reconfiguration of the Soviet leadership at the beginning of 1950 to the gathering of the XIX Party Congress in October

1952 was one of relative calm for Stalin's companions. The routine, every-day management of the country during those lengthy periods Stalin spent in the south encouraged the gradual consolidation of a small group of these leaders. The septet, which acted in the Politburo's name while Stalin was on leave, used the same methods of collective leadership characteristic of the Politburo in the 1930s, methods that would again become typical after Stalin's death. In the face of an ever-present threat from a decrepit and capricious leader, this ruling group—notwithstanding its own internal rivalries and conflicts—behaved in a restrained and careful manner, pre-ferring to concentrate on its official duties rather than engaging in in-trigues and internecine struggles. Stalin's companions had learned from the Leningrad Affair that any conflict could be used by the leader in a most destructive and unpredictable way.

However, the rhythms of Stalinist dictatorship suggested that any period of relative stability was likely to give way to new efforts by Stalin to firm up his position with the aid of cadre reshuffles and repressions. What remained to be seen was how, and to what purposes, Stalin planned to use his personal control over the punitive apparatus as his energy and state of health fell to a new low.

PART III

Stalin's Legacy

5

AWAKENING TO CRISIS

So far, we have focused on Stalin's personal relations with his inner circle and on his manipulation of political and economic structures. Yet as Stalin and his coterie went about pursuing their own goals, they left large swathes of their country in dire poverty. As became apparent from the mounting flow of complaints to the center, some sectors of the economy, most notably agriculture and the labor camp system were, after years of relentless exploitation, on the verge of crisis. In this chapter, we examine the leadership's response to these signs of crisis. Doing so allows us to reconstruct some of the informal understandings that emerged among Stalin's companions prior to his death. By looking at how information reached the leadership and how it was filtered through by ministers and Politburo members to Stalin, we shall also be able to establish more clearly what relations existed between the leadership and lower bureaucracies. An examination of policy formation and, equally, of policy rejection, will also enable us to assess the very real costs to the social system of Stalin's determination to pursue his own ends. It will show, in particular, how Stalin's personal logic was often at odds with what was rational for the social system as a whole.

We know little of the substance of Stalin's own positions on policy. What direct evidence we have suggests that Stalin was prone to reject out of hand any talk of "reforms."[1] At the same time, Stalin must have had an explanation of some kind for the increasingly desperate problems facing the country and, most probably, some notion of how these problems could be solved. What was Stalin's position on these matters?

Stalin's companions will have had their own views. Establishing these is by no means an easy task, not least because under Stalin, senior Soviet leaders were extremely wary of advancing major policy initiatives of their own. In this system, as we have seen, the monopoly on all major proposals belonged to Stalin. Any attempt to follow the responses to policy failure within Stalin's leadership (and, accordingly, to account for the sources of post-Stalin reform) is, in view of the reluctance of Stalin's deputies to express their views openly, necessarily provisional and dependent on indirect sources.

This chapter focuses on two policy areas that presented particular problems to the leadership in the late Stalin era and that would subsequently lie at the heart of the new course followed by the post-Stalin leadership: the labor camp system and the crisis in food supplies. The Gulag and the rural sector did not receive equal treatment from Stalin and his ruling circle. Open discussion of the situation in the Gulag almost never reached beyond the Ministry of Internal Affairs and the one or two Soviet leaders who oversaw this sector, and was not, as far as we can tell, ever the subject of Politburo deliberations. Nevertheless, the evidence suggests, albeit indirectly, that some of Stalin's companions had come to recognize the need for reform of the cumbersome penal apparatus that the Stalinist revolution had created. By contrast, the problems of feeding the population and of maintaining agricultural production were actively discussed in Stalin's presence. This case study gives us a clearer view of Stalin and his companions' positions, as well as affording insights into the mutual understandings and tactics of Stalin's colleagues.

The Gulag

In the early 1950s, the Gulag occupied an important place in Soviet life. On 1 January 1953, there were 2.5 million prisoners in the camps and colonies, over 150,000 in prisons, and a further 2.75 million persons in special settlements.[2] The various subdivisions of the Gulag stretched across the country like a net. Whole regions, especially in the north, were settled predominantly by convicts or former convicts. The formidable dimensions of the Gulag were a direct consequence of the regime's extremely severe penal policies. In the postwar years, mass repressions were carried out on three fronts. First, those exhibiting the slightest of deviations from the views of the regime were repressed, yielding a steady flow of political prisoners to the camps. Second, in the western regions of Ukraine, Belorussia, and the Baltic republics, large-scale arrests and deportations were the main instrument of accelerated Sovietization and of struggle with the partisan movement. This, too, ensured a ready stream of political convicts to the camps. Third, by the postwar period, penal policy had become a regular method for settling everyday socioeconomic problems. Very high conviction rates for labor indiscipline and for nonfulfillment of compulsory labor dues, as well as for theft, were the result. This, too, had direct implications for the size of the camp system.

The balance between different kinds of repression varied considerably under Stalin. After the war, the number of persons convicted for political crimes fell sharply, while the number of those sentenced for nonpolitical crimes remained high. Hence, whereas convictions for counterrevolutionary offenses fell steadily from a postwar high of 129,826 in 1946 to 69,233 in 1948, 53,179 in 1950, and 27,098 in 1952,[3] the numbers for those prosecuted on charges relating to the "wartime decrees" of shirking, unlawful quitting, and the nonfulfillment of labor dues remained buoyant, accounting for over 6.3 million convictions, or just under half of all sentences passed in the courts from 1946 to 1952.[4] Since the great majority of these convictions resulted in noncustodial sentences, however, it was convictions for other offenses that would have the greatest ramifications for the camps. A distinguishing feature of the postwar period was the application of extreme penalties for ordinary nonpolitical crimes, the most significant of which were theft of state and personal property which, according to two infamous decrees of 4 June 1947, were subject to measures of punishment of from five to twenty-five years.[5] This shift in the balance of penal policies toward ordinary nonpolitical crimes had a notable effect on the composition of the camp population. Within the camps themselves, the share of those convicted of counterrevolutionary offenses dropped from 59.2 percent in 1946 to 26.9 percent at the beginning of 1953.[6] Across the camps and colonies as a whole, those convicted of counterrevolutionary offenses accounted for 21.9 percent of inmates on 1 January 1953, as opposed to 42.3 percent convicted on the June 1947 decrees.[7]

The high levels of those convicted for ordinary crimes would create major long-term problems for the regime. The ultra-severity of ordinary criminal laws meant that a large share of those convicted as ordinary "criminals" were, in effect, political victims of the regime. The scale on which these laws were applied was such that practically any citizen stood a chance of landing in court. From 1946 to 1952, approximately 14 million people were convicted in the ordinary Soviet courts; at least 5.9 million of them were subjected to custodial sentences.[8] Apart from the effects on morale and the everyday psychology of Soviet citizens, the constant flow of new inmates created major managerial problems for the administrators of the camps and colonies, whose population of 2.5 million appeared, if anything, to be growing. If we take into account the large numbers of those sentenced or deported for long terms in earlier years, the cumulative impact of Stalin's penal policies threatened to push the scale of the Gulag beyond sustainable limits.

The archives of the Ministry of Internal Affairs contain numerous documents on the problems presented by the 5-million-plus army of prisoners and exiles. To begin with, the task of guarding the camps presented major difficulties. Staff limits, including the supervisory service and fire brigades, agreed to by the government for camps and colonies at the beginning of 1953 were, on average, 9.62 percent of the camp population (in some camps there were more staff, in the range of 10–12 percent). This meant that the camps and colonies would require approximately 240,000 guards. In reality, however, this figure was surpassed. At the beginning of 1953, there were 250,000 civilians, rank-and-file conscripts, and sergeants in the militarized guard of the camps and colonies. There were, in addition, several thousand officers and members of the fire and supervisory services. Finally, 1.2 percent of the prisoners themselves (approximately 30,000 people) were recruited to fill secondary guard positions.[9] The funds and energy put into maintaining and disciplining this vast 300,000-strong army of guards (to say nothing of the Gulag's sizable bureaucracy) were themselves a major drain on the state.

Despite the resources poured into their prevention, escapes by prisoners were common. According to official statistics (whose accuracy we may well question) 3,000 prisoners escaped from the camps in 1951; 250 of these were not caught. Following a strengthening of the guard in 1952, the corresponding figures fell sharply—to 1,500 and 163. In addition, during 1952, 24,600 attempted escapes, 4,500 of which were group-based, were prevented.[10] Although the Ministry of Internal Affairs' (MVD) leadership reported that a large majority of fugitives were caught, there were, in fact, many thousands of escaped prisoners roaming the country. Further, many of the escapees were armed, so that stopping them or chasing them once they had escaped inevitably led to casualties on both sides.

The camps also periodically witnessed various forms of mass unrest and hunger strikes. The history of mass opposition in the camps under Stalin has received little scholarly attention, but what is known suggests opposition on a scale that must have troubled the leadership.[11] Apart from rising levels of banditry among ordinary criminals, camp disturbances were whipped up by active opponents of the regime. This latter element, which included former members of the partisan movement in the western districts, as well as former soldiers of General Vlasov's Russian Liberation Army, had proven fighting experience and had swelled considerably since the war. There is also evidence that prisoners collectively undermined the informer networks that constituted a vital control mechanism for the authorities. The camp underground killed and manipulated informers, impeded the recruitment of new agents, and set up its own secret networks.[12]

Also extensive was the phenomenon of "camp banditry" and the murder of inmates by other prisoners. Despite the many convictions of bandits in the camp courts and the transfer of the most serious recidivists to prisons and special zones, 1,470 "bandit incidents" were officially recorded in

1951, as a result of which 2,011 people were killed and 1,180 injured; the following year there were 1,017 such incidents, with 1,299 killed and 614 injured.[13] The situation was sufficiently serious that at the beginning of 1953, the government passed special measures to combat murders in the camps. Passed on 13 January, the decree of the Presidium of the USSR Supreme Soviet, "On Measures to Strengthen the Struggle with Particularly Serious Instances of Banditry among Prisoners in Correctional Labor Camps," provided for the application of the death penalty to inmates who committed bandit attacks involving murder.

Officials of the MVD attributed these mounting problems in part to the general relaxation of camp regimes which had occurred in the preceding years. In fact, many camp authorities had taken to releasing large numbers of prisoners without escort and assigning them economic duties outside the camp zones. The main reason for this was that in the postwar period, the Ministry of Internal Affairs, already one of the most powerful of Soviet economic institutions, had come under increasing pressure to achieve economic targets set for it by the government. The MVD's main economic role lay in the area of construction. In 1952, the camp workforce received approximately 10 percent of all-union capital investments, which exceeded that of any other ministry. Bearing in mind that prisoners were sent to do the hardest labor at minimal economic cost, mainly in far-off regions, these figures in effect underestimate the true role of the Gulag in capital construction. More modest, but nonetheless significant, was the role of the MVD as an industrial ministry. Although gross industrial production by the MVD as expressed in prices accounted for approximately 2.3 percent of all Soviet industrial output, the MVD mined a significant share of the country's nonferrous metals (gold, nickel, cobalt, etc.), produced around 12–15 percent of the country's timber and sawtimber, and manufactured a variety of construction materials, machines, and mass-consumption goods.[14]

Under Stalin, the need to have forced labor on a large scale was never openly questioned. Not only was there a lack of ethical opposition; forced labor was also integral to some of Stalin's most cherished projects. State control of large contingents of prisoner-workers, who could be compelled to work at any time and under any conditions and who could be moved at will from one site to another, went hand in hand with economic voluntarism and the adoption of grandiose, labor-intensive projects. It was on the back of prisoner labor, for example, that huge hydroelectric stations on the Volga were constructed and that various hydraulic works, such as the Volga-Don, Volga-Baltic, and Turkmen Canals—known in official propaganda as the Stalinist Structures of Communism—were proposed.

At times, information on the Gulag's worsening problems passed beyond the walls of the MVD and caught the attention of individual Soviet leaders.

The Politburo member with the most detailed knowledge of these matters was Lavrentii Beria. In his capacity as deputy chair of the Council of Ministers, Beria oversaw the activities of the Ministry of Internal Affairs, which meant dealing with MVD matters on an almost daily basis. The list of documents Beria received from the Ministry of Internal Affairs takes up several large volumes.[15] From this correspondence it is evident that Beria was, above all, engaged in the economic affairs of the MVD and, in particular, in the use the ministry made of prisoner labor. Accordingly, it becomes important to establish what position the leadership of the MVD—and, by implication, Beria himself—adopted on economic matters. Although there was no direct criticism of the system of forced labor, it is clear that the leadership of the MVD found it increasingly difficult to meet the ever-higher economic targets set for it and to satisfy the constant requests for prisoner-workers. More significantly, it appears that the ministry had also become troubled by the very principle of using prisoners as a source of labor. We can trace two connected positions on these matters in the MVD during this period. First, we find repeated appeals from the MVD concerning the shortage of labor power, as well as outright refusals by it to allocate prisoners following requests from other ministerial and regional leaders. Second, we encounter numerous initiatives to alter the system of work incentives in the camps.

On the eve of the war, Beria, who had been Commissar of Internal Affairs since the end of 1938, had scrapped the system of "work cards," by which prisoners who had fulfilled their production norms were entitled to a preterm release. This decision had an enormous impact on the Gulag, for it led to an increase in the overall camp population on account of the decline in turnover, and it deprived prisoners of any incentive to work.[16] Under the extraordinary conditions of war, the problems of motivating the workforce temporarily diminished; with the end of the war, however, they resurfaced. Notwithstanding the strong legal prohibition against using work cards, the leadership of the MVD, now with the support of Beria, who had changed his own position on this issue, confirmed that these cards were the most effective way of motivating prisoners and resurrected the system on its more remote labor sites. As a result, by September 1950, work cards were used in camps accommodating 27 percent of all prisoners[17] and showed signs of spreading further. The extension of the work card system led to serious manpower shortages at individual MVD sites. The MVD leadership, however, recognized the merits of the system and, by implication, the ineffectiveness of pure forced labor.

As evidence of a conscious, albeit piecemeal, dismantling of the Gulag, we may cite the MVD leadership's early release of prisoners and the assignment of these prisoners to designated enterprises as civilian workers. In August 1950, on the basis of corresponding government resolutions, the USSR Minister of Internal Affairs ordered the early release of 8,000 prisoners and their assignment to construction work on the railways.[18] In January 1951, Minister Sergei Kruglov requested that Beria sanction the early release and transfer of a further 6,000 prisoners to work on the construction of the Kuibyshev and Stalingrad hydroelectric stations. Kruglov justified this request by reference to the fact that these construction sites lacked qualified cadres who could operate heavy machinery.[19] In February 1951, the Council of Ministers approved yet more proposals from the Ministry of Internal Affairs on the early release of groups of prisoners and their redeployment, "so as to increase the number of regular working cadres" at the Pechory coal field.[20] Despite the apparent advantages of total and unmediated control of prisoners, the state increasingly preferred to deal with relatively free workers, who, as well as being more productive, did not require such a refined and expensive system of containment and supervision.

To raise the productivity of prisoners, the MVD leadership introduced a wage system in certain camps at the end of the 1940s. Although this breached one of the main economic principles of forced labor—that camp work should be "free" to the state—the MVD widened this approach and insisted that prisoners everywhere receive a wage. On 13 March 1950, the government, accepting these demands, passed a resolution on the introduction of payment to prisoners in all correctional labor camps and colonies of the MVD, with the exception of special camps, which held "especially dangerous" ordinary and political criminals.[21] Before long, however, the system of wages was extended to these special camps as well. The priority assigned by MVD and Gulag officials to economic criteria is also reflected in the very wide use of so-called unescorted prisoners, who were not placed under guard. Unable to ensure that all prisoners were properly guarded during the production process, camp administrations either secured official permission to have prisoners unsupervised or introduced this system on the spur of the moment.

Taken together, these facts point to a clear tendency within the Gulag in the postwar period toward converting a significant portion of prisoners into partially civilian workers, in effect turning slaves into serfs. The logic of this process meant that the next step—the replacement of prisoners by genuinely civilian workers and the dismantling of the Gulag economy—was only a matter of time.

In view of the way in which the Soviet state machine operated, it is hard to imagine that the leadership of the MVD could have secured government decisions on the early release of prisoners, or on wages, in defiance of the views of the Politburo member, Beria, who oversaw this sector. In fact, Beria himself became actively involved not only in routine matters relating to the MVD economy but also in wider aspects of the economic effectiveness of the MVD. It was following a specific request from Beria, for example, that on 9 October 1950 Kruglov sent him a report on the cost of construction at the MVD compared to construction costs at other ministries. From this report Beria discovered that outlays on maintaining the camps were on such a scale that the cost of keeping each prisoner exceeded the average salary of civilian workers. Thus, for example, in building the Volga-Don Canal in 1949, the cost of housing, feeding, and guarding a single prisoner came to 470 rubles a month, while his salary (calculated according to the same criteria as for free workers) would have come to 388 rubles. For the camps to pay their way without subsidy, reported Kruglov, the ministry would have to lengthen the working day and raise work norms for prisoners.[22]

Indirect evidence of Beria's own position comes from the stance adopted by one of his closest aides and confidants, S. S. Mamulov.[23] From the time of his appointment as deputy Minister of Internal Affairs in 1946, Mamulov repeatedly recommended that the leadership of the MVD put a proposal to the government that, for several categories of convict, exile to remote regions be substituted for camp confinement.[24] Prisoners would be turned into special settlers, who would be linked to designated camps and who would serve their labor obligations at economic sites belonging to these camps. In a note to Kruglov in June 1951, Mamulov suggested extending these measures to over half of all prisoners—those convicted of theft, speculation, hooliganism, and official and economic crimes, among others. Such a measure, Mamulov argued, would lower state expenditure on the camps, make better use of prisoners for production, and reduce the number of escapes while improving provisions for guarding those prisoners still left in the camps.[25]

Kruglov instructed all his deputies and the head of the Gulag to familiarize themselves with Mamulov's note and to submit their suggestions. The MVD leaders were divided. Some fully supported Mamulov's proposal, while others supported it in principle but thought it premature. A third group put forward their own proposals, which differed from Mamulov's in their form, if not in their fundamentals.[26] Although it did not go beyond the MVD, and the proposal itself was not adopted, the discussion around Mamulov's initiative suggests that senior MVD managers were at the very least quite happy to consider a major reorganization of the Gulag which would have freed them from the need to keep over a million camp prisoners continuously under guard. It was another matter that Kruglov and his deputies could not yet bring themselves to present such reforms to the government.

Judging by the materials they sent to Stalin, it appears that the leadership of the MVD thought better than to bother the leader with core, strategic questions.[27] Instead, Stalin received from the MVD fairly general information on the fulfillment of economic plans, on the condition of prisoners of war in the camps, on incidents such as fires, crashes, major thefts investigated by the MVD, and the like. The nature of this information likely reflected Stalin's own limited interest in the problems of the Gulag. The difficulties of running the Gulag were, in fact, far more likely to attract the attention of Georgii Malenkov. As the Central Committee Secretary who presided over meetings of the Orgburo and the Secretariat, and as deputy chair of the Council of Ministers, Malenkov was obliged to look into various signals that Moscow received from the camps, as well as to resolve battles that arose between the Ministry of Internal Affairs and other economic agencies over allocation of the prisoner workforce. In addressing such matters, Malenkov would often interact with Beria.

Evidence of such cooperation between Malenkov and Beria can be found in the papers on camp investigations. For example, on 10 May 1950, the Secretary of the Sakhalin regional party committee, D. Mel'nikov, sent the Minister of Internal Affairs, Kruglov, and Malenkov a letter on abuses committed at the Sakhalin camp, which included beatings and murders of prisoners by guards, banditry, escapes, drunkenness, and abuse of office by the camp administration. Malenkov passed a copy of the letter on to Beria with an instruction: "Please read this." On Beria's orders, a commission, headed by the deputy Minister of Internal Affairs, Ivan Serov, was sent to Sakhalin. Beria also commanded the Minister of Internal Affairs, Kruglov, to report to Malenkov on all measures that had been taken.[28] This pattern of interaction between Malenkov and Beria appears to have been typical, for shortly afterward, it was repeated. On 24 August 1950, the procurator of the Karaganda camp, Moiseenko, sent a similar signal on his own malfunctioning camp to the center. Moiseenko told a similar tale of mass thefts, banditry, murders, and administrative chaos. In January 1951, Kruglov informed Beria about the results of the investigation into the camp. Beria, in turn, placed an instruction on the letter: "Let G. M. Malenkov know of this."[29]

Immediately after Stalin's death, Beria, then Minister of Internal Affairs, launched a major initiative aimed at dismantling the Stalinist Gulag. On 26 March 1953, Beria sent a memorandum, addressed to Malenkov at the Central Committee Presidium, stating that there were over 2.5 million people in the camps, prisons, and colonies, a large proportion of whom "do not represent a serious danger to society." Beria proposed implementing a broad amnesty that would lead to the release of approximately 1 million people, and he also suggested that criminal laws be reviewed and relaxed. "A review of criminal legislation is necessary," the report stated, "since every year over 1.5 million people are convicted, of whom just under 650,000 are given custodial sentences, and a large proportion of whom are convicted for crimes that do not represent a special danger to the state.

If we do not do this, then within one to two years the overall number of prisoners will climb again to 2.5 to 3 million people."[30] Beria's proposals on offering amnesty to over a million people were quickly implemented, although the review of criminal legislation took place more gradually and was spread out over a number of years.

In addition to reducing the Gulag, Beria sought its fundamental reorganization. On 17 March 1953, Beria sent Malenkov proposals on the basis of which the government passed a resolution the next day on transferring all construction and industrial enterprises from the MVD to economic ministries (a decision on the transfer of agricultural enterprises from the Gulag was taken in May).[31] At the same time, on Beria's instructions, the MVD apparatus also prepared plans for a major reduction in its own construction program. In contrast to the plans adopted under Stalin, in which the MVD was supposed to have built projects with an estimated overall cost of 105 billion rubles, including a plan for capital construction in 1953 of 13.34 billion rubles, the MVD now proposed jettisoning nearly half of its construction commitments and reducing the plan for capital construction for 1953 by 3 billion rubles. On 21 March 1953, Beria sent the resultant draft proposals to the Council of Ministers, where they were soon passed into law.[32] Beria's reorganization of the MVD was capped on 28 March 1953 by a Council of Ministers resolution on transferring the camps and colonies (with the exception of the special camps) from the MVD to the USSR Ministry of Justice.[33]

Beria and Malenkov's initiatives for reorganizing the penal system in the spring of 1953 appear to have been a logical continuation of their involvement in MVD and Gulag affairs under Stalin. With a steady flow of relatively accurate information on the state of the Gulag, the two were particularly well positioned to push for such a change. Although the lack of relevant documents does not allow us to say with any certainty whether the problems of the Gulag were discussed at the Politburo under Stalin, we can assume that the primary impetus for the reform of this sector in spring 1953 came from Malenkov and Beria, both of whom—unlike their Politburo companions—had been regularly apprised of the Gulag's economic and administrative deficiencies over the previous years.

Given Stalin's uncompromising views on punishment and his leanings toward grandiose projects based on forced labor, none of his companions would have dared to speak in favor of softening the state's criminal policy or to express any doubts as to the wisdom of maintaining such an extensive camp system. Instead, they—Malenkov and Beria included—preferred to demonstrate their resoluteness, severity, and absolute intransigence before anything that smacked of "liberalism." Such norms had, indeed, been widely cultivated within the party-state apparatus under Stalin. As we have seen, however, numerous facts suggest that, beneath the surface, there also existed more pragmatic and reasoned assessments of the Gulag's prospects. These would come to the fore after Stalin's death.

Problems in the rural sector, and in particular the breakdowns in food supplies that they led to, were a second area of difficulty at the end of the Stalin era. By contrast with the Gulag, reforms to the agrarian sector were given full consideration while Stalin was alive, and discussions of these involved not only Stalin but also a large group of his companions. Here we are in a better position to assess how news of the worsening situation was greeted by Stalin and his inner circle, and to see how Stalin's deputies, despite their reservations, were compelled to follow the dictator's lead.

Reforming the Countryside

The continual crisis of agricultural production and the poor living conditions of the peasantry, who still accounted for an absolute majority of the country's population, were a natural consequence of the socioeconomic policies pursued by Stalin's regime. Accelerated industrialization and the growth of military expenditure were carried out at the expense of the countryside, whose needs were discarded in order to secure a relatively high standard of living for the cities, on which the social stability of the regime depended. Soviet leaders were nonetheless forced to make certain concessions to the peasantry during those periods when tensions in the agrarian sector were strained beyond acceptable limits. One such instance would occur at the end of Stalin's rule.

To add to the traditionally low level of capital investment in agriculture, the late Stalin period saw a rise in the punishing tax burden on farmers and an increase in compulsory deliveries to the state, for which farmers received next to nothing. The average agricultural tax on a single collective farm homestead in 1952 was more than two and a half times what it had been in 1941,[34] when taxes had, in any case, been high in connection with preparations for the war. Requisitions by the state also ate into the time farmers could devote to their personal plots. A perverse consequence of this combination of relentless pressure and poor incentives was a progressive fall in overall agricultural output. This limited the state's ability to generate strategic reserves in case of war and to deliver grain abroad, above all to its needy new allies in Eastern Europe. Of greater concern was the fact that on the eve of Stalin's death, the consumption of major foodstuffs by the Soviet population had dropped to a disturbingly low level. According to calculations put together by the Central Statistical Administration (TsSU) in 1953, on a normal day, the average Soviet citizen consumed 500 grams of flour, groats, and pasta, approximately the same amount again of potatoes, and about 400 grams of milk and dairy produce (mainly cow and goat's milk). Given that other foodstuffs were consumed in negligible quantities, this formed the basis of daily consumption.[35] Strikingly, these amounts were approximately equal to the main norm for camp prisoners who, on an average day, were supposed to receive 700 grams of bread, 120 grams of groats and pasta, and 400 grams of potatoes (the rations for prisoners engaged in heavy work were higher), apart from which all prisoners were entitled to increments for overfulfilling norms.[36]

The figures presented in the TsSU paper on average consumption masked significant differences in living standards between different categories of the population. Privileged social groups, such as senior bureaucrats, military personnel, members of the security services, the creative intelligentsia, the labor aristocracy, workers in large factories, and the inhabitants of the larger cities (above all, Moscow) received significantly more than these beggarly norms. We get some notion of the distribution of resources from the following figures: of the 443,000 tons of meat distributed across the USSR via the state and cooperative network in 1952, 110,000 tons were sent to Moscow and 57,400 tons to Leningrad.[37]

The calamitous situation in which much of the rest of the population found itself was well known to the leadership due to the many appeals it received from ordinary citizens and reports sent from regional leaders. Thus, for example, on 1 November 1952, Malenkov received a letter from the Secretary of the Yaroslavl' regional party committee, V. Luk'ianov, who reported: "Owing to limited stocks of a number of major foodstuffs, trade in these goods in the towns and worker settlements of the Yaroslavl' region is proceeding unsatisfactorily. An especially serious situation has arisen in the fourth quarter of the current year with regard to the sale of meat, sausages, animal fats, sugar, herring, cheese, groats, and macaroni. The sale of these foods, even in the major industrial towns, such as Yaroslavl' and Shcherbakov, with a population of over 500,000, has been marked by major disruptions on account of the large queues."[38] Following an instruction from Malenkov, the matter was examined at the corresponding ministries, but Luk'ianov's request for additional foodstuffs was declined, a fairly typical outcome for such a petition.[39] Within only a few days, however, the situation would change.

At the beginning of November, another letter on the food shortages, this time from the Riazan' region, happened to catch Stalin's eye. Although Moscow received a vast number of similar signals from across the country, for some reason (most likely, quite by chance), Stalin decided to respond specifically to this letter and instructed that Malenkov have the complaint checked. Malenkov assigned the Central Committee Secretary responsible for regional party agencies, Averkii Aristov, to visit the region. On 17 November 1952, all ten Central Committee Secretaries congregated in Stalin's office, where he demanded an account of the situation in Riazan'. As described by Aristov,

> Stalin came in and said: "What's going on in Riazan'?" A silence fell. "Who's been to Riazan'?" At that point I got up: "I have been," I said. "So, what's going on? Are there disruptions?" "No, comrade Stalin," I answered, "but for a while now there has been no bread, oil, or sausage to speak of." "What sort of Secretary do we have there? A feeble person, clearly. Why has he not told us of this? Have him removed," Stalin shouted.... I began to object, saying that Larionov [Secretary of the Riazan' regional party committee] was not at fault, and that the bread situation was very similar in other cities.... Had comrades Khrushchev and Ignatov not come to my rescue, I really would have had it.... Nikita Sergeevich [Khrushchev] said: "Comrade Stalin, the Ukraine is wheat-based, but there is no wheat or white bread to be had there." Ignatov, similarly, declared that in Krasnodar the situation was much the same.[40]

The discussion of the situation in Riazan' drew attention to the fact, well known to the majority of Soviet citizens and to most of the country's leaders, that there were insufficient reserves to feed the country adequately. Despite this, Stalin continued to insist that the shortages were due to poor short-term planning and to the incorrect distribution of resources. On the same day, he authorized the following resolution: "The Bureau of the Presidium of the Council of Ministers must pay urgent attention to the *incorrect distribution* of market reserves of grain, groats, meat, sugar, vegetable oil, and animal fats which, in a number of regions (Ukraine, some central regions, the Kuban') has caused disruptions to supplies, and it must also plan measures for reassessing existing reserves."[41] The heightened activity of the government in response to this injunction became immediately apparent as, in an unusual step, both the Bureau of the Presidium and the Presidium of the Council of Ministers met over three consecutive days.[42] By 22 November, two resolutions had been adopted. The first confirmed Stalin's perception of the disruptions as a function of "poor distribution" and ordered that, in the remaining days of November and December 1952, market reserves of flour be raised by 120,000 tons, of groats by 30,000 tons, of sugar by 20,000 tons, of meat by 10,000 tons, of vegetable oil and animal fat by 3,000 tons each, and of cheese by 1,000 tons. Further, the Ministry of Trade was instructed to correct the mistakes that had crept into the planning of market reserves and to assess the distribution of stocks across republics and regions on a monthly basis, rather than quarterly.[43] The Bureau of the Presidium of the Council of Ministers also drafted a resolution, "On Facilitating Trade in the Riazan' Region," which, when confirmed,[44] provided for the construction of new shops and chambers of commerce, canteens, storage depots, vegetable stores, bread-baking plants, bake houses, and the like in Riazan'.[45] On 4 December 1952, a meeting of the Presidium of the Central Committee heard updates on the supply of foodstuffs around the country. The next week, following a telegram from the Kuibyshev regional committee, a Council of Ministers resolution on increasing market reserves in this region was pushed through with unusual speed.[46]

Stalin's companions knew full well that such a meager redistribution of resources could not address the real problems underlying the food shortages. Once these shortages had been acknowledged, the next logical step was to reevaluate the condition and future prospects of agriculture. Some members of the leadership certainly understood that the policy of continuously pumping resources out of the countryside could only be taken so far. Of particular interest in this respect was a paper presented to Malenkov by one of his closest associates, the head of the agricultural department at the Central Committee, A. I. Kozlov, in April 1952. On the basis of data from the TsSU, Kozlov showed that the rise in state procurements of meat, milk, and other stock-raising products had been obtained by increasing compulsory delivery norms. At the same time, "any further raising of compulsory delivery norms for meat and milk," Kozlov predicted, "will only reduce the amount of excess produce collective farmers can sell on the market." "The current procurement prices for compulsory deliveries of meat and milk (32 kopecks for one kilogram of fresh meat and 25–30 kopecks for one liter of milk)," he went on, "hardly let collective farms cover their costs." Kozlov recommended raising the prices at which the state obtained over-the-plan deliveries of meat and milk.[47]

Any project that presupposed raising state investments in agriculture and even a marginal rise in income stood little chance of success. The main obstacle to its adoption was Stalin, who viewed concessions to the peasantry as a blow to the very foundations of his long-term policy of accelerated growth in the military and heavy industry sectors. He once again confirmed his position at the first organizational plenum after the XIX Party Congress, where he launched a blistering attack on Molotov and Mikoian for having spoken sympathetically of the need to raise procurement prices for grain. After this, none of Stalin's companions would have dared to speak in favor of raising investments in agriculture. For this reason, any draft resolution on raising purchase prices in the last months of 1952 must have come from Stalin.

At the end of December 1952, proposals on increasing payment to collective farmers who raised cattle were tabled at the highest level. That Stalin should have blessed such a move was a measure of the sheer enormity of the crisis in livestock rearing in this period. The crisis had, in fact, been brewing for many years. The three-year plan of 1949 for the development of cattle rearing had done more to disguise the problem than to remedy it. By insisting on a growth in head of cattle on the collective farm at any cost, even at the expense of cattle from personal holdings, the plan had achieved a temporary rise in indicators for state procurements of meat and dairy products only by squeezing the last remaining disposable resources out of the farms. By 1952, any further opportunities for pumping out resources had been used up. There were by now 3.5 million fewer cows in the country than in the impoverished prewar years.[48] At the same time, over the spring of 1952 there was a major crisis in meat supplies. What scanty stocks there were of meat and butter were almost entirely earmarked for Moscow and for certain large industrial centers. On 18 September 1952, the USSR Minister of Agriculture, Ivan Benediktov, informed Malenkov, who oversaw the agricultural sector, that numbers of cattle and poultry had fallen significantly short of the plan. Moreover, in the collective farms of twenty-nine regions and republics, the number of cattle had actually declined. The minister was not able to offer any serious proposals.[49] As a result, the Council of Ministers resolution of 27 September 1952, "On Serious Shortcomings in the Fulfillment of the State Plan for the Development of Public Stock Raising on Collective Farms," contained a traditional assortment of largely empty demands to regional leaders—to secure the fulfillment of the plan, "to take measures," and "to carry out additional steps."[50]

All the while the situation with stock raising appeared to be getting worse. The issue was raised repeatedly at meetings of the government and at the Central Committee. On 3 December 1952, a report on the fall in head of cattle in thirty-eight republics and regions led the Presidium of the Central Committee to request a draft resolution on animal husbandry and to the establishment, on 11 December, of a commission under Khrushchev "for drawing up radical measures to secure the further growth of animal husbandry." Of major significance was the fact that the commission was asked to pay special attention to raising incentives for collective farmers to engage in stock raising.[51] This was a new element, which seemed to be taking agrarian policy in a quite different direction. How such a seemingly radical idea was mooted was later explained by a member of the commission, Anastas Mikoian. In response to a bland paper from Benediktov, from which one could have inferred that collective farmers simply "idled their time away, comrade Stalin [interjected], 'If our collective farmers are not taking care of our cattle properly, this means that they are not properly rewarded for public stock raising which, in turn, means that in order to develop stock raising, we shall need to make our collective farms more economically oriented.' "[52]

The banality of such a conclusion was understood full well by all of Stalin's companions. However, to come out with such proposals without fear of being charged with "right deviation" was something that Stalin alone could do. Reconstructing Stalin's line of thinking here is a complex matter. Some years later, Khrushchev asserted that he had directed Stalin's attention to the crisis in animal husbandry.[53] Mikoian also claimed credit for the move, arguing that it was only after his speech that Stalin gave the order to have Khrushchev's commission set up.[54] It is clear, however, that Stalin relied on a wider base of advice and information than the words of one or another of his companions. It is logical to suppose that the change in Stalin's plans took place either in October or November 1952, in the period following the adoption of the resolution on animal husbandry of 27 September. We may recall that in November, following the complaint from Riazan', the matter of food supplies had, on Stalin's orders, been reexamined. It was also in November that Stalin received a letter, from a vet in the Moscow region, N. I. Kholodov, explicitly describing the agricultural situation:

> Let us look at animal husbandry. One is ashamed even to speak of it— annual milk yields do not exceed 1,200 to 1,400 liters for a forage cow. That is absurd—you get as much from your average she-goat. One has to ask: "Why is this so?" Let me give you some reasons.
>
> 1. Cattle are put out to pasture in the spring completely emaciated, as a result of which productivity is low and the cows are very dry
> 2. As a rule cattle do not get green feed, since there are no crops for this, and in any case it is hard to find the people to do the mowing and carrying
> 3. Even at the best time of the year there are only two to three separate milkings a day since the milkmaids, without being paid for it, refuse to do four
> 4. Cattle are kept in unsanitary conditions (in some herds, their abdomens hover over the dung)
>
> At first I thought that this only happens in some of the industrial districts, but it turns out that no—the picture is quite the same, as I have found out, in a number of districts in the Vladimir, Riazan', Kursk, and Voronezh regions, to say nothing of other areas. . . .
>
> We need radical measures to change the situation of collective farms in the central regions.[55]

Kholodov's letter was dated 1 November 1952 and, judging by the official stamp on it, was received by the special sector on 5 November. While there is no conclusive evidence that Stalin saw the letter, the weight of circumstantial evidence suggests that he did. First, the letter is kept in Stalin's files where, as a rule, only those appeals that caught the leader's interest were deposited. Second, the copy of the letter in the archive carries a note: "To comrades Malenkov and Khrushchev. 10 November 1952." It is implausible that a secretary would have forwarded copies of the letter to such high-ranking recipients without an instruction from Stalin. Finally, on 3 December 1952, the Buro of the Presidium of the Central Committee instructed Khrushchev to examine the facts set out in Kholodov's letter. Again, such an instruction could not have been given without Stalin's knowledge. In a memorandum of 11 December to Stalin, Khrushchev acknowledged the truth of a number of the arguments in Kholodov's letter, but nonetheless averred that the vet had considered only the worst collective farms, while knowing little of how the more advanced farms fared. In conclusion Khrushchev informed Stalin that the question of personal incentives on collective farms would receive further scrutiny.[56]

Khrushchev's commission deliberated for two weeks. On 26 December, the commission presented Khrushchev with a draft resolution of the Council of Ministers "On Measures for the Further Development of Livestock Raising on State and Collective Farms," along with appendices and supporting information.[57] At the heart of these extensive documents were proposals on increasing payment to collective farmers with cattle, including raising procurement prices by three to four times for meat and by around 50 percent for milk.[58] It was also proposed that bonuses be increased for the handing over of cattle that were fattened and of higher nutritional value, and that over-the-plan deliveries of meat be stimulated by favored access to certain industrial goods for successful farmers. According to the calculations of the Ministry of Finance, the cost of these initiatives would be in the order of 3.4 billion rubles in 1953, 4.2 billion rubles in 1954, and 4.9 billion rubles the following year. Further, the cost of improving feed, stock, and equipment for cattle raising over the following three years would bring state capital investments in this sector to 6 to 7 billion rubles over what had been envisaged in the five-year plan.[59]

In the course of the commission's work, a conflict emerged that highlighted the nature of personal relations among Stalin's companions. It is likely that Stalin's colleagues feared being blamed by the leader for the patent failure of state policies on cattle raising. For this reason, Stalin's appointment of Khrushchev as head of the commission for animal husbandry was a mixed blessing. At the same time, Stalin chose not to include Malenkov on the commission, even though he had nominally been in charge of this area of agriculture. An offended Malenkov saw this as a demonstration of Stalin's lack of faith in him. Khrushchev tried to defuse the situation by first attempting to decline the offer and then proposing that the position be given to Malenkov.[60] Despite the propriety of Khrushchev's actions, Stalin insisted on his taking the position. According to Khrushchev, Malenkov began to nurse a grudge against him. Malenkov's dependents in the agriculture bureaucracy were asked to file regular reports for their patron on the work of the commission, while Beria implored Khrushchev "not to offend" Malenkov any more.[61] The situation turned out well for Khrushchev: not just Malenkov but even Beria were subsequently included on the commission.

How this happened can be roughly reconstructed. At the July 1953 plenum of the Central Committee, Mikoian asserted that the commission, while working without Malenkov, had presented Stalin with alternative draft resolutions that provided for a rise in basic procurement prices to either 70 or 90 kopecks a kilogram of cattle meat. Stalin proposed his own more modest variant—of raising these prices to 50–60 kopecks.[62] At the same time, Khrushchev claimed, Stalin proposed that the tax "on collective farms and on collective farmers" be raised by the extraordinary sum of 40 billion rubles.[63] Documentary evidence supporting Khrushchev's claims has not been found, and this figure sounds implausible since the overall agricultural tax in 1952 was in the order of 10 billion rubles.[64] It appears, however, that Stalin did indeed propose pushing up investment in stock raising on the basis of a corresponding increase in taxes on agriculture. Hence, the intended measures to stimulate stock raising would have turned into a simple redistribution of resources within agriculture itself, with the rise in income of stock raising coming at the expense of other branches in the agrarian sector. Such a plan was fully in line with Stalin's vision of agriculture as little more than a source of funding for industrial and military growth.

According to Mikoian, Stalin's rejection of the proposals from the Khrushchev commission and his demand that taxes on the peasantry be raised took place at one of the meetings of the leading group at Stalin's dacha. After hearing the leader's hard line, Khrushchev proposed—and Stalin agreed—that Malenkov and Beria be brought onto the commission to study the matter more fully.[65] Mikoian recalls that all members of the top leadership who served on the commission (Khrushchev, Malenkov, Beria, and him) believed that Stalin's instructions on raising the tax burden were simply unfeasible.[66] No working estimates on tax increases over the last weeks of Stalin's life have been discovered in the archives. Following Stalin's death, the question was swiftly buried and the new leadership undertook serious reforms of the countryside, raising procurement prices on agricultural goods and reducing taxes.

In contrast with the situation in the Gulag, the food crisis had been actively discussed at the highest circles while Stalin was alive. The transformation of the countryside carried out by his successors was thus, to a degree, the continuation of a course that had been worked out under Stalin. At the same time, it is clear that the discussion Stalin had initiated on food supplies bore little resemblance to the radical measures that would eventually be implemented. To the extent that Stalin was willing to contemplate agrarian reform—a rise in procurement prices for cattle—it was only in order to increase the supply of meat to the cities, and even this was to be at the cost of a corresponding rise in the tax burden on peasants. Stalin marked out the possibilities of reform and, to the last, his views remained unshakably conservative.

Although they nearly always left their concerns unsaid, it is likely that all of Stalin's close companions were to one degree or another aware of the underlying problems facing the country. It is reasonable to assume that the degree to which they were informed of these difficulties depended on the position they occupied in the party-state hierarchy. The dissemination of information on a "need-to-know" basis was a fixed rule at all levels of the Stalinist hierarchy. Accordingly, the leaders in possession of the highest grade information were most probably Malenkov and Beria. As Stalin's first deputy in the party, the former was privy to a very wide range of quite diverse and highly sensitive questions; the latter, on the other hand, oversaw such important sectors as the Ministry of Internal Affairs and the defense program. The high quality and range of information the two received could only have sharpened their awareness of the gravity of the situation across the country and, accordingly, inclined them to the relatively radical solutions they were to advance following Stalin's death.

Stalin and his companions were trapped in a self-perpetuating cycle of stalled reforms. Underpinning this cycle was the leader's monopoly on political initiatives. This monopoly was secured, on the one hand, by fear of the leader and, on the other, by a collective suspiciousness among Stalin's companions. In advancing a serious proposal, any member of the Politburo had to put up not only with the unpredictable nature of Stalin's reaction but with the probable aggression of his colleagues, who jealously followed each other's steps, especially if these trespassed on their own administrative responsibilities. It is in such a light that we should view the conflict between Khrushchev and Malenkov over the preparation of new policies on livestock raising.

With Stalin around, any proposals with "political" content were either completely repressed or heavily diluted before reaching the leader. Until the very end, Stalin's policy orientation remained extremely rigid, and he viewed any challenges to his long-cherished policy principles with extreme suspicion and hostility. Admittedly, in order to supply meat to the cities, Stalin agreed to raise the procurement price for cattle products, but even this came at the expense of a concomitant rise in the overall tax on the rural sector. Over the last year of his life, Stalin continued to be an unmovable roadblock to reform. It would be wrong, however, to view the dictator as little more than a stationary or an inhibiting force in this period. For a tired and aging man, he continued to show a surprising amount of energy and political enterprise in his dealings with colleagues. This would lead to a number of quite unexpected offensives during the last months of his rule.

(*Facing page*) XIX Party Congress, 5 October 1952. On the rostrum is Georgii Malenkov, who delivered the opening political report to the congress. Sitting at the presidium in the first row are Stalin, Kaganovich, Molotov, Voroshilov, Khrushchev, Beria, and Bulganin. In the second row are, from left to right: A. B. Aristov, the First Secretary of the Cheliabinsk regional party committee, who would be elected Secretary of the Central Committee after the congress; M. D. Bagirov, the First Secretary of the Azerbaijani central committee, a favorite of Stalin's who, unusually, had occupied his post as republican party chief for twenty years; O. V. Kuusinen, from the Karelian Republic; the First Secretary of the Leningrad regional party, V. M. Andrianov, one of Stalin's key agents in the Leningrad Affair; the First Secretary of the Uzbek central committee, A. I. Niiazov; the Prime Minister of Ukraine, D. S. Korotchenko; the First Secretary of the Kazakh central committee, Zh. Shaiakhmetov; and the First Secretary of the Belorussian central committee, N. S. Patolichev. In the back row are, from left to right, Stalin's aide Poskrebyshev, Mikoian, Kosygin, and Andrei Andreev. Molotov and Mikoian would be fiercely attacked by Stalin at the Central Committee plenum, which followed two days after the congress, and, in an unexpected step, neither made it to the new cabinet, the Buro of the Presidium of the Central Committee.

Stalin, speaking on the
last day of the XIX Party
Congress, 14 October 1952.
In the background
Malenkov, Beria, and
Bulganin can be seen
straining to make out
the dictator's words.

Unaltered photograph of
Stalin at the presidium of
the XIX Party Congress.
Contemporary newspapers
published retouched or old
photos of the leader, so that
it was hard to discern how
much he had aged.

6

STALIN'S LAST STRUGGLE

At the beginning of 1952, Stalin's personal physician, Professor V. N. Vinogradov, noted a marked deterioration in the leader's state of health. Despite flying into a rage and having Vinogradov dismissed, Stalin eventually came to heed his doctor's advice.[1] In the months that followed, the leader ceased smoking and further wound down his commitments. His physical condition came to be a source of concern to those around him, as the leader suffered from sudden memory losses, reduced stamina, and very sharp mood swings.[2] Some contemporaries went on to attribute the string of capricious actions that marked the last year of Stalin's life to his physical and even mental degradation. The public attacks on his oldest and most venerable colleagues, the sacking and imprisonment of his most intimate and long-serving aides, and the sudden descent of the leader into—even by his own standards—the most outlandish fits of paranoia, appeared to mark the onset of a deeply irrational state of mind.[3] Yet despite the occasional physical lapse and temper tantrum, the overall thrust of the leader's approach to rule over the last months of his life was entirely in keeping with the pattern of leadership he had established in earlier years. The aging dictator resorted to traditional—and, from his point of view, quite logical—maneuvers to keep his colleagues on their toes and to shore up his power and status despite his own uncertain health.

Over the last year of his life Stalin turned to techniques of leadership control favored earlier by the aging Lenin. Central to this approach were arrangements for a new party congress, which Stalin authorized in December 1951. The many conventions of the congress, which eventually met in October 1952, were skillfully deployed by Stalin to realign the leadership. The selection of leaders to deliver the main reports, for example, signaled the promotion of two relatively young figures, Malenkov and Khrushchev. Rather than being a purely vengeful act, Stalin's denunciation of his oldest comrades-in-arms, Molotov and Mikoian, at the post-congress plenum, was aimed at tainting those Stalin regarded as his closest rivals for the leadership, much as Lenin's "testament" had tarnished Stalin, Leon Trotsky, Lev Kamenev, and others in 1922. To add to the pressure on both groups, Stalin swelled the ranks of top leadership structures with an influx of relative unknowns, just as Lenin had proposed to draft a new generation of workers to the Central Committee thirty years earlier.

The congress afforded Stalin other opportunities for institutional restructuring. Since 1950, the Bureau of the Presidium of the Council of Ministers, which met without Stalin but attracted all other members of the Politburo, had acquired increasing institutional coherence, meeting on a near weekly basis. At the XIX Congress, Stalin brushed aside "established jurisdictions" within the state hierarchy. Flaunting his capacity to grant tasks and powers on an ad hoc basis, and to ensure personal loyalty to him rather than to any established "office," he set up entirely new spheres of competence within the party. By transferring senior political leaders from positions within the state to party bodies, he also lowered the reputation and credibility of the main Sovmin Bureau.

To this combination of organizational and personnel measures, the leader added the quintessentially Stalinist element of systematic high-level political intimidation. In the middle of 1951, he launched a purge of the Ministry of State Security. To keep his Politburo colleagues in check, he also set in motion a string of personal attacks, purges, and campaigns. While aimed primarily at specific targets, these campaigns touched on wider international tensions and threatened, in one case particularly, to engulf broader swathes of the population in a new wave of violence.

Although congress conventions allowed Stalin to realign the leadership, they also presented him with a difficulty. At earlier congresses, the keynote political report had been delivered by Stalin. In view of his weakened state of health, Stalin did not feel up to giving a long speech at such a major public occasion.[4] As an alternative, he opted to circulate a written report in advance.[5] The title of the report was to be Stalin's last major treatise, *The Economic Problems of Socialism in the USSR*, published on the eve of the congress. The work became, in effect, a surrogate chief political report and, as such, assumed the status of the main theoretical benchmark for others to follow. In tightly controlling the publication date of the work and in responding to comments on it in advance, Stalin was able to dictate the tone and policy direction of the congress.[6]

The Economic Problems
of Socialism and
the XIX Party Congress

The immediate pretext for the *Economic Problems of Socialism* was an academic debate over a textbook on political economy conducted within the premises of the Central Committee from November to December 1951. A draft had been sent to 250 academics, teachers, and economic leaders that summer. Stalin, who had over the years taken great personal interest in the textbook—and himself had rejected five earlier drafts—had bemoaned to the commission overseeing the project the lack of "fights over theoretical issues": "When the textbook is ready," he told them, "we shall place it before the court of public opinion."[7] The importance that Stalin accorded the debate was indicated by his asking his most senior party Secretary, Malenkov, to chair the sessions.[8] Rather than lasting two weeks, as originally intended, the debate ran for a month. Stalin, who was in Borzhomi for the duration of the conference, insisted on receiving summaries of the sessions nightly.

As the conference drew to a close in early December 1951, Stalin felt that he had acquired sufficient material on which he could base his own report to a party congress. With this in mind, on 4 December he telegraphed instructions to his Politburo colleagues in Moscow to convene a congress, to begin on 28 February 1952, which was to open with an "introductory speech" from the leader. Two days later, Stalin altered this formulation, choosing to delay the congress by eight months and to delete any reference to an opening speech. It was probably at this time that Stalin decided to confine his "report" to an exclusively published form. It was also at this point that Stalin resolved the key question, apparently on the minds of his Politburo colleagues, of who would deliver the political report—Malenkov—and who the report on the party rules—Khrushchev—decisions that made clear on which of his leaders he had bestowed his favor.[9]

Preparations for the congress, which were set in motion by the Politburo resolution of 7 December, subsequently followed two parallel courses. For his part, Stalin devoted himself almost entirely to writing up his "notes" to the November conference, even neglecting other tasks, such as the awarding of the Stalin prize on literature.[10] On 1 February 1952, Stalin sent a copy of his notes, which were instantly approved, to members of the Politburo. Six days later, the notes were circulated to all members of the Central Committee and to the participants of the November conference.[11] On 15 February, at a Politburo meeting attended by the sixteen coauthors of the political economy textbook, Stalin provided authoritative guidance on the content of his notes. Whereas the November discussion had included a number of innovative topics, with sessions on incentives and self-accounting, both Stalin's notes and his replies at the Politburo meeting closed off any further discussion of these themes. Although Stalin's notes were sent out with an invitation for recipients to engage Stalin in correspondence, the patent intention was that the recipients should seek "clarification" from Stalin rather than stimulate any genuine debate. Indeed, when one of the correspondents, Leonid Iaroshenko, ventured to claim authorship of one of Stalin's ideas, Voroshilov proposed, and Stalin agreed, that he be arrested.[13]

Stalin carefully stage-managed the dissemination of his work on political economy so that it should set the tone for the forthcoming congress. At the meeting with the economists on 15 February, he sidestepped their requests to have his notes published by arguing that the textbook and conference on which they were based had themselves not been published.[14] Stalin similarly dismissed a request from the chief editor of the periodical *Bol'shevik* to have his notes published; indeed, he even refused to have a paper on his notes, which had already been delivered by Shepilov in February and which had received the blessing of the Central Committee apparatus, appear in print before the congress.[15] Stalin's notes went on to form the substance of his *Economic Problems of Socialism in the USSR*, which would also include three letters, written in response to queries from correspondents.[16] In order to maximize its effects, *Economic Problems of Socialism* was published in *Pravda* on the very eve of the congress, on 3 and 4 October 1952, and it went on to structure and inform debate at the congress, much as Stalin's political reports had done at earlier congresses.

In addition to *Economic Problems of Socialism*, preparations for the congress also revolved around the bona fide reports, including the general report, the report on the party rules, and the directives on the five-year plan, which were delivered by Malenkov, Khrushchev, and Saburov, respectively. In the first instance, following the announcement of the congress in December, responsibility for gathering materials for the reports rested with the speakers themselves. On 9 June 1952, a commission under Malenkov was then set up to look into Khrushchev's draft, and two weeks later, on 23 June, a second commission, headed by Molotov, was established to look at the Saburov report.[17] Following some editing, especially, according to Khrushchev, the reduction of text by Beria, both drafts were approved by the Politburo.[18] On 15 August, for the first time in over five years, the Central Committee plenum met in full session in order to discuss arrangements for the congress.[19] In addition to approving the draft directives on the five-year plan and the new draft party rules, the plenum set up Stalin's decision not to deliver the political report by ruling that "political reports of the Central Committee at party congresses should not necessarily be delivered by the First Secretary of the Central Committee."[20] Five days later, on 20 August, *Pravda* published the draft directives on the plan and the draft party rules and finally revealed to the public that preparations were under way for a congress, which was to commence on 5 October.

Three themes dominated the XIX Party Congress. Stalin's theses were explored in Malenkov's opening political report and referred to in subsequent speeches. Unlike Khrushchev and Saburov's speeches, Malenkov's report was not referred to a commission and may have been cowritten with Stalin. Certainly, Malenkov's declaration that in the Soviet Union the "grain problem . . . has been solved, solved definitely and finally" bore the direct imprimatur of the dictator.[21] A second theme of the congress was the emphasis on vigilance, the divulgence of state secrets, and economic discipline. "A spirit of negligence has penetrated our party organizations," Malenkov announced.

> There are cases of party, economic, Soviet, and other executives relaxing their vigilance and failing to see what is going on around them; there are cases of the divulgence of party and state secrets. Some people occupying responsible positions . . . forget that we are still in a capitalist encirclement, that enemies of the Soviet state are working persistently to smuggle their agents into our country and to utilize unstable elements in Soviet society for their own malignant ends.[22]

In accordance with the heightened emphasis on watchfulness, new provisions were inserted into the party rules on observing party and state discipline, on reporting errant officials, on adhering to the new rules on secrecy, and on vigilance.[23]

In its emphasis on vigilance and in the attention it lavished on Stalin's *Economic Problems of Socialism*, the congress moved in a direction that pleased Stalin. The tributes to Stalin's volume flattered the leader, while the attacks on "enemies of the Soviet state" set the scene for a post-congress purge. Stalin may, however, have been indifferent toward the third theme of the congress, the need to resurrect the democratic structures of the party. This issue had been highlighted in the run-up to the congress and received ample support at the congress itself. Several speeches emphasized the qualities of collegiality, the need for "political" as opposed to "economic" leadership, and closer ties between the party apparatus and the rank and file.[24] As with the emphasis on vigilance, the stress on the party's democratic credentials found expression in the new party rules, which, among other things, insisted that regional and district party plenums meet more often, enjoined party members to "develop criticism and self-criticism," and insisted that aktivs, subgroups of party enthusiasts, be formed in all district and city organizations and that they be convened "not for show and celebratory approval of decisions, but for genuine discussion."[25]

Following several days' absence, Stalin appeared at the congress on the very last day, 14 October. Ending speculation among delegates as to whether he would address the congress, he delivered a short oration, whose every paragraph was greeted with a round of prolonged, rapturous applause. "We all reached the conclusion," recalled Khrushchev, "about how physically weak he must be feeling if reading out a speech of seven minutes should have presented him with such improbable difficulties."[26] It would, however, be unwise to read too much into Stalin's faltering performance at the congress. While the leader suffered from chronic fatigue, he could still muster the energy and confidence to dominate a more intimate and better-known audience.

Countersuccession:
The Leninist Legacy

Two days after his congress speech, on 16 October, Stalin spoke, without notes, to the Central Committee for over an hour and a half, in terms displaying his "characteristic iron logic."[27] One feature of this address, which attracted the attention of the writer Konstantin Simonov, was the fact that Stalin "did not speak about himself, instead he spoke of Lenin, of his fearlessness in the face of any circumstances."[28] The reference to Lenin was neither accidental nor entirely an act of modesty. As Stalin neared his own death, he took every measure to stifle the aspirations of what he regarded as his closest challengers for the leadership. In this he appears to have followed—possibly quite consciously—Lenin's approach to succession.

Stalin followed two courses of action which had been pioneered by Lenin. The first involved enlarging the top committees of the party and filling them with new blood. Much as Lenin had advised in his testament of December 1922, Stalin increased the membership of the Central Committee, in this instance by over two-thirds.[29] Arguably of greater significance was the expansion of the Politburo which, under the pretext of a merger with the now dissolved Orgburo, came to be known as the "Presidium." From a membership of nine full members and two candidates elected at the XVIII Congress, the new Presidium would have twenty-five full members and eleven candidates. While this expansion has been attributed to the "job-slot" system, whereby those occupying senior positions in the economy, the armed services, and other branches of state administration were given ex officio representation on the party's top committees,[30] a less charitable explanation appears to be more convincing. By bringing in a new cohort of younger, relatively unknown figures as potential leaders, Stalin was placing the more senior incumbents under pressure. A year before the congress, Stalin had threatened his senior colleagues: "You have grown old, I shall replace you!" By swelling the ranks of the cabinet, Stalin made the senior leaders feel that much more expendable. "If, say, out of twenty-five people," recalled Mikoian, "five or six vanish in between congresses, it will not be viewed as a major change. If the same five or six disappear from a group of nine Politburo members, then that would be noticed."[31] The proceedings of the October plenum confirmed these suspicions. Ahead of the plenum, Stalin had dispensed with the consultative session of the Politburo which had traditionally preceded Central Committee meetings. At the plenum itself, he took out a sheet of paper on which were typed the names of the thirty-six-man Presidium, as well as of a nine-man Presidium Buro that he had selected on his own. Brushing aside a Politburo convention, Stalin now even did away with the pretense that the most powerful committee in the country would be chosen collectively.[32]

The second Leninist legacy that Stalin honored was to blacken the names of his political rivals. The similarity of tone and phrasing between Stalin's assessment of his heirs-apparent and Lenin's is striking. In his testament of 1922, Lenin had famously expressed his reservations about his likely successors: Nikolai Bukharin, he wrote, had been too "scholastic," Georgii Piatakov had "too much zeal . . . for the administrative side of his work," Lev Kamenev and Grigorii Zinoviev's "October episode" had, "of course, [been] no accident," Trotsky displayed "excessive self-confidence," while it was far from clear to Lenin whether the young Stalin "would always be capable of using [his] authority with sufficient caution."[33] In a conversation with his own ruling circle, most probably some time in 1950, Stalin had followed suit.

> Who will we appoint chairman of the Council of Ministers after me? Beria? No, he is not Russian, but Georgian. Khrushchev? No, he is a worker, we need someone more educated. Malenkov? No, he can only follow someone else's lead. Kaganovich? No, he won't do, for he is not Russian but a Jew. Molotov? No, he has already aged, he won't cope. Voroshilov? No, he is really not up to it. Saburov? Pervukhin? These people are only fit for secondary roles. There is only one person left and that is Bulganin.[34]

In fact, although Stalin had indeed promoted Bulganin as the sole First Deputy Chair of the Council of Ministers in April 1950, Bulganin's appeal lay in his predictability and trustworthiness as a functionary; he patently lacked the qualities of a potential leader and, as such, did not pose a serious threat to Stalin. By the spring of 1951, Bulganin had, in any case, lost this position.

As Lenin had done, Stalin cast doubt on the leadership qualities of his potential successors. In the preceding years, Stalin had regularly trampled on the ambitions of Politburo members while cultivating their dependence on his own stewardship. "He liked to repeat to us," Khrushchev recalled, "You are blind like kittens, without me the imperialists will throttle you."[35] He saved, however, his most venomous remarks for those he regarded as his closest challengers for the leadership. Out of the enlarged new Presidium, Stalin had created a Buro of the Presidium consisting of nine members. The fact that Stalin's two most senior lieutenants—Molotov and Mikoian—were left out of this buro was no accident. Stalin regarded these two, and in particular the former, as his most formidable challengers. Certainly, Stalin's relentless attacks on Molotov since the war had already taken their toll on Molotov's standing at the highest levels. "If we, people of the prewar generation," Khrushchev wrote, "had earlier viewed Molotov as the future leader of the country, who might replace Stalin when he died, now this was out of the question. At every meeting Stalin attacked Molotov and Mikoian, he 'laid into them.' "[36] A leading functionary from the Council of Ministers similarly recalls: "Although the 'people' (narod) continued to view [Molotov] as the second leader after Stalin, his influence on affairs in the country had waned before our eyes."[37] At the same time, ever conscious of Molotov's standing in the country, Stalin now felt impelled to finish off the leadership prospects of a man still regarded as his natural heir by the public at large.[38]

After the XIX Party Congress, Stalin decided to share his misgivings about Molotov with a wider audience. To the astonishment of the whole of the Central Committee, Stalin openly accused Molotov of cowardice, capitulationism and, critically, of personal betrayal. These accusations were all the more astonishing for the fact that they ran against the widely held perception of Molotov as Stalin's most firm and unbending follower. Although Stalin had privately hurled accusations at Molotov before, this, in Khrushchev's words, was no longer "a conversation at a dinner table among five to seven people."[39] According to Konstantin Simonov, the audience was aghast. "It was so unexpected that at the beginning I did not believe my own ears; I thought perhaps I had misheard, or had not fully understood." The Politburo figures seated immediately behind Stalin were stunned, with faces that had "turned into stone, had become tense and motionless."[40]

To some extent, Stalin appears to have let his emotions get the better of him. Simonov speaks of Stalin talking in such a "rage" that it "sometimes even seemed as if he had lost control."[41] Nevertheless, the length and "iron logic" of Stalin's attack on Molotov suggest that it contained a strong element of calculation, while the content of the attack provided some indication of Stalin's motivations. Stalin's charges centered on Molotov's misconduct in the autumn of 1945, when he had stood in for Stalin, which was precisely the time that rumors had surfaced in Moscow of Molotov succeeding Stalin as leader.[42] This was something that Stalin could not easily forget, and it was a memory that reemerged with particular vigor now that Stalin had aged and become physically weak. Repeated private humiliations of Molotov since the late 1940s therefore did not prevent Stalin from unleashing a more public frontal attack on Molotov in 1952.

The mauling of Molotov was followed by a savage attack on Mikoian, supported by charges that dated from the same period, including the "business with Lozovsky," which had now become all the more pertinent since Lozovsky had been executed for counterrevolutionary crimes two months earlier, on 12 August.[43] In a manner reminiscent of the 1930s, Stalin went on to accuse the two of right-wing deviations and, according to one source, he even went on to talk of a "split" within the leadership, with Molotov pursuing an anti-Leninist position and Mikoian a Trotskyist one.[44] With this, both Molotov and Mikoian were cursed and, in the months that followed, the two were, in effect, thrown out of the ruling circle.[45]

Redrawing the Boundaries

As well as striking out at individual Politburo leaders, Stalin erected fresh organizational structures and shunted colleagues to new positions. In redrawing jurisdictions and in switching Politburo members between them, Stalin reminded his colleagues, some of whom may have been lulled into a shallow sense of bureaucratic security, that their primary allegiance was to the ruler and not to their "office."

Three main organizational reforms were implemented at the time of the XIX Congress. The first concerned the organization of the internal party bureaucracy. The doubling of Secretaries (from five to ten) and the new division of responsibilities at the Secretariat reflected the impulse of the congress to activate the party and to highlight the distinctive "political" role of the party bureaucracy, in contrast to the more specialized and technocratic functions of state, ministerial, and economic bureaucracies. In the aftermath of the congress, all Secretaries, with the exclusion of Stalin, were assigned specific "political" roles and, in order to accommodate the rise in party-based business generated by the congress, all ten were invited to a succession of cabinet meetings.[46] At a meeting of the Presidium on 18 October and, then, two days later, of Secretaries at Stalin's office, the party's traditional role in cadre selection and ideology was underscored. To this end, a new department for the selection and assignment of cadres was established, with a wider remit than its predecessor.[47] In addition, two Secretaries were now assigned to oversee ideology—Suslov, who was to take overall charge of this field, and Nikolai Mikhailov, who was to head a revitalized agitation and propaganda department.[48] In order to spread the lessons of the congress to the provinces, three of the Secretaries—Suslov, Ignatov, and Ponomarenko—were to visit the republics and regions.[49]

The second major organizational innovation was the formation of three standing Presidium commissions. The largest, with a membership of fifteen, was the commission on foreign affairs under Malenkov, which was to supervise the Ministry of Foreign Affairs, the Ministry of External Trade, and other agencies that had dealings with international organizations.[50] A second commission, under Bulganin, with a membership of eleven, was entrusted with overseeing the ministries of defense and of military-naval affairs and other activities relating to military-industrial production.[51] The third and smallest of the Presidium commissions, with a membership of five, was the ideology commission. First under the leadership of Shepilov and then under his replacement, A. M. Rumiantsev, the ideology commission was asked to improve the work of the party's journals, most notably *Kommunist*, and to raise the theoretical level of cultural journals such as *Novyi mir* and *Znamia*.[52]

All the commissions were active prior to Stalin's death, with the commission on external affairs convening eighteen times, and both the defense and ideology commissions meeting eleven times.[53] Their chief significance, however, lay in shifting policy-making authority away from the Council of Ministers, from which Stalin had been estranged since the war. Since the end of 1949, the main Sovmin Bureau in its near weekly meetings had allowed the most senior Politburo members to confer and to discuss—in Stalin's absence—matters of national importance, including, as of 1950, a variety of top-level secret issues. In doing this, it had been served by several sectoral bureaus consisting of experts, who could advise it on the finer points of policy making.[54] In establishing entirely new institutions—the Presidium commissions—Stalin severed the ties of leading political figures to Sovmin and set up parallel authoritative policy-making and supervisory bodies at the Central Committee.[55] On 10 November, the Bureau of the Presidium ruled that Malenkov, who needed to concentrate on his duties at the Central Committee, had been "freed from his obligations as Deputy Chair of the Council of Ministers, and from his duties as a member of the Bureau of the Presidium and of the Presidium of Sovmin." Two other rising stars who had been members of the Sovmin Bureau, Bulganin and Khrushchev, were also relieved of their responsibilities there.[56] Henceforth, save for one meeting on 21 November, none of the three attended any sessions of the Bureau of the Presidium of Sovmin, which hitherto had been the most powerful committee in government. In the following days and weeks, all three of the new Presidium commissions were bolstered with an influx of service staff from the Council of Ministers.[58] Thus, Stalin reallocated resources and leading personnel from the previously formidable Bureau of the Council of Ministers to new cabinet structures within the Central Committee.

The third and most significant organizational reform was the creation of the Buro of the Presidium of the Central Committee, to act as an executive committee for the new Presidium. In violation of established norms, Stalin had not consulted the existing Politburo on the composition of the new Buro but, instead, read out a self-prepared list directly at the post-congress plenum on 16 October 1952. In setting up the Presidium Buro, Stalin was almost certainly mindful of the parallel Sovmin Bureau. Apart from the fact that it replicated the exact title of the Presidium Bureau at Sovmin,[59] the membership of the new party Buro was almost identical to that of the Sovmin Bureau that had met over the previous months.[60] The exceptions, however, were significant. In accordance with his charges at the plenum, the Politburo veterans Molotov and Mikoian were dropped from the new Buro.[61] More significantly, whereas Stalin had never presided over sessions of the Sovmin Bureau, he chaired and directly controlled all meetings of the new Presidium Buro. With the creation of the new Buro at the Central Committee Presidium, the balance between the executive committees of party and state was transformed.[62] In addition to forcing three of the most dynamic and upwardly mobile of leaders, Malenkov, Khrushchev, and Bulganin, to surrender their ties to the Sovmin Bureau, Stalin saw to it that the Presidium Buro, whose predecessor, the ruling group of the Politburo, had recently shrunk to a rump of five leaders, was regenerated with the addition of new members, regular meetings, and a stable workload.[63] Waving aside existing jurisdictions, Stalin, in setting up the Presidium Buro, altered the institutional allegiance of his subordinates and regained direct control over his heirs-apparent.

The Doctors' Plot

The last year of Stalin's life witnessed the unfurling of a complex net of crosscutting purges. The key to interpreting the progress of these "plots" was Stalin's absolute need to maintain control of the security agencies. To the very end, Stalin insisted that the instruments of repression—and in particular the Ministry of State Security and its administration for investigating especially important cases—be directly subordinate to him. He regularly dictated the questions investigators put to "suspects" and routinely reviewed transcripts of the interrogations.[64] According to the code of the time, "subordination of the Ministry of State Security to the Central Committee"—a phrase often used, especially during interrogations—meant the ministry's direct accountability to Stalin.[65] Even as the leader's stamina had begun to wane, and certain matters of national importance were referred elsewhere, he always made time to read interrogation reports.

The convulsions that rocked the security agencies over the latter part of Stalin's life had their origins in the MGB Affair of July 1951. It is likely that one of the reasons for Abakumov's arrest that month had been his inability to make charges stick against members of the Jewish Anti-Fascist Committee (EAK), who had been held in custody for over two years.[66] What, however, appears to have particularly incensed Stalin was the claim that Abakumov had obstructed a parallel investigation into the activities of the "Jewish nationalist" doctor, Iakov Etinger.[67] Following Abakumov's removal, Stalin had the "medical connection" pursued with fervor. On the basis of a Politburo resolution of 11 July, a special group of investigators was set up to examine case histories of patients at the Kremlin hospital, as well as to go over the activities of all doctors who had at any one time served at the Kremlin medical center.[68] To carry out these tasks, Stalin would rely on a fresh team at the security police which included the new minister, Ignat'ev; a new deputy minister, Goglidze; and, most important, the new head of the administration for investigating especially important cases, Abakumov's nemesis Mikhail Riumin.[69]

Stalin's relationship with the security organs from the summer of 1951 onward reveals, on the one hand, the ruler's susceptibility to fantasies, but, on the other, the pragmatic calculations that continued to guide his relations with the leadership. Beginning in the summer of 1951, Stalin for three months was fed with a stream of fantastic allegations by Riumin on a network of Jewish conspiracies, which had footholds in the worlds of culture, the medical profession, and the security organs. This clearly played into Stalin's own views, for on 19 October, Riumin was rewarded for his efforts with promotion to deputy Minister of State Security.[70] It was at around this time that Stalin gave Riumin license to arrest a number of senior MGB officials, beginning with those directly involved in the Etinger case, but eventually embracing all Jewish department chiefs at the MGB as well as two former deputy ministers, N. N. Selivanovskii and E. P. Pitovranov.[71] On 12 February 1952, Abakumov's own case was transferred from the Procuracy to Riumin's jurisdiction at the security police.[72] At the same time, Riumin followed a second line of inquiry, which had been opened in the summer, into the conspiratorial activities of Jewish doctors. Focusing on one of the defendants in the ongoing case against the Jewish Anti-Fascist Committee, the doctor Boris Shimeliovich, Riumin made inquiries about Jewish physicians in Shimeliovich's circle who had treated Kremlin officials.[73] As with the arrest of MGB officials, this, too, appeared to have Stalin's blessing. Hence the same Politburo resolution that transferred the Abakumov case to the MGB also gave Riumin the authority to look into a potential criminal plot between "doctor-wreckers" and their protectors at the MGB. Evidence on these lines of inquiry was presented to Stalin on 9 April.[74] The investigative front was given further momentum on 13 March, two weeks before the preliminary investigation into the EAK case drew to a close, when a decision was taken to launch inquiries into the activities of 213 individuals whose names had come up in the course of investigations for the forthcoming EAK trial.[75]

While appearing to indulge in his fantasies, Stalin's underlying approach toward Riumin was at all times coldly pragmatic: what he sought from Riumin was serviceable evidence that he could present to his Politburo colleagues. Although the trial of the members of the Jewish Anti-Fascist Committee eventually took place from May to July 1952, leading to the execution of all but one of their number on 12 August, investigations into the broader "conspiracies" proceeded slowly. Apart from confessions from the clearly insane Shwartzman, by September 1952, Riumin had obtained little in the way of convincing testimony. "In September 1952," Riumin later recalled during an interrogation, "Ignat'ev reproached me for the fact that our information from the investigations paled by comparison with that which had been supplied by Abakumov . . . and he repeatedly emphasized that if we did not obtain the necessary testimonies from the arrested Jewish doctors, then we would both be dismissed and maybe even arrested."[76] When, at around this time, the evidence of a conspiracy under Abakumov collected by Riumin was presented to the deputy head of the administration for especially important cases, Sokolov, the latter "shrugged his shoulders and said that although in the dossier there was talk of a group, there was not, as far as he could tell, any evidence or testimonies to show that such an anti-Soviet group in fact existed."[77] "Stalin's imagined plots did not," concludes the historian Kiril Stoliarov, "deprive him of his shrewdness, and all the charges had to be supported by more or less convincing evidence."[78] In desperation, Riumin threw all he had into exposing the MGB Affair in the early autumn of 1952, but he failed to come up with any corroborating materials and, on 14 November, was fired.[79]

At the end of 1952, Stalin could indeed dispense with Riumin's limited talents. The special investigation group set up a year earlier to examine the personal histories and attitudes of doctors who had served at the Kremlin hospital had now begun to yield fruitful leads. Availing themselves of all undercover and surveillance information, the group had accumulated a wealth of incriminating materials against leading physicians, including charges that some had led decadent lives, held anti-Soviet views, or concealed ties to or sympathies for landowners, Socialist Revolutionaries, and Jewish nationalists. Especially damaging was the accusation that leading doctors had incorrectly diagnosed and treated the serious heart conditions of the Politburo members Andrei Zhdanov and A. S. Shcherbakov.[80] The central piece of evidence here was the claim from a former cardiogram specialist, Lydia Timashuk, who had visited the Lubianka twice over the summer, that the doctors P. I. Egorov, Vinogradov, and G. I. Maiorov had forced her to change her reading of a cardiogram for Zhdanov, with fatal consequences.[81]

The first step against the doctors was the removal of Egorov as head of the medical administration of the Kremlin on 1 September 1952.[82] With Stalin's permission, the arrests of over twenty-five physicians soon followed, including of Professor Egorov himself on 18 October, Stalin's own consultant Professor Vinogradov on 4 November, and Professor M. S. Vovsi on 11 November.[83] It appears that some time toward the end of November, after Riumin's dismissal, Ignat'ev presented Stalin with a report based on findings from the interrogations of the doctors.[84] This report would prove to be critical in two respects. First, it gave Stalin a foundation—however rudimentary—for directing public attention to the Jewish origins of the doctors. "Initially," the pathologist Iakov Rapoport has written, "the Doctors' Plot had no nationalistic coloring; both Russian and Jewish doctors were implicated."[85] Soon, however, the anti-Semitic orientation of Stalin's position became unmistakable. "Jewish nationalists," he told a session of the Presidium on 1 December, "believe that their nation has been saved by the United States (there they can become rich, bourgeois, and so on). They believe they are obliged to the Americans. Among the doctors there are many Jewish nationalists."[86]

Second, the Ignat'ev report allowed Stalin to be far bolder in drawing a connection between the "doctors' conspiracy" and the MGB Affair. Spotting a link between the doctors who had reportedly misdiagnosed Zhdanov and the then head of the MGB, Abakumov, Stalin commented: "[Zhdanov] did not simply die, he was killed by Abakumov."[87] Agendas of high-level meetings were structured to reflect the ties between the two investigations. When the Presidium convened from 1–4 December, the first day of its proceedings was dominated by two items, "On wrecking in the Doctors' Affair" and "Information on the situation at the USSR Ministry of State Security" which, by the last day, had merged into a single item, "On the situation in the MGB and on wrecking in the Doctors' Affair."[88] Following the Ignat'ev report, Stalin also moved in a new direction by openly implicating Western intelligence agencies in the plot. Riumin's replacement as head of the administration for investigating especially important cases, Goglidze, was charged by Stalin with uncovering evidence of an international terrorist network sponsored by Western states. On 4 December, Goglidze presented the Presidium with evidence of these connections, which led to a resolution on the need to find the "organizers" of the Doctors'

Plot.[89] At the same time, the resolution of 4 December also ruled that it was a "most important and pressing task of the party and of leading party agencies to gain control of the Ministry of State Security."[90] As had been the case in the 1930s, submitting the security police to the "control of the party" meant, in effect, placing it under the authority of agents personally designated by the ruler.

At the October plenum, Stalin had breached Politburo protocol by airing his suspicions of Molotov and Mikoian before a rather wide audience. At the December meeting of the Presidium, he did the same with the Doctors' Plot by removing the matter from his inner circle and presenting it to a broader group.[91] The next step was to bring the Doctors' Plot to the public domain. To do this, Stalin charged four senior officials with pushing the campaign forward. The first two were party Secretaries, Suslov and Mikhailov, while the second two, Dmitrii Chesnokov and Shepilov had, over the autumn, taken on press positions of special responsibility, the latter as chief editor of the party daily, *Pravda*.[92] It was a measure of the importance of these individuals that the first three had been made full members of the nominal cabinet, the Presidium, in October.

Typically, Stalin aimed to swing his ideological apparatus into action by applying pressure on his agents and by playing them off against one another. On 24 December, *Pravda* carried an article, ostensibly by Suslov, but commissioned and edited by Stalin, on the errors of the former deputy head of Agitprop, P. N. Fedoseev.[93] The charges against Fedoseev were convoluted in the extreme, but they served as a rough pretext for publishing, for the first time, the whole of the Central Committee decree, "On *Bol' shevik*," of 13 July 1949.[94] Its publication significantly raised the stakes surrounding the ongoing debate on Stalin's book, *Economic Problems of Socialism*, by tying it to the purges of 1949.[95] Those holding "unmarxist" views were now openly associated with the work of one of the victims of the 1949 purges, Nikolai Voznesenskii.[96] The article also increased the pressure on those officials attacked in the 1949 decree who still held senior positions. These included the new editor of *Pravda*, Shepilov, who, as head of Agitprop in 1949, had been explicitly reprimanded in the final section of the decree.[97] Printing the decree enabled Stalin to step up the heat on his own ideological apparatus.

Leaning on the editor of *Pravda* proved fruitful at the beginning of 1953, as Stalin sought to make public his allegations against the doctors. On 9 January, Stalin sent members of the Presidium Buro a draft press bulletin, dictated by him, breaking the news that a "group of terrorist doctors" had "made it their goal, by means of sabotage, to curtail the lives of Soviet leaders."[98] In graphic language, it described how one group of "doctor-murderers" and "monsters in human form" had served the international Jewish bourgeois-nationalist organization Joint, while another had been "long-standing agents of the British security service." Stalin also decided that the affair deserved greater prominence than that afforded it by the appearance of a TASS notice on the inside pages of the national papers. Accordingly, he ordered Shepilov to compose a lead article for *Pravda* to accompany the bulletin, which Stalin then heavily edited.[99] Stalin's amendments revealed the leader's continued fondness for the purge formulations of the 1930s. Labels such as "enemies" and "enemies of the people" were prodigiously inserted in Stalin's hand, while those foes referred to by Shepilov as "opportunists" were now, in a politically symbolic move reminiscent of earlier times, labeled by Stalin "*right* opportunists."[100]

The eventual publication of the lead article and the bulletin on the pages of *Pravda* and other national papers on 13 January 1953 triggered members of Stalin's ideology team into action. On 21 January, Mikhailov delivered a keynote speech warning of spies and murderers and drawing the attention of his audience, in line with Stalin's own amendments, to "live persons" and "hidden enemies of our people."[101] Three days later, the new coeditor of *Kommunist*, Chesnokov, gave a talk on the intensification of the class struggle at a meeting of the Institute of Philosophy.[102] In what appeared to be an oblique swipe at the recently discredited members of the Politburo, Molotov and Mikoian, a January article in *Kommunist* touched on Stalin's recent injunction against "right opportunists": "Leninism," wrote Chesnokov, "teaches that the imperialists cannot be 'appeased' by minor concessions as suggested by various liberals, who have broken with the theory of the class struggle and descended into right-wing opportunism."[103] Further, in a development that corresponded closely to the pre-purge practices of the 1930s, Chesnokov and Shepilov also set about soliciting signatures from respected and ostensibly "loyal" members of the Jewish intelligentsia for an open letter endorsing the campaign against the "spy group of doctor-murderers."[104]

According to some observers, the attacks on the doctors were to lead to a show trial. Others have argued that plans were afoot to deport large numbers of Jews from western industrial cities to special camps in Birobidzhan and other closed zones in Siberia, much as Chechens, Kalmyks, Ingush, Balkartsy, and other ethnic groups had been "cleansed" and relocated during the war.[105] The archival evidence, however, tends to lean against both hypotheses. Unlike the geographically concentrated ethnic groups that had been deported earlier, the Jews were socially and geographically assimilated and, as such, deporting them would have presented incalculable logistical problems. Certainly, no preparatory documents for such an operation have ever been uncovered. Amidst the tens of thousands of incriminatory documents unearthed to discredit Stalin in the late 1950s and the communist system as a whole in the 1990s, no instructions or directives sanctioning or preparing for such a deportation have ever been found.[106] Similarly, the archival evidence does not lend support to the view that Stalin was preparing a show trial for the doctors. Indeed, at the beginning of February 1953, Stalin rejected as too sharp a hard-line letter from loyal Soviet Jews attacking the actions of the plotters, which some have viewed as a scene-setter for such a trial.[107] Certainly, both a show trial and a mass deportation would have been out of keeping with Stalin's behavior in the postwar period. Since the war, Stalin had spurned any show trials, preferring to have even Voznesenskii and Kuznetsov convicted at a secret hearing. In contrast to the mass expulsions of ethnic groups of the war and prewar periods, which ran into the hundreds of thousands, after the war Stalin had opted for surgical, targeted operations on a far more limited scale.

In keeping the security police on a tight leash and in placing the ideological apparatus on alert, Stalin's maneuvers over his last few months did not depart significantly from earlier patterns of behavior. Even so, Stalin's actions in this period did cross conventions and violate bonds he had honored for over twenty-five years. Here, Stalin's ailing health may have played a role. While neither the archives nor memoirs give us a full picture of the events of this period, they do suggest that relations between the leader and his entourage were heading toward new, uncharted territories.

Stalin at the Edge

Already an ill man, from the summer of 1952 onward, Stalin became more prone to bouts of frustration and ill temper. For this reason, he may have become less willing to abide by traditional, self-imposed restraints. In private, the leader had, for years, tossed anti-Semitic quips at his colleagues or launched into wild accusations against his erstwhile comrades, Molotov and Mikoian. Now, to the astonishment of those around him, he had assailed two of his closest allies and indulged in an open rant against the Jews in the semipublic forum of the Central Committee Presidium. In the past, Stalin had been careful to keep his dealings with the security police behind closed doors, meeting with investigators and police ministers alone in the privacy of his office. Now, recalled Khrushchev, Stalin phoned Ignat'ev, the security minister, and would "speak to him in our presence, going off his head, wailing and threatening that he would grind him to dust. He demanded that the doctors be relentlessly beaten, that they be mercilessly thrashed and put in chains."[108]

Stalin's relationship with his colleagues was such that while he was alive, there could not have been any hint of outright opposition to his leadership. To the end, his management of the security police and of the ideological apparatus remained complete and unchallenged. Nonetheless, it appears that by the beginning of 1952, the leader had truly begun to feel his age.[109] In the past, Stalin had made a point of presiding over all meetings of the Politburo while he was in Moscow and of rejecting any reference to others "presiding over" cabinet meetings in his absence. In a break with this precedent, the Buro of the Presidium resolved on 10 November 1952 that "in case of the absence of comrade Stalin, chairmanship over meetings of the Buro of the Presidium and of the Presidium of the Central Committee be carried out by comrades Malenkov, Khrushchev, and Bulganin," and that these three be given the right "to consider and to decide on current issues."[110] This formalization of contingency arrangements for taking charge of cabinet meetings was a marked break with tradition. Further, although Stalin would attend all seven formal meetings of the Presidium Buro prior to his death, he did not, again in a break with tradition, attend an impromptu meeting of the Buro on 9 January 1953.[111]

Stalin was also less able to extend himself to fields that traditionally had been within his domain. By contrast with the attentiveness to matters of high-level international diplomacy which he had shown only months earlier, by the end of December 1952 it took Stalin ten days to reply to a telegram from Mao Tse-tung.[112] At this time, Stalin was also forced to neglect another favorite area, the selection of cadres. Scholars had formerly assumed that Stalin appointed little known figures with few ties to other leaders to the cadres apparatus in order to have his own people take charge of a future purge.[113] In fact, the most powerful cadres section in the party bureaucracy was to be the new department for the selection and assignment of cadres, set up after the XIX Congress, to oversee the most senior party and state appointments. The new head of this department was N. M. Pegov who, far from being in any sense an "independent," was closely tied to Malenkov, with whom he had worked for over four years.[114] It was a measure of Pegov's overall responsibility on the cadres side that he, along with Suslov (ideology) and Malenkov (general leadership), were the Secretaries in whose hands, according to a decision of the Buro of the Presidium of 17 November 1952, chairmanship of the Secretariat was to be rotated.[115]

In fact, there appears to have been a more general shift in the upper reaches of the party bureaucracy away from Stalin's direct control. Traditionally, the work of the Politburo had been processed through the special sector which, under Poskrebyshev's leadership, had, in effect become Stalin's personal staff.[116] The special sector continued to function after the XIX Congress,[117] but increasingly had to compete with the new general department, some of whose functions appeared to overlap with its own.[118] The apparatus of the cabinet was no longer Stalin's personal preserve. On

10 November 1952, the Presidium Buro for the first time assigned a member of the leadership, Khrushchev, to focus on the organization of the Buro,[119] thereby giving him the chance to intercede in the mechanics of the cabinet bureaucracy. Stalin also appears to have dispensed with the services of his long-standing aide and the head of the special sector, Poskrebyshev, a month or so before his death.[120] The loss of what had been, for over twenty years, a key functional relationship with a top leading aide could not but have complicated Stalin's lines of control over the key gatekeeping functions of the cabinet apparatus.

In focusing his attention on some areas, such as the agencies of repression and ideology, Stalin had less time and energy to spend on other activities. Following the transfer of leading personnel from Sovmin to Presidium commissions in October 1952, a primary area of neglect, as it had been since the war, was the Council of Ministers. Although the Presidium and the Bureau of the Presidium of Sovmin were, according to a ruling of 10 November 1952, to be jointly chaired by Beria, Saburov, and Pervukhin,[121] Beria took advantage of Stalin's distractions elsewhere to hijack the Council of Ministers for his own ends. Organizing sessions of the Sovmin Presidium and the Bureau of the Presidium without consulting either of his co-chairs, Beria also structured agendas, canceled voting, and steered pecuniary rewards, in the form of prizes, pensions, and the awarding of flats and country houses, toward his own clients.[122] According to the head of the chancellery of the Council of Ministers, M. T. Pomaznev, Beria distanced and elevated his own personal secretariat over that of the Sovmin chancellery, and by allowing his own aides to summon and order around Sovmin officials, he in effect usurped the bureaucratic authority of Sovmin and vested it in his own people.[123]

Although they showed no inkling of rebellion, Stalin's colleagues did privately begin to question his judgment. From the early summer of 1952 on, there was, according to Malenkov's aide, Sukhanov, a feeling in the Central Committee that Stalin was in decline and one of growing incredulity and disbelief over some of his allegations.[124] " 'I can tell you,' " Bulganin would reveal to the Central Committee plenum in June 1953, " 'that even while Stalin was alive, we, the members of the Presidium, among ourselves, it must be owned, said that the Doctors' Plot is a forgery. Even when Stalin was alive, we said this to ourselves. Isn't that right, comrades?' . . . Voices from the Presidium: 'Yes, that's right.' "[125] According to another version, mild reservations over some aspects of the Doctors' Plot were even voiced at meetings of the Presidium; certainly errors of detail by Stalin did not help convince his colleagues of the veracity of the accusations.[126] It appears, too, that Stalin's allegations against Molotov and Mikoian were met with deep unease by his colleagues. Certainly, Stalin's displeasure toward Mikoian and Molotov had virtually no bearing on the attitudes of other top leaders toward the two, who were covertly told of leadership meetings even after Stalin's onslaught at the October plenum.[127]

The strength of these reservations was underlined by the speed with which Stalin's steps against Molotov and Mikoian and concerning the Doctors' Plot were reversed after his death. Even while the leader was still technically alive, the veteran leaders were invited to all four meetings of the Presidium Buro on 2 and 3 March to discuss Stalin's health, and both were included on the ten-man presidium at the joint meeting of the Presidium and the Central Committee on 5 March.[128] Indeed, at the June 1953 plenum, both Malenkov and Khrushchev openly attacked Stalin's October onslaught against Molotov and Mikoian.[129] Similarly, a couple of days after Stalin's death, the investigations against the doctors were effectively terminated.[130]

Despite their reservations, there is no evidence that any members of the leadership took any steps to stop Stalin. His hold over his colleagues was such that faced with a decision to expel Molotov or Mikoian from the party, his inner circle would almost certainly have complied. Notwithstanding their concerns over the Doctors' Plot, all members of the Presidium Buro signed the resolution of 9 January on publication of the news release on the plot. We may indeed be permitted a measure of skepticism when we read Khrushchev's reflections on this period: "I believe that we, members of the Presidium, did too little at the end of 1952. I reproach myself for that. We should have shown more decisiveness at the time, and not allowed this wild campaign to go on."[131]

On the evening of 28 February 1953, Stalin stayed on late at the Kremlin to watch a film and then invited four members of his inner circle for a drink at his dacha, where they stayed until about 4:00 A.M. Unusually, over the following day, 1 March, the leader did not call on his domestic staff. At 10:30 P.M. the assistant warden of the dacha, bringing in the mail, found Stalin lying on the floor. Malenkov and Beria, who were the first to be informed, arrived at 3:00 A.M. on 2 March, followed by Khrushchev at 7:30 A.M., and a group of doctors an hour later, who announced that the leader had suffered a brain hemorrhage.[132] On this news, the ruling circle quickly swung into action, convening a meeting of the Buro of the Presidium at noon that day.[133] On 3 March, Stalin's doctors informed the ruling group that the leader had no hope of a recovery, and the following morning a radio bulletin on Stalin's health was broadcast.[134] By 8:00 P.M. on 5 March, while Stalin was technically still alive (he died at 9:50 P.M.), the ruling group had convened a joint session of the Presidium and of the Central Committee, and the process of jockeying for position in the post-Stalin leadership had begun in earnest.[135]

Within a few months of Stalin's death, amidst the rough and tumble of the succession struggle, memories had begun to fade of how, until only recently, Stalin had kept his companions in a psychological vice. Yet keeping his colleagues in line is exactly what, over the last phase of his life, Stalin had managed to do. To achieve this he had resorted to what, for him, were a number of quite traditional strategies. By way of his *Economic Problems of Socialism in the USSR* he had single-handedly dominated the ideological content of the XIX Party Congress. Immediately after the congress, he had carved out new jurisdictions and offices at the Council of Ministers and at the Central Committee and moved leading politicians from office to office like marionettes. To the very end, even in the context of worsening food shortages, he had blocked any talk of serious policy reform in agriculture or, indeed, in any other policy realm. Finally, barely two months before his death, he unleashed a vicious campaign against the "doctor-murderers," which he forced all his cabinet colleagues to sign up to. Shakily pulling the levers of the last section of the party-state machinery over which he had undivided control, Stalin had nudged the apparatus of repression and ideological discipline into one final offensive.

CONCLUSION

The Russian archives, on which much of this book is based, do not allow us to see into Stalin's mind. They do, however, provide evidence of a pattern in Stalin's behavior and, more broadly, they present a picture of symbiosis between Stalin and the system he had created. After twenty years of cajoling and personal manipulation, the leader had learned how to steer and how to break his colleagues. He also knew better than anyone how to operate the levers of his system. Over two decades, Stalin had learned how to "work" the party, how to mobilize campaigns, and how to instigate purges. These talents would come to the fore in Stalin's final years, as the leader leaned almost instinctively on the dual apparatus of ideology and repression.

Stalin was in many respects a patrimonial leader. In his last years, much official business was transacted in private meetings between Stalin and his entourage. The leader secured the loyalty of his colleagues over and above their commitment to any office and, to underline this, he completely re-shaped and renamed posts and committees, maneuvering his companions between them at will. Stalin was not, however, interested in maintaining this cozy system of governance for its own sake. He was always concerned with his own status as the leader of a great power. Although prone to fantasies and bouts of paranoia, as a leader he was pragmatic to the core. So as not to compromise the state's longer term economic and geopolitical ambitions, he accepted innovations, such as the separation of the Politburo from the Council of Ministers, which would make the administrative system more effective. It is this occasional will to delegate and to rationalize that characterizes his rule as neo-patrimonial.

Once Stalin died, the tension between a patrimonial leadership style and a well-ordered system of administration quickly dissolved and, in its stead, a new cleavage emerged. Under Stalin, Malenkov had successfully resisted pressures to ally himself with either party or government by keeping feet in both camps. Lacking Stalin's patrimonial authority, he was unable to combine a senior position in both bodies and was forced, on 13 March 1953, to take sides.[1] In the knowledge that according to a tradition going back to Lenin, sessions of the Politburo (Presidium) would be chaired by the head of the Council of Ministers, Malenkov opted for the leadership of Sovmin, relinquishing his secretaryship of the Central Committee in the process.[2] Malenkov had his aides transferred to the Council of Ministers apparatus and began to identify institutionally with the government an 1 managerial groups in a way that, Molotov later recalled, did not befit "a true member of the Central Committee."[3]

Malenkov's decision was accompanied by a shift in the center of gravity from the party to the state apparatus.[4] Certainly, judging by the frequency of its meetings prior to Beria's arrest at the end of June 1953, it was the Sovmin Presidium, rather than the Central Committee Presidium, that was the more active decision-making body. From 13 March to the beginning of July 1953, the Presidium of Sovmin met over three times as often as the rival Presidium of the Central Committee, and it began to discharge functions that earlier had been the prerogative of the Politburo.[5] Only the most senior Soviet leaders attended meetings of the Sovmin Presidium, whose sessions may be regarded as gatherings of the new ruling circle.[6]

This institutional shift was in fact the continuation of an underlying trend that had been apparent since the war. Stalin's delegation of responsibilities after the war, especially in the economic realm, had led to a growing autonomy of decision making in areas where expertise mattered and from which "political" issues as such appeared to be absent. This was most apparent at the Council of Ministers and, especially, at its core committee, the Sovmin Bureau. From the late 1940s and, especially, from 1950, the Sovmin Bureau, which consisted of all members of Stalin's leading circle with the exception of Stalin himself, had met on a weekly basis. At these meetings, a Stalin-less leading group considered matters of national economic importance and acquired an experience of collective decision making that would put them in good stead once Stalin died. The rise of the Council of Ministers in the early post-Stalin period was thus little more than a continuation of its increasingly prominent role under Stalin.

Although somewhat harder to discern, there were also underlying continuities in policy. Among the issues the government now considered was the growing crisis afflicting the countryside and the Gulag. In both areas, Stalin had insisted on a highly coercive regime throughout his tenure, a regime that extracted the maximum possible surplus from the peasantry and imposed the highest custodial terms on offenders. In their joint deliberations, members of the government had recognized the crushing cost of such policies and approached Stalin with reforms. The leader's steadfast refusal to countenance reforms markedly deepened the crisis in these areas. It was, at the same time, a measure of the general consensus throughout the governmental apparatus that reforms in both areas were implemented almost immediately once Stalin died.

Stalin's death opened the gates for the so-called new course on a variety of domestic and foreign policy issues, many of which were steered by the new collective leadership at the Council of Ministers.[7] It was only a matter of days, for example, before a series of political cases that had been fabricated under Stalin—including the Doctors' Plot, the Mingrelian Affair, and the Aviators' and Artillery Officers' Affairs—were reviewed. Molotov's wife, Polina Zhemchuzhina, and Kaganovich's brother, Mikhail, who had committed suicide at the very beginning of the war following charges of belonging to a "right-Trotskyist organization," were fully rehabilitated, as were various other victims of political repression. While this early selective rehabilitation may have served the personal interests of the country's new leaders, it also paved the way for a more general release of the victims of Stalinist terror. Over the spring and summer of 1953, the Gulag was transformed: a mass amnesty for prisoners convicted of nonpolitical crimes halved the camp population, while numerous enterprises and construction sites previously under the MVD's control were handed over to economic ministries. The list of regions covered by the restrictive passport regime was reduced, and the general softening of the state's repressive policies led to a drop in the flow of new prisoners. The new leadership also reduced tensions in the western parts of the Ukraine and in the Baltic states, where partisan divisions continued to operate. To obtain the support of the native populations and local intelligentsia, it was proposed that party-state bureaucracies be indigenized. Important changes were announced and, in part, achieved, in the economic sphere. A drop in taxes on the peasants and a rise in procurement prices were accompanied by a contraction in capital spending in heavy industry and a reduction in outlays on administration and on the military sector.

Stalin's successors were also to demonstrate their relatively peaceful disposition on the international stage. The ending of the Korean War served as a distinctive symbol of these changes. On 19 March 1953, a resolution of the Council of Ministers confirmed a policy of "concluding the war in Korea as soon as possible."[8] Following intensive negotiations, an armistice was agreed on 27 July 1953. With Moscow's encouragement, there was also significant liberalization of the communist regimes in Eastern Europe. This was most pronounced in Germany. On 2 June 1953, a Council of Ministers directive encapsulated the main criticisms the Soviet leadership had of the East German government and looked for measures to improve the political situation in the country.[9]

With Stalin's death and the ending of the patrimonial dimension of supreme decision making, no leader was able to straddle the top institutions in the way that Stalin had done. Malenkov and the Council of Ministers had to contend with a new dynamics of personal and institutional competition. Here, too, the late Stalin legacy played an important role. The XIX Party Congress in autumn of 1952 had seen a feverish wave of activity within party structures as redundant party committees were convened, elections held, and debates conducted ahead of the congress, the first in thirteen years. The general momentum built up by the congress campaign was to prove decisive on Stalin's death, when a group of party democratizers, led by Khrushchev, built on the political energy of the congress period by heading a campaign for the further reform of party structures.[10]

Not long after Stalin's death, and especially after the arrest of Beria in June, the battle between Malenkov, now firmly tied to Sovmin, and Khrushchev, linked to the party, fully came out into the open. While the party's cadres apparatus afforded Khrushchev the capacity to appoint allies to important posts, Khrushchev also took advantage of a continuity in ideological line not available to Malenkov and, by way of his populist leadership style, was able to forge a direct relationship of authority with officials that was somewhat reminiscent of the one Stalin had achieved through the cult of personality.[11]

This study of Stalin's leadership in the postwar period fills an important gap in our understanding of twentieth-century European dictatorships. An examination of the Soviet political system in the postwar period provides, in particular, a picture of dictatorship not available from the two other best known European dictatorships of the time: unlike the German or Italian cases, in the Soviet Union we see an autocrat and his system continuing to evolve and to adjust to the demands of running a mature, postwar order.

That Stalin survived the war was not the only factor that distinguished him from his German and Italian counterparts. Far more so than Hitler and more than Mussolini, Stalin was a machine politician. Never the grand orator that Hitler and Mussolini had been, Stalin was most at home scrutinizing files, intriguing on committees, and pulling the levers of the vast bureaucratic empire he had helped create. Far from shunning dossiers and files, as had been Hitler's wont,[12] before the war Stalin had sat on committees, solicited documents, and positively craved information from below on the functioning of his system. When, as happened after the war, his capacity to process data declined, he sought other, more economic, ways of obtaining information. One such method was the stimulation of conflicts and disagreements. Rather than shying away from personal conflict, as was Hitler's tendency,[13] Stalin actively courted it. "I cannot know everything," he told the Minister of Communications, I. V. Kovalev, "that is why I pay particular attention to disagreements, objections, I look into why they started to find out what is going on."[14]

By the postwar period, Stalin had honed his techniques of personal confrontation not only to elicit information about the inner workings of his system but also to intimidate and subjugate his companions. Immediately following the hostilities, Stalin moved methodically from one member of his inner circle to another with direct personal showdowns. Integral to these was a ritual of humiliation that involved a debasing apology and a statement of loyalty from the victim, usually in written form. Stalin often attacked his companions obliquely, either through his trademark arrests of relatives (for example, of Molotov's wife) or by demoting associates (such as Beria's confidant Merkulov), and then demanding the unconditional support of all his colleagues for the action, including, most of all, the leader whose relative or aide had been targeted. Stalin also had other ways of unnerving his companions and of reminding them who was in charge. He was often inclined, for example, to leave excluded colleagues in limbo, as he did Malenkov in the summer of 1946, letting him agonize while the leader lingered over his fate.

Stalin's ability to manipulate his colleagues was facilitated by an intimate knowledge of his own political system. Nowhere was the symbiotic relationship of leader and system more apparent than in the periodic purges that flared up after the war. As well as cleansing bureaucracies and rooting out enemies, purges were, for Stalin, a means of keeping his colleagues and agents under pressure. Purges increased the stress on officials and thereby heightened the chances of squeezing out information (as in the case of Riumin) or of converting functionaries feeling the pinch (for example, Shepilov) into special agents for campaigns, purges, and other leader-assigned duties. In purges, the broader goal of jolting bureaucracies into action coincided perfectly with Stalin's own power requirements.

Yet by the late Stalin period, the impulse to purge was more circumscribed than it had been in the 1930s. By now, there were a number of forces that kept Stalin's relations with his colleagues, and with their bureaucracies, at bay. Many sectors of the state, not least the criminal justice system, were now more institutionally robust than they had been in the early 1930s, and consequently less prone to the meltdown they had experienced later that decade.[15] Following the experience of the Great Terror, Stalin may himself have been aware of the incalculable consequences of another society-wide blood purge and, accordingly, he may have chosen to exercise a certain inner restraint. For their part, Stalin's colleagues appear to have become aware of their own interest in preserving the balance of power and in preventing any sudden movements at the apex of the system. From bitter experience, they had come to know that antagonizing the leader or rousing his suspicions was an extremely hazardous business. Once inflamed, Stalin's suspicions could easily claim more high-ranking victims, including, quite possibly, themselves.

Within the late Stalinist leadership, every leader had his role. In defining these roles, Stalin appears to have been as hardheaded and utilitarian as ever. Older comrades, such as Molotov and Mikoian, were important to the leader as symbols and co-architects of the Stalinist system. Attacks on them were usually qualified and tended to be confined to smaller audiences. Lacking symbolic value of this kind, the use of younger figures such as Malenkov, Beria, and Khrushchev resided entirely in their work qualities, which the leader tested at regular intervals. With lower level figures, Stalin was equally pragmatic. Although he appears to have gone along with Riumin's fantasies of Jewish conspiracies for a time, once the evidence dried up, Stalin swiftly dispensed with his chief investigator's services. "Stalin," concludes the writer Kiril Stoliarov, "did not tolerate chatterboxes."[16]

Stalin manipulated not only people but also the political structures around him. By the postwar period, the traditional cabinet, the Politburo, had been entirely remolded to fit with Stalin's personal preferences and lifestyle. In contrast to the formal Politburo, which had been chosen after the XVIII Party Congress in 1939, the de facto Politburo, or ruling group, was handpicked by Stalin and met at his convenience. Without set procedures, agendas, minutes, or even prearranged meeting times, the Politburo complied entirely with the norms laid down by the leader. The Politburo was nonetheless valuable to Stalin. It allowed him to bind his companions and co-rulers in an easily monitored circle. Further, through the system of cosignatures on which he insisted, Stalin was able to lock his companions in a system of joint responsibility, much as a gang of criminals might undertake a blood oath.

Stalin's immediate legacy was a relatively secure and self-confident Soviet Union. Apart from gaining buffer states in Eastern Europe and new-found allies in Asia, the Soviet Union at the time of Stalin's death had tested an atom bomb and was on the verge of possessing the means to detonate it on its adversaries. In addition, the social and political system that Stalin had helped construct was to prove sufficiently sturdy to survive his death. At the same time, Stalin's own power goals had set the Soviet Union off on a frightful path. Apart from the human suffering they inflicted, Stalin's policies were, even in their own terms, not always successful. On the international stage Stalin committed blunders, some of which caused great damage to his country's reputation.[17] The costs, moreover, of Stalin's policies to Soviet society were monumental. They led not only to hundreds of thousands of needless arrests, tortures, and executions but to cramped, unhealthy housing, to near subsistence levels of nutrition, and to a sharply distorted internal distribution of resources.

Despite the major reforms of the early post-Stalin period, the legacy of Stalin's method of rule was profound. Twenty years after Stalin's death, the head of the security police, Iurii Andropov, informed the General Secretary of the Central Committee, Leonid Brezhnev, that the record of Stalin's speech to a meeting of a Presidium commission on intelligence, dating from November 1952, had been recovered. Andropov wrote:

> Nearly all the observations of I. V. Stalin are fully relevant even today, in large part because they are general and are fit for all times. What personally struck me most was his comment that "communists who look askance at the intelligence services, at the work of the Chekha, *who are frightened of soiling themselves*, should be thrown head first down the well." In its form, this sentiment is a little Asiatic, but in essence it is as true now as it was in that distant age of the cult of personality.[18]

The Stalinist legacy, inherited from the postwar period, included a distribution of resources skewed toward arms production and heavy industry, a bipolar world locked in mutual suspicion and conflict, and a role for informers and security agents who were not "frightened of soiling themselves." To this we can add the reinforcement by Stalin of a traditional desire in Russia for a tough, powerful leader, who could show the way forward and save the country and the political order from itself.

NOTES

Introduction

1. This is described in some detail in V. F. Zima, *Golod v SSSR 1946–1947 godov: Proiskhozhdenie i posledstviia* (Moscow: IRIRAN, 1996).

2. See [Joseph Stalin], "Komissarov chertova gibel'," *Istoricheskii arkhiv* 5–6 (1997): 218.

3. One, albeit formal, measure of this is that from July 1945 to July 1947, the number of communists in the countryside more than doubled, from 827,000 to 1,896,000. See B. A. Abramov, "Organizatsionno-partiinaia rabota KPSS v gody chetvertoi piatiletki," *Voprosy istorii KPSS* 3 (1979): 63.

4. The overwhelming majority of the 680,000 people deported to special settlements from 1946 to 1952 were from the newly occupied or reoccupied western regions of Western Ukraine, Belorussia, the Baltic republics, and Moldavia. See Iu. A. Poliakov, ed., *Naselenie Rossii v XX veke*, vol. 2 (Moscow: Rosspen, 2001), 171–172. To the extent that there were expulsions of "internal" groups (for example, 3,000 Leningraders in 1949 and 10,000 Mingrelians in 1951), these were relatively limited and targeted in nature.

5. Convictions for counterrevolutionary offenses fell from 129,826 in 1946 to 69,233 in 1948, 53,179 in 1950, and 27,098 in 1952. Figures for the postwar period also reflect a marked decline from prewar levels. Whereas 480,000 people were convicted for "counterrevolutionary crimes" from 1946 to 1952, 1,380,000 had been convicted over an equivalent period from 1930 to 1936, and 1,370,000 were convicted during the Great Terror of 1937–1938. The number of executions also fell sharply. In the postwar period there were 7,700, in comparison to 40,000 from 1930 to 1936 and 680,000 from 1937 to 1938. See GARF f.R-9492 op.6a d.14 l.8; V. P. Popov, "Gosudarstvennyi terror v Sovetskoi Rossii, 1923–1953 gg,"*Otechestvennye arkhivy* 2 (1992): 28; GARF f.R-9401 op.1 d.4157 ll.201–205; *GULAG. 1918–1960* (Moscow: Materik, 2000), 431–434; and J. Arch Getty and Oleg V. Naumov, *The Road to Terror: Stalin and the Self-Destruction of the Bolsheviks, 1932–1939* (New Haven, Conn.: Yale University Press, 1999), 561.

6. Cf. T. H. Rigby, "Was Stalin a Loyal Patron?" in *Political Elites in the USSR: Central Leaders and Local Cadres from Lenin to Gorbachev* (Aldershot, U.K.: Edward Elgar, 1990), 141.

7. O. V. Khlevniuk, *Politbiuro: Mekhanizmy politicheskoi vlasti v 1930-e gody* (Moscow: Rosspen, 1996), 237–246, 249–250.

8. See ibid., 237.

9. Apart from Stalin himself, veteran Stalinists, including Molotov, Kaganovich, Mikoian, Voroshilov, and Andreev, always accounted for at least a half of the full postwar Politburo (i.e., excluding candidate members).

10. Khlevniuk, *Politbiuro*, 231–234.

11. Asked whether Beria had intrigued against him in 1952, when Molotov had been removed from the cabinet, Molotov replied: "Beria? No. I think that he probably even defended me in that business. When he saw that even Molotov had been pushed aside, he must have thought to himself, 'Watch out Beria! If Stalin does not even trust Molotov, then he could wipe out the rest of us in a minute!' " Feliks Chuev, *Sto sorok besed s Molotovym* (Moscow: Terra, 1991), 471. All translations from the Russian are the authors'.

12. Ibid., 258–259.

13. In the speech Stalin set out a list of compulsory long-term targets for certain producer goods. See I. V. Stalin, *Sochineniia*, vol.3. Edited by Robert H. McNeal (Stanford, Calif.: Hoover Institution Press, 1967), 10–11, 20.

14. This is discussed at greater length in chapter 2.

15. P. A. Sudoplatov, *Spetsoperatsii. Lubianka i Kreml' 1930–1950* (Moscow: Olma Press, 1997), 383.

16. Since this was itself a state secret, it has not been possible to establish Stalin's movements in the south with absolute precision. From the memoir literature, it does appear, however, that Stalin resided at a number of southern dachas in this period. Two of his main dachas appear to have been at Miussery and Gagry (on Lake Ritsa), both of which were near Sochi in the Krasnodar region of southern Russia. At other times he stayed at dachas in the Crimea, in Tskhaltubo and Borzhomi in Georgia, and in Novyi Afon in Abkhazia. It is likely that in the course of any one summer, he moved from one dacha to another. On the construction of the dacha complex near Lake Ritsa, see *Politbiuro TsK VKP(b) i Sovet Ministrov SSSR 1945–1953* (Moscow: Rosspen, 2002), 404.

17. Kiril Stoliarov, *Palachi i zhertvy* (Moscow: Olma Press, 1997), 21, 59.

18. Two are discussed in some detail in this book: the campaign against the cultural and artistic intelligentsia in 1946–1947, and that against the "Zionist" doctors in 1952.

19. This is discussed in greater detail in Yoram Gorlizki, "Ordinary Stalinism: The Council of Ministers and the Soviet Neo-patrimonial State, 1945–1953," *Journal of Modern History* 74, 4 (2002): 699–736.

20. For a more detailed discussion, see ibid., 701 n.3.

21. See Max Weber, *Economy and Society: An Outline of Interpretive Sociology*, vol. 2 (Berkeley: University of California Press, 1978), 1028–1029; and the useful discussion in Robin Theobold, "Patrimonialism," *World Politics* 34, 4 (1982): 555.

22. "In all political matters proper," Weber wrote, "the ruler's personal discretion delimits the jurisdiction of his officials. Jurisdiction is at first completely fluid—if we want to use this specifically bureaucratic concept here at all." See Weber, *Economy and Society*, 1029. Also see the discussion in Reinhard Bendix, *Max Weber: An Intellectual Portrait* (Berkeley: University of California Press, 1977), 345, 424–425.

23. Particularly useful are the works by Robert Conquest, *Power and Policy in the USSR: The Study of Soviet Dynastics* (London: Macmillan, 1961), chaps. 4–8; and Werner G. Hahn, *Postwar Soviet Politics: The Fall of Zhdanov and the Defeat of Moderation, 1946–1953* (Ithaca, N.Y.: Cornell University Press, 1982), chaps. 1–5. On the strength of painstaking analyses of the central and regional press, such works provide useful background information and remain, in certain respects, more accurate than later studies whose authors enjoyed access to Russian archives. Iurii Zhukov, for example, who has benefited from access to archival materials, has recently argued (in his *Tainy Kremlia. Stalin, Molotov, Beria, Malenkov* [Moscow: Terra, 2000], 561) that the Mingrelian Affair was initiated by Malenkov. As we shall see in chapter 4, however, this is almost certainly wrong. The more accurate assessment, provided by Conquest four decades ago (*Power and Policy*, 140–141), was that the affair was started and coordinated entirely by Stalin.

24. Particularly widely used to complement newspaper articles were Khrushchev's secret speech to the XX Party Congress and the two volumes of his memoirs. See N. S. Khrushchev, "Secret Speech of Khrushchev Concerning the 'Cult of the Individual,' " in *The Anti-Stalin Campaign and International Communism* (New York: Columbia University Press, 1956), 1–89; N. S. Khrushchev, *Khrushchev Remembers* (London: Andre Deutsch, 1971); and N. S. Khrushchev, *Khrushchev Remembers: The Last Testament* (London: Andre Deutsch, 1974).

25. Thus, for example, on the basis of their disappearance from the press, Conquest (*Power and Policy*, 177) implies that a number of senior officials, such as the Minister of Labor Reserves, V. P. Pronin, the Minister of Geology, P. A. Zakharov, and the Minister of the Communications Equipment Industry, G. V. Alekseenko, may have been arrested or executed on the eve of Stalin's death. In fact, however, all survived and retained their posts. See *Gosudarstvennaia vlast' SSSR. Vysshie organy vlasti i upravleniia i ikh rukovoditeli. 1923–1991* (Moscow: Rosspen, 1999), 196, 315, 483.

26. Particularly useful in this respect are Chuev, *Sto sorok besed*; Anastas Mikoian, *Tak bylo. Razmyshleniia o minuvshem* (Moscow: Vagrius, 1999); M. A Men'shikov, *S vintovkoi i vo frake* (Moscow: Mezhdunarodnye otnosheniia, 1996); and V. A. Malyshev, "Dnevnik narkoma," *Istochnik* 5 (1997): 103–147.

27. Boris Nikolaevsky, for example, significantly overestimated Malenkov's position in relation to Stalin, referring to the former as "First Secretary of the Central Committee" in 1946, writing of a " 'Malenkov' period of Soviet foreign policy" from February 1948 on, and mistakenly ascribing to Malenkov the power to appoint senior leaders, such as Voznesenskii, to high-ranking positions. See Nikolaevsky, "Malenkov: His Rise and His Policy," *New Leader*, 23 March 1953, 6; Nikolaevsky, "How Malenkov Triumphed," *New Leader*, 30 March 1953, 17–18. Posthumously published writings by Nikolaevsky on the

Politburo's efforts to "hasten Stalin's death" are in Boris I. Nikolaevsky, *Tainye stranitsy istorii* (Moscow: Izdatel'stvo Gumanitarnoi literatury, 1995), 7–8. A recent attempt to argue that the Politburo marginalized Stalin from power is Iurii N. Zhukov, "Bor'ba za vlast' v rukovodstve SSSR v 1945–1952 godakh," *Voprosy istorii* 1 (1995): 38–39; and see Zhukov, *Tainy Kremlia: Stalin, Molotov, Beria, Malenkov* (Moscow: Terra, 2000).

28. This, for example, is the view of Hahn, who presents Zhdanov as a consistent advocate of "moderation" from 1946 until his death in 1948, while presenting his opponent Malenkov as the patron of "dogmatist" protégés. Hahn, *Postwar Soviet Politics*, preface and chapters 1–2.

29. On some secondary issues, such as administrative reform within the party apparatus, in which Stalin himself took little interest, the leader may have tolerated or even encouraged different positions among his subordinates. We also argue that more coherent positions did emerge toward the very end of Stalin's life, especially from the XIX Party Congress onward, as a covert battle for Stalin's succession began to gather pace. See Yoram Gorlizki, "Party Revivalism and the Death of Stalin," *Slavic Review* 54, 1 (1995): 1–22; and chap. 6 of this book.

30. T. H. Rigby, "The Government in the Soviet Political System," in *Executive Power and Soviet Politics: The Rise and Decline of the Soviet State*, ed. Eugene Huskey (Armonk, N.Y.: M. E. Sharpe, 1992), 31, 27. Also see Leonard Schapiro, *Totalitarianism* (London: Macmillan, 1972), 60–61; and Merle Fainsod, *How Russia Is Ruled* (Cambridge, Mass.: Harvard University Press, 1963), 109.

31. For a different view, see Amir Weiner, *Making Sense of War: The Second World War and the Fate of the Bolshevik Revolution* (Princeton, N.J.: Princeton University Press, 2001), 154; and Weiner, "Nature, Nurture, and Memory in a Socialist Utopia: Delineating the Soviet Socio-ethnic Body in the Age of Socialism," *American Historical Review* 104, 4 (1999): 1115, 1119.

32. Zhukov, for example, in his *Tainy Kremlia*, relies almost exclusively on f.17 op.3 of the RGASPI archive, the repository of *podpis'nye protokoly*.

33. Fonds 82 op.2, 77 op.3, 83 op.1, 81 op.3, and 558 op.11, respectively.

34. A full list of these interviews is given in the bibliography.

1: A Return to Order

1. During the war Stalin was concurrently Chair of the State Defense Committee (GKO), Chair of the Council of Ministers, Minister of Defense, General Secretary of the Central Committee, and Supreme Commander in Chief of the Soviet Armed Forces.

2. The State Defense Committee was originally proposed at a meeting between Molotov, Malenkov, Beria, and Voroshilov and formed, with Stalin's consent, on 30 June 1941. Its first members were Stalin (chair), Molotov (deputy chair), Voroshilov, Malenkov, and Beria. They were joined on 3 February 1942 by Mikoian and Voznesenskii, by Kaganovich on 20 February 1942, and by Bulganin, who replaced Voroshilov, on 22 November 1944. The GKO, which reigned supreme over all party, police, and military committees, operated

through the apparatus of the Central Committee and the Council of People's Commissars. Unlike the other institutions that directed the war effort, the GKO was an entirely civilian body. Of the 9,971 resolutions it passed, approximately two-thirds were concerned with the military economy and military production. See Iu. A. Gor'kov, "K istorii sozdaniia goskomiteta oborony," *Novaia i noveishaia istoriia* 4 (1999): 17–18; and A. A. Pechenkin, "Gosudarstvennyi komitet oborony v 1941 godu," *Otechestvennaia istoriia* 4–5 (1994): 126, 131.

3. On 10 October, the London correspondent of *Paris Press* claimed that Stalin had suffered from a serious bout of angina at the Potsdam Conference; a similar story in the *Chicago Tribune* followed the next day. On 11 November, the French journal *Bref* ran a story that Stalin had suffered a heart attack on 13 September and that he had retired to the south in order to compose his political "testimony." More serious allegations along these lines were to appear in December. These articles are all collected in Stalin's personal files. See RGASPI f.558 op.11 d.97 ll.35–36; d.99 ll.29–34.

4. This group had in fact emerged, albeit in a looser form, earlier on in the war. Thus, for example, the powerful Operational Bureau of GKO, which had been established on 8 December 1942, comprised all members of the "quartet" (i.e., the "quintet" apart from Stalin).

5. This was entirely consistent with Stalin's position on the eve of the war, when he had made it clear that he wanted to combine hardworking older cadres with the most promising recruits from the younger generation. See O. V. Khlevniuk, *Politbiuro: Mekhanizmy politicheskoi vlasti v 1930-e gody* (Moscow: Rosspen, 1996), 234, 247–49; *Stalinskoe Politbiuro v 30-e gody* (Moscow: AIRO-XX, 1995), 172–173.

6. RGASPI f.17 op.163 d.1463 l.76.

7. Thus Stalin had read all the reports outlined in note 3 of this chapter. See RGASPI f.558 op.11 d.97 ll.35–36; d.99 ll.29–34. In addition, an article in the American magazine *Newsweek* claimed that during the Potsdam Conference, Stalin had had two minor heart attacks. See Vladimir Pechatnov, "Soiuzniki nazhimaiut na tebia dlia togo, chtoby slomit' u tebia voliu," *Istochnik* 2 (1999): 79.

8. If Stalin had suffered either a stroke or a heart attack, he made a remarkable recovery. Thus, for example, in the early morning of 13 October, only four days after he had left Moscow, Stalin sent the quartet very detailed instructions on the need to have transcripts of speeches from the foreign ministers meetings prepared. On 18 October, he wrote to the quartet that he was quite happy to receive the American ambassador Averell Harriman in Sochi. RGASPI f.558 op.11 d.97 ll.61, 71. Having visited him on 24 and 25 October, Harriman informed the press two days later that "Generalissimus Stalin is in good health and rumours of his ill health have no foundation whatsoever." Pechatnov, "Soiuzniki," 80.

9. Molotov recalled that after the war Stalin had announced: "Let Viacheslav take over now" [pust' Viacheslav teper' porabotaet]. See Feliks Chuev, *Sto sorok besed s Molotovym* (Moscow: Terra, 1991), 271.

10. RGASPI f.558 op.11 d.97 l.96.

11. Pechatnov, "Soiuzniki," 79.

12. Ibid., 73–74; Vladislav Zubok and Costantine Pleshakov, *Inside the Kremlin's Cold War: From Stalin to Khrushchev* (Cambridge, Mass.: Harvard University Press, 1996), 96–97.

13. Pechatnov, "Soiuzniki," 80.

14. RGASPI f.558 op.11 d.771 l.5; Pechatnov, "Soiuzniki," 81–82.

15. RGASPI f.558 op.11 d.771 l.6 (italics ours). Molotov also got into trouble for agreeing, at a banquet on 7 November, to give an interview to Churchill's son, a journalist, who happened to be in Moscow at the time. His decision was subsequently overturned. RGASPI f.558 op.11 d.99 l.104.

16. Iu. G. Murin, *Iosif Stalin v obiatiakh sem'i. Iz lichnogo arkhiva* (Moscow: Rodina, 1993), 95.

17. RGASPI f.558 op.11 d.771 ll.9–12; d.99 l.86.

18. As the quartet were later to explain in a message on 6 December, the piece had been filed by the Moscow correspondent of the *New York Times* on 30 November, before appearing in the paper the following day; it was only distributed by TASS, however, on 3 December. RGASPI f.558 op.11 d.99 l.92.

19. Pechatnov, "Soiuzniki," 82.

20. The message was sent at 1:15 A.M. on 5 December. In it Stalin claims to have read the *New York Times* piece "today," probably referring to 4 December. RGASPI f.558 op.11 d.99 l.86.

21. As the quartet explained, the *New York Times* piece had been filed from Moscow on 30 November and published on 1 December, before Stalin's conversation with Molotov. RGASPI f.558 op.11 d.99 ll.92–93.

22. RGASPI f.558 op.11 d.99 l.95.

23. RGASPI f.558 op.11 d.99 ll.103–104.

24. RGASPI f.558 op.11 d.99 l.120.

25. RGASPI f.558 op.11 d.99 l.121.

26. The message was addressed "to Molotov for the quartet." Mentioned six times in the space of four paragraphs, the need to maintain "our firmness" (*nasha stoikost'*) or the "policy of firmness" (*politika stoikosti*) was the dominant theme of this message. RGASPI f.558 op.11 d.99 l.127. The attack on Molotov was motivated not only by the need to keep his deputy in check. Stalin also wanted to maintain a hard line in foreign affairs, and he suspected Molotov's deputies—especially Litvinov and Lozovsky—of seeking to weaken it. RGASPI f.558 op.11 d.99 l.95. During the years 1946–1947, Molotov's deputy ministers Dekanozov, Litvinov, and Lozovsky were sacked and replaced by younger specialists. See N. V. Romanovskii, *Liki stalinizma, 1945–1953* (Moscow: RAGS, 1995), 36.

27. For a minor rebuff in December 1946, see Vladimir Pechatnov, "Na etom voprose my slomaem ikh antisovetskoe uporstvo," *Istochnik* 3 (1999): 98–99, 104; also see V. D. Esakov and E. S. Levina, *Delo KR. Sudy chesti v ideologii i praktike poslevoennogo stalinizma* (Moscow: IRIRAN, 2001), 84.

28. See Khlevniuk, *Politbiuro*, 241–244; O. V. Khlevniuk, "Stalin i Molotov," in *Stalin. Stalinizm. Sovetskoe obschestvo* (Moscow: IRIRAN, 2000), 277, 279. For Stalin's wartime admonitions of Molotov, especially during the latter's stay in

London, see O. A. Rzheshevsky, *War and Diplomacy: The Making of the Grand Alliance* (Amsterdam: Harwood, 1996).

29. As Abakumov would later write, "sometimes during [his] vacation certain questions are decided more severely." See Kiril Stoliarov, *Palachi i zhertvy* (Moscow: Olma Press, 1997), 59.

30. That is, using the *ty* form. See Anastas Mikoian, *Tak bylo: Razmyshleniia o minuvshem* (Moscow: Vagrius, 1999) 352. Men'shikov, who was close to Mikoian, claimed that Stalin only used the familiar form with Molotov. See M. A. Men'shikov, *S vintovkoi i vo frake* (Moscow: Mezhdunarodnye otnosheniia, 1996), 124.

31. Mikoian, *Tak bylo*, 494–498. This was to prove an extremely serious charge, since Lozovsky was arrested in connection with his work for the Jewish Anti-Fascist Committee in January 1949 and executed in August 1952.

32. RGASPI f.558 op.11 d.732 ll.43, 45.

33. A. A. Danilov, "Stalinskoe Politbiuro v poslevoennye gody," in *Politicheskie partii Rossii* (Moscow: Izdatel'stvo Moskovskogo Universiteta, 2000), 204–205; and see *Politbiuro TsK VKP(b) i Sovet Ministrov SSSR 1945–1953* (Moscow: Rosspen, 2002), 224 n.2.

34. RGASPI f.558 op.11 d.732 l.42; d.765 l.115.

35. RGASPI f.558 op.11 d.732 l.42. In a further attack on Mikoian, also at the end of 1946, Stalin accused him of "Menshevism" given the breakdown of supplies, for which Mikoian was responsible, to an American firm. See Men'shikov, *S vintovkoi*, 98–99.

36. RGASPI f.558 op.11 d.765 ll.113-114.

37. This at least was Malenkov's interpretation, as retold by Khrushchev. See N. S. Khrushchev, *Vospominaniia. Vremia, liudi, vlast'* (Moscow: Moskovskie novosti, 1999), 2:26.

38. Danilov, "Stalinskoe Politbiuro," 200. Shakhurin was formally sacked as minister on 5 January 1946. See *Gosudsarstvennaia vlast' SSSR. Vysshie organy vlasti i upraveleniia i ikh rukovoditeli. 1923–1991* (Moscow: Rosspen, 1999), 58.

39. R. G. Pikhoia, *Sovetskii soiuz. Istoriia vlasti, 1945–1991* (Moscow: RAGS, 1998), 46–47. The fact that this had been going on for "about two years" was significant since although Shakhurin had been commissar since January 1940, he had only been supervised by Malenkov since 1942, that is, for the period encompassing the previous two years. Shakhurin was eventually tried by the military panel of the supreme court on 11 May 1946. *Gosudarstvennaia vlast'*, 594–595.

40. Pikhoia, *Sovetskii soiuz*, 48, 59; *Lavrentii Beria. 1953. Stenogramma iul'skogo plenuma TsK KPSS i drugie dokumenty* (Moscow: MFD, 1999), 59–61.

41. Malenkov would not attend sessions of the Bureau of the Council of Ministers from 13 March until his reappointment as deputy premier on 8 August. *Politbiuro TsK VKP(b) i Sovet Ministrov SSSR 1945–1953*, 463–474.

42. The new draft was submitted to Stalin on 10 April. In the first draft the new Secretary, Kuznetsov, had only been given the right to "oversee" the cadres administration, rather than "lead" it, as was the case in the final version. APRF f.3 op.22 d.14 l.158; d.41 l.158; RGASPI f.17 op.163 d.1480 ll.4–6.

43. The phrase is Mikoian's. See his *Tak bylo*, 555.

44. RGASPI f.83 op.1 d.11 ll.2, 6.

45. RGASPI f.17 op.163 d.1489 ll.56–57.

46. Werner G. Hahn, *Postwar Soviet Politics: The Fall of Zhdanov and the Defeat of Moderation, 1946–1956* (Ithaca, N.Y.: Cornell University Press, 1982), 51.

47. After his dismissal as party Secretary, Malenkov did occupy a number of interim positions. On 13 May, he was appointed chair of the special committee on jet technologies and on 10 July, chair of the radar commission. See Pikhoia, *Sovetskii soiuz*, 58.

48. Over the three months after his expulsion from his party posts, Malenkov's positions were not formally passed on to anyone else. It was only on 2 August—the day on which Malenkov was made deputy premier—that the chair of the Orgburo was formally handed on to Zhdanov. RGASPI f.17 op.163 d.1487 ll.131–134, esp. point 11. As was often the case, Stalin liked to sit on the matter. In fact, the draft resolution transferring command of the Orgburo had already been delivered to him on 10 May 1946, that is, three months before it was finally passed. APRF f.3 op.22 d.41 l.70.

49. Cf. Hahn, *Postwar Soviet Politics*, 51, who suggests that Malenkov "hit his low point" in autumn 1946.

50. GARF f.5446 op.1 d.275 l.35.

51. See the resolution of the Council of Ministers of 28 March 1946. GARF f.5446 op.1 d.275 ll.121–122.

52. Beria had been released as Commissar of Internal Affairs on 29 December 1945, a post in which he had served for over seven years, "in view of his overwork in other central areas." The latter phrase was written in by Stalin. RGASPI f.17 op.163 d.1471 l.4. As with all commissariats, the Commissariat of Internal Affairs (NKVD) was renamed the Ministry of Internal Affairs (MVD) in March 1946. Hence the terms "commissar" and "minister" and "commissariat" and "ministry" are used here interchangeably.

53. Mamulov had been the head of Beria's personal secretariat. See Danilov, "Stalinskoe Politbiuro," 204.

54. These were reflected in an exchange between Stalin in the south and Malenkov and Beria in Moscow, in which the latter, in a message of 31 October 1945, recommended V. S. Riasnii as the new First Deputy Commissar of State Security, "so that in one to two months time we shall be able to confirm him as commissar." RGASPI f.558 op.11 d.97 l.136.

55. On this and on the appointment of ministry deputy chairs two days later, see *Politbiuro TsK VKP(b) i Sovet Ministrov SSSR 1945–1953*, 207–208.

56. Although the content of these mistakes was not revealed, it is possible that they were connected to the defection of Igor Guzenko, a cipher clerk in Ottawa, who had betrayed Soviet spy rings in North America. See Zubok and Pleshakov, *Stalin's Cold War*, 146.

57. The resolution stated that "comrade Merkulov, occupying a responsible position, has not conducted himself with full honesty, has not informed the Central Committee of the serious situation at the security services, and he has concealed from the Central Committee, until the very last moment, the failure

of its work abroad." The original version of the resolution, drafted by Stalin, is in RGANI f.2 op.1 d.10 l.195.

58. For the final version of the resolution and the correspondence vote, see RGANI f.2 op.1 d.9 l.3.

59. *Neizvestnaia Rossiia. XX vek* (Moscow: Istoricheskoe nasledie, 1993), 3: 73–74.

60. A long-standing member of the Politburo, Voroshilov, who had been on the receiving end of considerable abuse from Stalin during the war, was admonished by the Politburo on 24 October 1945 for permitting, without authorization from Moscow, the four leading Hungarian parties to issue a pre-election declaration. *Vostochnaia Evropa v dokumentakh Rossiiskikh arkhivov, 1944–1953* (Moscow/ Novosibirsk: Sibirskii Khronograf, 1997), 276–277. Aside from Malenkov and Beria, the other "young" member of the Politburo, Khrushchev, was set back by the Politburo's decision, on 27 February 1947, to replace him with Lazar Kaganovich as First Secretary of the Ukrainian Central Committee. RGASPI f.17 op.163 d.1496 l.195. There is a useful discussion of Khrushchev's arguments with Stalin at the 21–26 February 1947 plenum in Hahn, *Postwar Soviet Politics*, 64. In the 1930s, the arrival of a Politburo pleni-potentiary could have spelled doom for a deposed incumbent. In the event, however, Khrushchev retained his position as Chair of the Ukrainian Council of Ministers and, on 15 December, saw Kaganovich return to Moscow and himself reappointed to his old post as First Secretary. RGASPI f.17 op.163 d.1507 l.13.

61. For a good description of this, see Seweryn Bialer, ed, *Stalin and His Generals: Soviet Military Memoirs of World War II* (London: Souvenir Press, 1970), 296.

62. Based on his experiences as a Moscow-based journalist, Alexander Werth wrote tellingly: "During the war and for a short-time after [Stalin] wanted to be seen by the Russian people *as a soldier above all else*, as head of the government second, and as head of the party as a bad third." Werth, *The Post-war Years* (New York: Taplinger, 1971), 16 (italics ours). This point was elaborated on by Khrushchev in his secret speech. See "Secret Speech of Khru-shchev Concerning the 'Cult of the Individual,' " in *The Anti-Stalin Campaign and International Communism* (New York: Columbia University Press, 1956), 54. Also see David Holloway, *Stalin and the Bomb: The Soviet Union and Atomic Energy, 1939–1956* (New Haven, Conn.: Yale University Press, 1994), 225.

63. The new Commissariat of Armed Forces united the former Commissar-iat of Defense, which Stalin had headed since the beginning of the war (he had taken over on 19 July 1941) and the dissolved Commissariat of the Navy. Thus, the new commissariat brought under its jurisdiction all ground, air, and naval forces. See *Gosudarstvennaia vlast'*, 171.

64. See N. V. Petrov, "Pervyi predsedatel' KGB general Ivan Serov," *Otechest-vennaia istoriia* 5 (1997): 28–29.

65. Pikhoia, *Sovetskii soiuz*, 44, 47–48, 54.

66. G. K. Zhukov, "Korotko o Staline," *Pravda*, 20 January 1989, 3, cited in Holloway, *Stalin and the Bomb*, 224.

67. Pikhoia, *Sovetskii soiuz*, 48–49.

68. Some of his colleagues were not so lucky. At the beginning of 1947, on the basis of denunciations and, especially, defamatory conversations picked up by bugging devices lodged in their homes, three of Zhukov's associates, generals Kulik, Gordov, and Rybal'chenko, were arrested and subsequently executed. Pikhoia, *Sovetskii soiuz*, 49–53.

69. This took place at the Politburo session of 29 December 1945. The move was carried out in the guise of setting up a "commission on external affairs" at the Politburo, whose membership consisted of Stalin, Molotov, Beria, Mikoian, Malenkov, and Zhdanov. RGASPI f.17 op.163 d.1471 ll.2, 6.

70. This, for example, was the reading of Werth, *Russia*, chap.11; and of Harold Swayze, *Political Control of Literature in the USSR, 1946–1959* (Cambridge, Mass.: Harvard University Press, 1962).

71. It was only Zhdanov's decline in 1948, so it has been argued, which ushered in a period of genuine ideological regimentation and repression in these areas. See Hahn, *Postwar Soviet Politics*, preface and chaps. 1–3.

72. Two decrees, of August and December 1941, had made it possible for any soldier "who had distinguished himself in battle" to join the party with a minimum of formalities and after only a three-month-long candidate stage. See Werth, *Russia*, 100. By the end of the war, over half of the party's 6 million members were from the armed forces, and a high proportion of these had joined during the war. A. V. Krasnov, ed., *Bor'ba partii i rabochego klassa za vosstanovlenie i razvitie narodnogo khoziaistva SSSR (1943–1950 gg.)* (Moscow: Mysl', 1978), 53.

73. See points 1b and 6 of the resolution in RGASPI f.17 op.163 d.1480 ll.4–6.

74. B. A. Abramov, "Organizatsionno-partiinaia rabota KPSS v gody chetvertoi piatiletki," *Voprosy istorii KPSS* 3 (1979): 56, 59; Iurii N. Zhukov, "Bor' ba za vlast' v rukovodstve SSSR v 1945–1952 godakh," *Voprosy istorii* 1 (1995): 27.

75. Mikoian, *Tak bylo*, 563, claims that the two "sincerely related well to each other, loved each other as genuine friends," while Andrei Zhdanov's son, Iurii, recalls that "the foundation of their association was work rather than friendship." Interview with Iurii Andreevich Zhdanov, 23 October 1993. One writer who sees an active enmity between the two is Zhukov, "Bor'ba," 27–28.

76. See point 1(v) of the Politburo resolution of 13 April, RGASPI f.17 op.163 d.1480 l.4. On Kuznetsov's subsequent role in reforming the nomenklatura, see Mikhail Levin [Moshe Lewin], "Nomenklatura—Arcanum Imperii," in *Kuda idet Rossiia?* (Moscow: Intertsenter, 1997), 71, 73; Abramov, "Organizatsionno-partiinaia rabota," 58.

77. Intended to restore the authority of the Central Committee in controlling the work of regional party organizations, the new administration consisted of Moscow-based "inspectors"—most of whom were themselves formerly regional party bosses—who were given unmediated on-the-spot authority to direct the work of local officials. It was a measure of their status that all the inspectors were either full members (Andrianov, Borkov, Zodionchenko, Korotchenko, Mikhailov, Nikitin, Patolichev, and Pegov) or candidates (Gusarov, Denisov, Zhavoronkov, and Ignat'ev) of the Central Committee. N. S. Patolichev,

Ispitanie na zrelost' (Moscow: Politizdat, 1977), 281–283; Abramov, "Organizat-sionno-partiinaia rabota," 61; RGANI f.2 op.1 d.9 l.1. On Patolichev's long-term association with Zhdanov, see Patolichev, *Sovest'iu svoei ne postupis'* (Moscow: Sampo, 1995), 73. According to Zhdanov's son, Iurii, Patolichev had been close to his father, more so than Kuznetsov. Interview with Iu. A. Zhdanov, 23 October 1993.

78. Although it was only formalized on 2 August, Zhdanov's assumption of the chair of the Orgburo in fact took place at the beginning of May. See APRF f.3 op.22 d.41 l.70. Cf. point 11 of the resolution of 2 August and point1(a) of the resolution of 13 April. RGASPI f.17 op.163 d.1487 l.134; RGASPI f.17 op.163 d.1480 l.4. From March to August 1946, the leadership functions of the Orgburo were significantly enhanced. See Yoram Gorlizki, "Stalin's Cabinet: The Politburo and Decision Making in the Post-war Years," *Europe-Asia Studies* 53,2 (2001): 299–301; and Patolichev, *Sovest'iu*, 14–15.

79. *Vlast' i khudozhestvennaia intelligentsiia* (Moscow: Demokratiia, 1999), 587–591. The resolution was followed by two others, "On the Repertory of Theaters and on Measures for Its Improvement," of 26 August, and "On the Film *Bol'shaia zhizn'*," of 4 September.

80. *Pravda*, 21 September 1946.

81. For such a view of Zhdanov, see Werth, *Russia*, 202–209, esp. 204.

82. See D. L. Babichenko, *Pisateli i tsenzory. Sovetskaia literatura 1940-x godov pod politicheskim kontrolem TsK* (Moscow: Rossiia Molodaia, 1994), 117–118; RGASPI f.17 op.163 d.1480 l.6; RGASPI f.77 op.1 d.976 l.40.

83. This decision was probably only made by Stalin in mid-summer. At the April Politburo meeting, Stalin had not indicated that the targets would be Leningrad-based writers and journals. He had, in fact, singled out *Zvezda* and the Moscow-based *Novyi mir* as the worst culprits and held up *Oktiabr'* and *Znamia* as examples of the finest journals. Babichenko, *Pisateli*, 118.

84. Ibid., 119, 121, 129, 135, 143.

85. Ibid., 130–131; and *Vlast' i khudozhestvennaia intelligentsiia*, 570, 581. Malenkov's role was such that Babichenko even suggests, mistakenly, that it was Malenkov who chaired this meeting (121, 131).

86. RGASPI f.558 op.11 d.1128 ll.16, 19.

87. RGASPI f.77 op.1 d.802 ll.4–5, cited in Babichenko, *Pisateli*, 146 n.54. Zhdanov delivered two speeches in Leningrad, one to the party aktiv, and one to the Writers' Union, on 15 and 16 August, respectively.

88. See Romanovskii, *Liki stalinizma*, 106.

89. Khrushchev, *Vospominaniia*, 2:91.

90. RGASPI f.558 op.11 d.732 ll.1-3. Among several changes to the text, Stalin crossed out a preamble on how Zhdanov had been "assigned by the Central Committee of the party to explain the resolution of [14 September]." Instead, presumably in order to represent the resolution and the Leningrad speech as Zhdanov's idea, Stalin had the piece retitled: "An Address from Comrade Zhdanov on the Journals *Zvezda* and *Leningrad*." RGASPI f.558 op.11 d.732 l.4.

91. The connection with the events in 1947 is made in V. D. Esakov and E. S. Levina, "Delo KR," *Kentavr* 2 (1994): 55.

92. RGASPI f.558 op.11 d.732 l.19.

93. In Stalin's telegram to the quartet on 10 November 1945, he had denounced, albeit in a different rendering, "servility [*ugodnichestvo*] before Western figures." Cited in Danilov, "Stalinskoe politbiuro," 195. One of the associated tenets of this campaign, that the Soviet people should not underestimate their own strengths, also appears to have been inspired by Stalin. In his speech on the eve of the February elections, Malenkov had declared: "We need to believe in our own strengths. Comrade Stalin teaches us that we must not underestimate our own strength." *Pravda*, 8 February 1946, 2.

94. V. D. Esakov, "K istorii filosofskoi diskussii 1947 goda," *Voprosy filosofii* 2 (1993): 87.

95. "Diskussiia po knige G. F. Aleksandrova," *Voprosy filosofii* 1 (1947).

96. Ibid., 369; Hahn, *Postwar Soviet Politics*, 73–74, 76.

97. Resolution of 17 September 1947 in RGASPI f.17 op. 163 d.1504 l.67. Suslov had been made Central Committee Secretary on 22 May 1947, in the first instance as head of the administration for checking party organs, a position vacated following Patolichev's departure for Ukraine at the beginning of March. RGASPI f.17 op.163 d.1499 l.51.

98. See "Postanovlenie SM i TsK 'O sudakh chesti . . . ' 28 March 1947," *Istochnik* 1994 (6): 68–69; Iu. G. Murin, "Sudy Chesti," *Izvestiia TsK KPSS* 11 (1990): 135–137; Nikolai Krementsov, *Stalinst Science* (Princeton, N.J.: Princeton University Press, 1997),136–137.

99. Krementsov also suggests that Zhdanov used the "KR [Kliueva-Roskin] affair," to embarrass rivals, most notably Molotov. *Stalinist Science*, 130, 135, 156.

100. On 20 June 1946, the U.S. ambassador, Walter Bedell Smith had visited Kliueva's laboratory at the Institute of Epidemiology, Microbiology, and Contagious Diseases; in September, two eminent American physicians, Stuart Mudd and Robert Leslie, also visited the lab. Then, in the late autumn, the academician secretary of the Academy of Medical Sciences, Vasilii Parin, took the manuscript of Kliueva and Roskin's book, *The Biotherapy of Malignant Tumors*, and several samples of their "preparation," designed to cure malignant tumors, on a scientific visit to the United States. Esakov and Levina, *Delo KR*, 58–60; Krementsov, *Stalinist Science*, 132, 134.

101. See Esakov and Levina, *Delo KR*, 90.

102. Ibid., 100, 102.

103. Ibid., 112–114.

104. Ibid., 117–121, 122, 124, 133.

105. In a note of 25 March 1947, three days before the resolution was passed, Zhdanov wrote to Stalin: "*In accordance with your instructions, I am sending you a draft of the Central Committee resolution 'On honor courts in ministries and central institutions'* " (italics ours). See ibid., 130.

106. On 7 May, Stalin received, for his approval, a draft of the letter laying out the charges against the scientists. On 29 May, Stalin also received a draft of Zhdanov's statement to the honor court at the health ministry, with a request for comments. Ibid., 142–143; Esakov and Levina, *Delo KR*, 64; RGASPI f.558 op.11 d.732 ll.87–91; and Krementsov, *Stalinist Science*, 138.

107. There were few signs in the early stages that Kliueva and Roskin would emerge as the targets of the trial. On 28 January, Zhdanov had met with them to seek assurances about the significance of Parin's delivery of the manuscript to the Americans, which had taken place on 26 November 1946. On 17 February, at an expanded meeting of the leadership, Kliueva told Stalin that the book did not contain the key to her and Roskin's preparation and that the declassification of their work had been authorized, against their will, by Parin and the Minister of Public Health, Miterev. It was in the light of this that on 18 February the Orgburo agreed to release—and to increase the circulation of—copies of Kliueva and Roskin's book, and that Parin was arrested and Miterev dismissed. It only appears to have been in April that Kliueva and Roskin were chosen as the chief defendants. RGASPI f.558 op.11 d.732 ll.88–89; Esakov and Levina, *Delo KR*, 48–57, 62–63, 67–83; Krementsov, *Stalinist Science*, 134–135, 137.

108. Esakov and Levina, *Delo KR*, 137.

109. Ibid., 41–43.

110. Ibid., 71.

111. RGASPI f.558 op.11 d.732 l.91.

112. See Esakov and Levina, *Delo KR*, 64–65,143–145; Krementsov, *Stalinist Science*, 137.

113. "O dele Professorov Kliuevoi i Roskina," in Esakov and Levina, *Delo KR*, 66–68.

114. On the effect of the Marshall Plan on the Soviet Union's relations with the West, see Zubok and Pleshakov, *Stalin's Cold War*, 74.

115. Arguably, Zhdanov's most famous proclamation was the thesis, announced at the founding conference of the Cominform (Informational Bureau of Communist Parties) in late September 1947, that the world had divided into "two camps." It now appears most likely that this phrase, too, was Stalin's. According to Zubok and Pleshakov, Stalin had summoned Zhdanov to his vacation spot near the Black Sea in August and charged him with working out a blueprint for the Cominform. The critical phrase *two camps* is absent from all the early drafts of the speech in Zhdanov's personal archive. Zubok and Pleshakov, *Kremlin's Cold War*, 129–130, 133.

116. According to Zhdanov's son, Iurii, doctors had advised his father in the summer of 1947 to step down from his work for health reasons. Interview with Iu. A. Zhdanov, 23 October 1993. Cf. Hahn, *Postwar Soviet Politics*, 98; Zubok and Pleshakov, *Kremlin's Cold War*, 136. There are also numerous references in the literature to Andrei Zhdanov's alcoholism. See, for example, N. S. Khrushchev, *Khrushchev Remembers* (London: Andre Deutsch, 1971), 284; Milovan Djilas, *Conversations with Stalin* (London: Hart-Davis, 1962), 140; Mikoian, *Tak bylo*, 562–563.

117. Krementsov, *Stalinist Science*, 156–157.

118. The evolution of this struggle, which had begun in the 1930s and had reached a stalemate over the second half of 1947 and the first half of 1948, is treated at length in ibid., 58–83, 143–155.

119. Ibid., 178–180.

120. The connection between the worsening international climate and Sta-

lin's involvement in the Lysenko affair is excellently made in ibid., 158–159, 181.

121. Ibid., 173–174. In addition, on 23 July, Lysenko had sent Stalin a preliminary draft of his report, which Stalin read and edited, making numerous corrections. Ibid., 168.

122. Iu. A. Zhdanov, "Vo mgle protivorechii," *Voprosy filosofii* 7 (1993): 66–67.

123. Ibid., 69–71. Interview with Iu. A. Zhdanov, 23 October 1993.

124. Krementsov, *Stalinist Science*, 146–149.

125. For an extended summary of the speech, see Zhdanov, "Vo mgle," 74–86, esp. 75–76, 81, 85–86.

126. Ibid., 74, 86; Krementsov, *Stalinist Science*, 164–165.

127. V. A. Malyshev, "Dnevnik narkoma," *Istochnik* 5 (1997): 135.

128. Kremenstov, *Stalinist Science*, 166.

129. Malyshev, "Dnevnik narkoma," 135.

130. This is the argument of Kremenstov, *Stalinist Science*, 167–169.

131. Zhdanov, "Vo mgle," 87.

132. See Pravda, 7 August 1948, 3.

133. Kremenstov, *Stalinist Science*, 173–174.

134. Ibid., 272–273. In spite of forcing the younger Zhdanov into submission, Stalin felt a personal affinity for Iurii. In 1949, he coerced his daughter Svetlana into an unsuccessful marriage with the scientist. Iurii continued to visit Stalin on a social basis, seeing him in Sochi in the summer of 1951. In fact, Iurii Zhdanov stayed on as head of the natural science sector at Agitprop while, for his part, Stalin continued to act as his protector until his death. Interview with Iu. A. Zhdanov, 23 October 1993.

135. According to Kostyrchenko, Zhdanov originally left for the south, which he found too hot, before moving on to the Dolgie Borody sanatorium near Valdai. See G. V. Kostyrchenko, *Tainaia politika Stalina: Vlast'I antisemitism* (Moscow: Mezhdunarodnye otnosheniia, 2001), 638; and Esakov and Levina, *Delo KR*, 317–318.

136. For a detailed discussion of Zhdanov's physical state at the end of August, see Viktor Malkin, "Sem' pisem Lidii Timashuk," *Novoe vremia* 23 (1993): 39.

2: State Building Stalin-Style

1. Apart from Andreev, who was absent, the meeting of 29 December was attended by the full Politburo members elected at the XVIII Congress in 1939: Voroshilov, Zhdanov, Kaganovich, Kalinin, Mikoian, Molotov, Stalin, and Khrushchev. The candidate members of 1939, Beria and Shvernik, were now joined by Voznesenskii and Malenkov, who had become candidate members in 1941. Other participants included the Central Committee members Bulganin and Kosygin, both of whom would later join the Politburo. RGASPI f.17 op.163 d.1471 ll.2, 7.

2. These were formal sessions, with preannounced agendas sent out to all members of the Politburo, as well as to influential members of the Central

Committee. RGASPI f.17 op.163 d.1471 ll.2, 7; f.17 op.3 d.1055 l.1; f.17 op.3 d.1056 l.1; f.17 op.3 d.1058 l.1; and f.17 op.163 d.1489 ll.1–2.

3. A. A. Pechenkin, "Gosudarstvennyi komitet oborony v 1941 godu," *Otchestvennaia istoriia* 4–5 (1994): 130.

4. Ibid.; and see also Seweryn Bialer, ed., *Stalin and His Generals: Soviet Military Memoirs of World War II* (London: Souvenir Press, 1970), 370–371.

5. Although this was a practice dating back to the 1920s, it assumed a more stable form in the late 1930s. In April 1937, Stalin established two "commissions" which, in the wake of the Great Terror, were merged into a single subgroup consisting of Stalin, Molotov, Voroshilov, Kaganovich, and Mikoian. Heralding a practice that would become common in the postwar period, this group was referred to as the "quintet." In the last two years before the war, this quintet came to sideline the official Politburo, and it was a revised version of it that had formed the basis of the State Defense Committee. See O. V. Khlevniuk, *Politbiuro. Mekhanizmy politicheskoi vlasti v 1930-e gody* (Moscow: Rosspen, 1996), 237–239, 249–250.

6. With this resolution, the quintet became the sextet, consisting of Stalin, Molotov, Beria, Mikoian, Malenkov, and Zhdanov. RGASPI f.17 op.163 d.1471 ll. 2, 6.

7. That is, expanded sessions attended by all Politburo members for which agendas were prepared and of which records were kept. In addition to Politburo members, up to thirty Central Committee members and other officials attended these sessions. RGASPI f.17 op.163 d.1506 ll.1–3; f.17 op.163 d.1525 ll.1–6.

8. See N. S. Khrushchev, *Khrushchev Remembers* (London: Andre Deutsch, 1971), 299.

9. Reference to the *uzkii sostav* may be found in Anastas Mikoian, *Tak bylo. Razmyshleniia o minuvshem* (Moscow: Vagrius, 1999), 500, 564; the *blizhnii krug* is referred to in A. A. Danilov, "Stalinskoe Politbiuro v poslevoennye gody," in *Politicheskie partii Rossii. Stranitsy istorii* (Moscow: Izdatel'stvo Moskovskogo Universiteta, 2000), 193.

10. In the early postwar period, the members of the official Politburo excluded from the ruling group were Andreev, Kaganovich, Kalinin, Khrushchev, and Voroshilov (of the full members) and Shvernik (of the candidate members).

11. This is at least as far as we can tell, since no materials of this kind have surfaced in the archives. Decisions of the ruling group were effected either as resolutions of the Politburo or of the Council of Ministers. Contrast this with the agenda for the formal session of the Politburo of 13 April 1946, the supporting materials for which were distributed three days earlier, on 10 April. RGASPI f.17 op.163 d.1480 l.1

12. An exception was the dismissal of Malenkov as Central Committee Secretary at the expanded Politburo session of 4 May 1946.

13. Note that one of the Politburo commissions set up in April 1937, a forerunner of the sextet, had been assigned to look at "secret matters, including issues of foreign policy." Khlevniuk, *Politbiuro*, 237–238.

14. Danilov, "Stalinskoe Politbiuro," 204–205; and *Politbiuro TSK VKP (b) i Sovet Ministrov SSSR 1945–1953* (Moscow: Rosspen, 2002), 38.

15. Ibid., 38.

16. Svetlana Allilueva, *Twenty Letters to a Friend* (London: World Books, 1967), 194.

17. "The main thing [at those dinners]," Khrushchev recalled, "was to occupy Stalin's time so that he wouldn't suffer from loneliness. He was depressed by loneliness and he feared it." Khrushchev, *Khrushchev Remembers*, 299.

18. Some of the most important Politburo resolutions in this period were passed by the ruling group. The decision to abolish the State Defense Committee was made by the quintet from 11:00 to 12:00 P.M. on 4 September 1945, with other Politburo members voting later by correspondence. RGASPI f.17 op.163 d.1463 l.76; *Istoricheskii arkhiv* 4 (1996): 110–111. The decision on 2 August 1946 to rehabilitate Malenkov by appointing him deputy chair of the Council of Ministers was made by the sextet and, again, was later confirmed by correspondence. Numerous other high-profile cadre decisions were made by the "commission." So, for example, the decision of 15 December 1947 (two days after the expanded session of 13 December) to appoint Kaganovich as head of Gosplan and "to recommend" that Khrushchev return to his former post as First Secretary of the Ukrainian Communist Party was made by the septet. RGASPI f.17 op.163 d.1507 l.13. Cf. *Istoricheskii arkhiv* 5–6 (1996), 23.

19. See, for example, M. A. Men'shikov, *S vintovkoi i vo frake* (Moscow: Mezhdunarodnye otnosheniia, 1996), 120–121, 123–124.

20. For a more detailed discussion of this, see Yoram Gorlizki, "Stalin's Cabinet: The Politburo and Decision Making in the Post-war Years," *Europe-Asia Studies* 53, 2 (2001): 294–295, 297, 308 n.49.

21. Both in his secret speech and in his memoirs Khrushchev recalled: "Sometimes he would glare at you and say, 'Why don't you look me in the eye today? Why are you averting your eyes from mine?' or some such stupidity. Without warning he would turn on you with real viciousness." Khrushchev, *Khrushchev Remembers*, 258; also Khrushchev, "Secret Speech Concerning the 'Cult of the Individual,'" in *The Anti-Stalin Campaign and International Communism* (New York: Columbia University Press, 1956), 40. Also see Mikoian, *Tak bylo*, 535.

22. G. K. Zhukov, "Korotko o Staline," *Pravda*, 20 January 1989, 3, cited in David Holloway, *Stalin and the Bomb: The Soviet Union and Atomic Energy, 1939–1956* (New Haven, Conn.: Yale University Press 1994), 224.

23. V. A. Malyshev, "Dnevnik narkoma," *Istochnik* 5 (1997): 131. For an example of the leadership invoking the authority of the Politburo in this way, see Men'shikov, *S vintovkoi*, 122, 135; and interview with B. F. Bratchenko, 23 February 1999, 9.

24. At both the XVIII Party Congress in March 1939 and the XVIII Party Conference in February 1941, there had been 139 members of the Central Committee. See Evan Mawdsley and Stephen White, *The Soviet Elite from Lenin to Gorbachev: The Central Committee and Its Members, 1917–1991* (Oxford: Oxford University Press, 2000), 93. One hundred and forty-four people attended the February 1947 plenum. RGANI f.2 op.1 d.9 l.1.

25. Procedural issues included the renaming of commissars as ministers and the replacement of Kalinin as head of state by Shvernik. The personnel

changes consisted of the election of Malenkov and Beria as full members of the Politburo, and of Bulganin and Kosygin as candidate members, the appointment of a new fifteen-man Orgburo, and the promotion of Kuznetsov and Popov as Central Committee Secretaries. See RGANI f.2 op.1 d.7 ll.42–44; [Joseph Stalin] "Kommisarov chertova gibel'" *Istoricheskii arkhiv* 5–6 (1997): 217–218.

26. The Central Committee discussed a paper from the Politburo, entitled "On Measures to Improve Agriculture in the Postwar Period," drafted in response to the worsening food crisis. In addition, it formalized the expulsion of Shakhurin, Zhukov, and others from the Central Committee and ratified the elevation of Voznesenskii as a full member of the Politburo. The plenum also accepted Stalin's resignation as Minister of Armed Forces. RGANI f.2 op.1 d.9 ll.1–3; f.2 op.1 d.14 l.32.

27. The votes in 1946 were on the Aviators' Affair on 4–6 May, and on Merkulov from 21–23 August; the votes in 1947 were on the expulsion of G. N. Pal'tsev from the Central Committee on 28–30 January, and on the appointment of M. A. Suslov as Central Committee Secretary from 23–24 May; two of the votes in 1948 (on 16–18 February and on 3–4 September) were on promotions—of Bulganin and Kosygin—to the Politburo; the other two, in May and July, concerned the honor court and the appointment of Malenkov and Ponomarenko as Central Committee Secretaries. RGANI f.2 op.1 d.9 ll.3–4; and f.2 op.1 d.19 l.3.

28. In continuing to refer to "factions" (*fraktsionnye grupirovki*), claimed Zhdanov, the existing statutes underestimated "the moral and political unity of the party." They also failed to reflect organizational changes, such as the introduction of the new administration for checking party organs and the expansion of the Orgburo. See RGANI f.2 op.1 d.14 ll.21–25, 27–29, esp. 21,

29. See rule 29 of the 1939 party statutes in Graham Gill, *The Rules of the Communist Party of the Soviet Union* (Basingstoke, U.K.: Macmillan, 1988), 171–172.

30. Editorial in Pravda, 28 April 1964, cited in Werner G. Hahn, *Postwar Soviet Politics: The Fall of Zhdanov and the Defeat of Moderation, 1946–1953* (Ithaca, N.Y.: Cornell University Press, 1982), 38–39.

31. See RGASPI f.83 op.1 d.6 l.67.

32. This was a point made by Stalin in his election speech a week earlier, on 9 February 1946. "The war was nothing other than a test of our Soviet system, of our state, our government, our communist party." See I. V. Stalin, *Sochineniia*, vol. 3. Edited by Robert H. McNeal (Stanford, Calif.: Hoover Institution Press, 1967), 4–5.

33. See [Joseph Stalin], "Komissarov chertova gibel'," *Istoricheskii arkhiv* 5–6 (1997): 218.

34. In the 1920s, under Rykov, Sovnarkom had enjoyed a measure of independence from the Politburo. From Molotov's takeover in 1930 onward, however, Sovnarkom became fully integrated into party and, especially, Politburo structures. In the last few months prior to the war, the Politburo and the new leading committee of Sovnarkom, the Sovnarkom Bureau, were virtually merged. See Khlevniuk, *Politburo*, 25, 40, 50 255–256; and O. V. Khlevniuk,

"Stalin i Molotov," in *Stalin. Stalinizm. Sovetskoe obschestvo* (Moscow: IRIRAN, 2000), 277–279; and G. A. Kumanev, *Riadom so Stalinym. Otkrovennye svidetel'stva* (Moscow: Bylina, 1999), 386.

35. The existence of two Sovnarkom bureaus resulted from the transformation in September 1945 of the GKO operational bureau, under Beria, into an operational bureau of Sovnarkom, which now joined the existing Sovnarkom bureau, reestablished, under Molotov's leadership, in December 1942. The division of labor between the two bureaus proved, however, to be highly contrived. According to a Politburo resolution of 6 September 1945, the Molotov bureau was to supervise the affairs of thirty-three agencies spread across the departments of defence, the navy, agriculture, food, trade, finances, health, education, and culture; Beria's bureau, by contrast, was assigned responsibility for thirty-two agencies embracing the industrial commissariats and the railway system. The overlap between the two bureaus is suggested by the fact that two members, Voznesenskii and Mikoian, sat on both. RGASPI f.17 op.163 d.1471 ll.110–12.

36. On 20 March, the two Sovnarkom bureaus were unified in a single Sovmin Bureau under Beria's leadership. GARF f.5446 op.1 d.275 l.35. Eight days later, a second resolution rationalized the activities of the Bureau by dividing supervisory responsibilities over ministries among the chair and eight deputy chairs of Sovmin. GARF f.5446 op.1 d.275 ll.121–124.

37. The precursor of the Sovmin Bureau, the Sovnarkom Bureau, had been established on 21 March 1941 as a successor to two Sovnarkom committees, the Defense Committee (Komitet oborony) and the Economic Council (Ekonomsovet), both of which had been established in 1937. As with its postwar successor, the Sovnarkom Bureau, meeting weekly, was endowed with many powers of the full Sovnarkom, which, with the proliferation of commissariats in the late 1930s, was now considered too large. While legislation on the Sovnarkom Bureau in 1941 had insisted that plans, budgets, and military orders passed at the Bureau be confirmed by the full Sovnarkom and by the Central Committee, the February 1947 resolution included no such provision. RGASPI f.17 op.163 d.1495 l.125; Khlevniuk, *Politbiuro*, 251–255.

38. A Council of Ministers resolution of 28 March 1946 had accorded Beria, in his capacity as deputy chair of Sovmin, the right to oversee the activities of the Ministries of Internal Affairs, State Security, and State Control. GARF f.5446 op.1 d.275 l.122. By contrast, the resolution of 8 February stated that "all questions relating to the Ministry of Foreign Affairs, the Ministry of Foreign Trade, the Ministry of State Security, financial and hard currency matters, as well as the most important issues relating to the Ministry of Armed Forces—be concentrated in the Politburo." The Politburo also continued to control all important cadre appointments and to initiate organizational reforms. See RGASPI f.17 op.163 d.1495 l. 126. That this document was drafted by Stalin is apparent from the fact that parts of the original are in his hand. See ibid., ll.128–130.

39. As an example of the uncertain division of responsibilities between the Politburo and Sovmin concerning relatively minor individual issues, Stalin, in

March 1946, had split two adjoining items in the same letter by referring one, on the construction of an irrigation system, to the Council of Ministers, while converting the other, on the length of secondary education in Georgia, into a Politburo resolution. RGASPI f.17 op.163 d.1481 ll.115–116.

40. Stalin's address as paraphrased by Malyshev, "Dnevnik narkoma," 131–132.

41. GARF f.5446 op.59 d.100 l.17. Notwithstanding this intervention, Stalin's involvement in economic affairs was already fairly limited. A good example of his estrangement from the Sovmin Bureau just prior to the February resolution is provided by Malyshev. At a meeting of 28 December 1946, Stalin gave Malyshev a dressing-down for producing a particular kind of locomotive "without authorization of the government." "Although I had actually obtained permission from the Sovmin Bureau (with Beria's signature)," Malyshev later recounted, "I decided to keep mum and to shoulder the blame." See Malyshev, "Dnevnik narkoma," 130.

42. The one area where Stalin did interfere in the work of the Sovmin Bureau after February 1947 was the formulation of annual plans. For these purposes, the Sovmin Bureau might even be convened in his office. An example of one such meeting, attended by non-Politburo deputy premiers such as Malyshev and Saburov, was that of 25–26 December 1947 (and then continued five days later), which discussed the plan for capital investments for 1948. Possibly in view of the fact that they were held in Stalin's office and in Stalin's presence, Malyshev refers to these meetings as sessions of the "Politburo." See his "Dnevnik narkoma," 134.

43. The February resolution did contain the provision—never observed—that the "Bureau of the Council of Ministers of the USSR consists of the Chair of Sovmin I. V. Stalin, the First Deputy Chair V. M. Molotov, the deputy chairs of Sovmin and the head of Gosplan." RGASPI f.17 op.163 d.1495 l.125. Cf. "O raspredelenii obiazannostei" of 28 March 1946, GARF f.5446 op.1 d.275 l.124.

44. RGANI f.2 op.1 d.14 l.32. For the Central Committee resolution on Stalin's resignation, which took effect on 3 March, see RGANI f.2 op.1 d.9 l.3.

45. See N. V. Novikov, *Vospominaniia diplomata. Zapiski 1938–1946* (Moscow: Politizdat, 1989), cited in Holloway, *Stalin and the Bomb,* 427 n.1

46. "Ob obrazovanii biuro Soveta Ministrov SSSR," 20 March 1946, and "O raspredelenii obiazannostei v Sovete Ministrov SSSR," 28 March 1946. See GARF f.5446 op.1 d.275 ll.35, 121–124; RGASPI f.17 op.163 d.1471 ll.110–12.

47. There had been fifty meetings of the Bureau from its formation on 20 March 1946 until the February resolution. Of the eight deputy chairs only one, Molotov, failed to make most meetings. See *Politbiuro TsK VKP(b) i Sovet Ministrov SSSR 1945–1953* (Moscow: Rosspen, 2002), 464–488.

48. That is, the *Biuro pri Soveta Ministrov* as opposed to the main Sovmin Bureau, the *Biuro Soveta Ministrov.* In fact, the section on the sectoral bureaus (part 1) took up the bulk of the February resolution, accounting for five of its eight pages; the section on the main Bureau (part 2), by contrast, only accounted for a page and a half. See RGASPI f.17 op.163 d.1495 ll.120–124 and ll.125–126.

49. See RGASPI f.17 op.163 d.1495 l.120, 123 part 1, point 3.

50. The resolution of 28 March 1946 had assigned supervision of ministries to individual deputy premiers rather than to committees. This was a continuation of the prewar practice, first introduced on 21 March 1941, whereby deputy premiers were to supervise two to three commissariats each. The only equivalent to the postwar sectoral bureaus were the five economic councils, set up in April 1940 under the leadership of five junior deputy premiers: Bulganin, Malyshev, Voznesenskii, Pervukhin, and Kosygin. On 17 January 1941, Stalin had sung these councils' praises: "We need to put an end to the parliamentarism [of the Ekonomsovet] and to deal with matters in a businesslike way. We need to conduct all our work through the economic councils. Questions are prepared more thoroughly there, by summoning factory directors, heads of workshops, and designers." There were, however, key differences with the sectoral bureaus: the sectoral bureaus were headed mostly by Politburo members, whereas the councils were led by relatively junior figures; and heads of sectoral bureaus sat ex officio on the main Sovmin Bureau, while the councils did not slot into any supraministerial structure. In any event, the councils were dissolved on 21 March 1941, the same day as the main Sovnarkom Bureau was established. See Malyshev, "Dnevnik narkoma," 114, 144 n.55; GARF f.5446 op.1 d.275 ll.121–124; Khlevniuk, *Politbiuro*, 252, 255.

51. Part 1, point 4. RGASPI f.17 op.163 d.1495 ll.123-4.

52. Some ministries and commissions, such as the Ministry of State Control, the Ministry of Justice, and the main supply agencies bypassed the sectoral bureaus and were directly subordinate to the main Sovmin Bureau. In addition, some committees and ministries outside the sectoral bureaus were directly subordinate to individual members of the inner cabinet. The MVD, for example, was supervised by Beria, and the Ministry of Finance by Voznesenskii. RGASPI f.17 op.163 d.1495 ll.125–126.

53. At the time of the February resolution, five of the eight sector heads (Malenkov, Beria, Mikoian, Kaganovich, and Voroshilov) were Politburo members. Two weeks later, on 22 February, Voznesenskii, who had been a member of the septet since October 1946, was made a full member of the Politburo. See RGASPI f.17 op.163 d.1495 ll.124, 128.

54. The Bureau convened forty-seven times in 1947, fifty-three times in 1948, and fifty-three times in 1949. The figure for 1949 included the Presidium, the successor to the Bureau, which was created on 30 July 1949. Unlike 1946, which had seen a seven-week gap from 4 October to 20 November, the years 1947–1950 had no similar slack periods. Full agendas for these meetings are not yet available, though lists of approximately half of the items considered at each meeting can be found at RGAE f.1562 op.329 dd.1483–84, 1919–20, 2279, 2680–81.

55. The monthly rate of full Sovmin resolutions bearing Stalin's stamp grew from 184 in 1946 to 369 in the three months after the February resolution. See GARF f.5446 op.49a d.5061 ll.75–76. A report on 22 December 1947 from Serov, the Deputy Minister of Internal Affairs, also noted a sharp increase in correspondence handled by the courier office at Sovmin. To deal with this, Serov requested that the dispatch office be allocated a further six cars, in ad-

dition to the sixteen already at its disposal. See GARF f.9446 op.50a d.6958 ll.97–98a.

56. In each case, attendance at the Bureau followed shortly after appointment as deputy premier. The relevant meetings were as follows: Bulganin (27 March 1947), Malyshev (20 December 1947), Krutikov (29 July 1948), Efremov (10 March 1949), Tevosian (23 June 1949), and Pervukhin (19 January 1950). Not all of the new deputies headed sectoral bureaus. Bulganin's appointment was in connection with his promotion as Minister of Armed Forces on 3 March; Malyshev became deputy premier in December 1947, on becoming chair of the state committee for technology. RGASPI f.17 op.163 d.1507 l.7; d.1526 l.166; d.1541 l.71; *Gosudarstvennaia vlast'* SSSR, 25; *Politbiuro TsK VKP(b) i Sovet Ministrov SSSR 1945–1953*, 490–537.

57. *Gosudarstvennaia vlast'*, 25.

58. Jeremy R. Azrael, *Managerial Power and Soviet Politics* (Cambridge, Mass.: Harvard University Press, 1966), 106; William O. McCagg, *Stalin Embattled, 1943–1948* (Detroit: Wayne State University Press, 1978), 93, 354 n.94. Apart from the new deputy premiers, others listed by McCagg as "managers" were Nosenko, Sokolov, Akopov, Parshin, Ustinov, and Goremykin.

59. See Yoram Gorlizki, "Ordinary Stalinism: The Council of Ministers and the Soviet Neo-patrimonial State, 1945–1953," *Journal of Modern History* 74, 4 (2002): 711 n.34.

60. The significance of such a heavy presence of senior Politburo figures was not lost on Zhdanov, who himself was never a member of the Sovmin Bureau: "How can anyone say that the Council of Ministers has been forsaken? . . . [In fact,] our most important economic agencies have members of the Politburo and of the Central Committee sitting on them." RGASPI f.77 op.3 d.21 ll.12–13.

61. See Gorlizki, "Ordinary Stalinism," 712 n.36.

62. For example, GARF f.5446 op.75 d.6 ll.1102–3.

63. GARF f.5446 op.50a d.6964 ll.8, 27; d.6965 ll.14, 34, 53–54, 106; d.6962 ll.70, 76; d.6963 l.19; d.6960 l.43; d.6961 l.112.

64. See Gorlizki, "Ordinary Stalinism," 713 n.40.

65. RGASPI f.17 op.163 d.1510 l.6. From 29 March 1948 until Voznesenskii's removal in March 1949, chairmanship of the Bureau was shared equally between Voznesenskii (thirteen times), Beria (seventeen times), and Malenkov (sixteen times).

66. Gorlizki, "Ordinary Stalinism," 713 n.42. Control over the Bureau was then further dispersed on 1 September 1949, when chairmanship of its successor, the Presidium, was handed to five deputy premiers, Beria, Bulganin, Malenkov, Kaganovich, and Saburov, who henceforth headed meetings strictly in turn. RGASPI f.17 op.163 d.1530 l.61.

67. Part 1, point 7 of the resolution of 8 February. RGASPI f.17 op.163 d.1495 l.124.

68. See, for example, the memberships of the bureau for metallurgy and geology, established on 6 April 1949, and of the bureau for transport and communications, established on 13 February 1950. RGASPI f.17 op.163 d.1523 l.3; f.17 op.163 d.1542 ll.6, 86.

69. The resolution of 8 February specified that "each bureau have a member engaged exclusively in the organization of checking implementation and be freed from other functions" (see point (b) part 4 in RGASPI f.17 op.163 d.1495 l.126.) This was in fact a minimum. Some bureaus, such as the bureau of metallurgy and geology, established in 1949, and the bureau for transport and communications, established in February 1950, had two each. RGASPI f.17 op.163 d.1523 ll.2–3 f.17 op.163 d.1542 l.86.

70. Gorlizki, "Ordinary Stalinism," 714 n.47.

71. The February resolution had spoken of the sectoral bureaus facilitating the "more expeditious consideration and resolution of important economic questions" by allowing them to "decide on current questions." RGASPI f.17 op.163 d.1495 ll120, 123. On other forms of decentralization at Sovmin in this period, see, for example, A. G. Zverev, *Zapiski ministra* (Moscow: Politizdat, 1973), 228.

72. The February resolution had stipulated that "decisions of the bureaus could be issued in the form of orders [*rasporiazheniia*] of the Council of Ministers when accompanied by the signature of the corresponding deputy chair of Sovmin." Accordingly, enterprises could bring their case directly to the bureau without bothering the main Sovmin Bureau. RGASPI f.17 op.163 d.1495 l.124. See, for example, the appeals in 1948 from Ural'mash to Saburov, as head of the machine-building buro, for additional supplies of cast iron, electric power, ball bearings, and transformers. GARF f.5446 op.50 d.529 ll.30–31, 52, 80, 146.

73. Gorlizki, "Ordinary Stalinism," 715 n.50.

74. RGASPI f.17 op.163 d.1513 l.37.

75. By 12 July, the Orgburo, under Malenkov, assigned a special commission to look into the distribution of departments, and by 9 August, it had approved a new structure along with a list of relevant personnel. RGASPI f.17 op.115 d.727 ll.103–4; f.17 op.116 d.365 ll.9–43.

76. For a discussion of the background to this, see Gorlizki, "Ordinary Stalinism," 715–716 n.53.

77. Of the departments set up at the Central Committee, four had direct analogues in existing sectoral bureaus at Sovmin and a further two corresponded roughly with Sovmin bureaus. The direct analogues are the department of transport, which matched the bureau for transport and communications, the department of agriculture, which corresponded to the bureau for agriculture, the department of machine-building, which paralleled the bureau for machine-building, and the department of heavy industry, which shadowed the bureau for metallurgy and chemicals. There was also a rough correlation between the departments of light industry and of planning, finance and trade and the bureaus for food industry and for trade and light industry. Compare RGASPI f.17 op.163 d.1513 l.75; f.17 op.163 d.1495 l.124.

78. Milovan Djilas, *Conversations with Stalin* (London: Hart-Davis, 1962), 73–74; also see 144.

79. See note 38.

80. Part 3, RGASPI f.17 op.163 d.1495 l.126.

81. See Zverev, *Zapiski ministra*, 231–33, 273.

82. The main goal of the Politburo resolution of 16 February 1948 was to replace Zverev with Kosygin as Minister of Finance. Compare part 2.2.4 in RGASPI f.17 op.163 d.1495 l.125 with f.17 op.163 d.1509 ll.112–113.

83. The 10 December entry of Malyshev's diary, "Dnevnik narkoma," 133–134; for the original resolution, see RGASPI f.17 op.163 d.1507 l.8.

84. See point 2.2 (a) in RGAPI f.17 op.163 d.1495 l.125.

85. See RGASPI f.17 op.163 l.160.

86. See part 5 in RGAPI f.17 op.163 d.1495 l.126.

87. On 1 December 1947, the Politburo authorized a tariff of salaries for the Chair and Deputy Chairs of Sovmin, as well as for Central Committee Secretaries. RGASPI f.17 op.163 d.1506 l.137; also see GARF f.5446 op.75 d.5 ll.174–75.

88. *Neizvestnaia Rossiia. XX vek* (Moscow: Istoricheskoe nasledie, 1993), 3: 73. Also see P. A. Sudoplatov, *Spetsoperatsii. Lubianka i Kreml' 1930–1950* (Moscow: Olma Press, 1997), 285–286. On how the Aviators' Affair was channeled through Abakumov's counterintelligence service (SMERSH), see RGASPI f.17 op.163 d.1482 l.56.

89. See the Politburo resolution of 8 February 1947, "Ob organizatsii raboty Soveta Ministrov SSSR," section 3, in RGASPI f.17 op.3 d.1063 l.36.

90. RGASPI f.17 op.163 d.1509 l.222; and O. V. Khlevniuk, "Stalin i organy gosudarstvennoi bezopasnosti v poslevoennyi period," *Cahiers du monde russe* 42, 2–4 (2001): 537–538.

91. RGASPI f.17 op.163 d.1514 ll.9-14, 138-143. Cf. part 2.2(v) in RGASPI f.17 op.163 d.1495 l.125.

92. See Mikoian, *Tak bylo*, 355, 522.

93. Stalin openly defended "censorship" in his interview with Harold Strassen on 9 April 1947. See Stalin, *Sochineniia*, 3:83. For the view that it was specifically "Stalin who made secrecy all-embracing," see N. V. Romanovskii, *Liki stalinizma, 1945–1953* (Moscow: RAGS, 1995), 55.

94. These lectures, led by a veteran of earlier vigilance campaigns, the chair of the criminal panel of the USSR Supreme Court, V. V. Ul'rich, enjoined officials to reexamine their "trust" in those around them. Talks included sections on "personal and official acquaintances at work and their goal," on "discussing work at home or with colleagues," and on "the use of information for personal goals in reports and lectures." Officials were also given instructions on how secret materials were to be subjected to rigorous procedures for registration, safekeeping, copying, and redistribution. GARF f.5446 op.50a d.6957 ll.4–5.

95. The secret department at Sovmin sought an increase in staff from 204 on 1 November 1948 to 347 at the beginning of 1949. This was to cover an increase in the number of incoming secret documents registered by Sovmin from 98,300 in the first ten months of 1947 to 188,500 in the first ten months of 1948; the volume of secret documents sent out by its dispatch office grew from 122,000 to 173,500 over the same period. GARF f.5446 op.50a d.6958 ll.181–182.

96. Although the resolution of 8 June 1947 was not a secret, and was published in the press two days later, the resolution of 1 March 1948 on its implementation was itself categorized as a state secret. Over 99,000 copies of

the resolution had to be distributed to all union and republican ministries, as well as to committees affiliated with Sovmin. See GARF f.5446 op.50a d.6957 ll.14–20.

97. In October 1948, the deputy minister of light industry, Aleksandr Rybakov, complained that although the directive obliged tens of thousands of officials "to take important measures to preserve state secrets," the fact that the decree was itself "strictly secret" (*sovershenno sekretno*) meant that many of these same officials could not be told about it. GARF f.5446 op.50a d.6957 l.32.

98. See Gorlizki, "Ordinary Stalinism," 722–723 n.75.

99. N. K. Baibakov, *Ot Stalina do El'tsina* (Moscow: Gazoil Press, 1998), 42; Baibakov, *Sorok let v pravitel'stve* (Moscow: Respublica, 1993), 19, 27. According to the head of the Chancellery at the Ministry of Justice, ministerial officials would gaze at Stalin's window and wait for his light to go off before leaving their desks. Interview with N. F. Chistiakov, April 1993.

100. Men'shikov, *S vintovkoi*, 146.

101. Ibid., 100, 137.

102. Interview with N. F. Chistiakov, April 1993.

103. See the letter of 6 December 1948, from the typist, V. D. Galaktionova, at the administration of affairs at the Council of Ministers, complaining of the difficulties of returning by train to her home, fifty kilometers outside of Moscow, when her shift ended at 6:00 A.M. GARF f.5446 op.50a d.6958 l.28.

104. In a letter to Stalin from Sochi, dated 5 January 1947, Zhdanov, who noted that his trip was doing wonders for his health, pleaded: "I dearly request of you, comrade Stalin, that you extend my break, which ends on 15 January, by 10 days, to allow me to return to Moscow on 25 January." RGASPI f.17 op.163 d.1494 l.118. For a request to Stalin that a work deadline be extended, this time from Voznesenskii, Beria, and Malenkov, see RGASPI f.17 op.163 d.1519 l.11.

105. RGASPI f.74 op.1 d.429 ll.13-38. Voroshilov, who left Moscow on 22 April, did not attend the main Sovmin Bureau meetings from 3 April to 26 June 1947. RGASPI f.17 op.163 d.1497 l.223. After missing another three weeks in March 1948, Voroshilov's doctors advised him, in light of the stress he had been under, not to work more than four hours a day. RGASPI f.74 op.1 d.429 ll.13-38, entry of 17 March 1948.

106. RGASPI f.83 op.1 d.35 ll. 35, 22.

107. "One of the causes of the above-mentioned illnesses," it stated, "is the intensive work not only during the day, but also at night, and sometimes even on holidays." RGASPI f.77 op.3 d.3 l.6.

108. GARF f.5446 op.37 d.49 ll.237–245.

109. RGASPI f.77 op.3 d.3 l.6.

110. RGASPI f.82 op.2 d.396 l.138.

111. For example, Voroshilov's letters to Stalin of 22 June and 29 August 1949. GARF f.5446 op.54 d.67 ll.110–111; and Men'shikov, *S vintovkoi*, 126–127.

112. A new binding schedule was approved by the Council of Ministers only after Stalin's death in August 1953. "Postanovlenie Soveta Ministrov SSSR o

rezhime rabochego dnia v ministerstvakh, vedomstvakh i drugikh sovetskikh uchrezhdeniiakh," GARF f.5446 op.87 d.2112 l.92. The resolution, which warned that work discipline among functionaries had "gone to pieces," announced that the working day should begin at 9:00 A.M. and end at 6:00 P.M., with lunch to last for one hour.

113. The merging of the Politburo and the Council of Ministers had taken place over several stages from 1937 to 1941. First, in 1937, two committees, the Committee of Defense and the Economic Council, both filled with Politburo members, were established at Sovnarkom. Then, on 21 March 1941, a Bureau of the Sovnarkom was set up as a successor to these committees. The bureau, which met once a week, also acquired executive decision-making rights over the full Sovnarkom. On 4 May 1941, Stalin became head of Sovnarkom; three days later, membership of the Sovnarkom Bureau was increased to thirteen and, finally, a day later, the number of deputy premiers was increased to fifteen. As a result, virtually all Politburo members now sat on the SNK Bureau. According to the head of administration at the SNK, Ia. E. Chadaev, meetings of the SNK Bureau took place immediately before those of the Politburo, with Stalin chairing both. See Kumanev, *Riadom so Stalinom*, 385–386; and Khlevniuk, *Politbiuro*, 251–255.

3: The Politburo's Last Purge

1. For these and other figures for 1948, see the report of Gosplan, presented to the Bureau of the Council of Ministers of the USSR: GARF f.R-5446 op.51a d.5443 ll.1–44.

2. For more on this, see O. V. Khlevniuk, "Sovetskaia ekonomicheskaia politika na rubezhe 1948–1950-kh godov i 'delo Gosplana,' " *Otechestvennaia istoriia* 3 (2001): 77–82.

3. The Jewish Anti-Fascist Committee was denounced as a "center of anti-Soviet propaganda" and as a purveyor of "anti-Soviet information to foreign intelligence agencies." *Evreiskii antifashistskii komitet v SSSR. 1941–1948* (Moscow: Mezhdunarondnye otnosheniia, 1996), 371–372. For more on the anti-cosmopolitican campaign, see G. V. Kostyrchenko, *Tainaia politika Stalina: Vlast' i antisemitism* (Moscow: Mezhdunarodnye otnosheniia, 2001).

4. *Vostochnaia Evropa v dokumentakh Rossiiskikh arkhivov. 1944–1953* (Moscow/Novosibirsk: Sibirskii Khronograph, 1997), 1:7.

5. See G. P. Murashko and A. F. Noskova, "Sovetskoe rukovodstvo i politicheskie protsessy T. Kostova i L. Raika (po materialam rossiiskikh arkhivov)," in *Stalinskoe desiatiletie kholodnoi voiny. Fakty i gipotezy* (Moscow: Nauka 1999), 23–35.

6. GARF f.R-5446 op.1 d.346 ll.52–53.

7. Among the institutions and geographical units assigned new names were two districts in Moscow and Leningrad, a Moscow street, a number of enterprises (including one of the oldest Russian factories, the Sormovskii), and Leningrad University. GARF f.R-5446 op.1 d.349 ll.54–55.

8. The positions in question were deputy head of the department of propaganda and the department of foreign relations. RGASPI f.83 op.1 d.5 l.91.

9. RGASPI f.17 op.116 dd.355 ff.

10. RGASPI f.17 op.116 d.358 l.3.

11. RGASPI f.17 op.163 d.1514 l.186.

12. *Gosudarstvennaia vlast' SSSR. Vysshie organy vlasti i upravleniia i ikh rukovoditeli. 1923–1991. Istoriko-biograficheskii spravochnik* (Moscow: Rosspen, 1999), 370; *Sovet Narodnykh Komissarov SSSR. Sovet Ministrov SSSR. Kabinet Ministrov SSSR. 1923–1991. Entsiklopedicheskii spravochnik* (Moscow: Mosgorarkhiv, 1999), 316.

13. Kosygin, who had earlier headed this bureau, was asked to concentrate on the Ministry of Finance. RGASPI f.17 op.163 d.1513 l.73.

14. Anastas Mikoian, *Tak bylo. Razmyshleniia o minuvshem* (Moscow: Vagrius, 1999), 527–528.

15. Vladimir Pechatnov, "Shtrikhi k portretu genseka," *Istochnik* 3 (2000): 101–102.

16. RGASPI f.83 op.1 d.5 l.89.

17. RGASPI f.83 op.1 d.5 l.88.

18. Mikoian, *Tak bylo*, 567.

19. D. T. Shepilov, "Vospominaniia," *Voprosy istorii* 6 (1998): 15; Mikoian, *Tak bylo*, 565.

20. G. A. Kumanev, *Riadom so Stalinym. Otkrovennye svidetel'stva* (Moscow: Bylina, 1999), 428, 435; Mikoian, *Tak bylo*, 565–566; N. K. Baibakov, *Ot Stalina do El'tsina* (Moscow: Gazoil Press, 1998), 101–103.

21. APRF f.45 op.1 d.771 l.150.

22. *Stalinskoe Politbiuro v 30-e gody* (Moscow: AIRO-XXX, 1995), 171–172.

23. Feliks Chuev, *Sto sorok besed s Molotovym* (Moscow: Terra, 1991), 475.

24. RGASPI f.17 op.3 d.1073 l.56. Some of these charges would resurface at the trials of the Jewish Anti-Fascist Committee in 1952. See Joshua Rubenstein and Vladimir P. Naumov, eds., *Stalin's Secret Pogrom: The Postwar Inquisition of the Jewish Anti-Fascist Committee* (New Haven, Conn.: Yale University Press, 2001).

25. Chuev, *Sto sorok besed*, 473.

26. The vote was carried out by correspondence. From Poskrebyshev's notes it is apparent that Stalin, Bulganin, Voroshilov, Voznesenskii, Shvernik, Kaganovich, Mikoian, Andreev, Beria, Malenkov, and Kosygin voted to have Zhemchuzhina expelled, while "comrade Molotov abstained." RGASPI f.17 op.163 d.1518 l.162.

27. Stalin also insisted that the triumvirate he had written to about Molotov in 1945 be sent reminders. The original correspondence is discussed at greater length in chapter 1 of this book on pages 21–23.

28. RGASPI f.17 op.163 d.1518 l.164; A. A. Danilov, "Stalinskoe Politbiuro v poslevoennye gody," in *Politicheskie partii Rossii. Stranitsy istorii.* (Moscow: Izdatel'stvo Moskovskogo Universiteta, 2000), 210–211.

29. G. V. Kostyrchenko, *V plenu u krasnogo pharaona* (Moscow: Mezhdunarodnye otnosheniia, 1994), 136.

30. RGASPI f.17 op.163 d.1521 l.78.

31. G. M. Adibekov, *Kominform i poslevoennaia Evropa. 1947–1956 gg.* (Moscow: AIRO-XX, 1994), 19–21.

32. RGASPI f.17 op.163 d.1523 l.67.

33. Ibid.

34. RGASPI f.17 op.163 d.1523 l.3.

35. RGASPI f.82 op.2 d.393 ll.83-85.

36. RGASPI f.17 op.163 d.1523 l.3.

37. RGASPI f.17 op.163 d.1523 l.87.

38. RGASPI f.17 op.163 d.1523 l.87 ob.

39. RGASPI f.17 op.163 d.1523 l.169.

40. Mikoian, *Tak bylo*, 529.

41. Although the Soviet blockade was only finally lifted in May 1949, the failure of the policy had already become apparent at the beginning of March. While they were largely formal in nature, Western concessions did offer Stalin the opportunity to come out of the conflict with his dignity in tact. William Taubman, *Stalin's American Policy: From Entente to Détente to Cold War* (New York: Norton, 1982), 203–208.

42. Mikoian, *Tak bylo*, 566–567. This is discussed in greater detail later on in this chapter.

43. RGASPI f.17 op.163 d.1526 l.166.

44. RGASPI f.17 op.163 d.1542 l.6.

45. N. I. Egorova, "Evropeiskaia bezopasnost' i 'ugroza' NATO v otsenkakh stalinskogo okruzheniia," in *Stalinskoe desiatiletie kholodnoi voiny* (Moscow: Nauka, 1999), 72. In order to assess more fully the procedures for adopting foreign policy decisions and Molotov's role in this process, it would be necessary to study the original "special records" of the Politburo (the so-called special files or *osobye papki*), which contain resolutions on the more important foreign policy decisions, as well as information on how these were confirmed and implemented. These documents remain out of bounds to scholars.

46. Indeed, as the former diplomat Oleg Troianovskii recounts, the main consequence of Molotov leaving the Ministry of Foreign Affairs was not that Molotov's stature diminished but, rather, that the institutional authority of the ministry itself declined. He writes: "After the replacement of Molotov by Vyshinsky [in 1949], who was not a Politburo member, the role of the ministry in determining the course of the Soviet Union in international affairs noticeably decreased, and became all but ancillary." Troianovskii, *Cherez gody i rasstoianiia. Istoriia odnoi sem'i* (Moscow: Vagrius, 1997), 166.

47. RGASPI f.17 op.163 d.1540 l.183.

48. The classified records of the commission are kept in Mikoian's personal file at RGASPI (f.84 op.1).

49. RGASPI f.17 op.163 d.1541 l.141.

50. A somber example of this was Mikoian's announcement to his sobbing daughter-in-law, Alla Kuznetsova, that her father had been involved in a conspiracy against Stalin. "I, of course, had to tell her the official version." Mikoian, *Tak bylo*, 568.

51. *Reabilitatsiia. Politicheskie protsessy 30-50-kh godov* (Moscow: Politizdat, 1990), 313–314.

52. Ibid., 314.

53. It is quite possible that, at around this time, Stalin also received other

information on the Leningraders, such as signals on rigging during the vote at a conference of the Leningrad party organization, which had taken place at the end of December 1948. Ibid., 314.

54. RGASPI f.17 op.163 d.1519 l.104.

55. RGASPI f.17 op.163 d.1520 l.30.

56. Makarov's initials were not given in the visitors' book to Stalin's office. "Posetiteli Kremlevskogo Kabineta I. V. Stalina. 1947–1949 gg." *Istoricheskii arkhiv* 5–6 (1996): 48.

57. RGASPI f.17 op.163 d.1520 l.125.

58. *Reabilitatsiia*, 316.

59. It was thus, for example, Stalin (i.e., the words were written in his hand) who added to the original version of the reprimand against Voznesenskii the mitigating clause acknowledging that Voznesenskii had pointed out the error of Popkov's proposal on patronage.

60. Kovalev told this story to the writer Konstantin Simonov. See Konstanin Simonov, *Glazami cheloveka moego pokoleniia* (Moscow: Novosti, 1990), 160–161. These observations are confirmed by others who came across Voznesenskii, including Simonov himself, who observed Voznesenskii's behavior at an award ceremony for the Stalin prize. "He sticks in my memory not so much because I liked him, but because I was struck by the unrestrained and abrupt way in which he spoke and by the firmness with which he explained, in response to Stalin's questions, the various changes which had been made to the original decisions of the Science and Technology Prize Committee, by how often, and how resolutely and sharply, he stood his ground. In a word, his behavior was quite out of line with how the others spoke." Simonov, *Glazami cheloveka*, 158–159 What Stalin viewed as a virtue, many of those around Voznesenskii may have seen as a personality flaw. Mikoian, who was largely sympathetic to Voznesenskii, all the same wrote: "As a person, Voznesenskii had certain shortcomings. For example, [there was] his ambitiousness and his haughtiness. In the small circle of the inner Politburo, this was noticeable to all." Mikoian, *Tak bylo*, 559.

61. Aleksandr Pyzhikov has suggested that there were policy differences between the Leningraders and Beria and Malenkov's group. The victory of the latter, in his view, represented the triumph of the military-industrial complex over the "purely civilian sphere." See A. V. Pyzhikov, *Konfiguratsiia i funktsionirovanie vlasti v SSSR. 1945–1953* (Moscow: Nauchnaia Kniga, 1999), 26–27. There is, however, at present no evidence to back this position, and in particular the view that Zhdanov, Voznesenskii, and Kosygin actively spoke in favor of "moving economic priorities towards group 'B' industries."

62. It has been argued that unlike the ministries, Gosplan was not, in principle, directly held responsible for economic performance. It thus had no incentive to distort the upward flow of information and could be used by the political leadership as a third-party truth-telling agency. See Paul R. Gregory, *Restructuring the Soviet Economic Bureaucracy* (Cambridge: Cambridge University Press, 1990), 18–19, 20–21. Yet one of the big problems for Voznesenskii as the head of Gosplan was that he was also, in effect, held responsible for achieving the Politburo's growth targets for the first quarter of 1949. He was thus

caught between two stools: that is, he was expected to be *both* a purveyor of honest information and a hierarchical economic agent responsible for performance.

63. In order to fulfill their annual plans, Soviet enterprises tended to "storm" production over the last quarter of each calendar year. As a rule, this was followed by a spell of relaxation and economic slack in the first quarter of the following year. This is what Stalin hoped to avoid in 1949.

64. "It seemed," writes Mikoian, that "the psychological circumstances were such" that Voznesenskii had no choice but to agree. Mikoian, *Tak bylo*, 560.

65. RGASPI f.82 op.2 d.530 ll.8–10.

66. It is most probable that Pomaznev's note was part of an offensive by Beria and Malenkov against Voznesenskii. Certainly, it appears to have been no accident that Pomaznev was soon appointed to the influential post of head of administration at the Council of Ministers and that he should have been removed from it immediately after Beria's arrest in 1953.

67. It was typical in such circumstances that the report should have been cosigned by Voznesenskii, who was, in effect, now criticizing himself.

68. RGASPI f.82 op.2 d.530 ll.19–32.

69. Mikoian, *Tak bylo*, 560–561.

70. Although the original version of this resolution has not been found, and we do not therefore know what amendments were made by Stalin, its language and style suggest that Stalin had a major hand in its composition.

71. RGASPI f.17 op.163 d.1521 l.82.

72. Ibid.

73. Ibid., l.86.

74. Ibid., ll.88, 91.

75. *Molotov, Malenkov, Kaganovich. 1957. Stenogramma iun'skogo plenuma TsK KPSS i drugie dokumenty* (Moscow: MFD, 1998), 202.

76. *Reabilitatsiia*, 316; GARF f.R-8131 op.32 d.3289 ll.49–50.

77. APRF f.3 op.34 d.158 ll.118–121. Voznesenskii's book, *Voiennaia ekonomika SSSR v period otechestvennoi voiny*, had been published, to great acclaim, in December 1947.

78. The letter has appended to it a note from Stalin's aide Poskrebyshev: "To comrade Malenkov." RGASPI f.83 op.1 d.5 l.96.

79. RGASPI f.17 op.135 d.16 ll.83–89.

80. *Reabilitatsiia*, 317.

81. APRF f.3 op.54 d.26 ll.78-91.

82. RGASPI f.17 op.163 d.1530 l.154.

83. GARF f.R-8131 op.32 d.3989 l.63.

84. *Reabilitatsiia*, 319-320.

85. RGASPI f.17 op.135 d.38 l.1.

86. Ibid., ll.1–3.

87. RGASPI f.82 op.2 d.530 l.46.

88. GARF f.R-5446 op.51a d.5437 ll.1–14.

89. On this issue, Malenkov's statement to the June 1957 plenum of the Central Committee—which was overwhelmingly hostile to him—is convincing: "It is easy to establish that at no time was I the organizer of the Leningrad

Affair. *There are enough comrades here* who would confirm that it all happened on the personal orders of comrade Stalin"; "What, I told Stalin what to do [Ia rukovodil Stalinym]? People will just laugh." See *Molotov, Malenkov, Kaganovich,* 49, 491 (italics ours).

90. RGASPI f.558 op.11 d.762 ll.36–39.

91. Certainly some of the charges outlined in the letter appear to have been contrived. Thus, for example, the episode at the banquet (if it occurred at all) must have taken place no less than two years earlier, in 1947.

92. RGASPI f.558 op.11 d.762 ll.30–31.

93. Later, Malenkov inserted a telling amendment to the resolution, so that it was formally recorded in the following way: "To appoint a Politburo commission, comprising comrades Malenkov, Beria, Kaganovich, and Suslov, to carry out an examination of the activities of comrade G. M. Popov *in light of the circumstances noted in the letter of the three engineers*" (italics ours). Malenkov opted for a formulation that repeated, word for word, the original proposal from Stalin's letter. RGASPI f.17 op.163 d.1583 ll.263–265.

94. RGASPI f.17 op.163 d.1538 ll.30–33.

95. "Posetiteli Kremlevskogo Kabineta I. V. Stalin. 1947–1949 gg." *Istoricheskii arkhiv* 5–6 (1996): 60.

96. RGASPI f.17 op.163 d.1538 ll.24–26.

97. Ibid.

98. He eventually died peacefully, already a pensioner, in 1968.

99. N. S. Khrushchev, "Vospominaniia," *Voprosy istorii* 11 (1994): 72.

100. Bulganin's promotion was agreed at the February meeting of the Central Committee and was then ratified, on 3 March, by the Supreme Soviet. RGANI f.2 op.1 d.9 l.3.

101. RGASPI f.17 op.163 d.1497 l.25.

102. RGASPI f.17 op.163 d.1505 l.113.

103. RGASPI f.17 op.163 d.1509 l.116.

104. Bulganin was succeeded as Minister of Armed Forces on 24 March by Marshal A. M. Vasilevskii. RGASPI f.17 op.163 d.1523 l.88; f.17 op.163 d.1522 l.90.

105. In light of this, supervision of the Ministry of Finance was passed on to Kosygin. RGASPI f.17 op.163 d.1524 l.70; f.17 op.163 d.1522 l.91.

106. GARF f.R-5446 op.1 d.377 l.198.

107. RGASPI f.17 op.163 d.1530 l.61.

108. RGASPI f.17 op.163 d.1545 l.163. Bulganin was involved in preparing the resolution of 7 April. It was he who presented Stalin with a draft resolution on 6 April, to which Bulganin attached an accompanying note saying that neither Molotov, Beria, Kaganovich, nor Mikoian "have any objections to the draft." RGASPI f.17 op.163 d.1545 l.164. What immediately attracts attention is the absence of Malenkov from the original membership of the Bureau. We cannot be sure of the reasons for this. It is conceivable that Stalin first had in mind a purely party-based role for Malenkov or that, for some reason or other, Stalin wanted to show his displeasure toward Malenkov. At any rate, Stalin quickly changed his mind. The newly created Bureau met only three times—

on 8, 11, and 15 April 1950—without Malenkov. On 15 April, the Politburo passed a resolution on admitting Malenkov to the Bureau. RGASPI f.17 op.163 d.1546 l.106; *Istoricheskii arkhiv* 1 (1997): 11.

109. Khrushchev, *Vospominaniia* 2: 102.

110. Chuev, *Sto sorok besed*, 323.

4: Peaceful Coexistence

1. G. V. Kostyrchenko, *V plenu u krasnogo pharaona* (Moscow: Mezhdunarodnye otnosheniia, 1994), 207–288.

2. *Nepravednyi sud. Poslednyi stalinskii rasstrel.* Edited by V. P. Naumov (Moscow: Nauka, 1994), 9.

3. V. I. Pasat, *Trudnye stranitsy istorii Moldovy. 1940–1950-e gody.* (Moscow: Terra, 1994), 612–615, 637–639.

4. Matias Rakosi, "Ludiam svoistvenno oshibat'sia," *Istoricheskii arkhiv* 5–6 (1997): 7–8. The very fact that the January 1951 conference took place at all has been corroborated by the Czech historian Karel Kaplan, who bases his work on the testimony of another participant, the Czechoslovak Minister of Defense Aleksei Chepichka. Kaplan's interpretation diverges in important respects from that of Rakosi. According to Kaplan, Stalin, alluding to the war in Korea, highlighted the military weakness of the United States and claimed that over the next four or five years the socialist bloc would enjoy a temporary military advantage in Europe. "The socialist countries," Stalin is reported to have said, "should use these four to five years in order to change the face of Europe, free it from capitalism by means of military force, and turn the continent socialist." Hence, argues Kaplan, Soviet military officials and the East European defense ministers agreed to specific targets at the meeting which "each country was to fulfil within four years, as well as those tasks that would lie ahead in the course of the 'European campaign.' " On this point Kaplan's account seems implausible. If Stalin, as Kaplan writes, believed that the military predominance of the socialist camp in Europe was only transitory, and would last for no more than four or five years, then why should he choose to delay the "European campaign"? That such a belligerent declaration of intent could have been made at all—even among the most senior of East European leaders—also appears dubious. In light of these reservations, it is more probable that the meeting matched the description given by Rakosi. In view of the increasing hostility of the West, as it appeared to the Soviet leadership, Moscow proposed that its allies join in the arms race. The key issue addressed at the meeting was how to compel the East European states to take on a part of the military burden that had, by this stage, exceeded what the Soviet Union could carry on its own. Karel Kaplan, "Vozvyshenie i padenie Alekseia Chepichki," *Voprosy istorii* 10 (1999): 85–86.

5. RGAE f.1562 op.329 d.3873 ll.27, 138.

6. These statistics are based on the four ministries established after Stalin's death—the Ministries of Defense (uniting the former War and Naval Ministries), Defense Industries (based on the former Arms Ministry), Aviation In-

dustry, and Medium Machine-Building. These four ministries accounted for the overwhelming bulk of military spending.

7. RGAE f.4372 op.11 d.677 ll.9–10.

8. N. S. Simonov, *Voenno-promyshlennyi kompleks SSSR v 1920–1950-e gody* (Moscow: Rosspen, 1996), 210–266.

9. A. A. Danilov and A. V Pyzhikov, *Rozhdenie sverderzhavy. SSSR v pervye poslevoennye gody.* (Moscow: Rosspen, 2001), 92–93.

10. GARF f.R-5446 op.816 d.6645 ll.1–4.

11. For more on this, see chapter 5 of this book.

12. The program was approved in a Council of Ministers resolution of 19 February 1953.

13. RGASPI f.82 op.2 d.393 l.82.

14. Apart from Bulganin himself, the bureau included all the relevant ministers. RGASPI f.17 op.163 d.1577 ll.22–23.

15. The dissolved bureaus were for fuel industries, agriculture and procurements, transport and communications, metallurgy and geology, and culture. RGASPI f.17 op.3 d.1088 l.2.

16. Responsibility for overseeing sectors formerly covered by the branch bureaus was now vested directly in their former heads who, as deputy chairs of Sovmin sat ex officio on the Sovmin Presidium. To help in this task, each deputy chair of Sovmin was asked to identify "necessary aides."

17. The Politburo resolution of 15 March was clearly initiated by Stalin: the first draft of the resolution contains a host of Stalin's corrections, including some in his own hand. RGASPI f.17 op.163 d.1580 l.1.

18. RGASPI f.17 op.163 d.1519 l.22.

19. In fact, from February 1947 until Stalin's death, Andreev never made it to Stalin's office. Andreev's position had also been of little help in protecting his wife, Dora Khazan, from virulent persecution during the anti-Semitic campaigns of 1949. Having already been sacked as Deputy Commissar of the Textile Industry and demoted to the lesser post of director of a scientific research institute, she was, amidst an unseemly scandal, driven out of the institute in 1949. Kostyrchenko, *V plenu*, 137; RGASPI f.17 op.118 d.562 ll.115, 125–128.

20. The original draft of his letter to Stalin, in which Andreev fully admitted his mistakes and requested a meeting with the leader, has been preserved in the archives. RGASPI f.73 op.2 d.23 l.143; f.17 op.163 d.1542 l.136.

21. See, for example, GARF f.R-5446 op.54 d.67 l.110; RGASPI f.17 op.3 d.1077 l.8; d.1078 l.6

22. APRF f.3 op.52 d.252 ll.24–48.

23. RGASPI f.17 op.163 d.1556 l.92.

24. *Politbiuro TsK VKP(b) i Sovet Ministrov SSSR 1945–1953* (Moscow: Rosspen, 2002), 539–561. In January 1951, Khrushchev was also charged with overseeing the work of the Ukrainian Central Committee. RGASPI f.17 op.163 d.1574 l.94.

25. V. M. Loginov, *Teni Stalina. General Vlasik i ego soratniki* (Moscow: Sovremennik, 2000), 133. Vlasik, who was, one might note, a fervent enemy of Beria's, dates this meeting to 1950, although, clearly, the atomic factor must

have played a significant role in Beria's favor earlier than this, for the first successful test had already been carried out in August 1949.

26. RGASPI f.17 op.163 d.1577 l.23.

27. On Stalin's role in this, see *Lavrentii Beria. 1953* (Moscow: MFD, 1999), 77.

28. *Istoricheskii arkhiv* 4 (1998): 8–9.

29. See the information on Stalin's breaks in RGASPI f.558 op.11 d.1481.

30. "Posetiteli Kremlevskogo Kabineta I. V. Stalina. 1950–1953 gg." *Istoricheskii arkhiv* 1 (1997): 25. This was linked to the fact that, after a long break, which had gone on until 21 December 1951, Stalin came down with the flu in January 1952. RGASPI f.558 op.11 d.1483 ll.74–78.

31. See, for example, RGASPI f.17 op.163 d.1611 l.140. In documents from the period, the group was referred to as the septet (*semerka*). The septet, however, rarely met in full, since at any one time members of the group may have been on holiday or on a work-related visit.

32. RGASPI f.17 op.163 d.1598 l.60 (italics ours).

33. RGASPI f.17 op.163 d.1604 l.186 (italics ours).

34. See, for example, RGASPI f.17 op.163 d.1561 ll.105–108; d.1562 l.112; d.1565 l.30; d.1598 ll.43, 125; d.1599 l.150; d.1602 ll.42, 118.

35. Stalin was also included on the original membership of the Bureau of the Presidium, but he never actually attended its meetings. RGASPI f.17 op.163 d.1545 l.163. From September 1950 on, Khrushchev regularly attended sessions of the Bureau. Prior to this he had occasionally attended sessions of the Presidium, for example on 3 April, 13 April, 4 May, 27 May, 27 June, 6 July, 20 July, 10 August, and 24 August. See *Politbiuro TsK VKP(b) i Sovet Ministrov SSSR 1945–1953*, 539–543. The admission of Khrushchev is significant since he was not a deputy premier and, indeed, held no position at Sovmin. His inclusion underlines the general cabinet functions of the Bureau of the Presidium.

36. The Presidium, by contrast, convened twenty, eighteen, and twelve times in these years. See *Politbiuro, TsK VKP(b) i Sovet Ministrov SSSR 1945–1953*, 539–562.

37. This is discussed at greater length in chapter 5.

38. These were different from the formal meetings of the Bureau of the Council of Ministers referred to earlier, whose proceedings were officially recorded and which convened on a regular, near weekly basis. These meetings were never attended by Stalin. See *Politbiuro, TsK VKP(b) i Sovet Ministrov SSSR 1945–1953*, 539–563.

39. These decisions were drawn up as Politburo resolutions after Vyshinsky informed Poskrebyshev that the matter had been confirmed at a Politburo meeting. As a rule, the dates given by Vyshinsky correspond to the days on which Politburo sessions, attended by Vyshinsky himself, had been held in Stalin's office. Thus, according to Vyshinsky, questions relating to the Ministry of Foreign Affairs were confirmed on 22 and 31 March, 22 April, 19 and 24 May, 9 and 25 June, and 20 and 22 August of 1952. RGASPI f.17 op.163 d.1615 l.95; ll.167–169; d.1618 ll.74–80; d.1620 ll.153–174; d.1622 ll.148–155; d.1624 ll.6–

10; d.1628 ll.8, 28. On these days Vyshinsky attended Stalin's office along with other members of the Politburo. "Posetiteli Kremlevskogo Kabineta I. V. Stalina. 1950–1953 gg." *Istoricheskii arkhiv* 1 (1997): 26–30.

40. RGASPI f.17 op.163 d.1627 l.160. It is apparent from Vyshinsky's notes on the original Politburo record that a whole welter of such proposals from the Ministry of Foreign Affairs was confirmed on 13 August. RGASPI f.17 op.163 d.1627 ll.138–149.

41. We cannot be sure of this. It is conceivable that a decision had been reached unilaterally by Stalin and then conveyed to Vyshinsky by phone. It would have been strange, however, for Stalin to have instructed Vyshinsky on this matter and not Poskrebyshev directly.

42. RGASPI f.17 op.163 d.1622 l.43. Likewise, on two other drafts, Vyshinsky wrote: "Comrade A. N. Poskrebyshev. I understand from comrade V. M. Molotov that this was confirmed on 17 June 1952. Please have this drawn up." RGASPI f.17 op.163 d.1622 ll.61, 63. On neither of these days, on 6 or 17 June, were there meetings in Stalin's office.

43. RGASPI f.17 op.163 d.1623 l.99. When decisions were taken unilaterally or in a small cabal, the draft resolution was often circulated "by correspondence" to the other members of the Politburo. Such a procedure, however, required Stalin's consent. So, on 23 July (seemingly at a meeting in Stalin's office in the Kremlin), Vyshinsky received Stalin's permission to have a number of foreign policy questions voted on "by correspondence." The subsequent vote, which involved Malenkov, Bulganin, Kaganovich, Mikoian, Khrushchev, and Beria (the agreement of the latter was conveyed by his aide, Ordyntsev) was taken in stages over 25 July and 1–2 August. RGASPI f.17 op.163 d.1626 ll.100–101; d.1627 ll.19–20.

44. For a meticulous earlier account of these events based on published sources, see Robert Conquest, *Power and Policy in the USSR: The Study of Soviet Dynastics* (London: Macmillan, 1961), chaps. 6 and 7.

45. APRF f.3 op.30 d.159 l.76. First published in *Otechestvennye arkhivy* 1 (1994): 44 (prepared by V. P. Popov).

46. Feliks Chuev, *Sto sorok besed s Molotovym* (Moscow: Terra, 1991), 362.

47. D. T. Shepilov, "Vospominaniia," *Voprosy istorii* 6 (1998): 32.

48. RGASPI f.17 op.163 d.1581 l.13.

49. Chuev, *Sto sorok besed*, 362.

50. Shepilov, "Vospominaniia," *Voprosy istorii* 6 (1998): 32.

51. Later, Khrushchev's misdemeanor would be famously alluded to in Malenkov's speech at the XIX Party Congress. It is also no coincidence that when Khrushchev himself acceded to power, he had the Central Committee's resolution overturned and declared erroneous. See " 'Vtoroi i vazhneishii etap' (ob ukreplenii kolkhozov v 50-e–nachale 60-kh godov)." *Otechestvennye arkhivy* 1 (1994): 49–50.

52. Conquest, *Power and Policy*, 140–141. Iurii Zhukov contests this view and suggests that the Mingrelian Affair was initiated by Malenkov. However, he supplies no evidence to support this thesis. Iurii N. Zhukov, *Tainy Kremlia. Stalin, Molotov, Beria, Malenkov.* (Moscow: Terra, 2000), 561.

53. Kiril Stoliarov, *Palachi i zhertvy* (Moscow: Olma Press, 1997), 163.

54. That Vlasik should have passed on these signals was entirely logical. Vlasik was at the time locked in a head-to-head struggle with the Ministry of Internal Affairs, which was overseen by Beria, and could demonstrate to Stalin his adherence to "principles," while at the same time indirectly implicating Beria, whose brief also included supervision of Georgia.

55. Stoliarov, *Palachi i zhertvy*, 225–226.

56. Ibid., 167–168.

57. RGASPI op.163 d.1604 ll.57-60.

58. Stoliarov, *Palachi i zhertvy*, 169–172.

59. *Lavrentii Beria. 1953*, 34–35, 399.

60. RGASPI f.558 op.11 d.418 ll.9-10.

61. Ibid. Apart from his role in authoring it, Stalin also titled the resolution. The draft has an amendment in Poskrebyshev's hand, again almost certainly dictated by Stalin. RGASPI f.17 op.163 d.1615 ll.134, 138.

62. Stoliarov, *Palachi i zhertvy*, 185–190.

63. There is a copy of this document in Stalin's archive, with corrections by the leader. Judging from its style, the letter had originally been dictated by Stalin. RGASPI f.558 op.11 d.135 l.89.

64. RGASPI f.558 op.11 d.135 l.89.

65. RGASPI f.17 op.163 d.1622 l.141.

66. RGASPI f.558 op.11 d.135 l.88.

67. That Beria himself viewed the repressions in Georgia as a personal threat is reflected in the fact that one of Beria's first moves following Stalin's death was to stop the Mingrelian Affair and to release and promote to leading positions the arrested "Mingrelians." *Lavrentii Beria. 1953*, 29–40.

68. *Molotov, Malenkov, Kaganovich. 1957* (Moscow: MFD, 1998), 748.

69. Ibid., 203.

70. P. A. Sudoplatov, *Razvedka i Kreml'. Zapiski nezhelatel'nogo svidetelia* (Moscow: Too "Geia," 1996), 383.

71. GARF f-R.8131 op.32 d.3289 ll.48–57.

72. RGASPI f.17 op.163 d.1543 ll.49–52.

73. RGASPI f.17 op.163 d.1543 ll.49, 50.

74. For testimony that Riumin presented his denunciation of Abakumov to Malenkov's personal aide, Dmitrii Sukhanov, and that Malenkov forwarded the charges to Stalin, see D. N. Sukhanov, "Iz vospominaniia Sukhanova D. N. byvshego pomoshchnika Malenkova G. M," manuscript deposited at RGANI, 1992, d.2 l.14; also see Stoliarov, *Palachi i zhertvy*, 320, as well as 115–116, 178. Stoliarov even implies that the Riumin letter was in some ways solicited by Malenkov (*Palachi i zhertvy*, 14–15). As of yet, there is no solid evidence on this. Nonetheless, as Stalin's favorite henchman in the early postwar period, Abakumov had certainly made powerful personal and institutional enemies including, among the former, Malenkov, whose involvement in the Aviators' Affair he had investigated in 1946, and, among the latter, the Ministry of Internal Affairs, with whose Deputy Minister, Ivan Serov, Abakumov had crossed swords on several occasions over the preceding years. See N. V. Petrov, "Pervyi predsedatel' KGB general Ivan Serov," *Otechestvennaia istoriia* 5 (1997): 28–30, 33–34.

75. Stoliarov, *Palachi i zhertvy*, 42.

76. RGASPI f.17 op.163 d.1590 l.135; R. G. Pikhoia, *Sovetskii soiuz. Istoriia vlasti, 1945–1991* (Moscow: RAGS, 1998), 82.

77. "Posetiteli Kremlevskogo Kabineta I. V. Stalina. 1950–1953 gg.," *Istoricheskii arkhiv* 1 (1997): 21.

78. The following day, on July 12, Abakumov was arrested. Abakumov's arrest was accompanied by a clear-out of his colleagues, including the dismissal of two deputy ministers, Selivanovskii and Pitovranov. For slightly differing interpretations of Abakumov's arrest and subsequent interrogations, see Stoliarov, *Palachi i zhertvy*, 11, 20, 47; and Pikhoia, *Sovetskii soiuz*, 81–82.

79. The resolution of 11 July was placed in a "special file" (*osobaia papka*) and has not yet been unearthed by researchers, although the closed letter, which contains the text of the resolution in full, has been published. See "Zakrytoe pis'mo TsK VKP(b)," *Svobodnaia mysl'* 1 (1996): 90–93.

80. According to D. N. Sukhanov, Malenkov's aide, Stalin insisted that a figure from the party apparatus head the MGB. Initially, three persons were considered: N. G. Ignatov, S. D. Ignat'ev, and N. M. Pegov. Eventually, Stalin settled for Ignat'ev. Sukhanov, "Iz vospominaniia Sukanova D. N.," d.2, l.14. Ignat'ev had served as head of the department of party, trade union, and Komsomol agencies since 29 December 1950. See RGASPI f.17 op.163 d.1573 l.43.

81. RGASPI f.17 op.163 d.1595 l.130.

82. Ibid.

83. Their fate after Stalin's death tells us something about their affiliations. While Goglidze, with Beria's support, received a top position at the new Ministry of Internal Affairs, Ogol'tsov was arrested.

84. The original record of the resolution on Riumin's appointment suggests that it was adopted on the basis of a note by Ignat'ev. The resolution itself, which was written up by a secretary, did not contain any reference to a vote, which suggests that the decision was made jointly by Stalin and Ignat'ev. RGASPI f. 17 op.163 d.1602 l.30.

85. Pikhoia, *Sovetskii soiuz*, 92; Stoliarov, *Palachi i zhertvy*, 70–77.

86. RGASPI f.558 op.11 d.117. A comparison with analogous registers for 1945 shows that there was a drop in the volume of materials forwarded by the MGB to Stalin while the leader was in the south. In 1945, Stalin had received 215 materials over a period half as long (from early October to the middle of December 1945). RGASPI f.558 op.11 d.117. This decline was largely due to the incomplete forwarding (judging by their issue numbers) of reports. One may assume that on his last break in the south, Stalin was only sent the most important reports, while in 1945 he had been sent all.

87. RGASPI f.17 op.3 d.1086 l.84.

5: Awakening to Crisis

1. This, for example, would become apparent at the Central Committee plenum of October 1952, when Stalin launched into Molotov and Mikoian for

their proposals on raising procurement prices. This is discussed at greater length in chapter 6 of this book.

2. *GULAG. 1918–1960* (Moscow: Materik, 2000), 435, 447; V. N. Zemskov, "Massovoe osvobozhdenie spetsposelentsev i ssylnykh (1954–1960)," *Sotsiologicheskie issledovaniia* 1 (1991): 5.

3. See GARF f.9492 op.6a d.14 l.8.

4. Of the 14,030,000 convictions in the ordinary courts from 1946 to 1952, 6,371,000 were on charges relating to the wartime legislation which, apart from the three main offenses of unlawful quitting, shirking, and nonfulfillment of labor dues, included other edicts on violations of discipline, desertion, and evasion of military service. GARF f.9492 op.6s d.14 ll.6, 9.

5. See Peter H. Solomon Jr., *Soviet Criminal Justice under Stalin* (Cambridge: Cambridge University Press, 1996), chap. 12; and Yoram Gorlizki, "Rules, Incentives, and Soviet Campaign Justice after World War II," *Europe-Asia Studies* 51, 7 (1999): 1249–1254.

6. V. N. Zemskov, "Gulag. Istoriko-sotsiologicheskii aspekt," *Sotsiologicheskie issledovaniia*, 6 (1991): 11.

7. *GULAG. 1918–1960*, 437.

8. These custodial sentences included 4,356,000 for crimes involving preliminary investigations and 1,530,000 for prosecutions on charges relating to the wartime decrees. The figure of 14,030,000 convictions for the period 1946–1952 relates only to the ordinary courts, not to the line, transport, and camp courts, or to the military tribunals, which would bring the figure up to 15,597,000. If we take into account the latter jurisdictions, the overall number of custodial sentences rises to approximately 7 million. Calculations from GARF f.9492 op.6s d.14 ll.6, 10, 30; and see A. Kokurin and Iu. Morukov, "Gulag. Struktury i kadry," *Svobodnaia mysl'* 12 (2001): 98–101.

9. GARF f.R-9401 op.1 d.4109 ll.279–280.

10. GARF f.R-9401 op.1 d.4109 l.281.

11. The book *Soprotivlenie v Gulage* (Moscow: Vozvrashchenie, 1992), 204–210, records nine major armed escapes, hunger strikes, and disturbances from 1947 to 1952. This list, however, is clearly incomplete. Thus, in 1951 alone, the Gulag files recorded seven major disturbances and collective assaults by prisoners on camp officials. The armed attacks led to large-scale casualties among the prisoners and the camp guards (GARF f.R-9414 op.1 d.326 ll.140–141).

12. Marta Kraveri, "Krizis Gulaga. Kengirskoe vosstanie 1954 goda v dokumentakh MVD," *Cahiers du monde russe* 36, 3 (1995): 321–322.

13. GARF f.R-9414 op.2 d.411 l.7.

14. GARF f.R-5446 op.86a d.8339 ll.224-226; d.8335 l. 362.

15. *Arkhiv noveishei istorii Rossii*, vol. 4, "Osobaia papka" L. P. Berii. Iz materialov Sekretariata NKVD-MVD SSSR. 1946–1949. Katalog dokumentov (Moscow: Gosarkhiv, 1996).

16. See Oleg Khlevniuk, ed., *The History of the Gulag: 1930–1941*, vol.2 (New Haven, Conn.: Yale University Press, forthcoming), chap.5.

17. GARF f.R-5446 op.80 d.7561 l.42.

18. GARF f.R-9414 op.1 d.1363 l.10.

19. GARF f.R-5446 op.80 d.7384 ll.26–27.

20. GARF f.R-5446 op.81b d.6557 ll.83–84, 124.

21. GARF f.R-5446 op.80a d.7641 ll.51–54.

22. GARF f.R-5446 op.81b d.6645 ll.19–23.

23. Mamulov had first served under Beria for many years in Georgia. Following Beria's appointment at the end of 1938 as Commissar of Internal Affairs, Mamulov took over as the head of Beria's secretariat, then after the war became deputy Minister of Internal Affairs. After Stalin's death, Mamulov was once again immediately appointed as head of Beria's secretariat at the new USSR Ministry of Internal Affairs. Following a short stint there, Mamulov was moved to another post of strategic significance for Beria, the head of the department of party, trade union, and Komsomol agencies at the Georgian Central Committee. In the wake of Beria's own arrest in June 1953, Mamulov was also apprehended and sentenced to a prison term of fifteen years. Mamulov's career path indicates how closely linked he was to his patron and suggests—although we cannot be absolutely certain of this—that he was attuned to Beria's own views and policy preferences.

24. GARF f.R-9401 op.1 d.2643 ll.235–239.

25. GARF f.R-9401 op.1 d.3586 ll.274–276.

26. GARF f.R-9401 op.1 d.3586 ll.280–298.

27. *Arkhiv noveishei istorii Rossii*, vol.1. *"Osobaia papka" I. V. Stalina. Iz materialov Sekretariata NKVD MVD SSSR 1945–1953 gg.* Edited by V. A. Kozlov and S. V. Mironenko (Moscow: Gosarkhiv, 1994).

28. GARF f.R-5446 op.80a d.7743 ll.2–20.

29. GARF f.R-5446 op.81b d.6528 ll.2–23.

30. *Lavrentii Beria. 1953* (Moscow: MFD, 1999), 19–21.

31. *GULAG. 1918–1960*, 786–788; GARF f.R-5446 op.57a d.133 ll.21–24; d.134 l.9.

32. *GULAG. 1918–1960*, 788–791; GARF f.R-9401 op.1 d.4155 ll.21–29.

33. *GULAG. 1918–1960*, 791–793; GARF f.R-5446 op.57a d.133 ll.26–28.

34. GARF f.R-5446 op.87 d.1202 l.69; V. P. Popov, *Ekonomicheskaia politika Sovetskogo gosudarstva. 1946–1953 gg* (Moscow-Tambov: Izdatel'stvo TGTU, 2000), 205.

35. Around 170 grams of vegetables and gourds, 66 grams of meat and fat, one egg every five to six days, several spoonfuls of sugar a day, and very small quantities of fish.

36. Prisoners were also entitled to a daily norm of 20 grams of meat, 160 grams of fish, and 250 grams of other vegetables. See *GULAG. 1918–1960*, 543–551.

37. GARF f.R-5446 op.87 d.1162 l.171.

38. GARF f.R-5446 op.86 d.2552 l.176.

39. GARF f.R-5446 op.86 d.2552 ll.177, 179–180.

40. *Molotov, Malenkov, Kaganovich. 1957* (Moscow: MFD, 1998), 193.

41. GARF f.R-5446 op.87 d.1162 l.279 (italics ours).

42. *Politbiuro TsK VKP(b) i Sovet Ministrov SSSR 1945–1953* (Moscow: Rosspen, 2002), 561.

43. The full title of the first resolution was, "On the Incorrect Distribution of Market Reserves of Grain and Certain Foodstuffs That Have Caused Disruptions to Trade in Various Regions, and on Measures for Eliminating Shortcomings in this Area." GARF f.R-5446 op.87 d.1162 ll.271–272.

44. The draft was prepared at the beginning of December and confirmed on 16 December. GARF f.R-5446 op.86 d.2233 ll.10, 11, 22.

45. *Postanovleniia Soveta Ministrov SSSR za dekabr' 1952 g.* chast' 1, 373–375.

46. That is, "On Measures to Secure the Delivery of Certain Industrial Goods and Foodstuffs to the Trade Organizations in Kuibyshev and Kuibyshev region." GARF f.R-5446 op.86 d.5128 ll.2, 9–10.

47. The effective confiscation of livestock deliveries had risen from 9.8 percent in 1940 to 13.8 percent in 1952. GARF f.R-5446 op.87 d.2337 ll.94–99.

48. RGAE f.7486 op.47 d.260 l.26.

49. GARF f.R-5446 op.86 d.4403 ll.157–160.

50. GARF f.R-5446 op.86 d.4403 ll.167, 179–180.

51. *Lavrentii Beria. 1953,* 417.

52. Ibid., 171. Mikoian suggests that the exchange took place in November 1952, but it appears to have taken place either on 3 or 11 December.

53. *Molotov, Malenkov, Kaganovich,* 492.

54. Anastas Mikoian, *Tak bylo: Razmyshleniia o minuvshem* (Moscow: Vagrius, 1999), 577.

55. RGASPI f.558 op.11 d.903 ll.42–46. This letter has also been published by A. Ponomarev on the basis of a copy deposited in the former Moscow party archive. *Istochnik* 4 (2000): 98–102.

56. *Istochnik* 4 (2000): 98, 107.

57. RGASPI f.17 op.138 d.414 ll.2–124.

58. The increase for meat would have been from 24 kopecks to 1 ruble for a kilogram of cattle meat and from 72 kopecks to 3–5 rubles for pork, depending on its type; the increase for milk would have been from between 25 to 30 to between 35 to 40 kopecks a liter.

59. RGASPI f.17 op.138 d.414 ll.105-106, 108, 124.

60. *Molotov, Malenkov, Kaganovich,* 487; Mikoian, *Tak bylo,* 577.

61. *Molotov, Malenkov, Kaganovich,* 493.

62. *Lavrentii Beria. 1953,* 171.

63. Ibid.; *Molotov, Malenkov, Kaganovich,* 487.

64. GARF f.R-5446 op.87 d.1202 l.69.

65. Mikoian, *Tak bylo,* 578. Mikoian's knowledge of this event was almost certainly obtained secondhand—most likely from Khrushchev—since he was no longer invited to meetings of the ruling group, but his version is corroborated by later events. On 19 February 1953, a resolution of the Buro of the Presidium of the Central Committee ruled that Malenkov and Beria be added to "the Central Committee commission for drawing up radical measures to secure the further growth of animal husbandry." The draft resolution has notes on it indicating that Stalin, Malenkov, Beria, Bulganin, and Khrushchev voted in favor of their inclusion. According to the visitors' book, there were no meetings of the ruling group at Stalin's office in the Kremlin on or around 19

February. We can therefore assume that the meeting took place at Stalin's country house. "Posetiteli Kremlevskogo Kabineta I. V. Stalina. 1950–1953 gg." *Istoricheskii arkhiv* 1 (1997): 38.

66. Mikoian, *Tak bylo*, 578.

6: Stalin's Last Struggle

1. Stalin saw Vinogradov for the last time on 19 January. RGASPI f.558 op.11 d.1483; and G. V. Kostyrchenko, *Tainaia politika Stalina: Vlast' i antisemitism* (Moscow: Mezhdunarodnye otnosheniia, 2001), 636. Also see Yakov Rapoport, *The Doctors' Plot of 1953* (Cambridge, Mass.: Harvard University Press, 1991), 218; and Zh. A. Medvedev, "Zagadka smerti Stalina," *Voprosy istorii* 1 (2000): 86. Stalin's health appears to have deteriorated quite sharply at the end of 1951. Cf. Svetlana Allilueva, *Twenty Letters to a Friend* (London: World Books, 1967), 207.

2. For one of the best examples of Stalin's sudden loss of memory, see N. S. Khrushchev, *Vospominaniia. Vremia, liudi, vlast'* (Moscow: Moskovskie novosti, 1999), 2:75, 98.

3. The most consistent advocate of this view was Khrushchev. See ibid., 2: 89, 125.

4. This was reportedly cited by Stalin as one of the chief reasons why, party rules notwithstanding, a congress had not been convened earlier. *Pravda*, 28 April 1964, 5.

5. Khrushchev, *Vospominaniia*, 2:95.

6. This point was first made by Werner G. Hahn, *Postwar Soviet Politics: The Fall of Zhdanov and the Defeat of Moderation, 1946–1953* (Ithaca, N.Y.: Cornell University Press, 1982), 150.

7. See L. A. Openkin, "I. V. Stalin. Poslednii prognoz budushchego (iz istorii napisaniia raboty 'Ekonomicheskie problemy sotsializma v SSSR')," *Voprosy istorii KPSS* 7 (1991): 116.

8. The original chair—whose name was crossed out by Stalin—was to have been Suslov. RGASPI f.17 op.163 d.1602 l.168.

9. For a sense of the anticipation on this, see Khrushchev, *Vospominaniia*, 2:95–96. The draft resolutions of 4 and 6 December are in RGASPI f.17 op.163 d.1608 ll.105–106, 103–104. The Politburo resolution was then confirmed by a correspondence vote of the Central Committee from 8–11 December. RGANI f.2 op.1 d.19 ll.7–8.

10. See Konstantin Simonov, *Glazami cheloveka moego pokoleniia. Razmyshleniia o I. V. Staline* (Moscow: Novosti, 1990), 177. Cf. 140–150, 169–174. Stalin did see fit, however, to get involved in a minor literary controversy surrounding Latsis's novel *K novomu beregu*, even going so far as to edit a letter from a "group of readers," which was published in *Pravda* on 25 February 1952. RGASPI f.558 op.11 d.205 ll.133–136.

11. See RGASPI f.558 op.1 d.1270 ll.35–38, 89.

12. RGASPI f.558 op.11 d.1267 ll.4–17; and f.558 op.11 d.418 ll.5–6.

13. Khrushchev, *Vospominaniia*, 2:106–107, 110–111.

14. RGASPI f.558 op.11 d.1267 l.4.

15. See Abalin's letters of 12 February and 21 April 1952. Shepilov's paper only eventually appeared in *Kommunist* after the congress, in November. RGASPI f.558 op.11 d.1270 ll.107–109, 148-158.

16. The text of Stalin's notes can be found in I. V. Stalin, *Sochineniia* (Stanford, Calif.: Hoover Institution Press, 1967), 3:188–245. The three letters were to Notkin on 21 April, to Iaroshenko on 22 May, and to Savin and Venzher on 28 September (ibid., 3:246–257, 258–290, 291–304).

17. RGASPI f.17 op.163 d.1622 l.147; f.17 op.163 d.1623 l.138; Khrushchev, *Vospominaniia*, 2:96.

18. For a marked difference between the English and Russian versions of Khrushchev's memoirs on this matter, compare N. S. Khrushchev, *Khrushchev Remembers* (London: Andre Deutsch, 1971), 277, and Khrushchev, *Vospominaniia*, 2:96.

19. Central Committee members were invited to the plenum in a Politburo resolution of 9 August. RGASPI f.17 op.3 d.2233 ll.11, 89.

20. RGANI f.2 op.1 d.19 ll.1–3. As it was held in mid-summer, not all members of the Central Committee made it to the plenum, though 88 of the 139 full and candidate members were present.

21. Robert Conquest, *Power and Policy in the USSR: The Study of Soviet Dynastics* (London: Macmillan, 1961), 126. Khrushchev recalled: "In his report, Malenkov devoted much attention to Stalin's work. And so did other speakers, with the exception of me. I did not speak of it not because I was 'clever and courageous' and was critical of the work, but because at the congress I spoke on the party rules, and so there was no need for me to allude to this work of Stalin's." Khrushchev, *Vospominaniia*, 2:107.

22. See Conquest, *Power and Policy*, 155–156.

23. See article 3 parts (f), (h), and (j) of the new party rules adopted at the XIX Congress, in Graham Gill, *The Rules of the Communist Party of the Soviet Union* (Basingstoke, U.K.: Macmillan, 1988), 185–186.

24. See Yoram Gorlizki, "Party Revivalism and the Death of Stalin," *Slavic Review* 54, 1 (1995): 4–7. Prior to the congress, letters to party committees and to newspapers had attacked the amoral conduct and conspicuous consumption of the elite. See N. V. Romanovskii, *Liki stalinizma, 1945–1953* (Moscow: RAGS, 1995), 32, 79.

25. Gorlizki, "Party Revivalism," 7.

26. Khrushchev, *Vospominaniia*, 2:98; also see Simonov, *Glazami*, 206–207.

27. Simonov, *Glazami*, 210–212. Even at his congress speech, Stalin made every effort to ensure continuity between ovations "lest the form of one of the strictly constructed paragraphs of his speech be violated." Ibid., 207. For other evidence of Stalin's lucidity at this time, see the text of his conversations with Zhou Enlai on 20 August and on 3 and 19 September, reproduced in "Stalin's Conversations," *Cold War International History Project Bulletin* 6–7 (1995–1996): 9–19.

28. Simonov, *Glazami*, 211. In his original notes, Simonov recorded that when one of the speakers declared himself a " 'devoted follower of comrade Stalin,' Stalin replied: 'We are all followers of Lenin.' " Ibid., 209. Also see [L. N. Efremov,] "Neopublikovannaia rech' I. V. Stalina na plenume TsK KPSS," in

Dos'e glasnosti. Spetsvypusk, 13 December 2001, 11; [A. M. Rumiantsev,] "Mistika tsifr upravliaet istoriei," *Obshchaia gazeta*, 14–20 October 1999.

29. The number of full members rose from 71 to 125, and the number of candidate members from 68 to 111. In his testament, the first item in the list of Lenin's proposed changes was an "increase in the number of members of the Central Committee [from twenty-seven] to several tens or even up to a hundred." Although the number of members was not increased at the XII Congress in April 1923, as Lenin had hoped, it had more than doubled by the XIV Congress in December 1925. See Evan Mawdsley and Stephen White, *The Soviet Elite from Lenin to Gorbachev: The Central Committee and Its Members, 1917–1991* (Oxford: Oxford University Press, 2000), 36 n.1, 103.

30. Ibid., 103–104.

31. Anastas Mikoian, *Tak bylo: Razmyshleniia o minuvshem* (Moscow: Vagrius, 1999), 573.

32. According to Mikoian, Stalin had discussed the composition of the new Presidium with Politburo members at the end of the congress. He did not, however, discuss either the existence or the composition of the Presidium Buro with them. See Mikoian, *Tak bylo*, 572–574; on this also see Khrushchev, *Vospominaniia*, 2:99. The original, typed list with amendments by Stalin is in RGANI f.2 op.1 d.22 l.1.

33. Moshe Lewin, *Lenin's Last Struggle* (London: Faber and Faber, 1968), 79–80.

34. Khrushchev, *Vospominaniia*, 2:102.

35. Ibid., 2:81.

36. Ibid., 2:96.

37. [Mikhail Smirtiukov,] "Do 90 let on ezdil" *Kommersant' vlast'*, 21 March 2000, 48.

38. "For many many people," wrote Simonov of the autumn of 1952, "and the wider the circle the greater the proportion, the name of Molotov was called out or remembered directly after that of Stalin." Simonov, *Glazami*, 213.

39. Khrushchev, *Vospominaniia*, 2:102. For earlier examples of Stalin accusing Molotov of being an American spy, see ibid., 2:80–81.

40. Simonov, *Glazami*, 211, 212.

41. Ibid., 212.

42. N. G. Kuznetsov recalled that in his condemnation of Molotov, Stalin read out from foreign sources, presumably the *Daily Herald* (London) and Reuters reports of December 1945. See Kuznetsov, "Krutye povoroty," *Pravda*, 27 July 1988, 3. Molotov's indiscretion in 1945 and the rumors of his succession are described in some detail in chapter 1 of this book.

43. Mikoian, *Tak bylo*, 498. On Lozovsky's execution, see Joshua Rubenstein and Vladimir P. Naumov, *Stalin's Secret Pogrom: The Postwar Inquisition of the Jewish Ant-Fascist Committee* (New Haven, Conn.: Yale University Press, 2001), 495.

44. Rumiantsev, "Mistika"; Mikoian, *Tak bylo*, 574, also talks of Stalin accusing Molotov of "reflecting the line of the right deviation." Efremov, "Neopublikovannaia rech'," 11, by contrast, has Stalin likening Mikoian to Frumkin, a member of the right opposition.

45. Although they attended the first meeting of the Buro of the Presidium on 27 October, they were not invited to any of the six subsequent sessions prior to Stalin's death (10 November, 22 November, 11 December, 16 December, 29 December, and 26 January). See *Politbiuro TsK VKP(b) i Sovet Ministrov SSSR 1945–1953* (Moscow: Rosspen, 2002), 432–436.

46. At the meeting of 18 October, the three senior Secretaries (Stalin, Malenkov, and Khrushchev) were reserved for general leadership functions, while the seven junior Secretaries (Pegov, Aristov, Suslov, Ignatov, Ponomarenko, Mikhailov, and Brezhnev) were assigned to specifically political, noneconomic roles. APRF f.3 op.22 d.15 l.7. All ten Secretaries attended the fourth, fifth, sixth, and seventh meetings of the new cabinet, the Buro of the Presidium of the Central Committee, on 11, 16, and 29 December 1952, and on 26 January 1953. See ibid., 434–435.

47. Resolution of the Buro of the Presidium of the Central Committee of 26 January 1953, points 1(b) and 5.

48. Resolution of the Buro of the Presidium of the Central Committee of 27 October, points 2(a), (c), and (d).

49. Item 8 of the Presidium meeting of 18 October 1952. APRF f.3 op.22 d.15 l.7.

50. For more on the membership, functions, and staff of the commission, see RGASPI f.17 inventory for op.164 l.14; APRF f.3 op.22 d.12 l.2; d.13 ll.4, 7.

51. See RGASPI f.17 inventory for op.164 l.15; APRF f.3 op.22 d.13 ll.14, 26–27.

52. APRF f.3 op.22 d.12 l.2. In connection with Shepilov's appointment as chief editor of *Pravda* on 18 November, he was replaced as head of the commission by Rumiantsev. APRF f.3 op.22 d.13 ll.46–47. On the commission's relationship to Agitprop, see points 2 and 3 of the resolution of the Buro of the Presidium "O raspredelenii obiazannostei mezhdu sekreteriami" of 27 October 1952 in *Politbiuro TsK VKP(b) i Sovet Ministrov SSSR 1945–1953*, 93.

53. See RGASPI f.17 inventory for op.164 ll.15–17.

54. See Gorlizki, "Ordinary Stalinism," 707–715, 728–731.

55. On 18 October, Stalin freed Molotov from overseeing the Ministry of Foreign Affairs and Mikoian from supervising the Ministry of Foreign Trade, with both functions being transferred to the new Presidium commission for foreign affairs. At the same time, a third elder figure, Kaganovich, was released as chair of Gossnab. APRF f.3 op.22 d.12 l.2.

56. Bulganin was to concentrate on his new post as head of the defense commission, while Khrushchev was to focus on the Moscow party oganization and on the Buro of the Presidium. APRF f.3 op.22 d.12 l.3.

57. See *Politbiuro TsK VKP(b) i Sovet Ministrov SSSR 1945–1953*, 560–561.

58. Thus, for example, on 12 November, M. G. Mel'nikov and D. I. Tsareva, as well as two members of the technical staff, were moved from the Council of Ministers apparatus, where they had previously worked for Malenkov, to serve as aides to Malenkov at the Central Committee. RGANI f.4 op.9. d.3 ll.119–120.

59. Thus, the new Buro of the Presidium of the Central Committee was an exact replica of the Bureau of the Presidium of Sovmin, just as the Presidium

at the Central Committee was a copy of the Presidium of the Council of Ministers. Although the terms are identical in Russian, for the sake of consistency with other party committees such as the Politburo and the Orgburo, and in order to distinguish the party from the equivalent state body, we have rendered the new party committee as the Buro (not Bureau) of the Presidium of the Central Committee.

60. At its last meeting prior to the congress on 18 September 1952, the Bureau of the Presidium of the Council of Ministers had consisted of Bulganin, Beria, Kaganovich, Malenkov, Mikoian, Molotov, Pervukhin, and Khrushchev. See *Politbiuro TsK VKP(b) i Sovet Ministrov SSSR 1945–1953*, 560.

61. Apart from the subtraction of these two, the only other difference with the Sovmin Bureau was the addition of Voroshilov and Saburov. Although Mikoian, *Tak bylo*, 576–577, claimed that Stalin convened three sessions of the Buro and that he and Molotov attended all, there were actually seven sessions before Stalin fell ill and, according to the records, the two men only attended the first of these, on 27 October. See *Politbiuro TsK VKP(b) i Sovet Ministrov SSSR 1945–1953*, 432–435.

62. Item 4 and resolution 68 of Presidium Buro meeting of 10 November 1952. See *Politbiuro TsK VKP(b) i Sovet Ministrov SSSR 1945–1953*, 433.

63. The informal ruling group of the preceding months had consisted of Stalin, Malenkov, Beria, Khrushchev, and Bulganin. To this group Voroshilov, Pervukhin, Kaganovich, and Saburov were now added. The Buro, which met seven times, handled matters that previously had been the prerogative of the Politburo, as well as proposals from the new Presidium commissions. See ibid., 432–436.

64. See Simonov, *Glazami*, 241–242. Also see N. S. Khrushchev, "Secret Speech of Khrushchev Concerning the 'Cult of the Individual,' " in *The Anti-Stalin Campaign and International Communism* (New York: Columbia University Press, 1956), 64; R. G. Pikhoia, *Sovetskii soiuz: Istoriia vlasti, 1945–1991* (Moscow: RAGS, 1998), 89–93, esp. 92; Rapoport, *Doctors' Plot*, 150; Kiril Stoliarov, *Palachi i zhertvy* (Moscow: Olma Press, 1997), 77; Kostyrchenko, *Tainaia*, 643.

65. Stoliarov writes: "Any reference to the Central Committee or to the government should not be interpreted literally, for the text invariably refers to Stalin, who was categorically forbidden from being mentioned in the protocols." Stoliarov, *Palachi i zhertvy*, 20, 59, 64.

66. Virtually all had been held in custody since January 1949 or earlier. Although the investigations had been completed by the spring of 1950, it was felt that the testimonies beaten out of the accused might not stand scrutiny in court, and so the case had been deferred. See *Nepravednyi sud. Poslednii Stalinskii rasstrel* (Moscow: Nauka, 1994), 7–9; Rubenstein and Naumov, *Stalin's Secret Pogrom*, xvii, 42–46.

67. Having been arrested on 18 November 1950, Etinger was moved to Lefortovo on 5 January 1951 and died in custody on 2 March 1951, having been transferred, on Abakumov's orders, to a cold cell there. The significance of the Etinger case is suggested by the importance accorded it by the Malenkov commission on Abakumov in July 1951. Pikhoia, *Sovetskii soiuz*, 82–83; Kostyrchenko, *Tainaia*, 632.

68. Pikhoia, *Sovetskii soiuz*, 88–89.

69. On Riumin's role in the original Etinger investigation, see Kostyrchenko, *Tainaia*, 632–633.

70. RGASPI f.17 op.3 d.1091 l.22. Although there is little evidence that Malenkov or any other member of Stalin's immediate entourage were anti-Semitic, Riumin seems to have had a pathological hatred of Jews. See Stoliarov, *Palachi i zhertvy*, 178–179.

71. Kostyrchenko, who suggests that the arrests began in October, the month of Riumin's promotion, gives the names of nine such "Zionist plotters." Kostyrchenko, *Tainaia*, 460–461; also see Pikhoia, *Sovetskii soiuz*, 90; and Stoliarov, *Palachi i zhertvy*, 47.

72. Kostyrchenko, *Tainaia*, 637.

73. Thus, for example, on December 19, 1951, Riumin asked Shimeliovich about Dr. Evgeniia Lifshitz, a pediatrician who had treated the children and grandchildren of Kremlin officials. See Rubenstein and Naumov, *Stalin's Secret Pogrom*, 54, 61.

74. Kostyrchenko, *Tainaia*, 637.

75. The preliminary investigation into the EAK case was completed on 22 March, the official indictment approved on 31 March, and the text sent to Stalin three days later, on 3 April. Rubenstein and Naumov, *Stalin's Secret Pogrom*, xvii–xix; *Nepravednyi sud*, 9.

76. Stoliarov, *Palachi i zhertvy*, 200–201.

77. Ibid., 239.

78. Ibid., 116–117.

79. Ibid., 203–204.

80. Ignat'ev's report to Stalin in November, cited in Pikhoia, *Sovetskii soiuz*, 88–89.

81. Timashuk visited the MGB headquarters on 24 July and 11 August 1952, where she was interrogated by V. N. Garkush and I. I. Eliseev. Kostyrchenko, *Tainaia*, 638. Timashuk claimed that the electro-cardiogram she had taken of Zhdanov in Valdai on 28 August 1948 had shown that he had clearly suffered a coronary thrombosis or heart attack (*infarkt*), but that professors Egorov and Vinogradov and Dr. Maiorov had ordered her to change the wording to "functional violation of the heart's activity." This meant that Zhdanov was allowed to walk in the park, whereas a person in his state should have been confined to bed. Timashuk later claimed that it had been purely in order to cover herself that she had written three letters on the matter, first to Stalin's guard Vlasik, and then to the Central Committee Secretary A. A. Kuznetsov in 1948. See Viktor Malkin, "Sem' pisem Lidii Timashuk," *Novoe vremia* 23 (1993): 39–40.

82. RGASPI f.17 op.163 d.1628 l.148.

83. The arrests, which occurred cumulatively over four months, commenced with the detention of three doctors at the end of September 1952 and culminated in the apprehension of over half a dozen physicians in January, bringing the total of arrested doctors to twenty-eight in the first half of February 1953. See Kostyrchenko, *Tainaia*, 643, 645, 652, 660.

84. Pikhoia, *Sovetskii soiuz*, 88–91.

85. Rapoport, *Doctors' Plot*, 221. One should note that of the nine doctors named in the *Pravda* announcement of 13 January, three (Vinogradov, Egorov, and Maiorov) were not Jewish.

86. M. A. Malyshev, "Dnevnik narkoma,"*Istochnik* 5 (1997): 140–141.

87. Pikhoia, *Sovetskii soiuz*, 90.

88. *Politbiuro TsK VKP(b) i Sovet Ministrov SSSR 1945–1953*, 434.

89. Later in December, a new main intelligence directorate with a special "anti-Zionist" department was set up at the MGB under S. I. Ogol'tsov. See Kostyrchenko, *Tainaia*, 649, 657–658.

90. Malenkov later referred to the directive as "prepared under the guidance of comrade Stalin." *Lavrentii Beria. 1953* (Moscow: MFD, 1999), 222.

91. Thirty-two members of the Presidium attended the meeting of 1–4 December. See *Politbiuro TsK VKP(b) i Sovet Ministrov SSSR 1945–1953*, 433–434.

92. Mikhail Suslov had been Secretary with special responsibilities for ideology since 1947; Nikolai Mikhailov, who had served for ten years as head of the Komsomol, had been made head of Agitprop in October. Dmitrii Chesnokov, who had previously served as editor of the journal *Voprosy filosofii* and as deputy director of the Institute of Philosophy, was appointed joint chief editor of the party's ideological flagship, *Kommunist*, and head of the department of philosophical and legal sciences and higher educational institutions at the Central Committee. On his own appointment, see D. T. Shepilov, "Vospominaniia," *Voprosy istorii* 7 (1998): 33–34.

93. The piece assailed Fedoseev for articles published in *Izvestiia* earlier that month. A version of the letter, signed by Suslov on 23 December, and marginally edited by Stalin, may be found in Stalin's personal files in RGASPI f.558 op.11 d.205 ll.173–180. Stalin's management of this publication is also indicated by the presence of Fedoseev's repentant reply of 31 December in the leader's file. A very different version of this letter was published in *Pravda* on 2 January 1953. RGASPI f.558 op.11 d.205 ll.171–172.

94. Fedoseev, claimed Suslov, in articles published in *Izvestiia* that month, had accused others of holding "unmarxist" positions, while not mentioning that as editor of *Bol'shevik* from 1947 to 1949, he had himself given credence to such views.

95. This point was first made by Conquest, *Power and Policy*, 178–179. Also see Hahn, *Postwar Soviet Politics*, 152, 155.

96. See Hahn, *Postwar Soviet Politics*, 152–153; and Conquest, *Power and Policy*, 105–109.

97. Point 5 of the 1949 decree had been devoted to Shepilov's errors and, in particular, to Shepilov's decision to have his department recommend the Voznesenskii volume as a textbook for raikom party secretaries and propaganda cadres. RGASPI f.17 op.163 d.1528 l.15.

98. The original version of this, in Malenkov's hand with minor amendments by Stalin, may be found in RGASPI f.558 op.11 d.157 ll.29–33. The bulletin appears to have been discussed at an impromptu meeting of the Presidium Buro which met without Stalin. See Kostyrchenko, *Tainaia*, 658–659; Pikhoia, *Sovetskii soiuz*, 94.

99. From the draft sent in by Shepilov, it is not readily apparent whether any parts of this text had been dictated by Stalin. Many of the terms used, such as *terrorist groups, doctor-wreckers, doctor-murderers*, and *monsters in human form* had, however, been lifted from Stalin's original TASS communiqué. See RGASPI f.558 op.11 d.157 ll.7, 9–14.

100. See RGASPI f.558 op.11 d.157 l.12. Altogether, Stalin inserted the term *enemies* five times in the amended text, two of which came in the form *enemies of the people*. The phrase *hidden enemies of the people* had also been used in the original TASS communiqué dictated by Stalin. See RGASPI f.558 op.11 d.157 ll.12–14, 30.

101. *Pravda*, 22 January 1953.

102. Stalin had personally inserted the phrase "*live persons*, hidden enemies of the people" (emphasis original) when editing Shepilov's draft. See RGASPI f.558 op.11 d.157 l.13. Mikhailov's speech was reported in *Pravda*, 28 January 1953.

103. *Kommunist* 2 (1953): 22. This was also the centerpiece of Kozlov's article in *Pravda* on 6 February.

104. Malyshev, "Dnevnik narkoma," 143–146; A. A. Fursenko, "Konets ery Stalina," *Zvezda* 12 (1999): 178–179; and Rapoport, *Doctors' Plot*, 80–81.

105. This position appears to be based on the following grounds: First, that a commission for deporting the Jews, headed by Suslov, had been set up by Stalin; second, that Chesnokov wrote a brochure, with a print run of 1 million copies, entitled *Why It Is Necessary to Expel the Jews from the Industrial Centers of the Country*; third, that barracks to house the Jews were already under construction in Birobidzhan and other closed zones; and finally, that lists were being prepared across the country of citizens of Jewish extraction. For an extended discussion of these arguments, as well as of the counterarguments, see Samson Madievsky, "1953: La déportation des Juifs soviétiques était-elle programmée?" *Cahiers du monde russe* 41, 4 (2000): 561–568.

106. For a useful discussion of the archival evidence of a deportation, see Madievskii, "1953: La déportation," 563–567; and Kostyrchenko, *Tainaia*, 676–677.

107. It appears to have been at Stalin's behest, for example, that the call for the "most merciless punishment of the criminals" in the original letter was crossed out. See Kostyrchenko, *Tainaia*, 681–682.

108. Khrushchev, *Vospominaniia*, 2:93.

109. Certainly, after his return from the south in December 1951, Stalin no longer presided over meetings, for example, for the awarding of Stalin prizes, which he would customarily have chaired in the past. Thus, for example, it was Malenkov who chaired the meeting of 26 February 1952 on awarding the Stalin prize for literature. See Simonov, *Glazami*, 176, 186, 203. Similarly, it was Malenkov who presided over the expanded meeting of 10 March 1952 on the awarding of Stalin prizes for science, inventions, and the introduction of new work technologies. RGASPI f.558 op.11 d.418 ll.7–8. For a description of Stalin's lesser role on military committees after his return in December 1951, see Kuznetsov, "Krutye povoroty," 3.

110. Point 4, item 68, protocol 2 from the meeting of 10 November 1952. APRF f.3 op.22 d.12 l.3. The Buro of the Presidium also resolved, on 26 January, that a triumvirate of Beria, Malenkov, and Bulganin should take control of work with what were referred to as the special agencies (*rabota spetsial'nykh organov po osobym delam*). APRF f.3 op.22 d.12 l.8. The triumvirate met four times during 2–23 February 1953.

111. A list of the seven formal Buro meetings is given in *Politbiuro TsK VKP(b) i Sovet Ministrov SSSR 1945–1953*, 432–436. A reference to the ad hoc Buro meeting of 9 January 1953, with a list of those who attended, is given in Kostyrchenko, *Tainaia*, 658–659.

112. "Stalin's Conversations," 79–80.

113. Conquest, for example, suggests that Aristov, the new head of the party agencies department at the Central Committee, was an independent figure who was being groomed by Stalin to lead a purge. Although he may have overstated Aristov's role on the cadre side, it could be, as Conquest suggests, that Aristov had been selected by Stalin to take over as the new head of the secret police. The party organs department had been a traditional recruiting ground for this post, and the sitting minister, Ignat'ev had, according to Khrushchev, suffered a heart attack and for that reason had missed the Presidium meeting of 1 December 1952. See Conquest, *Power and Policy*, 181; Hahn, *Postwar Soviet Politics*, 145–146; and Khrushchev, *Vospominaniia*, 2:93.

114. Pegov's closeness to Malenkov was underlined in an interview with Malenkov's aide, D. N. Sukhanov, on 1 April 1994.

115. "O rabote Sekretariate TsK KPSS," item 74, protocol 3 of the Buro of the Presidium of the Central Committee.

116. The special sector, which was largely devoted to technical matters, had six sections: for drawing up decisions of the Politburo and the Central Committee; for preparing materials directly for Stalin; for decoding correspondence; for household provisions; an archive; and a library.

117. Indeed, under a proposal from Poskrebyshev of December 1952, it was to be renamed the Secretariat of the Buro of the Presidium, retaining similar functions. The new secretariat was to have six departments: a department for preparing cabinet and Central Committee resolutions; an archive; the former archive of the Comintern; a decoding department; a section for letters to Stalin; and one for the household economy. APRF f.3 op.22 d.65 ll.55–56.

118. On the surface, the general department appeared to be a direct successor to the Tekhsecretariat—the main chancellery of the now dissolved Orgburo. Its functions and staff were, however, broader. In addition to receiving 114 technical staff directly from the Tekhsecretariat on 27 November (RGANI f.4 op.9 d.5 ll.189–198; f.4 op.9 d.543 ll.38–161), the general department also picked up over 60 experienced personnel, many of whom were classed as "line officials" (*otvetsvennye rabotniki*) from a variety of departments within the Central Committee apparatus and from the chancellery of the Council of Ministers from the beginning of November onward. RGANI f.4 op.9 d.3 ll.121–134; d.4 ll.161–168, 190–191; d.6 l.64; d.8 l.18, d.12 l.169. On 3 February 1953, a deputy head of a section at the special sector, N. R. Khodov, was made head of the third section and deputy head of the general department. RGANI f.4

op.9 d.22 l.116. The broader functions of the general department were such that, among other things, some of its functionaries were seconded to help out at the new Presidium commissions. RGANI f.4 op.9 d.8 l.197. Shortly after Stalin's death, most staff from the special sector—and three of its six sections— were completely swallowed up by the burgeoning general department. Thus, the first, fourth, and fifth sections of the former special sector were directly absorbed by the general department on 18 March 1953. On the same day, the chancellery of the Presidium was formed out of the other remnants of the special sector. RGANI f.4 op.9 d.32 ll.95–99. It is also telling that some of the staff of the new Presidium chancellery came directly from the general depart- ment. RGANI f.4 op.9 d.744 ll.211–215.

119. APRF f.3 op.22 d.12 l.3.

120. The origins of Poskrebyshev's dismissal went back to an investigation into the head of Stalin's guard, Vlasik, which had begun the previous year. In the autumn of 1951, while Stalin was in the south, he had ordered that Pos- krebyshev carry out an investigation into Vlasik's expenses. In April 1952, Vlasik was dismissed and sent to a lowly position in the Urals, and on 16 December he was arrested. Vlasik, in turn, made allegations against Poskre- byshev which, together with Stalin's belief that Poskrebyshev had mislaid ma- terials from his book, resulted in Poskrebyshev's dismissal in February. See Poskrebyshev's letter to the Presidium of 19 July 1954, RGANI f.2 op.1 d.65 ll.26, 28–29; Interview with D. N. Sukhanov, 1 April 1994; RGASPI f.83 op.1 d.7 ll.75–76, cf. 73; Khrushchev, Vospominaniia, 2:109–110; Malkin, "Sem' pi- sem," 40; Stoliarov, Palachi i zhertvy, 293, 295; Kostyrchenko, Tainaia, 656.

121. Point 5 of item 68 of the Buro of the Presidium protocol 2 of 10 November 1952. APRF f.3 op.22 d.12 l.3.

122. "Dokladnaia zapiska M. T. Pomazneva," in Lavrentii Beria, 1953, 82, 363–364.

123. Ibid., 364.

124. Interview with D. N. Sukhanov, 1 April 1994.

125. Lavrentii Beria. 1953, 113.

126. P. K. Ponomarenko, then a party Secretary, refers to a meeting of the Presidium where he cast doubt on the charges against the doctors: "I expressed doubt; perhaps there was the odd person who had sold out or who had got entangled and had been recruited long ago, but that there should be so many respected and well-known doctors [involved in this matter]?" At a later meeting, in retaliation for Ponomarenko's defiance, Stalin warned: "We shall extirpate not only the poisoners, but also those who inspired them," and went on to accuse Ponomarenko of having dined twice at Professor Vinogradov's and once at Professor Egorov's house, the latter of whom had already been arrested. By this stage, however, it appears that Stalin's grasp of detail had begun to fail him, making it all the more difficult to spin a compelling story. After Stalin accused Ponomarenko of passing over a report from a Central Committee func- tionary, Olga Mishakova, concerning irregularities in the health system, it turned out that the report was an exact copy of a paper that had already been sent to the leader by the Minister of Health, under Ponomarenko's supervision. This account is based on an interview with a friend of Ponomarenko's. See

Natalia Sokolova, "Kak Stalin zemli delil," *Literaturnaia gazeta*, 9 December 1992, 3.

127. Even in his outburst at the October plenum, Stalin had tempered his attacks on Molotov and Mikoian with comments about their bravery and valiance. "He had to do so," recalled Mikoian, "since, to the extent that we were members of the Politburo and the participants at the plenum knew us well, the whole plenum was stunned by his attacks on the two of us." Mikoian, *Tak bylo*, 557–558. Also see Kostyrchenko, *Tainaia*, 683–685.

128. The two attended the Presidium Buro meetings of 12:00 noon and 8:00 P.M. on 2 March and of 12:00 noon and 12:00 midnight on 3 March. See *Politbiuro TsK VKP(b) i Sovet Ministrov SSSR 1945–1953*, 436–437. Simonov, having observed that both Molotov and Mikoian were on the ten-man Presidium at the plenum held on 5 March 1953, two hours before Stalin's death, concluded: "Thus, [Stalin's] decision, clearly taken unilaterally at the [October] plenum was, as it were, simply ignored." Simonov, *Glazami*, 216.

129. *Lavrentii Beria. 1953*, 224, 240.

130. See Rapoport, *Doctors' Plot*, 19–20.

131. Khrushchev, *Vospominaniia*, 2:93.

132. A. T. Rybin, "Riadom s I. V. Stalinym," *Sotsiologicheskie issledovaniia* 3 (1988): 92–94. Rybin's account, based on the reminiscences of Stalin's staff, is one of the two main eyewitness accounts of these events. The other, Khrushchev's, differs mainly in the claim that Khrushchev and Bulganin accompanied Malenkov and Beria on their first visit to the dacha, though they did not themselves go in to see Stalin. See Khrushchev, *Vospominaniia*, 2:129–131; and Medvedev, "Zagadka," 88.

133. *Politbiuro TsK VKP(b) i Sovet Ministrov SSSR 1945–1953*, 436–437.

134. A. L. Miasnikov, "Konchina," *Literaturnaia gazeta*, 1 March 1989.

135. *Politbiuro TsK VKP(b) i Sovet Ministrov SSSR 1945–1953*, 101–104.

Conclusion

1. In the first division of power of 3 March, before Stalin died, Malenkov retained his position as Central Committee Secretary while becoming Prime Minister. Following the meeting of the Presidium on 13 March, however, he was forced to relinquish the secretaryship in order to focus on the Council of Ministers. Iurii N. Zhukov, "Bor'ba za vlast' v partiino-gosodarslvennykh verkhakh SSSR vesnoi 1953 goda," *Voprosy istorii* 1 (1995): 40–41, 46. Malenkov's aide, D. N. Sukhanov, also recounts that Malenkov believed it better to head the state than the party apparatus after Stalin's death. See "Stalin poshevelil pal'tsami," *Novoe vremia* 48 (1991): 33. Also see Konstantin Simonov, *Glazami cheloveka moego pokoleniia: Razmyshleniia o I. V. Staline* (Moscow: Novosti, 1990), 227, 238–239.

2. Stalin had abolished the position of General Secretary of the Party at the XIX Congress, so that, strictly speaking, all party Secretaries were of equal rank. On this and on the Leninist norm that the head of Sovnarkom chair Politburo meetings, see Feliks Chuev, *Sto sorok besed s Molotovym* (Moscow: Terra, 1991), 325, 334–325, 354. Kaganovich suggests that, at the time, the

head of Sovmin was regarded as the most important position in the country. See Feliks Chuev, *Tak govoril Kaganovich: Ispoved' Stalinskogo apostola* (Moscow: Otechestvo, 1993), 85.

3. See Chuev, *Sto sorok besed*, 337. On the transfer of Malenkov's aides, see Yoram Gorlizki, "Party Revivalism and the Death of Stalin," *Slavic Review* 54, 1 (1995): 17. Even those, such as Azrael, who deny that Malenkov had a distinctly "managerial" cast of mind under Stalin, accept that he allied himself with the managerial elite after Stalin's death. See Jeremy R. Azrael, *Managerial Power and Soviet Politics* (Cambridge, Mass.: Harvard University Press, 1966), 124–126.

4. Evidence included the liquidation of the standing commissions at the Central Committee Presidium and the restoration to their former ministerial positions of Molotov and Mikoian. At their meeting of 5 March 1953, Stalin's successors demolished other party structures erected by the leader in October 1952. Instead of the Presidium and the Buro of the Presidium of the Central Committee, a new, significantly reduced Presidium was created, which accommodated the previously out-of-favor Molotov and Mikoian, while finding no room for some of those recently promoted by Stalin.

5. There are only eleven records of Central Committee Presidium meetings, as opposed to thirty-seven of the Sovmin Presidium, for this period. Principal foreign policy decisions—on the situation in Germany and ending the war in Korea—were now drawn up as directives and resolutions of the Council of Ministers.

6. This seems to be confirmed by the fact that, apart from Malenkov, Beria, Molotov, Kaganovich, Bulganin, Mikoian, and Voroshilov, the meetings were attended by Khrushchev, who was not formally a member of the Sovmin Presidium.

7. For the leading documents on these reforms see *Lavrentii Beria. 1953* (Moscow: MFD, 1999), 18–64; *Reabilitatsiia. Kak eto bylo* (Moscow: MFD, 2000), 15–16, 19–20, 38, 41, 50.

8. A. V. Torkunov, *Zagadochnaia voina. Koreiskii konflikt, 1950–1953 godov.* (Moscow: Rosspen, 2000), 272–279.

9. This was largely in response to the large-scale flight of East German citizens to the West. See *Lavrentii Beria. 1953*, 55–59; Iu. V. Aksiutin, *Poststalinskoe obschestvo. Problema liderstva i transformatsii vlasti* (Moscow: Nauchnaia kniga, 1999), 30–34.

10. Gorlizki, "Party Revivalism," 10–11, 17–19.

11. For more on the question of ideological continuity, see ibid., 5–11; for more on Khrushchev's populism and on Stalin's direct relationship with officials and masses achieved through his cult, see George Breslauer, *Khrushchev and Brezhnev as Leaders: Building Authority in Soviet Politics* (London: Allen and Unwin, 1982), 10–11, 52–58. Although the leadership struggle should not be viewed as a straightforward conflict between "party" and "state," the two leaders did increasingly align themselves with constituencies from these respective institutions. T. H. Rigby, "The Government in the Soviet Political System," in *Executive Power and Soviet Politics: The Rise and Decline of the Soviet State* (Armonk, N.Y.: M. E. Sharpe, 1992), 29.

12. On Hitler's infamous lack of discipline for systematic work, his dislike of administrative and organizational matters, and his aversion to files, see, from a voluminous literature, Ian Kershaw, *Hitler, 1889–1936: Hubris* (Harmondsworth, U.K.: Penguin, 1999), 20, 39, 156, 300, 534.

13. On Hitler's aversion to personal conflict and on his reluctance to manipulate the personal rivalries of his deputies, see Hans Mommsen, "Hitler's Position in the Nazi System," in *From Weimar to Auschwitz: Essays in German History* (Cambridge: Polity, 1991), 171–172; and Martin Broszat, *The Hitler State: The Foundation and Development of the Internal Structure of the Third Reich* (London: Longman, 1981), 202.

14. Simonov, *Glazami*, 160–161

15. Yoram Gorlizki, "Rules, Incentives, and Soviet Campaign Justice after World War II," *Europe-Asia Studies* 51 (7) 1999: 1255–1262.

16. Kiril Stoliarov, *Palachi i zhertvy* (Moscow: Olma Press, 1997), 116–117.

17. Stalin's diplomatic failures, especially the lifting of the Berlin blockade in May 1949, are discussed in Vladislav Zubok and Constantine Pleshakov, *Inside the Kremlin's Cold War: From Stalin to Khrushchev* (Cambridge, Mass.: Harvard University Press, 1996), 46–47, 52.

18. "Razvedka—sviatoe, ideal'noe dlia nas delo," *Istochnik* 5 (2001): 130 (emphasis original).

GLOSSARY

Agitprop   Agitation and propaganda administration of the Central Committee

aktiv   Party enthusiasts who take on special responsibilities

Bureau of Sovmin   The chief executive committee of the government after 1946. The term lowercased refers to the subordinate sectoral bureaus that supervised different branches of the economy

Buro of the Presidium of the Central Committee   Supreme executive organ of the All-Union Communist Party from October 1952 to March 1953

Central Committee   Supreme decision-making body of the All-Union Communist Party between congresses. Rarely convened in this period

Chekists   Officials from the security police

Cominform   Informational Bureau of Communist Parties, Moscow-dominated organization of European communist parties founded in September 1947

Council of Foreign Ministers   Postwar body designed to draft the outlines of peace treaties with Germany and its former satellites, Hungary, Bulgaria, and Rumania (CFM)

dacha   Russian country house

EAK   Jewish Anti-Fascist Committee, one of five antifascist committees set up in March 1942 to help win support from the West. Dissolved in November 1948

GKO   State Defense Committee, wartime cabinet formed in June 1941 and dissolved in September 1945

Gosplan   State planning commission (committee from 1948)

Gossnab   State committee for material and technical supplies

Gostekhnika   State committee for the introduction of new technologies

GULAG   Main administration of the camps at the Ministry of Internal Affairs, often used as a shorthand for the camp system

Kolkhoz   Collective farm

Komsomol   All-Union Leninist Youth League (VLKSM): Communist party youth wing

MGB   Ministry of State Security

MVD   Ministry of Internal Affairs

nomenklatura   Technically the lists of posts to be filled (and of persons to fill them) by a party committee. Often used more broadly to describe the general system for appointing top-level officials or to denote the Soviet elite as a whole

Orgburo   Executive body of the Central Committee in charge of the party's general organizational work, dissolved in October 1952

Politburo   Political bureau of the Central Committee. Highest executive organ of the party and ruling Cabinet of the country. Dissolved in October 1952

Presidium of the Central Committee   Set up in October 1952 as successor to the Politburo and Orgburo. Powers quickly usurped by the Buro of the Presidium of the Central Committee

raikom   District party committee

Secretariat   Executive body of the Central Committee in charge of the party's current organizational work, subordinate to the Orgburo

Sovnarkom   Council of People's Commissars, the government prior to its re-naming as the Council of Ministers in March 1946

Sovmin   Council of Ministers, the government after March 1946

SNK   See Sovnarkom

TASS   Telegraph Agency of the Soviet Union, published official press releases

TsK   Central Committee of the All-Union Communist Party (see Central Committee)

TsSU   Central Statistical Administration

VASKhNIL   Lenin All-Union Academy of Agricultural Sciences

VKP(b)   All-Union Communist Party (Bolshevik)

VPK   Foreign policy commission of the Central Committee

BIBLIOGRAPHY

Archives

Rossiiskii Gosudarstvennyi Arkhiv Sotsial'no-Politicheskoi Istorii (RGASPI) Moscow

Fond 17 Opis'3. *Podpis'nye protokoly zasedanii Politbiuro TsK VKP (b).*

Opisi 115, 116, 118, 121. *Podpis'nye protokoly zasedanii Orgbiuro i Sekretariata TsK VKP (b) i materialy k nim.*

Opis' 135. *Upravlenie propagandy i agitatsii TsK VKP (b).*

Opis' 138. *Sel'skokhoziaistvennyi otdel TsK VKP (b).*

Opis' 163. *Podlinnye protokoly zasedanii Politbiuro Tsk VKP (b).*

Opis' 164. *Komissii Tsk VKP (b)-KPSS.*

Fond 73. *Andreev, Andrei Andreevich.*

Fond 74. *Voroshilov, Kliment Efremovich.*

Fond 77. *Zhdanov, Andrei Aleksandrovich.*

Fond 81. *Kaganovich, Lazar Moiseevich.*

Fond 82. *Molotov, Viacheslav Mikhailovich.*

Fond 83. *Malenkov, Georgii Maksimilianovich.*

Fond 558. *Stalin, Iosif Vissarionovich.*

Fond 592. *XIX s'ezd VKP (b).*

Rossiiskii Gosudarstvennyi Arkhiv Noveishei Istorii (RGANI), Moscow

Fond 2. *Plenumy TsK VKP (b)-KPSS.*

Fond 3. *Protokoly zasedanii Prezidiuma i Biuro Prezidiuma TsK KPSS.*

Fond 4. Opis' 9. *Podpis'nye protokoly zasedanii Sekretariata TsK KPSS.*

Rossiiskii Gosudarstvennyi Arkhiv Ekonomiki (RGAE), Moscow

Fond 1562. *Tsentral'noe statisticheskoe uprvalenie SSSR.*

Fond 4372. *Gosplan SSSR.*

Fond 7486. *Ministerstvo sel'skogo khoziaistva SSSR.*

Arkhiv Prezidenta Rossiiskoi Federatsii (APRF), Moscow

Fond 3. *Materialy k protokolam zasedanii Politbiuro (Prezidiuma) TsK VKP (b)-KPSS.*

Fond 45. *I. V. Stalin.*

Gosudarstvennyi Arkhiv Rossiiskoi Federatsii (GARF), Moscow

Fond R-5446 Opis' 1. *Podlinniki postanovlenii Soveta Ministrov SSSR.*

Fond R-5446 Opis' 37. *Sekretariat upravliaiushchikh delami Soveta Ministrov SSSR.*

Fond R-5446 Opisi 49a, 50, 50a, 51, 51a, 80, 80a, 81b, 86, 86a, 87. *Upravelnie delami Soveta Ministrov SSSR.*

Fond R-5446 Opis' 53. *Sekretariat zamestitelia predsedatelia Soveta Ministrov SSSR N. A. Voznesenskogo.*

Fond R-5446 Opis' 54. *Sekretariat zamestitelia predsedatelia Soveta Ministrov SSSR K. E. Voroshilova.*

Fond R-5446 Opis' 59. *Sekretariat zamestitelia predsedatelia Soveta Ministrov SSSR A. N. Kosygina.*

Fond R-5446 Opis' 75. *Sekretariat zamestitelia predsedatelia Soveta Ministrov SSSR A. I. Mikoiana.*

Fond R-8131. *Prokuratura SSSR.*

Fond R-9401. *Ministerstvo vnutrennykh del SSSR.*

Fond R-9414. *Glavnoe upravlenie mest zakliucheniia MVD SSSR (GULAG).*

Fond R-9492. *Ministerstvo iustitsii SSSR.*

Arkhiv Pravitel'stva Rossiiskoi Federatsii, Moscow

Tekushchii arkhiv.

Journals and Newspapers

Bol'shevik

Istochnik

Istoricheskii arkhiv

Izvestiia

Izvestiia TsK KPSS

Kentavr

Kommunist

Kul'tura i zhizn'

Literaturnaia gazeta

Otechestvennaia istoriia

Otechestvennye arkhivy

Partiinaia zhizn'

Pravda

Sotsialisticheskii vestnik

Svobodnaia mysl'

Voprosy ekonomiki

Voprosy filosofii

Voprosy istorii

Voprosy istorii KPSS

Atomnyi proekt SSSR. Dokumenty i materialy. Atomnaia bomba. 1945–1954. Vol.
2. Edited by L. D. Riabev. Moscow: RFIaTs-VNIIEF, 1999.

Evreiskii antifashistskii komitet v SSSR. 1941–1948. Dokumentirovannaia istoriia.
Edited by Shimon Redlikh. Moscow: Mezhdunarondnye otnosheniia, 1996.

GULAG (Glavnoe upravlenie lagerei). 1918–1960. Compiled by A. I. Kokurin and
N. V. Petrov. Moscow: Materik, 2000.

*Lavrentii Beria. 1953. Stenogramma iul'skogo plenuma TsK KPSS i drugie doku-
menty.* Compiled by V. Naumov and Iu. Sigachev. Moscow: MFD, 1999.

*Molotov, Malenkov, Kaganovich. 1957. Stenogramma iun'skogo plenuma TsK KPSS
i drugie dokumenty.* Compiled by N. Kovalev, A. Korotkov, S. Mel'chin, Iu.
Sigarev, and A. Stepanov. Moscow: MFD, 1998.

"Neizvestnaia initsiativa Khrushcheva (o podgotovke ukaza 1948 g. o vyselenii
krest'ian)." Compiled by V. P. Popov. *Otechestvennye arkhivy* 2 (1993): 31–
38.

Neizvestnaia Rossiia. XX vek. Compiled by V. A. Kozlov and S. M. Zav'ialov. Vols.
1–3. Moscow: Istoricheskoe nasledie, 1992, 1993.

*Nepravednyi sud. Poslednii Stalinskii rasstrel. Stenogramma sudebnogo protsessa nad
chlenami evreiskogo antifashistskogo komiteta.* Edited by V. P. Naumov. Moscow: Nauka, 1994.

"O dele Professorov Kliuevoi i Roskina." Resolution of the Central Committee,
16 July 1947. In "Delo KR," by V. D. Esakov and E. S. Levina, *Kentavr* 2
(1994): 66–68.

Politbiuro TsK VKP(b) i Sovet Ministrov SSSR 1945–1953. Compiled by O. V.
Khlevniuk, Y. Gorlizki, L. P. Kosheleva, A. I. Miniuk, M. Iu. Prozumenshchikov, L. A. Rogovaia, and S. V. Somonova. Moscow: Rosspen, 2002.

*Reabilitatsiia. Kak eto bylo. Dokumenty prezidiuma TsK KPSS i drugie materialy,
mart 1953–fevral' 1956.* Compiled by A. Artizov, Iu. Sigachev, I. Shevchuk,
and V. Khlopov. Moscow: MFD, 2000.

[Stalin, Joseph]. "Komissarov chertova gibel'." *Istoricheskii arkhiv* 5–6 (1997):
217–218.

———. "Bez khoroshei stolitsy net gosudarstva." *Istochnik* 4 (2001): 110–112.

Stalin i Kaganovich. Perepiska, 1931–1936 gg. Compiled by O. V. Khlevniuk, R. W.
Davies, L. P. Kosheleva, E. A. Rees, and L. A. Rogovaia. Moscow: Rosspen,
2001.

"Stalin's Conversations: Talks with Mao Zedong, December 1949–January 1950,
and with Zhou Enlai, August–September 1952." *Cold War International History Project Bulletin* 6–7 (1995–1996): 5–19.

Stalinskoe Politbiuro v 30-e gody. Compiled by O. V. Khlevniuk, A. V. Kvashonkin,
L. P. Kosheleva, and L. A. Rogovaia. Moscow: AIRO-XX, 1995.

" 'Tsk vskryl presmykatel'stvo pered zagranitsei.' Kak sozdavalis' 'sudy chesti'
v tsentral'nykh organakh." Compiled by Nikolai Sidorov. *Istochnik* 6
(1994): 68–81.

*Vlast' i khudozhestvennaia intelligentsiia Dokumenty TsK RKP(b)–VKP(b), VChK-
OGPU–NKVD o kul'turnoi politike. 1917–1953 gg.* Compiled by Andrei Artizov and Oleg Naumov. Moscow: Demokratiia, 1999.

Vostochnaia Evropa v dokumentakh Rossiiskikh arkhivov, 1944–1953. Vols. 1 and 2. Edited by G. P. Murashko, T. V. Volokitina, T. M. Islamov, A. F. Noskova, and L. A. Rogovaia. Moscow/Novosibirsk: Sibirskii Khronograf, 1997, 1998.

" 'Vtoroi i vazhneishii etap' (ob ukreplenii kolkhozov v 50-e–nachale 60-kh godov)." Compiled by V. P. Popov. *Otechestvennye arkhivy* 1 (1994): 37–50.

"Zakrytoe pis'mo TsK VKP(b)," *Svobodnaia mysl'* 1 (1996): 90–93.

Reference Works

Arkhiv noveishei istorii Rossii. Vol. 1. *"Osobaia papka" I. V. Stalina. Iz materialov Sekretariata NKVD-MVD SSSR, 1944–1953 gg. Katalog dokumentov.* Edited by V. A. Kozlov and S. V. Mironenko. Moscow: Gosarkhiv, 1994.

Arkhiv noveishei istorii Rossii. Vol. 4. *"Osobaia papka" L. P. Berii. Iz materialov Sekretariata NKVD-MVD SSSR. 1946–1949. Katalog dokumentov.* Edited by M. A. Kolerov. Moscow: Gosarkhiv, 1996.

Arkhiv noveishei istorii Rossii. Vol. 6. *"Osobaia papka" L. P. Berii. Iz materialov Sekretariata NKVD-MVD SSSR. 1950 g.–dekabr' 1952 g. Perepiska ministra vnutrennykh del L. P. Berii s Sovetom Ministrov SSSR I TsK VKP (b). Iz materialov Sekretariata MVD SSSR. Mart–iun' 1953 g. Katalog dokumentov.* Edited by V. A. Kozlov and S. V. Mironenko. Moscow: Gosarkhiv, 2000.

Gill, Graham. *The Rules of the Communist Party of the Soviet Union.* Basingstoke, U.K.: Macmillan, 1988.

Goliakov, I. T. *Sbornik dokumentov po istorii ugolovnogo zakonodatel'stva SSSR i RSFSR 1917–1952 gg.* Moscow: Gosiurizdat, 1953.

Gosudarstvennaia vlast' SSSR. Vysshie organy vlasti i upravleniia i ikh rukovoditeli. 1923–1991. Istoriko-biograficheskii spravochnik. Compiled by I. V. Ivkin. Moscow: Rosspen, 1999.

Politiuro, Orgbiuro, Sekretariat TsK RKP(b)-VKP(b)-KPSS. Moscow: Politizdat, 1990.

Politbiuro TsK RKB(b)-VKP(b). Povestki dnia zasedanii. Katalog. 1940–1952 gg. Vol. 3. Edited by G. M. Adibekov, K. M. Anderson, and L. A. Rogovaia. Moscow: Rosspen, 2001.

"Posetiteli kremlevskogo kabineta I. V. Stalina. Zhurnali (tetradi) zapisi lits, priniatykh pervym gensekom [1945–1953]." *Istoricheskii arkhiv* 4 (1996): 66–131 [1944–1946]; 5–6 (1996): 3–61 [1947–1949]; 1 (1997): 3–39 [1950–1953].

Resheniia partii i pravitel'stva po khoziaisvennym voprosam. 1941–1952 gg. Vol. 3. Moscow: Politizdat, 1968.

Sovet Narodnykh Komissarov SSSR. Sovet Ministrov SSSR. Kabinet Ministrov SSSR. 1923–1991. Entsiklopedicheskii spravochnik. Edited by S. D. Garniuk. Moscow: Mosgorarkhiv, 1999.

229 Kremlevskikh vozhdei. Politbiuro, Orgbiuro, Sekretariat TsK Kommunisticheskoi partii v litsakh i tsifrakh. Edited by A. D. Chernev. Moscow: Rodina, 1996.

Memoirs, Diaries, Speeches

Allilueva, Svetlana. *Twenty Letters to a Friend*. London: World Books, 1967.

Baibakov, N. K. *Sorok let v pravitel'stve*. Moscow: Respublica, 1993.

———. *Ot Stalina do El'tsina*. Moscow: Gazoil Press, 1998.

Chuev, Feliks. *Sto sorok besed s Molotovym. Iz dnevnika F. Chueva*. Moscow: Terra, 1991.

———. *Tak govoril Kaganovich. Ispoved' Stalinskogo apostola*. Moscow: Otechestvo, 1993.

Djilas, Milovan. *Conversations with Stalin*. London: Hart-Davis, 1962.

[Efremov, L. N.] "Neopublikovannaia rech' I. V. Stalina na plenume TsK KPSS." *Dos'e glasnosti. Spetsvypusk*, 13 December 2001, 11.

Khrushchev, N. S. "Secret Speech of Khrushchev Concerning the 'Cult of the Individual.' " In *The Anti-Stalin Campaign and International Communism*, edited by The Russian Institute, Columbia University. New York: Columbia University Press, 1956.

———. *Vospominaniia. Vremia, liudi, vlast'*. Vols. 1–4. Moscow: Moskovskie novosti, 1999.

Kuznetsov, N. G. "Krutye povoroty." *Pravda*, 27 July 1988, 3.

Malyshev, V. A. "Dnevnik narkoma." *Istochnik* 5 (1997): 103–147.

Men'shikov, M. A. *S vintovkoi i vo frake*. Moscow: Mezhdunarodnye otnosheniia, 1996.

[Miasnikov, A. L.] "Konchina. Iz vospominanii A. L. Miasnikova, uchastnika konsiliuma u posteli I. V. Stalina." *Literaturnaia gazeta*, 1 March 1989.

Mikoian, Anastas. *Tak bylo. Razmyshleniia o minuvshem*. Moscow: Vagrius, 1999.

Novikov, N. V. *Vospominaniia diplomata. Zapiski 1938–1946*. Moscow: Politizdat, 1989.

Patolichev, N. S. *Ispitanie na zrelost'*. Moscow: Politizdat, 1977.

———. *Sovest'iu svoei ne postupis'*. Moscow: Sampo, 1995.

Rakosi, Matias. "Liudiam svoistenno oshibat'sia." *Istoricheskii arkhiv* (1997) 3: 108–157, 4: 3–63, 5–6: 5–50, and (1998) 3: 3–59.

[Rumiantsev, A. M.], "Mistika tsifr upravliaet istoriei." *Obshchaia gazeta*, 14–20 October 1999.

Rybin, A. T. "Riadom s I. V. Stalinym." *Sotsiologicheskie issledovaniia* 3 (1988): 84–94.

Shepilov, D. T. "Vospominaniia." *Voprosy istorii* (1998) 3: 3–24, 4: 3–25, 5: 3–27, 6: 3–45, 7: 3–35.

Simonov, Konstantin. *Glazami cheloveka moego pokoleniia. Razmyshleniia o I. V. Staline*. Moscow: Novosti, 1990.

[Smirtiukov, Mikhail.] "Posle rasstrela Berii Malenkov vse vremia ulybalsia," *Kommersant' vlast'*, 8 February 2000, 53–55; 22 February 2000, 52–54; 21 March 2000, 46–48; 18 April 2000, 44–45; 2 May 2000, 52–55.

Stalin, I. V., *Sochineniia*. Vol. 3. Edited by Robert H. McNeal. Stanford, Calif.: Hoover Institution Press, 1967.

Sudoplatov, P. A. *Razvedka i Kreml'. Zapiski nezhelatel'nogo svidetelia*. Moscow: Too "Geia," 1996.

———. *Spetsoperatsii. Lubianka i Kreml' 1930–1950*. Moscow: Olma Press, 1997.

[Sukhanov, D. N.] "Stalin poshevelil pal'tsami." *Novoe vremia* 48 (1991): 32–34.

———. "Iz vospominaniia Sukhanova D. N. byvshego pomoshchnika Malen-kova G. M. Neopisannye memuary." Manuscript deposited at RGANI, 1992, d.2.

Troianovskii, Oleg. *Cherez gody i rasstoianiia. Istoriia odnoi sem'i.* Moscow: Va-grius, 1997.

Zhdanov, Iu. A. "Vo mgle protivorechii." *Voprosy filosofii* 7 (1993): 65–92.

Zverev, A. G. *Zapiski ministra.* Moscow: Politizdat, 1973.

Secondary Materials: Selected Books and Articles

Abramov, B. A. "Organizatsionno—partiinaia rabota KPSS v gody chetvertoi piatiletki." *Voprosy istorii KPSS* 3 (1979): 55–65.

Adibekov, G. M. *Kominform i poslevoennaia Evropa. 1947–1956 gg* Moscow: AIRO-XX, 1994.

Aksiutin, Iu. V. *Poststalinskoe obschestvo. Problema liderstva i transformatsii vlasti.* Moscow: Nauchnaia kniga, 1999.

Azrael, Jeremy R. *Managerial Power and Soviet Politics.* Cambridge, Mass.: Harvard University Press, 1966.

Babichenko, D. L. *Pisateli i tsenzory. Sovetskaia literatura 1940–x godov pod politicheskim kontrolem TsK.* Moscow: Rossiia Molodaia, 1994.

Bialer, Seweryn, ed. *Stalin and His Generals: Soviet Military Memoirs of World War II.* London: Souvenir Press, 1970.

Bugai, N. F. *L. Beriia–I. Stalinu: "Soglasno vashemu ukazaniiu."* Moscow: AIRO-XX, 1995.

Conquest, Robert. *Power and Policy in the USSR: The Study of Soviet Dynastics.* London: Macmillan, 1961.

Danilov, A. A. "Stalinskoe Politbiuro v poslevoennye gody." In *Politicheskie partii Rossii. Stranitsy istorii,* edited by N. D. Erofeev, Iu. I. Kir'ianov, V. V. Shelok-haev, and A. V. Gusev. Moscow: Izdatel'stvo Moskovskogo Universiteta, 2000.

Danilov, A. A., and A. V Pyzhikov. *Rozhdenie sverderzhavy. SSSR v pervye poslevoennye gody.* Moscow: Rosspen, 2001.

Dunmore, Timothy. *The Stalinist Command Economy: The Soviet State Apparatus and Economic Policy 1945–1953.* London: Macmillan, 1980.

Egorova, N. I. "Evropeiskaia bezopasnost' i 'ugroza' NATO v otsenkakh stalin-skogo okruzheniia." In *Stalinskoe desiatiletie kholodnoi voiny. Fakty i gipotezy,* edited by I. V. Gaiduk, N. I. Egorova, and A. O. Chubar'ian. Moscow: Nauka, 1999.

Esakov, V. D. "K istorii filosofskoi diskussii 1947 goda." *Voprosy filosofii* 2 (1993): 83–106.

Esakov, V. D., and E. S. Levina, "Delo KR." *Kentavr* 2 (1994): 54–65.

———. *Delo KR. Sudy chesti v ideologii i praktike poslevoennogo stalinizma.* Moscow: IRIRAN, 2001.

Filitov, A. M. "Stalinkskaia diplomatiia i Germanskii vopros. Poslednii god." In *Stalinskoe desiatiletie kholodnoi voiny. Fakty i gipotezy,* edited by I. V.Gaiduk, N. I. Egorova, and A. O. Chubar'ian. Moscow: Nauka, 1999.

Filtzer, Donald. *Soviet Workers and Late Stalinism: Labour and the Restoration of the Stalinist System after World War II.* Cambridge: Cambridge University Press, 2002.

Fursenko, A. A. "Konets ery Stalina." *Zvezda* 12 (1999): 173–188.

Gaiduk, I. V., N. I. Egorova, and A. O. Chubar'ian, eds. *Stalinskoe desiatiletie kholodnoi voiny. Fakty i gipotezy.* Moscow: Nauka, 1999.

Getty J. Arch, and Oleg V. Naumov. *The Road to Terror: Stalin and the Self-Destruction of the Bolsheviks, 1932–1939.* New Haven, Conn.: Yale University Press, 1999.

Goncharov, Sergei N., John W. Lewis, and Xue Litai. *Uncertain Partners: Stalin, Mao, and the Korean War.* Stanford, Calif.: Stanford University Press, 1993.

Gor'kov, Iu. A. "K istorii sozdaniia goskomiteta oborony." *Novaia i noveishaia istoriia* 4 (1999): 17–34.

Gorlizki, Yoram. "Party Revivalism and the Death of Stalin." *Slavic Review* 54, 1 (1995): 1–22.

———. "Rules, Incentives, and Soviet Campaign Justice after World War II," *Europe-Asia Studies* 51, 7 (1999): 1245–1265.

———. "Stalin's Cabinet: The Politburo and Decision Making in the Post-war Years." *Europe-Asia Studies* 53, 2 (2001): 291–312.

———. "Ordinary Stalinism: The Council of Ministers and the Soviet Neopatrimonial State, 1945–1953." *Journal of Modern History* 74, 4 (2002): 699–736.

Gregory, Paul R. *Restructuring the Soviet Economic Bureaucracy.* Cambridge: Cambridge University Press, 1990.

Hahn, Werner G. *Postwar Soviet Politics: The Fall of Zhdanov and the Defeat of Moderation, 1946–1953.* Ithaca, N.Y.: Cornell University Press, 1982.

Holloway, David. *Stalin and the Bomb: The Soviet Union and Atomic Energy, 1939–1956.* New Haven, Conn.: Yale University Press, 1994.

Kaplan, Karel. "Vozvyshenie i padenie Alekseia Chipichki," *Voprosy istorii* 10 (1999): 82–93.

Khlevniuk, O. V. *Politbiuro. Mekhanizmy politicheskoi vlasti v 1930-e gody.* Moscow: Rosspen, 1996.

———. "Stalin i Molotov. Edinolichnaia diktatura i predposylki 'oligarkhizatsiia.'" In *Stalin. Stalinizm. Sovetskoe obschestvo. K 70-letiu V. S. Lel'chuka,* edited by G. Sagatelian, B. Ilizarov, and O. Khlevniuk. Moscow: IRIRAN, 2000.

———. "Sovetskaia ekonomicheskaia politika na rubezhe 1948–1950-kh godov i 'delo Gosplana.'" *Otechestvennaia istoriia* 3 (2001): 77–89.

———. "Stalin i organy gosudarstvennoi bezopasnosti v poslevoennyi period." *Cahiers du monde russe* 42, 2–4 (2001): 535–548.

Kliuchevskii, Vasilii. *Kurs russkoi istorii.* 1904–1910. In *Sochineniia v deviati tomakh.* Vol. 2. Moscow: Mysl', 1988.

Kokurin, Aleksandr, and Iurii Morukov, "Gulag. Struktura i kadry," *Svobodnaia mysl'* 12 (2001): 89–110.

Kostyrchenko, G. V. *V plenu u krasnogo pharaona.* Moscow: Mezhdunarodnye otnosheniia, 1994.

————. *Tainaia politika Stalina. Vlast' i antisemitism.* Moscow: Mezhdunarodnye otnosheniia, 2001.

Krasnov, A. V., ed. *Bor'ba partii i rabochego klassa za vosstanovlenie i razvitie narodnogo khoziaistva SSSR (1943–1950 gg.).* Moscow: Mysl', 1978.

Kraveri, Marta. "Krizis Gulaga. Kengirskoe vosstanie 1954 goda v dokumentakh MVD." *Cahiers du monde russe* 36, 3 (1995): 319–344.

Krementsov, Nikolai. *Stalinist Science.* Princeton, N.J.: Princeton University Press, 1997.

Kumanev, G. A. *Riadom so Stalinym: Otkrovennye svidetel'stva.* Moscow: Bylina, 1999.

Lewin, Moshe. *Lenin's Last Struggle.* London: Faber and Faber, 1968.

————. "Stalin in the Mirror of the Other." In *Russia/USSR/Russia.* New York: New Press, 1995.

————[Mikhail Levin]. "Nomenklatura—Arcanum imperii." In *Kuda idet Rossiia?* edited by T. I. Zaslavskaia. Moscow: Intertsenter, 1997.

Loginov, V. M. *Teni Stalina. General Vlasik i ego soratniki.* Moscow: Sovremennik, 2000.

Madievski, Samson. "1953: La déportation des Juifs soviétiques: était-elle programmée?" *Cahiers du monde russe* 41, 4 (2000): 561–568.

Malkin, Viktor. "Sem' pisem Lidii Timashuk." *Novoe vremia* 23 (1993): 38–41.

Mawdsley, Evan, and Stephen White. *The Soviet Elite from Lenin to Gorbachev: The Central Committee and Its Members, 1917–1991.* Oxford: Oxford University Press, 2000.

McCagg, William O. *Stalin Embattled, 1943–1948.* Detroit, Mich.: Wayne State University Press, 1978.

Medvedev, Zh. A. "Zagadka smerti Stalina." *Voprosy istorii* 1 (2000): 83–91.

Murashko, G. P., and A. F. Noskova. "Sovetskoe rukovodstvo i politicheskie protsessy T. Kostova i L. Raika (po materialam rossiiskikh arkhivov)." In *Stalinskoe desiatiletie kholodnoi voiny. Fakty i gipotezy,* edited by I. V. Gaiduk, N. I. Egorova, and A. O. Chubar'ian. Moscow: Nauka, 1999.

Murin, Iu. G. "Sudy Chesti." *Izvestiia TsK KPSS* 11 (1990): 135–137.

————. *Iosif Stalin v obiatiakh sem'i. Iz lichnogo arkhiva.* Moscow: Rodina, 1993.

Nikolaevsky, Boris I. "Ideologicheskaia perestroika VKP." *Sotsialisticheskii vestnik* 26, 2 (1946): 35–39.

————. "Malenkov: His Rise and His Policy." *New Leader,* 23 March 1953, 2–6.

————. "How Malenkov Triumphed." *New Leader,* 30 March 1953, 15–19.

————. *Tainye stranitsy istorii.* Edited by Iu. G. Fel'shtinskii. Moscow: Izdatel'stvo gumanitarnoi literatury, 1995.

Novik, F. I. *"Ottepel'" i inertsiia kholodnoi voiny (Germanskaia politika SSSR v 1953–1955 gg.)* Moscow: Akademiia nauk, 2001.

Openkin, L. A. "I. V. Stalin. Poslednii prognoz budushchego (iz istorii napisaniia raboty 'Ekonomicheskie problemy sotsializma v SSSR')." *Voprosy istorii KPSS* 7 (1991): 113–128.

Pasat, V. I. *Trudnye stranitsy istorii Moldovy. 1940–1950-e gody.* Moscow: Terra, 1994.

Pechatnov, Vladimir. "Soiuzniki nazhimaiut na tebia dlia togo, chtoby slomit' u tebia voliu." *Istochnik* 2 (1999): 70–85.

———. "Na etom voprose my slomaem ikh antisovetskoe uporstvo." *Istochnik* 3 (1999): 92–104.

———. "Shtrikhi k portretu genseka." *Istochnik* 3 (2000): 97–104.

Pechenkin, A. A. "Gosudarstvennyi komitet oborony v 1941 godu." *Otechestvennaia istoriia* 4–5 (1994): 126–141.

Petrov, N. V. "Pervyi predsedatel' KGB general Ivan Serov." *Otechestvennaia istoriia* 5 (1997): 23–43.

Pikhoia, R. G. *Sovetskii soiuz. Istoriia vlasti, 1945–1991.* Moscow: RAGS, 1998.

Poliakov, Iu. A., ed. *Naselenie Rossii v XX veke. Istoricheskie ocherki. 1940–1959.* Vol 2. Moscow: Rosspen, 2001.

Popov, V. P. "Gosudarstvennyi terror v Sovetskoi Rossii, 1923–1953 gg." *Otechestvennye arkhivy* 2 (1992): 20–31.

———. *Ekonomicheskaia politika Sovetskogo gosudarstva. 1946–1953 gg.* Moscow-Tambov: Izdatel'stvo TGTU, 2000.

Pyzhikov, A. V. *Konfiguratsii i funktsionirovanie vlasti v SSSR. 1945–1953.* Moscow: Nauchnaia Kniga, 1999.

Rapoport, Yakov. *The Doctors' Plot of 1953.* Cambridge, Mass.: Harvard University Press, 1991.

Reabilitatsiia. Politicheskie protsessy 30–50-kh godov. Edited by A. N. Iakovlev. Moscow: *Politizdat*, 1990.

Rigby, T. H. "Was Stalin a Loyal Patron?" In *Political Elites in the USSR: Central Leaders and Local Cadres from Lenin to Gorbachev.* Aldershot, U.K.: Edward Elgar, 1990.

———. "The Government in the Soviet Political System." In *Executive Power and Soviet Politics: The Rise and Decline of the Soviet State*, edited by Eugene Huskey. Armonk, N.Y.: M. E. Sharpe, 1992.

Romanovskii, N. V. *Liki Stalinizma, 1945–1953.* Moscow: RAGS, 1995.

Rubenstein, Joshua, and Vladimir P. Naumov, eds. *Stalin's Secret Pogrom: The Postwar Inquisition of the Jewish Anti-fascist Committee.* New Haven, Conn: Yale University Press, 2001.

Rzheshevsky, O. A. *War and Diplomacy: The Making of the Grand Alliance.* Amsterdam: Harwood, 1996.

Simonov, N. S. *Voenno-promyshlennyi kompleks SSSR v 1920–1950-e gody.* Moscow: Rosspen, 1996

Solomon, Peter H., Jr. *Soviet Criminal Justice under Stalin.* Cambridge: Cambridge University Press, 1996.

Soprotivlenie v Gulage. Moscow: Vozvrashchenie, 1992.

Stoliarov, Kiril. *Palachi i zhertvy.* Moscow: Olma Press, 1997.

Swayze, Harold. *Political Control of Literature in the USSR, 1946–1959.* Cambridge, Mass.: Harvard University Press, 1962.

Taubman, William. *Stalin's American Policy: From Entente to Détente to Cold War.* New York: Norton, 1982.

Torkunov, A. V. *Zagadochnaia voina. Koreiskii konflikt 1950–1953 godov.* Moscow: Rosspen, 2000.

Weber, Max. *Economy and Society: An Outline of Interpretive Sociology.* Vol. 2. Berkeley: University of California Press, 1978.

Weiner, Amir. *Making Sense of War: The Second World War and the Fate of the Bolshevik Revolution.* Princeton, N.J.: Princeton University Press, 2001.

Werth, Alexander. *Russia: The Post-war Years.* New York: Taplinger, 1971.

Zemskov, V. N. "Massovoe osvobozhdenie spetsposelentsev i ssylnykh (1954–1960)." *Sotsiologicheskie issledovaniia* 1 (1991): 5–26.

———. "Gulag. Istoriko-sotsiologicheskii aspekt." *Sotsiologicheskie issledovaniia* 6 (1991): 10–27.

———. "Sud'ba 'kulatskoi ssylki' (1930–1954 gg.)." *Otechestvennaia istoriia* 1 (1994): 118–147.

Zhukov, Iurii N. "Bor'ba za vlast' v rukovodstve SSSR v 1945–1952 godakh." *Voprosy istorii* 1 (1995): 23–39.

———. "Bor'ba za vlast' v partiino-gosudarstvennykh verkhakh SSSR vesnoi 1953 goda." *Voprosy istorii* 5–6 (1996): 39–57.

———. *Tainy Kremlia. Stalin, Molotov, Beria, Malenkov.* Moscow: Terra, 2000.

Zima, V. F. " 'Vtoroe raskulachivanie' (agrarnaia politika kontsa 40-kh–nachalo 50-kh godov)." *Otechestvennaia istoriia* 3 (1994): 109–125.

———. *Golod v SSSR 1946–1947 godov. Proiskhozhdenie i posledstviia.* Moscow: IRIRAN, 1996.

Zubok, Vladislav, and Constantine Pleshakov. *Inside the Kremlin's Cold War: From Stalin to Khrushchev.* Cambridge, Mass.: Harvard University Press, 1996.

Zubkova, E. Iu. "Kadrovaia politika i chistki v KPSS. 1949–1953 gg." *Svobodnaia mysl'* (1999) 3: 117–127, 4: 96–110, 6: 112–120.

Unpublished Materials

Dijk, Ruud Van. "The 1952 Stalin Note Debate: Myth or Missed Opportunity for German Unification?" Cold War International History Project, Working Paper no.14, Washington, D.C., May 1996.

Gorlizki, Yoram. "Theft under Stalin: A Property Rights Analysis." PERSA Working Paper, University of Warwick, May 2001.

Khlevniuk, Oleg. "Zadavlennye oligarkhi: Stalin i ego okruzhenie v poslevoennye gody." Paper presented at "Rethinking the Stalin Era: The Impact of Archival Research" conference, University of Toronto, September 1999.

Lewin, Moshe. "The Soviet Nomenklatura." Paper presented for the seminar "Serving the State: Administrative Practices in the Soviet Union," École des Hautes Études en Sciences Sociales, Paris, December 2001.

Pollock, Ethan. "Conversations with Stalin on Questions of Political Economy." Cold War International History Project, Working Paper no.33, Washington, D.C., July 2001.

Weathersby, Kathryn. " 'Should We Fear This?' Stalin and the Danger of War with America." Cold War International History Project, Working Paper no.39, Washington, D.C., July 2002.

Wheatcroft, S. G. "Stalin and the Soviet Political Elite: The Private Meetings in

Stalin's Kremlin Office." Paper presented at "Stalin's Politburo, 1928–1953" conference, European University Institute, Florence, March 2000.

Interviews

The following interviews were commissioned under U.K. Economic and Social Research Council award number R000222676. The interviews, carried out by a Russian archivist from February 1999 to January 2001, were with senior party and ministerial officials from the late Stalin period and with relatives of Politburo members. Copies of the transcripts have been lodged at the Baykov Library, University of Birmingham.

Alliluev, Vladimir Fedorovich, nephew of Stalin's wife, Nadezhda Allilueva (20 November 2000), 14 pages.

Andreeva, Natalia Andreevna, daughter of Politburo member Andrei Andreev (5 January 2001), 15 pages.

Baibakov, Nikolai Konstantinovich, Minister of Oil Industry (25 October 1999), 17 pages.

Bratchenko, Boris Fedorovich, Deputy Head of the Secretariat of Sovnarkom, subsequently Deputy Minister and then Minister of Mining Industries (23 February 1999), 19 pages.

Chistiakov, Nikolai Fedorovich, Head of Secretariat at the Ministry of Justice (22 February and 25 April 2000), 19 pages.

Kalmyk, Nikolai Iosifovich, instructor at Agriculture Department, Central Committee (22 July 1999), 14 pages.

Kazakov, Georgii Aleksandrovich, Deputy Head of Sector at Agitprop, Central Committee (21 September 1999), 16 pages.

Kazanetz, Ivan Pavlovich, First Secretary of the Makeev Party Committee, later Minister of Ferrous Metals (16 February 1999), 9 pages.

Troianovskii, Oleg Aleksandrovich, diplomat and official at the Ministry of Foreign Affairs (9 March 2000), 22 pages.

Voznesenskii, Lev Aleksandrovich, nephew of Politburo member Nikolai Voznesenskii (3 August 2000), 18 pages.

The following interviews, with senior officials from the late Stalin period, were conducted by Yoram Gorlizki.

Chistiakov, Nikolai Fedorovich, Head of Secretariat at the Ministry of Justice (17 April 1993).

Startsev, Afanasy Aleksandrovich, aide to Central Committee Secretary Panteleimon Ponomarenko, and subsequently Deputy Head of the Administrative Agencies Department (30 October 1993).

Sukhanov, Dmitrii Nikolaevich, aide to Georgii Malenkov (1 April 1994).

Zhdanov, Iurii Andreevich, son of Andrei Zhdanov and Head of the Science and Higher Educational Institutions Sector at the Central Committee (23 October 1993).

INDEX

Abakumov Affair, 113–120, 154–155

Abakumov, Viktor, 7, 30, 85, 113–120, 154–155, 207 n.74, 208 n.78, 216 n.67

attacks Zhukov, 30

and Ministry of State Security, 28–29, 60–61

agriculture, 14, 24

and failure of reform, 133–141

Agritprop. *See* Central Committee apparatus

Akhmatova Anna, 32–34, 43

Albania, 70

Aleksandrov, G. F., 31, 43

criticized for his book *The History of Western European Philosophy*, 35

as Zhdanov's dependent, 35

Alekseenko, G. V., 175 n.25

Allilueva, Nadezhda, 75

Allilueva, Svetlana, 49

Andreev, Andrei, 5, 57, 63, 86, 87, 101–102, 174 n.9, 186 n.1, 187 n.10, 198 n.26, 204 n.19

Andrianov, V. M., 182 n.77

Andropov, Iurii, 171

Arbeiderbladet, 19

archives, Russian and Soviet, 12–13, 227–228

podlinnye protokoly and *podpis'nye protokoly*, 12

Aristov, Averkii, 134–135, 215 n.46, 220 n.113

Artillery Officers' Affair, 113, 119, 167

Aviators' Affair, 26–28, 30, 113, 167, 189 n.27, 207 n.74

Azerbaijani Council of Ministers, 61

Baku, 73

Balkartsy, 158

Baltic republics, 98, 124, 167, 173 n.4

Baramiia, M. I., 110, 111

Batumi, 73

Bedell Smith, Walter, 36–37, 184 n.100

Beletskii, Zinovii, 35

Belorussia, 98, 124, 173 n.4

Benediktov, Ivan, 41, 137

Beria, Lavrentii, 5, 7, 18, 22, 25, 26, 57, 63, 74, 76, 80, 86, 88, 89, 91, 92, 95, 101, 103–104, 105, 115, 116, 118, 140, 141, 146, 149, 162, 169, 174 n.11, 176 n.2, 180 nn.52, 54, 181 n.60, 182 n.69, 186 n.1, 187 n.6, 189 n.25, 190 nn.35, 36, 38, 191 n.41, 192 nn.52, 53, 196 n.104, 198 n.26, 200 n.61, 201 n.66, 205 n.43, 207 nn.54, 67, 208 n.83, 209 n.23, 211 n.65, 216

Beria, Lavrentii (*continued*)
 n.60, 220 n.110, 222 n.132,
  223 n.6
 arrest of, 166, 168
 attacked by Stalin, 28–29, 109–113
 career of, 26
 and Council of Ministers, 28, 93–
  94, 161, 193 nn.65, 66
 elected to Politburo, 28
 and Gulag, 128–132
 as Merkulov's patron, 29, 60, 169
 and Ministry of State Security, 7,
  28–29, 60
 and nuclear weapons, 104, 204–
  205 n.25
Bessarabia, 98
Bierrut, Boleslaw, 98
Birobidzhan, special camps in, 158,
 219 n.105
Bol'shevik, 85, 146, 218 n.94
Borkov, G. A., 182 n.77
Borzhomi, 145, 174 n.16
Brezhnev, Leonid, 171, 215 n.46
British security service, 158
Bukharin, Nikolai, 149
Bulganin, Nikolai, 54, 56, 74, 76, 91,
 93, 101, 103, 104, 105, 116,
 149, 152, 161, 176 n.2, 186 n.1,
 189 nn.25, 27, 192 n.50, 198
 n.26, 204 n.14, 206 n.43, 211
 n.65, 215 n.56, 216 n.60, 220
 n.110, 222 n.132, 223 n.6
 and Artillery Officers' Affair, 113
 and Council of Ministers, 56, 93–
  94, 104, 160
 promoted by Stalin, 49, 54, 92–94
Buro of the Presidium. *See* Central
 Committee, Presidium of

Central Committee, 39, 42, 43, 47,
 50, 52, 76, 82, 90, 162
 as byword for Stalin, 87, 108, 118,
  154, 180 n.57, 216 n.65
 membership of, 26, 29, 30, 38,
  48, 144, 148
 plenums of, 50–52, 54, 136, 140,
  146, 149, 153, 157, 162, 201
  n.89
 resolutions of, 11, 27, 29, 32, 38,
  51, 109, 117–118, 157
 subordinated to Politburo, 51

Central Committee apparatus, 60,
 115, 146, 177 n.2
 administration for checking party
  organs, 32, 182 n.77
 administrative agencies
  department, 114
 Agitprop, 34, 35, 157, 186 n.134,
  218 n.92
 agriculture department, 109, 136
 cadres administration, 27, 32, 160
 Commission of Party Control, 86–
  87, 111
 department of leading party
  agencies, 26
 department of party, trade union
  and Komsomol agencies, 116
 department for selection and
  assignment of cadres, 160
 general department, 160, 220–221
  n.118
 and purge of MGB, 114–118
 reorganization of, 58, 71, 119, 151–
  152
 science department, 40
Central Committee, Presidium of,
 131, 135–136, 148, 149, 151,
 157, 158, 160, 162, 166, 215–
 216 n.59
 Commissions of, 152–153, 161
 Buro of, 135, 149, 157, 160–161,
  162, 215–216 n.59
Central Statistical Administration
 (TsSU), 133–134, 136
Charkviani, K. N., 111
Chechens, 158
Chekists, 118. *See also* Ministry of
 State Security
Chepichka, Aleksei, 203 n.4
Chesnokov, Dmitrii, 157–158, 218
 n.92, 219 n.106
Chicago Tribune, 177 n.3
China, Peoples Republic of, 69, 78, 91
Churchill, W. S., 19–21
close circle (*blizhnii krug*). *See* ruling
 group
collective leadership, 10, 12, 14, 50,
 93–95, 98, 101–107, 124, 149,
 166–167
Cominform, 99, 185 n.115
Comintern, 220 n.117
Commissariat of Armed Forces, 30

Commissariat of Foreign Affairs, 22

Commissariat of Internal Affairs (NKVD). *See* Ministry of Internal Affairs

Congresses of Communist Party, 50
  XVIII, 18, 48, 170, 186 n.1, 188 n.24
  XIX, 13–14, 51, 107, 119, 136, 144–151, 160, 163, 168, 176 n.29, 206 n.51
  XX, 175 n.24

cosmopolitanism, 70

Council of Foreign Ministers
  London, 18, 20
  Moscow, 35

Council of Ministers (Sovmin), 7, 45, 50, 52–58, 77, 86, 93, 108, 119, 129, 152–153, 161, 166–168
  chancellery, 161
  economic responsibilities, 45, 57, 59–60, 80
  reforms hampered by Stalin, 61–62
  relationship to Politburo, 45–46, 53, 59–60, 61, 64, 190–191 n.39, 197 n.113
  reorganization of, 7, 52–58
  succeeds Sovnarkom as official government, 52

Council of Ministers, Bureau of, 10, 13, 28, 53–58, 84, 93–94, 106, 144, 152, 153, 179 n.41, 190 n.37, 191 nn.41, 42, 48, 192 nn.50, 52, 196 n.105, 205 n.38

Council of Ministers, Presidium of, 103–106, 152–153, 166, 204 n.16, 215–216 n.59
  Bureau of, 10, 93, 101, 103, 104, 105, 106, 107, 135, 144, 152–153, 161, 205 n.35, 215–216 n.59

Council of Ministers, sectoral bureaus, 45, 55–58, 192 n.50, 194 nn.69, 71, 72, 194 n.77
  bureau for agriculture, 55
  bureau for culture and health, 55
  bureau for food industry, 24–25, 55, 79
  bureau for fuel and electrical power stations, 55

bureau for machine construction, 55
  bureau for metallurgy and chemicals, 55
  bureau for metallurgy and geology, 77–78, 194 n.69
  bureau for military-industrial and military issues, 4, 13–14, 100–101, 104
  bureau for trade and light industry, 55, 72, 79
  bureau for transport and communications, 55, 78, 194 n.69
  creation of, 55
  dissolved, 101, 204 n.15

Council of Peoples Commissars (Sovnarkom SNK), 19, 46, 52–53, 55–57, 177 n.2, 189–190 nn.34, 35, 36, 37, 192 n.50, 197 n.113. *See also* Council of Ministers

Czechoslovakia, 70

Daily Express, 19
Daily Herald, 21
demobilization, 3, 31–32
Denisov, G. A., 182 n.77
Djilas, M., 58
Doctors' Plot, 14, 153–159, 161–163, 167, 217 nn.81, 83, 219 n.99, 221 n.126
Dubinin, Nikolai, 40
Dvinskii, B. A., 24–25

Efremov, Aleksandr, 56, 193 n.56, 214 n.44
Egolin, A. M., 34
Egorov, P. I., 156, 217 n.81, 221 n.126
Eliseev, I. I., 217 n.81
Erevan, 73
Etinger, Iakov, 117, 154, 216 n.67
Evang, Karl, 19

Fedoseev, P. N., 36, 157, 218 nn.93, 94

Gagry, 174 n.16
Garkush, V. N., 217 n.81

Georgian Communist Party, 110–113
  replacement of leadership, 111–
    112
Georgian Ministry of State Security,
    111–112
GKO. *See* State Defense Committee
Goglidze, S. A., 115, 118, 154, 156,
    208 n.83
Gorshenin, K. P., 105
Gosbank, 85
Gosplan, 49, 54, 77, 79–88, 188
    n.18, 200 n.62
  division of, 59
Gosplan Affair, 5, 6, 7, 13, 69, 82–
    85, 87–88, 94, 191 n.43
Gossnab, 59, 215 n.55
Gostekhnika, 59
Great Terror, 5, 23, 43, 80, 89, 95,
    169, 173 n.5, 187 n.5
Greece, 35
Grigorian, G. M., 27
Gulag, 14, 124–133, 166
  construction projects, 127, 130,
    132, 167
  discipline within, 126, 129–131,
    209 n.11
  dismantling of, 128–129, 131, 167
  reform of, 132–133, 167
  scale and cost of, 124–127, 130–
    132, 166–167, 209 n.8
Gusarov, N. I., 182 n.77
Guzenko, Igor, 180 n.56

Harriman, Averell, 20, 177 n.8
Hitler, Adolf, 168, 224 nn.12, 13
honor courts, 36–37, 40, 61, 184
    nn.105, 106, 189 n.27

Iaroshenko, Leonid, 146
Ideological apparatus. *See* Central
    Committee apparatus: Agitprop
Ignat'ev, S. D., 7, 105, 111, 116, 117–
    119, 135, 152, 159, 182 n.77,
    208 nn.80, 84, 220 n.113
  career of, 118
  and Doctors' Plot, 154–156
Ignatov, N. G., 208 n.80, 215 n.46
Ingush, 158
inner circle. *See* ruling group
intelligentsia, campaigns against, 4–5
  cultural intelligentsia, 31–36

scientific intelligentsia, 36–39, 40–
    42
Izvestiia, 218 nn.93, 94

Jewish Anti-Fascist Committee
    (EAK), 70, 75, 98, 154–155, 179
    n.31, 197 n.5
Jewish anti-Soviet youth
    organization, 117

Kaganovich, Lazar, 13, 55, 63, 75,
    91, 102, 105, 149, 176 n.2, 181
    n.60, 186 n.1, 187 nn.5, 10,
    188 n.18, 192 n.53, 193 n.66,
    198 n.26, 206 n.43, 215 n.55,
    216 nn.60, 63, 223 n.6
  admission into ruling group, 49
  dismissed as successor, 93–94, 193
    n.66
Kaganovich, Mikhail, 167
Kalinin, Mikhail, 186 n.1, 187 n.10,
    188 n.25
Kalmyks, 158
Kamenev, Lev, 144, 149
Kaplan, Karel, 203 n.4
Kaspustin, F. Ia., 82, 85–87
Kazakhstan, 111
Khabarovsk, 115
Kholodov, N. I., 138–139
Khrulev, A. V., 46
Khrushchev, Nikita, 5, 11, 34, 47,
    74, 85, 91, 105, 106, 113, 135,
    141, 149, 150, 152, 159, 162,
    168, 175 n.24, 181 n.60, 186
    n.1, 187 n.10, 188 nn.17, 18,
    21, 205 n.35, 206 nn.43, 51,
    211 n.65, 213 n.21, 215 nn.46,
    56, 216 nn.60, 63, 220 n.113,
    222 n.132
  and agriculture, 108–109, 136,
    138–140
  at Council of Ministers, 103, 223
    n.6
  dismissed as successor, 94
  at XIX Congress, 144–148
  as populist, 168, 223 n.11
  return to Moscow, 89–92, 103
Khudiakov, S. A., 26
Kliueva, Nina, 36–38, 43, 184
    n.100, 185 n.107
Kommunist, 152, 158, 218 n.92

Komosomol, 116, 118, 218 n.92
Korean War, 4, 97, 98, 167, 223 n.5
Korotchencko, D. S., 182 n.77
Kostov, Traicho, 70
Kosygin, Aleksei N., 55, 56, 71, 75–
  76, 102–103, 186 n.1, 189
  nn.25, 27, 192 n.50, 195 n.82,
  198 n.26, 200 n.61
  admitted to novenary, 71
  and Leningrad affair, 73–74
Kovalev, Ivan, 82, 169, 200 n.60
Kozlov, A. I., 108, 136
Krasnodar, 135, 174 n.16
Kremlin, 104, 105, 106, 107, 154
Kruglov, S. N., 28, 105, 129, 130,
  131
Krutikov, A. D., 56, 60, 81, 193 n.56
  early career of, 72
Kruzhkov, V. S., 36
Kuban', 135
Kuibyshev, 92, 136
  hydroelectric station, 129
Kul'tura i zhizn, 32
Kursk, 138
Kuz'min, A. N., 77–78
Kuznetsov, A. A., 6, 159, 182 n.76,
  189 n.25, 217 n.81
  and Andrei Zhdanov, 32, 73–74,
    182 n.75
  as Central Committee Secretary,
    32–33, 179 n.42, 189 n.25
  and Leningrad Affair, 80–82, 85,
    87, 88–89
  responsibility for secret police, 60,
    89
Kuznetsova, Alla, 78, 199 n.50

Larionov, A. N., 135
Lazutin, P. G., 81, 87
Lenin, V. I., 143, 148–150, 166, 214
  n.29
  "testament" of, 144
Leningrad, 80, 85, 134
Leningrad, 32, 34, 38, 183 n.90
Leningrad Affair, 5, 6, 7, 13, 49, 70,
  73–74, 79–88, 90, 92–95, 111,
  114, 119, 120, 201–202 n.89
Litvinov, M. M., 178 n.26
Lozovsky, Solomon, 24, 151, 178
  n.26, 179 n.31
Lubianka, 119, 156

Luk'ianov, V. V., 134
Lysenko, Trofim, 38–41
Lysenkoists, 39–40

Maiorov, G. I., 156, 217 n.81
Makarov, M., 81
Makarov, V. E., 114–116
Makarov, V. I., 81
Malenkov, Georgii, 5, 12–13, 18, 22,
  33, 71–74, 89, 141, 149, 152,
  160, 169, 175 nn.23, 27, 176
  n.28, 176 n.1, 180 n.54, 184
  n.93, 186 n.1, 189 n.25, 196
  n.104, 198 n.26, 200 n.61, 201
  n.89, 206 nn.43, 52, 213 n.21,
  215 nn.46, 58, 217 n.70, 219
  n.109, 220 n.110, 222 n.132,
  223 n.3
  and agriculture, 134, 136, 139–
    140, 211 n.65
  and Aviator's Affair, 26–28, 60,
    113, 179 n.39
  career of, 26
  as Central Committee Secretary,
    27, 28, 32, 58, 71, 80, 131,
    166, 187 n.12, 194 n.75, 189
    n.27, 222 n.1
  at Council of Ministers, 28, 55,
    57, 104, 166, 168, 179 n.41,
    188 n.18, 192 n.53, 193 n.65,
    216 n.60, 223 n.6
  demotion of, 30, 32, 169, 180
    n.47
  and the Gulag, 131
  and Leningrad Affair, 80, 82, 85,
    86, 88, 95, 201 n.66, 201–202
    n.89
  and MGB purge, 115, 116, 119,
    207 n.74, 216 n.67
  and XIX Party Congress, 144–147,
    206 n.51
  and the Pobeda, 73
  positions in both party and state,
    103
  and the ruling group, 49, 105,
    187 n.6, 216 n.63
Malyshev, V. V., 56, 191 nn.41, 42,
  192 n.50, 193 n.56
Mamulov, S. S., 28, 130, 210 n.23
Mao Tse-tung, 78, 160
Mekhlis, Lev, 61

Mel'nikov, D., 131
Mel'nikov, M. G., 215 n.58
Men'shikov, M.A., 72, 76–79, 105
Merkulov, Vsevolod, 7, 28, 30, 60,
    115, 168, 180–181 n.57, 189
    n.27
Merkurov, S. D., 71
Mgeladze, A. I., 111–112
Michurin, Ivan, 40
Mikhailov, Nikolai, 152, 157–158,
    182 n.77, 215 n.46, 218 n.92
Mikhoels, Solomon, 76
Mikoian, Anastas, 4, 7, 10, 14, 18,
    22, 28, 72, 76, 80, 91, 102,
    105, 114, 136, 137, 138, 140,
    158, 159, 161, 174 n.9, 176 n.2,
    182 n.69, 186 n.1, 187 nn.5, 6,
    190 n.35, 192 n.53, 198 n.26,
    199 n.50, 206 n.43, 211 n.52,
    214 n.32, 215 n.55, 216 n.60,
    223 nn.4, 6
  attacked by Stalin in 1946, 24–25,
    179 n.35
  attacked by Stalin in 1952, 151,
    158, 159, 161, 214 n.44
  and bureau for food industry, 24–
    25, 55
  dismissed as minister, 76–79
  expelled from ruling group, 149–
    150, 153, 211 n.65, 216 n.67
Milonov, B. V., 37
Mingrelian Affair, 5, 108, 109–113,
    119, 167, 175 n.23, 206 n.52,
    207 n.67
Mingrelians, 110, 113, 173 n.4
Ministry of Armaments, 54
Ministry of Armed Forces, 30, 54
Ministry of External Trade, 152
Ministry of Finance, 59, 139, 192
    n.52
Ministry of Foreign Affairs, 77, 107,
    152, 205 n.39
Ministry of Internal Affairs (MVD),
    28, 141, 180 n.52, 190 n.38,
    207 nn.54, 74, 208 n.83
  division from Ministry of State
    Security, 28
  economic responsibilities, 28, 127–
    128, 132
  as manager of Gulag, 126–132
Ministry of Justice, 192 n.52

Ministry of State Control, 28, 61,
    190 n.38, 192 n.52
Ministry of State Security (MGB), 7,
    28–29, 60, 86, 87, 98, 105,
    144, 167, 171, 190 n.38, 192
    n.52, 208 nn.80, 84
  and the Doctors' Plot, 153–157
  purge of, 114–119
  supervision of, 53, 60–61, 119,
    153–154
Ministry of Trade, 25, 135
Mishakova, Olga, 221 n.126
Miterev, Georgii, 36–37, 185 n.107
Mitin, Mark, 41
Miussery, 174 n.16
Moldovia, 173 n.4
Molotov, V. M., 4, 5, 6, 7, 10, 13, 25,
    91, 94, 102, 105, 108, 116, 146,
    158, 166, 169, 174 nn.9, 10, 11,
    176 n.2, 178 n.15, 182 n.69,
    186 n.1, 187 nn.5, 6, 189–190
    nn.34, 35, 191 nn.43, 47, 206
    n.42, 216 n.60, 223 nn.4, 6
  attacked by Stalin in 1945, 19–24,
    178 n.15, 198 n.27
  attacked by Stalin in 1949, 75–79
  attacked by Stalin in 1952, 14,
    136, 150–151, 159, 161, 214
    n.44
  dismissed as minister, 76–79, 199
    n.46
  expelled from ruling group, 153,
    219 n.61
  and foreign affairs, 20–23, 57, 70,
    75–79, 199 n.46, 215 n.55
  as Stalin's natural successor, 10,
    14, 18–19, 150–151, 177 n.9,
    214 n.38
  and Zhemchuzhina, P. S., 8, 75–
    79, 198 n.26
Morozov, Grigorii, 49
Moscow, 85, 91, 98, 103, 106, 111,
    112, 114, 117, 118, 119, 133,
    145
Moskovskaia Pravda, 108
Mussolini, Benito, 168

narod, 150
NATO, 98
neo-patrimonialism, 9–10, 46, 58–
    65, 165–168

New York Times, 21, 178 n.18
Nikitin, V. D., 182 n.77
nomenklatura, 112, 115, 182 n.76
Novikov, A. A., 30
Novyi mir, 152, 183 n.83

Odessa, 73
Ogol'tsov, S. I., 118, 208 n.83
Oktiabr', 40, 183 n.83
Orbeli, Leon, 42
Orgburo, 27, 31, 32, 33, 58, 71, 85,
    103, 131, 148, 180 n.48, 183
    n.78, 185 n.107, 189 nn.25, 28,
    194 n.75, 220 n.118
Ounovsty, 98

Pal'tsev, G. N., 189 n.27
Parin, Vasilii, 37, 184 n.100, 185
    n.107
Paris Press, 177 n.3
Patolichev, Nikolai, 32, 182 n.77,
    184 n.97
patronage, local, 112, 200 n.59
Pegov, N. M., 111, 160, 182 n.77,
    208 n.80, 215 n.46
Pervukhin, Mikhail, 55, 94, 105,
    149, 161, 192 n.50, 193 n.56,
    216 nn.60, 63
Piatakov, Georgii, 149
Pitovranov, E. P., 154, 208 n.78
Pobeda, 73
podlinnye protokoly and *podpis'nye
    protokoly. See* archives, Russian
    and Soviet
Poland, 70
Politburo, 18, 21, 24, 26, 28, 29, 33,
    37, 41, 42, 43, 79, 80, 83, 85,
    87, 89, 90, 91, 92, 93, 94, 95,
    98, 100, 101, 102, 103, 104,
    105, 106, 107, 108, 111, 112,
    114, 115, 116, 117, 119, 123,
    124, 129, 144, 145, 146, 148,
    150, 151, 152, 170, 174 n.9,
    197 n.113, 205 n.39
  Commission for Foreign Affairs, 47–
    48, 182 n.69 (*see also* ruling
    group)
  correspondence votes, 9, 50, 52,
    77, 198 n.26
  and Council of Ministers, 45–46,
    53, 59–60, 61, 64

de facto Politburo, 47–50 (*see also*
    ruling group)
de jure Politburo, 46–47
foreign policy commission (VPK),
    77
as instrument of Stalin's personal
    rule, 8–9, 45–51, 59, 107
postwar revival of, 46–47
resolutions of, decided on by
    ruling group, 49, 107
Pomaznev, M. T., 84, 161, 201 n.66
Ponomarenko, P. K., 86, 103, 152,
    189 n.27, 215 n.46, 221
    n.126
Popkov, P. S., 81–82, 85, 87, 200
    n.59
Popov, Georgii M., 90–92, 103, 189
    n.25
Poskrebyshev, A. N., 12, 63, 76, 98,
    105, 107, 108, 111, 115, 160,
    161, 198 n.26, 205–206 nn.39,
    40, 41, 42, 220 n.117, 221
    n.120
Potsdam Conference, 20, 177 n.3
Pravda, 19, 20, 39, 42, 61, 102, 108,
    146, 147, 157, 158, 215 n.52,
    218 n.93
Presidium. *See* Central Committee;
    Council of Ministers
Pronin, V. P., 175 n.25

Rajk, Laszlo, 70
Rakosi, Matias, 98–99
Rapoport, Iakov, 156
Reuters, 22
Riasnii, V. S., 180 n.54
Riazan', 134–136, 138
Rigby, T. H., 12
Riumin, M. D., 169, 170, 207 n.74,
    208 n.84, 217 nn.70–71
  and denunciation of Abakumov,
    115–117
  as deputy Minster of State
    Security, 118, 154
  and Doctors' Plot, 155–156
Rodionov, M. I., 80–81, 85, 87
Rokossovskii, K. K., 99
Roosevelt, Franklin D., 19
Roskin, Grigorii, 36–38, 43, 184
    n.100, 185 n.107
Rukhadze, N. M., 110–112

ruling group (*rukovodiashchaia grupa*),
3, 6, 7, 8, 10, 13, 17–19, 24,
26, 29, 36, 47–48, 81, 91, 98,
102, 105–107, 123–124, 133,
140, 149, 151, 153, 166, 169,
170, 187 n.10
admission to, 48–49
as Commission for Foreign Affairs,
47–48, 182 n.69
decisions issued as Politburo
resolutions, 49–50
as de facto Politburo, 49–50
and domestic policy, 48
and equilibrium of, 5–6, 12–13,
18, 24, 29
informal nature of, 47–49
as novenary, 49, 71
as octet, 49
postwar reorientation of, 17
as quartet, 20, 22, 23, 25, 28–30,
177 nn.4, 8, 178 n.15, 184 n.93
as quintet, 18–19, 24, 31, 47, 177
n.4, 187 n.5
reverts to prewar conventions, 45
as septet, 10, 49, 101, 105–106,
120, 188 n.18, 192 n.53, 205
n.31
as sextet, 31, 47–49, 187 nn.5, 13,
188 n.18
as Stalin's social circle, 49, 188
n.17
as triumvirate, 22–23, 198 n.27,
220 n.110
Rumania, 70
Rumiantsev, A. M., 152, 215 n.52
Russian Liberation Army, 126
Rybakov, Aleksandr, 196 n.97
Rybal'chenko, General, 182 n.68
Rykov, Aleksei, 189 n.34

Saburov, M. Z., 55, 56, 93–94, 100,
146, 147, 149, 161, 191 n.42,
193 n.66, 216 nn.61, 63
Safonov, G. N., 105
Sakhalin, 131
Salimanov, 117
Scherbakov, Aleksei S., 31, 117
Secretariat of Central Committee,
25, 27, 31, 35, 57, 71, 131, 151
select group (*uzkii sostav*). *See* ruling
group

Selivanovskii, N. N., 73, 154, 208
n.78
Serov, I. A., 131, 192 n.55, 207 n.74
Shakhurin, A. I., 26, 179 n.39, 189
n.26
Shcherbakov, A. S., 31, 117, 134,
156
Shepilov, Dmitrii, 41, 108, 146, 157–
158, 169, 215 n.52, 218 n.97,
219 n.99
and ideology commission, 152
Shimeliovich, Boris, 154
Shkiriatov, Matvei, 75, 86, 111, 116
Shtemenko, S. M., 98–99
Shvernik, N. M., 76, 186 n.1, 187
n.10, 188 n.25, 198 n.26
Shwartzman, L. L., 155
Siberia, 28, 158
Siluianov, N. M., 77
Simonov, Konstantin, 148, 150, 200
n.60, 214 n.38
Sochi, 20, 174 n.16, 177 n.8, 186
n.134
Society for Cultural Relations with
Foreign Countries, 77
Solov'ev, N. V., 85
Sotsialisticheskoe zemledenie, 108
Soviet relations with Eastern Europe,
70, 98, 167, 170, 203 n.4
Soviet relations with the West, 4, 6–
7, 11, 18, 20–23, 32, 35, 39, 69,
119, 144, 170
and Berlin crisis, 4, 70, 78, 199
n.44
and Eastern Europe, 5
and Far Eastern Control
Commission, 20, 22
and intelligentsia, 32, 34–35, 39,
43, 70
and Korean War, 4, 97, 203 n.4
and Marshall Plan, 38
and NATO, 98
and nuclear weapons, 5, 69, 119
and Truman Doctrine, 54
Soviet Union, 97, 100, 105
as confident superpower, 3–5, 11,
25, 52, 69, 170
Sovnarkom. *See* Council of People's
Commissars
Stalin, I. V., 176 n.2, 186 n.1, 187
n.5

and agriculture, 134, 136, 140–141
and anti-Semitism, 14, 75–76,
   156, 204 n.19, 219 n.105
and authority of ruling group, 50
as Chair of Council of Ministers,
   104, 191 n.43
death of, 12, 98, 100, 105, 106,
   107, 120, 123, 131, 133, 140,
   141–142, 148, 150–151, 152,
   161–163, 170, 175 n.25, 222
   n.132
delegation of powers, 3, 6, 105,
   165–166
distorts working of government,
   61–62
and Eastern Europe leadership, 70–
   71
and economic initiatives, 59
and *Economic Problems of Socialism
   in the USSR*, 144–147, 157, 163
and the Gulag, 130–133, 166–167
and honor courts, 61
and the intelligentsia, 4, 31–38,
   36–43, 97–98
and law on state secrets, 62
and MGB, 14, 60–61, 88–89, 113–
   114, 119, 153–159, 161
as Minister of Armed Forces, 30,
   54, 189 n.26
as neo-patrimonial leader, 9, 46,
   58–65, 165–171
and XIX Party Congress, 14, 52,
   144–148, 150
nocturnal routine, 62–64
and Politburo, 8–9, 45–52, 59
rationale for campaigns, 9–14, 17,
   23, 25, 29, 30, 35, 43–44, 70,
   73, 88–89, 92, 169–170
and reforms, 7, 123, 136, 140–
   142, 165, 166–167
reluctance to remove top
   leadership, 5–6, 43–44
restricts attacks, 5, 10, 24, 43–44,
   75, 79, 170, 222 n.127
and "servility before the West,"
   21, 34–38, 184 n.93
and Sovmin, 54
time away from Moscow, 8, 10,
   17, 19, 23, 28, 39, 40, 49, 58,
   76, 103, 104, 105, 106, 107,
   110, 116, 118, 120, 140, 145,

   180 n.54, 185 n.115, 196 n.104,
   205 n.30
wartime leadership, 29
Stalin, I. V., relations with
Abakumov, 113–120
Andreev, A. A., 5, 119
Beria, 5, 7, 26–30, 103–104, 109–
   110, 112–113, 149, 170, 204–
   205 n.25
Bulganin, 149
Kaganovich, 149
Khrushchev, 5, 108–109, 113,
   119, 149, 170, 188 n.21
Malenkov, 5, 26–31, 43, 113, 139,
   149, 166, 170
Mikoian, 10, 14, 24–25, 74–79,
   136, 144, 150–151, 157, 159,
   161–162, 170, 179 n.35, 208–
   209, n.1, 214 n.44, 222 n.127
Molotov, 5, 10, 14, 19–25, 43, 74–
   79, 136, 144, 149–151, 157,
   159, 161–162, 168, 170, 178
   n.26, 208–209 n.1, 214 nn.42,
   44, 222 n.127
Pervukhin, 149
Popov, G. M., 90–93
Saburov, 149
Voroshilov, 5, 149, 181 n.60
Voznesenskii, 5, 82–85, 200
   nn.59, 60, 61
Zhdanov, A. A., 31–43
Zhukov, 30
Zhemchuzhina, P. S., 5, 8, 75–79,
   198 n.26
Stalin, Vasilii, 26
Stalingrad hydroelectric station, 129
Starovskii, V., 99
State Defense Committee (GKO), 17–
   19, 24, 46, 57, 74, 176 nn.1, 2,
   177 n.4, 190 n.35
   dissolution of, 19, 24
Stoliarov, Kiril, 155, 170
Sudoplatov, P. A., 114
Sukhanov, D. N., 161, 207 n.74, 208
   n.80
Sukhumi, 110
Supreme Soviet, 51
Suslov, M. A., 36, 91, 103, 152, 157,
   160, 184 n.97, 189 n.27, 215
   n.46, 218 n.92, 94, 219 n.105
Svinelupov, M.G., 114–115

TASS, 21, 158, 178 n.18, 219 nn.99, 100
Tbilisi, 112
Tevosian, Ivan, 56, 77–78, 193 n.56
Timashuk, Lydia, 156, 217 n.81
Timizarev Academy, 40
Tito, 70
Trotsky, Leon, 144, 149
Truman, Harry S., 21, 35, 99
Tsareva, D. I., 215 n.58
Turkey, 35
Turkmen Canal, 127

Ukraine, 98, 102, 124, 135, 167
Union of writers, 77
United States, 87, 97, 99, 100, 156
Ustinov, Dmitrii, 100

Vasetskii, G. S., 36
Vasilevskii, A. M., 98
VASKhNIL (Lenin All-Union
   Academy of Agricultural
   Sciences), 38, 41
Viktorov, V. N., 37
Vinogradov, V. N., 143, 156, 217
   n.81, 221 n.126
VISMUT, 117
Vladimir region, 138
Vlasik, Nikolai, 103–104, 110, 204
   n.25, 207 n.54, 217 n.81, 221
   n.120
Vlasov, General, 126
Volga
   hydroelectric stations, 127
   Volga-Baltic Canal, 127
   Volga-Don Canal, 127, 130
Voprosy filosofii, 36, 218 n.92
Voronezh, 138
Voroshilov, Kliment, 5, 24, 55, 63,
   76, 94, 101–102, 146, 149, 174
   n.9, 176 n.2, 181 n.60, 186 n.1,
   187 nn.5, 10, 196 n.105, 198
   n.26, 216 nn.61, 63, 223 n.6
Vovsi, M. S., 156
Voznesenskii, Nikolai, 5, 55, 56, 57,
   59, 93, 157, 176 n.2, 186 n.1,
   189 n.26, 190 n.35, 192 nn.50,
   52, 53, 193 n.65, 196 n.104,
   198 n.26, 200 nn.59, 61, 62,
   201 n.66, 218 n.97

admission into ruling group, 49
appeals to Stalin, 86–87
and Gosplan Affair, 82–85
and hostility of Beria, 74, 84
and Leningrad Affair, 80–82, 87
and loss of documents, 86–87
VPK (foreign policy commission),
   77
Vyshinsky, Andrei, 105, 205–206
   nn.39, 40, 41, 42, 43
   as Minister of Foreign Affairs, 76–
   79, 107, 199 n.46

Yaroslavl', 134
Yugoslavia, 70

Zakharov, P. A., 175 n.25
Zhavoronkov, V. G., 81, 182 n.77
Zhdanov, Andrei, 13, 31–43, 51–52,
   155, 176 n.28, 180 n.48, 182
   nn.69, 71, 75, 183 nn.78, 90,
   184–185 nn.105, 106, 107,115,
   186 n.1, 187 n.6, 193 n.60, 196
   n.104, 200 n.61
   attacks cultural intelligentsia, 32–
   35
   and honor courts, 36–37
   and ideological purity, 31–36
   illness and death of, 42–43, 70–
   74, 217 n.81
   and Kliueva and Roskin, 37
   and "servility before the West," 34–
   35
   and son, Iurii Zhdanov, 41–42
   as Stalin's agent, 31, 34, 37, 43
   undermines own interests, 38
Zhdanov, Iurii, 39–42, 182 n.75, 185
   n.116, 186 n.134
Zhdanovshchina, 33
Zhebrak, Anton, 40
Zhemchuzhina, P. S., 8, 75–79, 167,
   169, 198 n.26
Zhukov, G. K., 30, 46, 50, 182 n.68,
   189 n.26
Zinoviev, Grigorii, 81, 149
Znamia, 152, 183 n.83
Zodionchenko, S. B., 182 n.77
Zoshchenko, Mikhail, 32–34, 43
Zverev, A. G., 59, 195 n.82
Zvezda, 32–34, 38, 183 nn.83, 90